Robert N. Burrows
FALL 1936

HORACE GREELEY

VOICE OF THE PEOPLE

by WILLIAM HARLAN HALE

HARPER & BROTHERS, PUBLISHERS, NEW YORK

FOR OLGA HALE, MY MOTHER

HORACE GREELEY, VOICE OF THE PEOPLE

Copyright, 1950, by William Harlan Hale. All rights in this book are reserved. No part of the book may be reproduced in any manner whatsoever without written permission except in the case of brief quotations embodied in critical articles and reviews. For information address Harper & Brothers. Manufactured in the United States of America by The Haddon Craftsmen, Scranton, Pa.

CONTENTS

	Foreword	iv
I	JOURNEYMAN	1
II	NEW YORKER	15
III	WHIG	31
IV	CAMPAIGNER	46
V	TRIBUNE	63
VI	UTOPIAN	91
VII	LOVER	108
VIII	TRIUMVIR	127
IX	MOVER	148
X	SHAKER	174
XI	PRESIDENT MAKER	202
XII	WARHAWK	226
XIII	ERRANT KNIGHT	244
XIV	PEACEMAKER	275
XV	THE OLD WHITE HAT	294
XVI	THE PARTIES' CHOICE	314
XVII	THE SAGE OF CHAPPAQUA	339
	Bibliography	355
	Index	368

FOREWORD

In the early 1850's Horace Greeley's ace roving reporter, Bayard Taylor, wrote his chief from one of his cross-country swings, "The *Tribune* comes next to the Bible all through the West."

The New York *Tribune* was then barely ten years old, and its founder had only just passed forty. Never before that time had an editor emerged as a daily oracle heard from one end of America to the other. And no editor afterward was to repeat Greeley's role and become oracular in quite the same sense as he.

His role was unique for many reasons, of which the most immediate was that he played it with exuberant showmanship. His very look and bearing were cast in part: his moon-faced stare, his flopping trousers, his squeaky slang, his sputtering profanities, his unpredictable oddities, and his general air of an owlish, rustic sage all helped make a popular legend of him in his lifetime. But beneath these trappings of an American original there also lay a uniqueness of intention. Horace Greeley not only wished to inform and entertain the mass of his friends, the people. He wished to convert them. He wished to uplift them. He dreamed, in fact, of uplifting and reforming the entire world.

His originality, then, did not rest simply in the size of his audience; many editors since have talked to far greater numbers than he ever did. Nor was he remarkable above all others for his news-gathering innovations. In his own time James Gordon Bennett of the rival *Herald* beat him more often than not with the latest headlines; and in times not long after, the city rooms of Pulitzer and Hearst, with their speed-driven staffs of police reporters, feature writers, cable editors, rewrite men, staff artists, gossip columnists, general managers, assistant general managers, and syndicate stars, were to make the *Tribune's* "old rookery," with its dozen-odd bewhiskered men scratching away at their roll-top desks, seem but an antique memory. Greeley's special quality lay in something else, namely his relationship with his readers. He spoke to them in earnest language, yet he brought his pulpit to their fireside. He talked so winningly even of his unpopular causes that he managed to make them popular. As a result he took hundreds of thousands with him even when he went off on his furthest crusades.

In this he differed from the run of professional liberals who can start a crusade today but not get a sizable audience to follow them. He differed also from those editors of great mass journals who fear that the heavens may fall if they risk any word which one advertiser might call "subversive." Horace Greeley, an independent mind in a time of sweeping American change, thought it his duty to risk such words. He was not only one of the nation's first modern popular editors. He was also one of the last of its searching popular moralists. This combination explains him, and it helps explain his own transitional time.

Bursting forth with expansive vigor from the rigidities of a tie-wig age, the nation's swelling people called for entertainers, popularizers, storytellers—a P. T. Barnum, a Davy Crockett, a Mark Twain. But those same people were still trained to stand under the spell of moral preceptors and spiritual tutors—a Beecher, an Emerson, a Channing, a Theodore Parker. In the shifting order the two types of spokesmen often dovetailed: Barnum was in his way a moralist, while the Reverend Henry Ward Beecher was also a first-class showman—and Horace Greeley was a friend of both who shared their double drives. The blend carried him to a phenomenal success: he became the one editor in our history who made liberalism pay—although, to be sure, he cared nothing for all the money his *Tribune* brought in.

He was experimental, self-contradictory, explosive, irascible, and often downright wrongheaded. He preached thrift and could not practice it himself. He promoted conservative Whiggism and became a socialist immediately thereafter. He talked pacifism, but turned into one of the foremost fomentors of the Civil War. He helped found the Republican Party, only to run against it himself for President as an insurgent backed by Democrats. Modern critics have gravely charged that Greeley was not a systematic thinker. Obviously he was not. Who was? Or what became of the tight little systems of those few who tried it, like the Federalists of one generation or John C. Calhoun in another? The new, swirling energies of the country engulfed them. For most men, the object was simply to keep afloat. Greeley at least tried to keep well up in the intellectual stream and not get lost in its eddies.

The man who barged so broadly through that age at the head of the New York *Tribune* was like many other mentors of his time—by turns dizzy with American success and laid low by the persistence of evil. As knights of progress these men traveled light and carried little armor for self-defense. But they remained moralists even while serving as promoters, and so their personal crises came when they encountered oppression hand in hand with triumph. They might try to dodge many an approaching issue, but they rarely did so for long and never successfully. In the end they had to grapple with them all—a new industrialism, a new flood tide of immigration, a new upsurge of labor, a new West, a rising disgust with slavery. On almost every issue Greeley changed his mind. Almost every result he saw failed to live up to his soaring expectations. The new material forces which he had welcomed disheartened him when they got out of hand. The moral revolution which he had helped inspire reached its flower and then as suddenly withered. Spirits as strong as Emerson and Garrison and Whitman wearied in middle flight and declined into silence or garrulity. That left just a few, like Wendell Phillips and Greeley himself, to carry on into the 1870's as perennial critics and crusaders—and then Greeley, giving a last flourish with a tattered Excelsior banner, went under.

Yet the very banner and his way of waving it, along with such things as the particular tilt of his country hat and the squeak of his high-pitched, irrepressible voice, had managed to endear Greeley to the nation—or rather to the northern half of it—to a degree matched only by Abraham Lincoln himself. He had little poise and less discretion, but he knew instinctively that there were other virtues more compelling than these. He thumped for socialism in the 1840's, and his readers took it. He talked labor unions and free homesteads, and saw both come into being. He went afield into vegetarianism and spiritualism and fell for all manner of quacks, cranks, and spurious healers, but plain readers agreed that even if he sometimes became absurd, he was still their Uncle Horace. He fell out with Lincoln during the war and gyrated wildly between extreme militance and abject defeatism, and even then his *Tribune* survived as an extraordinary power.

He died in disappointment, having failed—of all things—to be President himself. But he had lived richly, in spite of his devotion to a diet of milk and Graham crackers. His morals, to be sure, were often better than his judgments. As an editor he had the shrewdness to spot young spirits ranging from Charles Dickens and Whittier and Thoreau to Bayard Taylor, Charles A. Dana and Henry Villard as coming men, but as a politician his first choice for President in 1860 was Edward Bates and, in 1864, General Rosecrans. And if oddities are the issue, it must be recorded that Greeley was one of the few men ever to adore Margaret Fuller, and certainly the only known Republican to have employed Karl Marx.

He was also one of the prime movers of the party of Lincoln, although he did run against it when it had fallen into the hands of Grant. His purpose in the first instance was to build a common cause of American progressives and businessmen; in the second, to voice his disillusionment when he had seen the results. The fact that he ever made the attempt to bring the two together may make him seem an oddity today; yet he undertook it with all the burning sincerity of his hope for brotherhood, and his repulse marked the start of a schism that has remained unhealed ever since.

Foreword

The fame of editors has a high rate of mortality, and few men today remember, for instance, the name of the brilliant protégé of Horace Greeley who founded the New York *Times*. But Greeley's own name persists in folklore even among people who have no idea what he did, other than to be a sort of Johnny Appleseed of American journalism. Six towns and villages in the West bear his name, thereby recalling the numbers of forebears who once acted on his most famous piece of advice. And in New York City, in the square named after him, Greeley cast in bronze sits gazing northward at the building once occupied by his sharpest rival, Bennett's *Herald*, and now half demolished.

My interest in Horace Greeley first became aroused when as a boy in the early 1920's I heard Marie Hansen-Taylor, then in her nineties, vividly recall the famous editor she had known in her youth as the friend and employer of her husband, Bayard Taylor. Then I had the chance to hear the late Daniel Frohman, the theatrical producer, also tell stories of Greeley, whom he had observed with awe while serving as an office boy in the *Tribune*'s "old rookery" in the late 1860's. The trail of interest thereupon took me to other people through whom Greeley facts and legends had been handed down, and then to manuscript sources.

For access to Greeley's personal papers I am indebted above all to the curators of the MS. collections in the Library of Congress, the New York Public Library, the New York Historical Society Library, and the Harvard University Library. Files of Greeley's publications were consulted in the New York Public Library, and the New York *Herald Tribune*'s own records helped with authenticating detail on internal *Tribune* matters. For special information on Greeley or for assistance in securing it I am indebted to numerous scholars and newspapermen, including particularly Wayne Andrews, Harry W. Baehr, Lucius Beebe, Arthur Eugene Bestor, Jr., Francis Brown, Gordon Haight, the late Burton J. Hendrick, Kenneth B. Holmes, A. V. Miller, James Parton, Louis M. Starr, and M. R. Werner. To Henry Christman I owe a special debt for the loan of source materials from his own collection as well as for information generously given from his own researches in the period. The work of Jeter Allen Isely, author of *Horace Greeley and the Republican Party, 1853-1861*, shaped much of my thinking and guided me to many a source. My brother, Bayard Hadley Hale, took time to drive me on a tour of remote villages and countrysides associated with Greeley's youth, and my wife, Jean Barker Hale, patiently checked many a source for me and shrewdly suggested many an improvement.

There Greeley, grieving at a brother's woe,
Spits with impartial spite on friend and foe . . .
To each fanatical delusion prone,
He damns all creeds and parties but his own;
And faction's fiercest rabble always find
A kindred nature in the Tribune's mind;
Ready each furious impulse to obey,
He raves and ravens like a beast of prey.
— WILLIAM J. GRAYSON, 1856

Greeley . . . is as wrongheaded as a pig.
— THEODORE PARKER, 1858

Greeley's views would be reckoned advanced even today.
— VERNON LOUIS PARRINGTON, 1926

I. JOURNEYMAN

1

Midsummer haze hung on the northern Alleghenies and banked up over the prairies. In the Pennsylvania hills a young man was packing his belongings and making ready to set forth on a long trip. Five hundred miles westward, in central Illinois, a young man whom he did not know was doing the same. The two started out almost simultaneously, traveling light in the heat. Both wore a weathered, open shirt and coarse country trousers that did not reach down to the ankles. Both carried their possessions bundled in a kerchief tied to a stick that was slung over the shoulder. Both, as they tramped along trails and team roads, were tall, lean, unkempt and homely—two young men striking out from their fathers' cabins to make their way in the world. The first was Horace Greeley, aged twenty, pushing through the oak and beech forest toward the Erie Canal. The other was Abe Lincoln, aged twenty-two, heading through the tall grass of Coles County for the Sangamon.

When Lincoln reached the river he borrowed a canoe and paddled downstream past the willows and poplars along the bank. He drew up at the prairie hamlet of New Salem, Illinois—a gaunt, shaggy figure moving with a drifting, melancholy air. Horace Greeley, meanwhile, hurried across Chautauqua County in western New York, where drovers and teams of settlers bouncing westward along the post road saw an odd appearance coming the other way— a bustling youth with spindly shoulders bearing a head so outsized that he seemed to have to walk fast just in order to keep it balanced on top.

The shape of his head was startling in itself as it approached through the drovers' dust. It looked as smooth, as rounded, and almost as white as a magnified egg. It was both large and heavy: the young man's narrow shoulders were stooped under it, and he walked in a wide, swaying gait, holding it erect. At close hand, the head gleamed: its forehead was pale and high, its eyes were light blue behind glistening spectacles, its hair was wispy and tossed like straw, and the face beneath wore a look so shiny, smiling and simple that it might have been that of a child.

The two young men—one already gnarled and weather-beaten, and the other still wide-eyed and cherubic—moved on in opposite directions. Soon almost a thousand miles separated them. Many years were to pass before they met, and many more before their fates became interlocked. Abe Lincoln, hauling up his canoe at the New Salem river bend, set to work there keeping store. Horace Greeley, passing Buffalo, pushed on to Lockport and the canal, heading for New York.

2

Both young men, striking out alone in this summer of 1831, had covered great stretches of the country before. Lincoln had helped move his parents' teamload of goods from a Kentucky cabin to a claim in Indiana and then to another in central Illinois. Greeley vividly remembered the day when as a boy of nine he had helped his father escape the sheriff's hammer in New Hampshire and hurry away to the furthest corner of Vermont. Now his father, quitting Vermont, had struck root again amid west-Pennsylvania virgin timber; but Zaccheus Greeley was talking of pulling up stakes once more and moving on. Zac had not done well in Pennsylvania—just as the shiftless Lincolns had not done well in Indiana. But then, Zac Greeley had not done well anywhere. In fact, the further the Greeley family moved west, the poorer they became. Horace, the son, was now out to reverse the process and move just the other way.

His people had been living on the American land for almost two hundred years. The first Greeley, a yeoman farmer or artisan from the English Midlands, had settled in about 1640 in rudimentary Salisbury on the Merrimack estuary, one of the Massachusetts Bay Colony's northern outposts. His son Ezekiel had moved upriver to amass some property near the present Nashua in New Hampshire. But Ezekiel's son, in turn, had lost most of it (he was "kind, mild, easy-going, and never a thrifty citizen," Horace recalled), and the next of the line, Horace's father Zaccheus, helped lose what was left. Zac Greeley, a small, sandy-haired, straw-whiskered man, was perhaps the most amiable of the many Greeleys who had now spread out along the Merrimack valley, but also the most ineffectual as a farmer; he was slow, ignorant, and a "bad manager," Horace remarked, always dreaming of acquiring some better land further on, and always failing to get the best out of what he had. "I doubt that we ever harvested one bounteous crop," the son summed up of all their years in New Hampshire and Vermont; "I know I had the stuff in me for an efficient and successful farmer, but such training as I received at home would never have brought it out."

Horace, as he grew up, had little patience with his floundering father and what he called the whole "tribe of Zaccheus." All his leanings lay on the side of his mother, Mary, who had brought him a more vigorous inheritance. Early in the century before, the orderly port of Boston had been invaded by shiploads of turbulent immigrants of a stock till then unknown to America: the fighting Scotch-Irish had arrived. Feared in Ireland, where they had settled on confiscated Catholic estates, and disliked by the lords of London, who had just thrown them off those same estates, they had been unwelcome in Massachusetts, too—save on condition that they move far out into the wilderness and keep out of the way of anyone but Indians, whom they might battle as they pleased. This the Scotch-Irish Covenanters had done with enthusiasm, striking root so fast that one band from old Londonderry, hacking out a clearing far up the Merrimack which they called the new Londonderry, petitioned Boston before the end of their first year that "being so numerous . . . they may be erected into a township," pointing out that "being a frontier place, they may the better subsist by having government amongst them, and be more strong and full of inhabitants." One of that band was John Woodburn, listed in 1721 as a "proprietor" of Londonderry, where he built himself a blockhouse, reared eleven children, and became the ancestor of Mary Woodburn Greeley.

When Mary Woodburn in 1807 married her valley neighbor, Zac Greeley, it was her family that held good Londonderry tracts, while his was living off nearby bits and pieces. In order to establish himself, young Zac impulsively bought a forty-acre farm of his own, half a dozen miles across the Merrimack on the high ground of Amherst township. There Horace Greeley was born on 3 February, 1811, the third of Zac's and Mary's children, and the first to survive. The heavy-raftered, one-story Greeley farm cottage was new, and

Zac had borrowed heavily to furnish it and surround it with land and livestock. But the forty acres for which he had paid the high price of $1,800 were studded with gravel and granite, and their yield was so small that he could not find his way out of debt. He added more land and thereby more debt. Then he became confused and found relief in drink.

Mary, his wife, drank too. When the Greeleys went into the fields to harvest their potatoes, oats and hops, helped by such hands as they could hire for the day, the liquor jug was freely passed around, and the daughter of the crusty Woodburns took her turn at it. Both were known as "free and generous natures," and Mary Woodburn, leaning against a stump or rocking in her chair as the jug went round, joined the men also in lighting up a pipe. ("Both my father and mother have always used ardent spirits and tobacco," Horace Greeley remarked years later, unhappy in the recollection, "very moderately, they think, but greatly to their injury, I know.") But Mary, a big, fair-skinned, blowsy woman, was also strapping and vigorous, which Zac was not. "She could outrake any man in town," a Londonderry neighbor recalled; "she hoed in the garden; she labored in the field; and while doing more than the work of an ordinary man and an ordinary woman combined, would laugh and sing all day long, and tell stories all the evening." Horace's lifelong friend Beman Brockway wrote that it was she, rather than her husband, who had "the brains of the party." And another of her son's companions, the biographer James Parton, heard Mary Woodburn's New Hampshire neighbors recall even after several decades her "perpetual overflow of animal spirits."

For all his mother's Woodburn vigor, though, Horace himself came into the world a frail baby, blue-skinned and feeble. His eyes were weak. His hearing was morbidly sensitive: the mere rustle of rainfall outside sometimes made him violently ill. Taking on a transparent pallor, he looked so wraithlike that the neighbors' boys called him "the Ghost." Too sickly to join in their outdoor games, he stood apart with a solemn, owlish air that was exaggerated by the swollen size of his skull. Yet he was sent to school at three. Neighbors watched the white-faced youngster trudging over the High Range under the weight of his primers and spelling books. His very survival was a local phenomenon.

By next year, though, he had become a phenomenon in another respect. Far from being half dead, "the Ghost" was found to be precociously alive. At four, he was being entered in evening schoolhouse spelling bees against boys twice his age and beating them—although he often had to be nudged out of sleep to answer when his turn came. At five he was said to be reading the Bible fluently. Stories began to spread of the strange accomplishments of the feeble Greeley boy. High-Range people declared that he could win a spelldown as well asleep as awake. Others heard that, in order to keep up with the news of the outside world, the five-year-old was now regularly scanning the weekly Amherst *Farmer's Cabinet*.

Horace Greeley later derided these stories as "monstrous exaggerations," although he repeated some of them with relish. He said he owed his early skill at reading to his mother, who had trained him at her knee. Mary, unlike Zac, had grown up with an aspiring streak that reached far beyond the small world of valley farms, and this she tried to transmit to her eldest surviving child. "Having suddenly lost her two former children, just before my birth," Greeley wrote in his *Recollections of a Busy Life*, "my mother was led to regard me even more fondly and tenderly than she might otherwise have done; hence, I was her companion and confidant about as early as I could talk; and her abundant store of ballads, stories, anecdotes and traditions was daily poured into my willing ears." She told him old Scotch and Scotch-Irish tales, handed down by her Woodburn forebears: there were legends of the Woodburn men who had fought at the battle of the Boyne, and there was a peculiarly hair-raising yarn of one Woodburn grandmother who had been captured by pirates while on her way to America, and who "while in their hands" (so a Londonderry chronicler recalled it) "was delivered of her first child, which so moved the pirate band, and particularly the captain, who had a wife and family, that he permitted them to pursue their voyage, bestowing upon her some valuable articles of apparel." Thus mother and son drew together—to remain so even after four more children were born to her. For long hours, while he stood at her knee and she spun flax at her wheel, she read to him from a book in her lap, with the result that Horace learned to read the pages even sideways or upside down—"an absurd practice, in which I was stimulated to persist by those who should have known better," he remarked much later, but nevertheless a skill that had its uses for a boy who was one day to become a printer.

Then Mary sent Horace over to her father's broad farm in Londonderry to board there during termtime, since the Woodburn place lay nearer to a schoolhouse than Zac's. There he saw a more ample life than at home. The Woodburn patriarch showed off the grandson to his valley neighbors. A retired sea captain across the way lent Horace books and tested him before company on his reading: "How do you spell Nebuchadnezzar? Who fought the battle of Eutaw Springs?" The boy was now accumulating an audience. One day, when a girl arrived in the village bearing the name "Asenath," the elders asked themselves wherever she could have gotten it, and the seven-year-old Horace piped up with the answer that the name was to be found "in the forty-first chapter of Genesis, verse forty-five." So, at least, the elders recounted it, checking their Bibles and discovering that the astounding youngster was right.

In springtime, though, Zac pulled Horace out of school for weeks on end to help with the plowing in Amherst. Horace remembered riding a plow horse at five over his father's frost-bitten fields, where "occasionally, the plow would strike a fast stone and bring up the team all standing, pitching me over the horse's head, and landing me three to five feet in front." The stones remained, thicker than Zac's potatoes. Falling into arrears, Zac turned over his farm "on shares" to a brother and hired himself out to another farmer across the ridge in order to raise cash. But then the valleys found themselves hit by a sudden, nationwide business depression—the "Panic" of 1819—whose causes none of the Greeleys could quite fathom. Zac's brother failed with the farm, too; Zac's new employer defaulted; Mary could not salvage their home with the linen and tow cloth she was weaving for the market; and so all was lost. The sheriff and his men arrived on the place one day at dawn, and Zac hid in the woods to avoid being arrested for debt while they swarmed over the house and barn to attach his assets. Horace's younger sister, Esther, years after recalled her mother tearfully following the sheriff from room to room, "while Brother Horace, then a little white-haired boy, held her hand trying to comfort her, telling her not to cry—he would take care of her."

Esther's billowing story was possibly still another exaggeration. She was at the time just six years old. But the Greeleys' recollection of their hardships in the following winter was not exaggerated. After prospecting for a refuge in Vermont, Zac slipped back in December to bundle his dispossessed family into a hired sleigh along with all the chattels they could carry, and set out northwestward across New Hampshire, over the Connecticut River ice, and up into the frozen Green Mountains. Zac had fifty dollars left in his pocket and a job as a day laborer in the lumber country in prospect. Horace, on the way, kept bothering the teamster who drove them. "He asked me how far it was to this, that and t'other place," the man remembered; "but Lord! he told me a damned sight more than I could tell *him!*"

3

After three days' travel they reached the new home Zac had picked out for them—a remote village called Westhaven, lying along Vermont's western fringe opposite Lake George. The place was a dreary sight under the snow, and drearier when the blanket melted. Lying in knotty, gullied land along the edge of Rutland County's limestone knobs, Westhaven had attracted settlers only because of its stands of white pine; and once the best of the woods were torn down, what was left was clayey slopes and sandy bottoms overrun with thistles, alders and rank grasses. If Zac's Amherst acres had been unpromising, Westhaven's were discouraging. The Reverend Timothy Dwight of Yale College, jogging over its corduroy back roads a few years before Zac's arrival, had recorded that he saw only "one handsome farm" in Westhaven, in an area that was generally "rough and disagreeable," with valleys that were "sudden, deep and uncouth" and burned-over forests that were "either decayed or dead," at whose margins stood log cabins so poor that "I could not discern the remotest hope of any change for the better."

The "one handsome farm" Dr. Dwight saw was probably that of Christopher Minot, a Boston banker who had established himself here in manorial style, dreaming of leading an expansive life on the frontier. It was on Minot's lonely place that Zac went to work, cutting out timber and brush at fifty cents a day. Then the ambitious Mr. Minot died and his estate was declared bankrupt, leaving Zac stranded with only part of his pay. The Greeleys drifted from one log shack to another, variously trying lumbering and small farming. They ran a sawmill, without making a success of it; they planted corn, but the hard clay crust choked off most of it; they tried wheat, but midges destroyed it; they went in for maple-sugaring, without learning properly how to do it; they fought thickets and swamps, and all came down sick because of the bad water they were drinking at "Flea Knoll." Zac, as a result, took to thinking of moving on again, and Horace, for his part, began to dream of breaking away from his family's life entirely.

One day when he was eleven, having heard that a newspaper printer in Whitehall just across the New York State line was looking for an apprentice, he had trudged eight hilly miles to confront him and be told that he was too young for the job. Four years later another opening occurred on the weekly *Northern Spectator* over in East Poultney, a handsome Vermont valley town that boasted of two thousand people, six sawmills, and a stately green. Zac Greeley was just then on the point of pulling out for Pennsylvania. Hurriedly, before it might be too late, Horace tramped the dozen miles down the Rutland road to the white gate of Amos Bliss, East Poultney's town clerk, drygoods merchant and newspaper manager. Bliss was out back of his house planting potatoes in the spring sunshine.

"Are you the man that carries on the printing office?" said a high-pitched voice close behind him.

Amos Bliss looked up from his hoe. Years later he recalled the scene to James Parton, Greeley's first biographer, in terms that helped establish it as the start of a favorite American success story. Bliss said he saw a tall youngster of about fifteen, wearing rough farmer's clothes, worn-down shoes, no stockings, and a felt hat "of the old stamp, with so small a brim that it looked more like a two-quart measure inverted than anything else," which was pushed far back on a light-haired head "rocking on shoulders which seemed too slender to support its weight."

Restraining himself from laughing at the sight, Bliss admitted he was the man.

"Don't you want a boy to learn the trade?" asked the stranger.

"Well," said Bliss, "we have been thinking of it. Do *you* want to learn to print?"

"I've had some notion of it," said the backwoods boy.

Bliss gazed at him with astonishment. "Well, my boy—but, you know, it takes considerable learning to be a printer. Have you been to school much?"

"No, I haven't had much chance at school. I've read some."

"What have you read?"

"Well, I've read some history, and some travels, and a little of most everything."

"Where do you live?"

"At Westhaven."

"How did you come over?"

"On foot."

Bliss—who, among his other accomplishments, was also on the side an inspector of common schools—gave him a quick examination on his general knowledge on the spot, and then sent him over to the foreman at the *Northern Spectator* shop across the green. After a quarter hour Horace sauntered back to Bliss' garden waving a slip of proof paper bearing the foreman's notation, "Guess we'd better try him." Bliss, by now interested in the curious lad's knowledge and persuasiveness, interrogated him further and finally offered him an apprenticeship, provided of course Zac Greeley would agree.

"You're not going to hire that tow-head, are you?" one of the apprentices asked Bliss that evening.

"I am, and if you boys are expecting to get any fun out of him, you'd better get it quick, or you'll be too late. There's something *in* that tow-head."

Such was Horace Greeley's entry into journalism—at least as Bliss and Parton reported it.

4

"Mr. Greeley says his boy may stay as an apprentice in the printing business until he is twenty years of age. . . . If the boy stays till he is twenty years old he is to have forty dollars in clothing after the first six months, and have his board. The boy is to be faithful and serve with the best of his ability. . . ." So ran the articles of Horace's apprenticeship to the firm of Dewey & Bliss, dated April, 1826. Mary Greeley, about to take her three other children westward, did not interpose—although when the actual hour of parting came, Horace suddenly turned to her and wished in anxiety that she might. Six years before, in New Hampshire, a group of men headed by the minister of the neighboring village of Bedford had offered to send the bright youngster to Exeter Academy at their own expense; but "mother said she was not willing to part with me," Greeley wrote, and so the offer was turned down. Now, on the point of leaving for East Poultney, "A word from my mother, at the critical moment, might have overcome my resolution; but she did not speak it, and I went my way." The twelve-mile hike to newspaperdom, he recalled, "was one of the slowest and saddest of my life."

The gangling apprentice who now settled into Harlow Hosford's Eagle Tavern at the edge of East Poultney green caused his host some concern. He ate too much, he talked too much, and, worst of all, while wolfing his bowls of soup or stew in the taproom of the best inn west of Rutland, he held forth as a boy lecturer against the evils of drink and tobacco. Just why young Greeley should have turned teetotaler and "taken the oath" at thirteen, not many neighbors understood—unless they knew the Greeleys. At seventeen, he helped organize the first temperance society to sprout in town. That year he also made his first appearance in the narrow brick schoolhouse across the green as an adolescent orator on politics, proclaiming that the policies set forth by that sound New England protectionist, John Quincy Adams, were the right ones, while Andrew Jackson, just as certainly, was wrong. This was to the liking of practically everyone in Poultney, no matter what they thought of temperance. The odd young man at Hosford's loved to hold forth in his high-pitched, stringy voice, and at least he had read the papers. Devouring his platters, he took to answering taproom questions on Washington politics with the same assurance he had shown to the sea captain who asked him to spell "Nebuchadnezzar." He became a useful fixture, drawing in passing farmers who wanted to hear the news. And while they listened, they filled their pipes and ordered another round of Hosford's whisky.

Four houses down the street, in a second story above a law office and a harness shop, stood the meager plant of the weekly *Northern Spectator*—a few old desks and tables, some type cases and boxes of worn-down rules and ornaments, and an old-style wooden hand press. Greeley was put to work at the heaviest job, which was that of pulling the five or seven hundred copies individually off the creaking flat-bed. The paper was a sketchy product, made up chiefly of items copied from week-old Boston and Hartford journals and garnished with local notices of land sales and feed prices. It had no full-time editor; for a while the incumbent was "a sound, well-read theologian" (so Amos Bliss reported with pride) who alternated his *Spectator* duties with those of serving the countryside as a Baptist preacher. Horace Greeley learned the type case, and then practiced thinking up his own squibs and paragraphs at the composing stick, setting them into the pages as space allowed. There was usually space to spare, since the preacher-editor was often away preaching and Amos Bliss was kept busy keeping up his store.

Bliss was so busy, in fact, that his *Northern Spectator* soon fell into decline, having failed to persuade its dwindling rural subscribers to pay up. All Poultney, meanwhile, was relatively declining, too, as its settlers heard of better chances out West. Perhaps Zac Greeley had been right after all to move out of this tight backwash of the New England lumber country and to head for the open Alleghenies. Just when Horace's apprenticeship neared its end, the *Spectator* closed. He had already traveled out twice, on foot, during the summers, to see his family in their newest clearing. Now he made ready to go again. Harlow Hosford, sitting on his inn porch, was concerned about his boarder's lack of clothes for the long trip. He turned to another of his guests. "Now, there is that brown overcoat of yours," Hosford said to the man. "It's cold on the canal . . . Horace is poor and his father is poor. You are owing me a little, as much as the old coat is worth, and what I say is, let us give the poor fellow the overcoat, and call our account squared."

So Horace left East Poultney, remembering it with an adopted Vermonter's love. "I have never known," he wrote long afterward, "a community so generally moral, intelligent, industrious and friendly." Here for the first time he had found friends, productive work, and a regular audience. The townspeople looked back with liking on the irrepressible adolescent who had stood up at their Debating Society meetings in the schoolhouse to argue such questions as "Is novel-reading injurious to society?" "Is the Union likely to be perpetuated?" and "Is marriage conducive to happiness?" And Greeley, for his part, was always to feel himself more rooted in East Poultney than in any other place he had known: "Tell me about deaths, marriages, courtships or even scandals," he wrote his village friend, B. F. Ransom, almost a decade later from New York; "It can't be that you merely vegetate like oysters up there. Do stir up something."

Ransom, a drifting young man who tried his hand without success at poetry and editing, remained the first of Greeley's letter-writing confidants. But during the same years Horace had also made friends with a Poultney youth who was one day to become a great success. Often he had paced across the green past the tall Baptist steeple with George Jones, whose house stood down the street, and to whom he confessed his growing passion for the world of newspapers. Many years later it was this George Jones who was to emerge as a cofounder and publisher of Horace Greeley's most formidable rival—the New York *Times*.

5

"It was a mistake at his time of life to plunge so deeply into the primitive forest," Horace remarked of his father out in Erie County, Pennsylvania. Mother Mary, he said, "could never be reconciled" to her entry into the great western woods, whose shadow "oppressed her from the hour she first entered them. . . . I never caught the old smile on her face, the familiar gladness in her mood, the hearty joyfulness in her manner, from the day she entered those woods . . ."

Hillside beech, hemlock and ash had yielded slowly to her husband's ax. Zac had thrown together a log lean-to against the first winter's snow, but the following summers had left his charred clearing unable to sustain his family. Then he and Mary had tried sheep raising, but wolves had decimated their herd. There was no way out now from the crippling cycle of ignorance on the frontier. Horace, visiting home in 1830, saw that his mother was declining in mind and body. He hurried away from her cabin and picked up odd jobs as a printer in the nearest towns; but after several months in Jamestown, in Lodi, and on the *Gazette* in Erie, "work failed," he recorded, "and no printing office in all that region wanted a journeyman." It was then that he decided to strike out for New York.

At home, brother Barnes would help out; Barnes was a rough, outdoor growth, more Greeley than Woodburn, slow-moving but a good man for the woods. ("Have you seen any stray brother of mine," Horace wrote years later to his upstate friend, Obediah Bowe, "with a head like a yellow brick house? If not, you've missed a first-rate chance, for there's more fun in him than can be got out of me. He is a backwoodsman and a good Whig, and can beat [your people] in hunting stories and the like.") Sister Arminda—dull, heavy, and clearly another Greeley—would also help. (Distantly, years later, Horace was to record of her, "She is very stout in body and rather worldly in spirit . . . was married at fifteen to a husband of eighteen, and they hadn't the value of a poor cow between them. . . . The husband is an easy reckless fellow. . . . They keep a rough sort of country hotel; I believe she has had fourteen children.") Sister Esther would help, too, although she was different and had something of the Woodburn streak: years after would see her in New York, billowing, expansive and officious, and trying to keep up with Horace or at least to protect him from trouble.

But as another of Horace's friends, Beman Brockway, put it of the Greeley family as a whole, "They are a good sort of people, but lack energy and vigor. They are not thrifty. I think Horace had all the push there was in the family." Horace, on the other hand, was thrifty—at least up to a point. He had pocketed twenty-five dollars from his work on the Erie *Gazette* at fifteen dollars a month. Half of this he now gave to his father. With the other half he set forth. He had no doubts about parting this time.

6

He walked the towpath along the Erie Canal most of the night in search of an eastbound line boat. Now and then, in the darkness of the flat country with its mist-laden clearings, he could hear the slow thud of tow-horse hoofs coming the other way along the path, then the mumble of voices or the twang of a guitar afloat, and finally the creak of the towline as a boat hove into shape: these were westbound freighters, carrying immigrants into the interior. Toward dawn, when he finally hailed a barge bound east with Buffalo grain for Albany, he found some of its roughneck passengers still drinking on the cabin roof. They joshed him and asked him if he hadn't been spending the night with a woman out on the soft banks. He hurried below for some sleep.

The barge was towed in August morning sunshine along the giant stone aqueduct over the Genesee at Rochester, a town which the canal had turned overnight into a city of flour mills and five-story warehouses that tapped the West and now served the East. Then trackless timberland enfolded the narrow cut again, and no noise rose but that of wild fowl in the cedar swamps. But next one heard grinding mills, and here was Syracuse—a lonely settlement "surrounded by a desolate, poverty-stricken, woody country, enough to make an owl weep to fly over it," Colonel W. L. Stone of the New York *Commercial Advertiser* had said of it a decade before, yet now rising into "noble ranges of buildings, and two or three large, tasteful churches." Cotton textile mills were humming at Utica, where passengers could dine richly at Baggs' Hotel or eat for ten cents at the Oneida Temperance House while waiting for the boat to start the haul into the Mohawk Valley. Here red-and-gold canal packets came the other way, bearing ladies under parasols. Traffic thickened; high ridges and romantic glens closed in; and now canallers could be seen rafting oak timber to Schenectady to help in building America's newest innovation—a steam railroad.

Horace Greeley left the boat at Schenectady rather than stay with it for the long, slow descent through locks into the Hudson. He struck over the hills on foot to Albany, walking through a countryside that had just been startled by a revolutionary occurrence. A few days before, on freshly laid iron tracks, a gleaming, festooned locomotive named the De Witt Clinton had hauled a string of crowded cars from Albany on the first trial run of a passenger train in the North. First the stage-like coaches, each shackled to the next by chains, had started up with such a jerk that the first citizens of Albany were hurled out of their seats. Then the shower of boiler sparks had ignited their Sunday clothes and parasols, and when the De Witt Clinton pulled up short for water the cars had banged into one another again, throwing the smoldering guests into another heap. Farmers' horses along the way had taken fright and overturned their wagons. The inns were full of excited talk. But Horace Greeley hurried on without taking time to listen. He was bent on catching the first morning Hudson River boat to face his own future in New York.

II. NEW YORKER

1

Gleaming in white with its sidewheels thrashing, the day steamer carried him downstream, away from the inland stagnation and failure he had known. Luggers, schooners and fast packets bearing gold scrollwork and excursion crowds dotted the sun-speckled river. Above their private glens and steamboat landings stood the mansions of the valley lords, shimmering with porticos and pergolas and distant colonnades. At the busy town of Hudson one could see new cement works and whaling ships; then came handsome Newburgh, with its brick yards and iron foundry; and further down travelers pointed out the site of strange doings at an experimental free-love and socialist colony near Haverstraw. A canal and spur railroad had just been built westward to tap the coal of the upper Delaware Valley, and black barges bearing factory anthracite joined the river, heading for New York. Fishing smacks and ocean-going craft multiplied in the Tappan Zee. Then came Yonkers, with its wooded knobs and country seats; upper Manhattan Island, with its slopes and farms; a patch of houses at Greenwich Village; and finally the mass of brick fronts, warehouses, steeples and alleys that converged at the foot of the island at Whitehall where Horace Greeley's river boat swung against wharfside, discharging a passenger whose sensitive ears were tortured by the hiss of escaping steam.

He walked up cobble-laid Broad Street, with its rattling handcarts, spangled phaetons and lines of shops behind buff awnings, and inquired for rates at a boardinghouse near the corner of Wall. The proprietor asked six dollars a week. So Greeley retreated to the waterfront, where at McGoldrick's shelter for sailors and immigrants, board and lodging could be had for $2.50 a week. He moved in, paid his first $2.50 in advance, and thereupon discovered that McGoldrick's place was also a drinking dive. Then, with five dollars left in his pocket and no acquaintance to turn to within two hundred miles, he started on his job-hunting rounds of the city's print shops, many of which were working with a reduced force in the August lull.

A little over a century before, another young journeyman printer had reached Philadelphia, looking for a similar job. "I was dirty from my journey," Benjamin Franklin remembered of his arrival there, "and I knew no soul nor where to look for lodging. . . . My whole stock of cash consisted of a Dutch dollar and about a shilling in copper. . . ." Philadelphia, in that earlier time, had been on its way to becoming the first city of the colonies. But by now New York had overhauled it and made itself the first city of the republic—America's "Commercial Emporium," as it proclaimed itself. New York had grown suddenly—too suddenly to have time to take on the appearance of order and stability. It was a "hobble-de-hoy metropolis, a rag fair sort of place," grumbled the manorial Fenimore Cooper from upstate. It had broken out of its old Knickerbocker confines so boisterously in order to make itself a ruling business mart that it had skipped entirely the intermediate stage of a middle-sized, balanced community such as Boston or Philadelphia itself, and this made it a place of unresolved extremes: it was metropolitan and provincial at once.

Upward of 40,000 jostling immigrants were now landing each year at Whitehall and the Battery, but only a few steps away one could still find cowsheds, while Bowling Green remained the shaded preserve of families with old Dutch names. Big brokerage and commission houses were rising along Broadway, but hogs still rooted in its gutters. Rows of brick fronts were being run up northward across old farms and meadows beyond Canal Street to house the city's 200,000 dwellers, but in the gaps lay fetid back alleys, dumps and clapboard stews. A newly rich class of grain brokers, shipping operators, canal promoters, real-estate speculators, and contract-labor importers swarmed noisily over Park Place, and had just taken to the new craze of drinking champagne—a drink which, being new to it, they warmed before serving. Aaron Burr still walked past City Hall, an aging pariah who recalled tiewig Hamiltonian days, and sometimes on his way he passed a foulmouthed, semiliterate young steamboat captain named Cornelius Vanderbilt, who had just amassed his first $30,000 and was going into the shipping business on his own.

The fashionable Philip Hone, a leading local patron of the theatre, entertained the British star, Fanny Kemble, at his mansion and found her manners "somewhat peculiar. . . . Indeed, I think that she prefers married men." But British visitors also found New York's manners peculiar, and unpredictable as well. A singer named Sinclair, who was said to have made disparaging remarks about Americans, was hooted off the stage where he was performing in an operatic version of Sir Walter Scott's *Rob Roy* with shouts of "Off! Off! Go back to England! Tell them the Yankees sent you back!" Tyrone Power, the famous Irish player, was gratified that at his New York debut in *The Irish Ambassador* he found "no coats off, no heels up, no legs over boxes," as he had expected. Harriet Martineau, the doughty English lady traveler, enjoyed the city's earthy turbulence but was frightened by its exuberant new fire engines, which "run along the side-pavement, stopping for nobody." Power, for his part, was happy to get out of the noisy metropolis and visit "the woods of Hoboken," "the forest heights of Brooklyn," and "Harlaem, a pretty village eight miles from the city."

Horace Greeley took at once to New York—shirtsleeves, slums, theatres, Tammany parades and all. Yet the first job he found left him neither leisure to see its sights nor money to patronize them. He had gotten work at John T. West's upstairs print shop in old Chatham Street, but it was work of a sort which more experienced printers studiously avoided. It consisted in setting a pocket-sized New Testament in narrow columns of small type, with an even smaller column of notes in diminutive five-point type in the middle, the whole text being thickly studded with Greek letters, italics, and minuscule raised characters. The job, extraordinarily demanding and slow, was paid for at piecework rates current for setting much easier work. Horace Greeley stuck at it in spite of his weak eyes, and by working as long as fourteen hours a day was sometimes able to take home six dollars a week.

Fifteen years before, another young printer named Thurlow Weed, also just in from upstate, had gotten a job in a better shop in John Street setting a big quarto Bible, and had been paid twelve to thirteen dollars a week for it. Weed, bluff and strapping, had known how to push himself ahead at once; and since then, moving on from big Bibles to bigger operations on his own, Weed had made himself the editor of the Albany *Evening Journal* and a rising politician in the state. Before long Greeley began to hear of Weed and to think of emulating this husky fellow journeyman who had climbed the ladder so fast. But Greeley's own appearance and callow manners stood against him. David Hale, the editor of the New York *Journal of Commerce*, had thrown him out when he applied for a composing-room job there, telling him that he was "a runaway apprentice from some country office."

After finishing his New Testament, Greeley was let out of West's. He drifted for weeks between odd jobs. Finally he found work setting type on a new sporting and betting weekly called the *Spirit of the Times*. This marked the beginning of the New York newspaper career of the man who was one day to become the moral counselor to millions. Within a few months the *Spirit* failed.

2

Years after, when he had risen to fame, pious legends arose about Greeley's singular virtue as a young printer in the big city. James Parton, his first biographer, wrote of the hero's journeyman days at West's that "while the young men and older apprentices were roaming the streets, seeking their pleasure, he, by the light of a candle stuck in a bottle, was ekeing out a slender day's wages by setting up an extra column of the Polyglot Testament." The paragon, it appeared, never went out on Saturday-night forays, never smoked, never drank, never gambled, never wasted time, and always went to church. He was so good, in fact, that even the faithful Parton grew impatient with the legends: after asking old Amos Bliss in East Poultney in the 1850's to tell him what Greeley had really been like a quarter of a century before, he complained to Greeley that Bliss had "tried to make you out the primmest, dullest little moral philosopher that ever went to church."

For Parton knew that Greeley had played cards even then—and for money, too. Everyone who dealt with Greeley knew that he swore profanely. True, he stuck to spruce beer, but he was not above visiting a taproom to get it. One day at West's, when he had been ragged long enough by the other printers for coming to work in his worn-down country shirt and pants, he turned up in a second-hand suit of funereal black, which caused such a burst of laughter that he had to stand a drink all around. Far from being queered by his odd appearance, he learned how to make capital of it, to play the part of a pressroom original and prankster. He talked incessantly. One of his employers, the stereotyper J. S. Redfield, recalled how amazed he was to find that young Greeley's work totals by far exceeded those of anyone else in the shop, although the newcomer had been chattering all day long. And after work, hat shoved back on head, Greeley went off gregariously across town with his fellow journeymen, often ending up at the Old Bowery or the new Richmond Hill Theatre for an evening of song or melodrama.

Years after, as a responsible editor in charge of the moral *Tribune*, Greeley was to condemn the New York theatre as being "rather an injury than a benefit to the community—vicious, licentious, degrading, demoralizing." But in his early New York days he wholeheartedly enjoyed it, especially when the *Spirit of the Times* office gave him free tickets. He found himself "in raptures from first to last" at a performance of *William Tell* in which the hero's son was played by a Miss Mestayer, then in her early teens. Fanny Kemble's American debut in Milman's tragedy, *Fazio*, thrilled him. He loved Mrs. Duff as Lady Macbeth, and later thought that she played the part "better than it has since been done in the city, though she played for $30 per week."

New York glittered to an inland man. It was the first really expansive community he had known. Amherst, Westhaven, East Poultney, and the Pennsylvania seat of Zac Greeley's latest attempt to establish himself were all eddies, and all were already drying up: Amherst and Poultney, in fact, were soon to become forgotten villages, while Westhaven was virtually to die out, and no future lay ahead in the particular hills where Zac lived now. Even the lake town of Erie, where Horace had found work, was a place of some disappointment: "it dwells in my memory as a place which started with too sanguine expectations," he wrote of it, "and was thus exposed to a sudden check from which it has never fully recovered."

New York was a bustling refuge from all this, and in fact from all the loneliness and insecurity of the inner country. Yet New York was also a half-western town itself—or rather it was the eastern outlet where western produce, western shippers and western ambitions congregated, seeking quick cash and exuberant promotion. Horace Greeley reached it just at the time when it had entered on its unique role as a city that no longer simply belonged to the seaboard, as Boston or Philadelphia did, but now looked out broadly across the land. He came in on the tide set up by the Erie Canal—a new current that cut straight across the older drift which had carried inland commerce down the interior river system to the South. He came East with a cargo of Great Lakes wheat that five years before would have been rafted down the Ohio and Mississippi to New Orleans, and in this change of direction there now also changed the entire direction of strength in the country. He arrived at the moment when startling vistas of western growth and wealth opened to the men in their grubby shops and countinghouses on Broadway and Exchange Place. And he arrived in a year when record numbers of immigrants from Europe came ashore in New York—many of them people who could read and others who would still have to learn how to read, but all of them a vigorous, hopeful, restless breed whose hearts were set on advancement, whose minds were ready to discard the past, and whose men were going to exercise the vote.

The sight was intoxicating. New York, at this moment, was the place to be. It lacked a finished culture, it read little literature, it threw its feet up over the seats at the Old Bowery. Yet its very rawness had its promise, and even intellectual young men were gravitating toward it—some of them New Englanders who felt that more was stirring here than in their own Athens on Boston Bay. William Cullen Bryant, the grave, deep-browed young poet whose *Thanatopsis* had made him famous, had come down from the Berkshire hills to go to work on the *Evening Post*. Charles Fenno Hoffman, a lively broker in talent and ideas, was about to start in New York his literary *Knickerbocker Magazine*. Washington Irving, grown stout and garrulous, was still New York's own coffeehouse luminary, surrounded by his coterie of clay-pipe, Hudson Valley imitators; but new blood was moving in. The *American Monthly*, also just founded in town, was gathering new artists and writers around it. The imaginative Boston editor, Park Benjamin, moved his *New England Magazine* to New York, in search of vigorous talent and a bigger market. Here he published the short stories of his fellow New Englander, Nathaniel Hawthorne, and before long was making friends with Horace Greeley of Vermont.

3

Bryant, soft-spoken, blue-eyed and aloof, was a curious arrival in the brash world of New York journalism. "While I was shaving this morning at eight o'clock," Philip Hone told his diary for 20 April, 1831, "I witnessed from the front windows an encounter in the street nearly opposite between William C. Bryant, one of the editors of the *Evening Post*, and William L. Stone, editor of the *Com-*

mercial Advertiser. The former commenced the attack by striking Stone over the head with a cowskin; after a few blows the parties closed and the whip was wrested from Bryant and carried off by Stone." It was "a disgraceful affair," said Hone; but it was the kind of thing that happened often among editors. The year before, the handsome, strutting Colonel James Watson Webb of the *Courier and Enquirer* had gone forth to cane the editor of the Washington *Telegraph,* Duff Green. William Leggett of the *Evening Post,* in turn, one day spat upon and assaulted Colonel Webb. Webb, again, publicly beat up a new rival who had formerly worked for him—"an ill-looking, squinting man called Bennett." Editors were simply not gentlemen, the elegant Hone summed up; "they cannot adjust their affairs in an *honorable* manner." And Bryant himself remarked that as for the public attitude toward newspaper editors, "contempt is too harsh a word for it, perhaps, but it is far below respect."

This attitude had been conditioned by the newspapers themselves, which in general were conducted with an eye to the lowest sort of lampooning and mutual abuse. Leggett in print called the editor of the New York *American* a "detestable caitiff"; Webb called his enemy James Gordon Bennett a "beggar"; Bennett in turn called the rival New York *Sun* "a sneaking, drivelling nigger paper" produced by "the garbage of society." Up in Albany, young Thurlow Weed of the *Evening Journal* denounced his political opponent, Croswell of the *Argus,* as "Martin van Buren's pimp." Croswell in reply called Weed a "rapist."

Most newspaper editors resorted to this sort of thing simply in order to attract attention, or to divert it from the fact that their papers carried little that was recognizable as fresh news. The average four-page paper of 1830 was a dingy, ill-printed sheet, made up of a jumble of market and ship-movement items, "Foreign Intelligence" paragraphs often lifted from other papers which in turn had lifted them from European journals, speech extracts or sermons, all this being livened up with a column or two of the editor's thickest vitriol and padded with Poets' Corners, Local Gleanings, and Miscellany. Individual Washington bureaus, press associations, regular foreign correspondents, reportorial staffs trained to cover local and general news, "human-interest" features, sports pages—all these were unknown. The average newspaper of 1830 looked very much like the average paper of 1730, when colonial postmasters had turned out little "newsletters" as an adjunct to their business. Now the newspaper was often the adjunct of a print shop or of some local politician or faction; but in many cases it was still written and edited by one man alone, who served also as its printer.

Such a man was Thurlow Weed in Albany, a skillful journeyman, brisk paragraph writer and aspiring politician who had bought the chief interest in the *Evening Journal*. "I not only edited the paper without an assistant," he recalled, "but reported the proceedings of the Assembly and the courts. I rose early and awaited the arrival of the steamboat from New York, to obtain newspapers two hours earlier than they were delivered at the post office. I also visited before breakfast the chief hotels . . . After breakfast, until the publication hour, I labored at my editorial table. I also assisted the foreman in making up and putting the paper to press." Under such circumstances, not only did an editor's news remain sketchy, but his reaction to the latest events was also often intermittent and delayed. Speed, in fact, was not generally thought to be of much importance. Bryant remembered of the veteran *Evening Post* that its men moved slowly, feeling no need of pronouncing "a prompt judgement on questions of public nature the moment they arose." Under his own hand, when he succeeded to the editorship in 1829, the paper took on new force and distinction, and his assistant, William Leggett, a brusque and colorful Jacksonian agitator, wrote for it some of the most effective editorial copy of the day; but even so, the *Evening Post* remained a small concern, and in 1834 its daily run still hung at 2,000 copies.

Here and there a publisher experimented with a more pretentious type of journal, designed to meet in greater detail the needs of the reading class most able to pay. The result was the mercantile or businessman's gazette—a sheet which specialized in market news and showed off its importance by enlarging the size of its four pages to enormous proportions, without however enlivening them. The price of such "blanket sheets," as delivered to gentlemen's clubs and offices, also ran up until it reached eight and ten cents a copy. At that rate the most successful of these, the choleric Colonel Webb's *Courier and Enquirer*, could sell no more than 4,000 copies —the highest daily circulation figure reached in a city of two hundred thousand.

Webb and his rival, "Davy" Hale of the *Journal of Commerce*, had at least seen the value of speeding up news as a means of enabling their readers to score business beats over their competitors. Both papers had taken to hiring their own express riders to bring back advance news of Washington legislation, while other editors waited patiently to learn the latest from mailed copies of Frank Blair's semiofficial Washington *Globe*. Webb and Hale also went into the business of chartering fast boats to intercept incoming ocean packets off Sandy Hook in order to get their hands first on European market news. But with circulations in the low thousands, there was an obvious limit to the expense that could be incurred for such innovations. Meanwhile, though, a new potential audience was building up in New York in terms of tens of thousands. A revolution in the technique of printing was under way which would make it possible to reach such an audience speedily. All that was needed now was a new idea.

4

James Gordon Bennett—"an ill-looking, squinting man," as Philip Hone said—had come from Scotland years ago to knock about grubby newspaper offices north and south, sometimes working as a hack writer, often being left wholly unemployed. Nearing forty, he was a lonely, scrawny figure, sardonic by nature, amoral, contemptuous of his betters, and—what seemed worse—wholly irreligious; his one passion was an absorbed fascination in day-to-day human affairs, right down to the most trivial domestic talk and gossip, and his instinct told him that all this was worth airing. He had tried to do something of the sort as a Washington contributor to Webb's paper, sending up columns of amused chatter about the social life of the capital, its balls, its dowagers, its feuds, and what he called its "mad frolics." But Webb, although always ready to slash away with a pen or stick, could not see what possible impact such trivia might have. All this might be very lively, but it was not to the point, and—for the audience of the *Courier and Enquirer*—it was not dignified. So Bennett was out of work again. But, seeing that Webb was not selling more than a trickle of papers with his pretense of "dignity," Bennett came away with an idea of his own. It was this: "An editor must always be with the people—think with them—feel with them—and he need fear nothing, he will always be right."

Just when and how James Gordon Bennett met Greeley is uncertain, but at some point in the early 1830's this idea communicated itself from one to the other. Newspaper editors and journeymen printers, at that time, tended to congregate: their backgrounds were often the same, and their crafts had not yet drawn far apart. Bennett, in fact, thinking of putting his idea into practice, proposed to Greeley that they go in together in starting a new newspaper in New York.

By that time Greeley had already strode ahead rapidly on his own. From the *Spirit of the Times* he had graduated into a small printing partnership, launched with Francis V. Story, the pressroom foreman on that paper. The firm of Greeley & Story, 54 Liberty Street, had announced itself in business early in 1833, particularly soliciting "lottery printing, such as schemes, periodicals, etc." Greeley, a fast compositor and a good talker who could get a couple of cases of type and a hand press on loan, by then had moved to a middle-class boardinghouse on Chatham Street.

Meanwhile he, too, had begun to think and talk about the possibilities of another kind of journalism in New York. One could not look at the weekly shiploads landing at the Battery without wondering what effect these might have on America in general and the city in particular. They knew so little of their new home—and, in order to rise and prosper, they would need to know much. Many of them had never in their lifetime read a newspaper or general magazine. They would want one now. A few men were talking about editing some new sort of cheap paper for them. Greeley, for the moment, only wanted to get in on printing it. But he knew that it was not a long way from being a printer to being an editor in his own right.

At this point he and Story met a man named H. D. Shepard, who was by training a medical student but by vocation a dabbler in publishing. Shepard had hit upon the radical notion of getting out a daily paper priced at only one cent in order to reach New York's poorer public, and of selling it not over an office counter but by newsboys hawking through the streets. Greeley & Story put up $200 as printing partners and entered with Shepard on the *Morning Post*. The *Post* appeared on New Year's Day, 1833, amid a snowstorm which drove its newsboys to cover and almost killed it. Its amateur editor, moreover, said Greeley, was "neither a writer nor a man of affairs; had no editors, no reporters worth naming, no correspondents, and no exchanges even; he fancied that a paper would sell, if remarkable for cheapness, though remarkable also for the absence of every other desirable quality." Within a few weeks the paper was dead; and "we printers," Greeley wrote, "were hard aground on a lee shore, with little prospect of getting off."

Next came Benjamin Day, another printer and a successful one, who picked up Shepard's idea and added to it the missing ingredient of popular editorial appeal in order to create his own penny paper, the immediately successful New York *Sun*. But Day's paper went to the opposite extreme of anything that had been tried before and made no attempt to present serious news at all: it dealt almost exclusively in horror stories, backstairs scandal and lugubrious yarns of fallen girls, ghosts, miracles and monstrosities, frankly seeking to catch the gullible and the semiliterate. The *Sun*, as the first product of the new journalism, repelled Greeley. He had believed in disseminating information to a popular audience, but this was not what he had in mind at all. Bennett was talking of starting a somewhat similar paper, with improvements—that is, one that would combine the appeal to servant girls with more adult, earthy news directed also to their masters. But this still was not the formula Greeley himself was seeking. Bennett in 1835, in an act of historic impact on journalism, rented a cellar in Wall Street, slung a pair of boards across two flour barrels in order to make an editorial desk and sales counter for himself, and, with only $500 in hand and no man to help him, founded the New York *Herald*. Greeley had not given up the idea of going into journalism himself, though. The year before he had started his own little weekly, the *New Yorker*.

5

He was then twenty-three. He had moved on from the Chatham Street boardinghouse to a diet-reform "hotel" conducted by Dr. Sylvester Graham, who promoted vegetarianism and unseasoned puddings along with such other innovations as cold baths, loose clothing, and open windows at night. There Greeley was in a stage of writing Byronic poetry at night. His sister Esther recalled that he kept a trunkful of books of verse and "appeared in a perpetual rose dream." He had devoured novels, essays, travel books, summaries of philosophy, and even statistical discussions of the state of the national banks, and was yearning to express himself on each. He was filled with a desire to do his friends and the world some good: he had already begun handing out sizable portions of whatever weekly cash he earned to fellow journeymen, strays, alcoholics, promoters of causes, and improvident members of his own family. Nevertheless, living frugally, he found himself with almost $1,500 cash earned as a printer in hand. He had to do something with it. He decided to help inform, entertain and elevate the public. His partner and good friend, Story, had been drowned while swimming in the East River, but Greeley had found himself a new printing associate, Jonas Winchester, who had the mind of a promoter and the desire to be a publisher. So the firm of Greeley & Winchester came forth on 22 March, 1834, with the first issue of its sixteen-page weekly, the *New Yorker*.

"Our paper is not blazoned through the land as 'The Cheapest Periodical in the World,' or any of the captivating clap-traps wherewith enterprising gentlemen are wont to usher in their successive experiments on the gullibility of the Public," proclaimed the fledgling editor; "No . . . fashionable characters have been dragged in to bolster up a rigmarole of preposterous and charlatan pretensions." The *New Yorker* was simply to be a journal of "general literature," news and comment—with no "humbug" about it.

All the editing and a large part of the writing were done by Greeley, working without a helper in his second-floor office in the rear of 20 Nassau Street. Much of the actual type composition was his work too, and the well-designed pages and careful presswork showed his meticulous hand. Winchester handled subscriptions, bought paper, and hired pressroom apprentices while Greeley spent the week assembling his miscellany of material for a Friday night deadline and Saturday delivery. The paper set out with a paid circulation of fifty. By the end of its first year its weekly sales had passed 4,500.

Usually the *New Yorker* opened with several pages of "general literature," under which Greeley grouped leisurely travel letters (often lifted from English monthlies), moral essays, reveries on life and love and family by anonymous contributors, and an ample selection of swooning verse sent in by ladies signing themselves "Eloisa," "Calista," "Clarice" and "Cyllene." One week "Lutetia" led off the paper with this sentiment:

> In Sunset's lingering hues of gold,
>   Some far-off isle of rest,
> The hearts in this sad world grown cold
>   Aye, beckons to its rest . . .

And "Ella," several weeks later, got Greeley to print

> Oh! Lay me by the river's side,
>   Where the graceful lily bends,
> And o'er the waters far and wide
>   Its grateful fragrance sends . . .

Then came stories and sketches—some by Greeley, others anonymous, and then a few by an Englishman who signed himself "Boz" and who later turned out to be Charles Dickens. The editor himself leaned more toward poetry: "As to Prose," he wrote a Vermont friend, B. F. Ransom, who was also aspiring to verse, "it is not worth writing, except for bread; to live, it must be Poetry." So Greeley wrote and published threnodies on "The Death of William Wirt" and verses "To the Memory of a Friend," and one day, in a confessional mood, produced this:

FANTASIES

> They deem me cold, the thoughtless and light-hearted,
>   In that I worship not at beauty's shrine;
> They deem me cold, that through the year's departed,
>   I ne'er have bowed me to some form divine.
> They deem me proud, that, where the world hath flattered,
>   I ne'er have knelt to languish or adore;
> They think not that the homage idly scattered
>   Leaves the heart bankrupt, ere its spring is o'er.
>
> No! in my soul there glows but one bright vision
>   And o'er my heart there rules but one fond spell,
> Bright'ning my hours of sleep with dreams Elysian
>   Of one unseen, yet loved, aye cherished well;
> Unseen? Ah! no; her presence round me lingers,
>   Chasing each wayward thought that tempts to rove;
> Weaving Affection's web with fairy fingers,
>   And waking thoughts of purity and love.

But then his interest turned to more practical matters, and he threw in items on "What Are Buffaloes?" "Disorders in Mexico," local "Spirit Manifestations," "The Pink-Eyed Lady" (to be seen that week at the American Museum on Broadway) and "The Massacre at the Fejee Islands":

The Ship *Cyrus Hussey*, of Nantucket, just from the Pacific, reports having heard on her passage that three of the officers and three of the crew of the whale ship *Awashonka*, of Falmouth, were murdered by savages while getting refreshments at the Fejee Islands.

Science and invention absorbed him: he reported on new fertilizers, welcomed an improved plow, and reprinted articles by Professor Silliman of Yale on electromagnetism. Then, midway through his paper, he turned his attention to domestic politics. Here the *New Yorker* ceased being a rambling miscellany and became concentrated and pointed: it was clear that for all the editor had said about his love of poetry, his chief interest lay in the prose of political ideas and public events.

He could have satisfied many readers by giving them simply a conventional rehash of Washington and Albany news. Instead of this, he experimented with an entirely new idea. Believing that almost all papers were grossly partisan and haphazard in their political coverage, he made it his business from the outset to be extraordinarily accurate, detailed and objective. He began with the local scene, taking time to attend city legislative sessions, write up precise accounts of proceedings, assemble authentic election lists, and come out first after election day with carefully checked voting tabulations. He got legislators in Albany and Washington to send him advance texts of their bills and speeches, and made sure that these were printed speedily and with absolute accuracy. He held the paper open sometimes on Saturday for late news, and then berated subscribers who objected to delayed delivery by pointing at the importance of what he carried. He scoured the city, ward by ward, during the two-day presidential election of 1836, seeking early returns and exposing false rumors, and in his next issue rapped the knuckles of the dailies that had put out misleading news. This, he said, was "undermining their credit with the public. They must mend their manners..."

He sat down then and let himself go in editorials on every conceivable subject: on the dirtiness of New York's streets, on the spread of prostitution, on the need of a steam railway from the Battery to Harlem, on the bases of sound national banking, on the evils of alcohol and tobacco, on relations with Mexico, and on the essence of Christianity. His tones grew firm and self-assured. "The Secretary of War urges an increase in the Army," he began one day; "We are opposed to this... We honor Mr. Kendall [the Postmaster

General] for his plain speaking on the subject of abuses of the franking privilege. Let the members of Congress take the hint. They know very well for whom it is intended." Some of his readers wrote in to say that he was holding forth at too great length about politics. He answered that he did not agree it was presumptuous of him to discuss "questions of absorbing national interest ... We shall pursue unwaveringly the even tenor of our way."

In fact, as his audience grew, he rather enjoyed browbeating it. He made a point of acknowledging contributions in print on his editorial page, often with brusque rejection notices:

The *poet* who stole "Sir Cupid" from an old magazine, and imposed it upon us as an original production, is informed that we hope to be favored with no more of his efforts in the pilfering line.

"Say, What Is Beauty?" we have, on final reading, been compelled to decline. Such grammer as "has fell" will not do.

We regret to decline "Soliloquoy, or, Complaint of Mary, Queen of Scots"; but really there is no alternative. The Royal Martyr has been executed too often in our columns already.

When readers did not pay up their subscriptions, he hectored them by publishing their names and the amounts due. Sometimes he blew up:

H. C. Francis of South Leroy, N. Y., is indebted to us $4. We cannot wonder that he does not pay us, as there is a rumor afloat that he pays nobody.

He sailed into rival publications, too: "The *Knickerbocker* is but fair this month. . . ." "We do not like the February number of the *American Monthly Magazine* at all. . . ." "The *Evening Post* is generally understood to have lost patronage within the last three or four years. . . ."

Yet the audience enjoyed the spectacle of this brash young man throwing his type cases around. By the end of his second year Greeley could show 7,000 circulation, and by the end of his third, almost 9,000. Publisher Jonas Winchester turned out to be shifty and irresponsible, and Greeley got rid of him and took in a new man named Wilson, who was not much better. Even so, money accumulated, and now Greeley found he could afford editorial helpers. He took in for a while as literary editor the distinguished Park Benjamin. Later he hired a young unknown named Henry J.

Raymond, who was to become the first of his extraordinary discoveries. "The calm, dispassionate character of [the *New Yorker's*] articles," Raymond wrote afterward, when he had become the editor of the New York *Times*, "and the accuracy of its statements, won for Mr. Greeley a degree of public confidence sufficient to set up half a dozen men in any business where confidence was the main thing required."

He began to think of bigger ventures. With $5,000 newly earned capital in hand, he might buy a fast press and produce something far in advance over the *New Yorker*. The day of the slow-moving, one-cylinder, flat-bed press, in which the type body was rocked back and forth under rollers, was passing. The Hoe firm had built a new kind of steam press that could perform 4,000 impressions an hour. Still newer presses were under way in which the type itself was placed on turning cylinders, and these would be able to do up to 8,000 an hour. The time for new newspaper enterprise was here.

In the meantime, feeling himself for the first time prosperous and secure, Horace Greeley had set out to find happiness by wooing Mary Cheney of Cornwall, Connecticut, a fellow boarder in the strictly vegetarian Graham House on Barclay Street.

III. WHIG

1

Life at Graham's had been drab and dull for Horace Greeley until Mary Cheney arrived from Connecticut to stay there while she taught classes at a nearby girls' school. She was twenty-two, slim, talkative and extraordinarily well dressed—a startling and even lustrous presence to descend suddenly into a circle of subdued, frugal folk as they sat eating their meals of coarse bread, unseasoned beans and puddings.

She was not beautiful, and not even conventionally pretty; apart from her dark eyes and high, arched forehead, her features were spare and plain. But her eyes were so extraordinarily large, luminous and intense that they could light up the whole of her pale face and gave it a high-spirited, ardent air. In repose, she looked somewhat austere. But when she talked she became eager and impetuous. Strong will showed in her manner, along with taut nerves and high sensitivity. She was an independent Yankee girl in a time when not many broke away from home.

Coming from a line of Housatonic Valley farmers, she had decided before she was twenty to be a schoolmistress and strike out on her own. Cornwall township by the river's gorges, where her family had held land for three generations, had fallen into decline as many of its vigorous men struck out for the more rewarding West; it was another East Poultney, almost another Westhaven. Mary had some money of her own that helped her move away: "She was as rich as I was," Greeley remarked of her to Moses Cortland at the time of their marriage, meaning that she was then worth possibly $5,000. Like Greeley, she was a fugitive from inner New England valleys and a seeker for the outside world. Like Greeley, she carried with her into that outside world a burning earnestness and moral rigor: education was her passion, and it was Dr. Graham's farinaceous vegetarianism that brought the two together.

"She was a typical Yankee schoolmistress, crazy for learning," her house guest in later years, Margaret Fuller, remarked. Yet to people less accustomed to curiosities than Margaret Fuller, Mary Cheney did not seem typical at all. In fact, she was strangely exaggerated in all her ways. She was both vigorously feminist and extravagantly feminine. She was so ascetic that she preferred to live in bare, graceless rooms stripped of pictures, curtains, or any comfortable furniture whatever. On the other hand, she loved to decorate herself with luxurious finery unheard-of among schoolmistresses. "She was dressed in clouds of white muslin, cut low," Horace Greeley's plain sister, Esther, gushed after her first startled meeting with Mary, "and her neck and shoulders covered by massive dark curls, from which gleamed out an oriental-looking coiffure, composed of strands of large gold and pearls."

She read, she talked of intellectual things, and she prided herself on being above narrow thoughts of domesticity. She loved poetry —and Horace Greeley had written some. He fell in love with her, and between his late hours and her Grahamite rice puddings he courted her. It was undoubtedly his first experience. (The love poem which he had written in 1834, a year before meeting Mary— "In my soul there glows but one bright vision of one unseen, yet loved, aye cherished well"—was appropriately called "Fantasies.") Restraints had surrounded him; as he later confessed to his friend Charles A. Dana at Brook Farm, speaking of sexual adventures, "The temptations to that special sin have never been so strong with me as with some." Mary Greeley was high-strung and restrained, too; she found Greeley amid his innocence and his ambition and aroused him.

She may have had doubts about marrying him; she knew how ill-fitted she was for domestic life. In late fall or winter she left Graham's to teach at a girls' academy in faraway Warrenton in the North Carolina piedmont. In the spring, though, Horace Greeley followed her there. They were married, at her wish, in the Episcopalian Church. Horace was and remained a Universalist.

Thirteen years after, Greeley wrote and permitted to be published in *The Printer's Book* for 1849 a curious sonnet entitled "Portrait of a Lady":

> The blissful June of life! I love to gaze
>   On its sweet wealth of ripening loveliness,
> And lose the thoughts that o'er my saddening days
>   Grim Care has woven clouds which will depress,
> In spite of stoic pride and stern resolve:
>   Beauty like this the waste of life redeems;
> 'Round it—their sun—the coldest hearts revolve,
>   Warm'd back to youth and gladdened by its beams.
> But, lady! in that mild, soul-speaking glance,
>   Those lustrous orbs, returning heaven its hue,
> I greet an earlier friend—forgive the trance!
>   'Tis Nature only, imaged here so true
> That, briefly, I forgot the Printer's art,
>   And hailed the presence of a Queenly Heart.

This poem, outwardly so trite and conventional with its swooning images, told the story of what happened between Horace and Mary Greeley. He spoke of his early "trance" in the presence of her "Queenly Heart." The trance dissolved; she became "an earlier friend." He returned to his first love, "the Printer's art."

Often, in later years, Greeley confessed himself unable to understand what had gone wrong between them—and, in that state, he did little about trying to set it right. Sometimes he sensed that he was making Mary unhappy by being so engrossed in his work. But one reason for his being so engrossed in his work was that he had become unhappy with Mary. Where did the fault begin, and on whose side did it lie? He never could unravel the tangled chain of cause and effect. Before long, though, he became a distracted and long-absent husband, and Mary a sharp-tongued, malingering wife, barely recognizable as the spirited and ornamental schoolmistress he had married.

Long after the fact he let drop a hint of their life together in a letter to Mrs. Emma Whiting Newhall, one of the woman friends to whom he turned to exchange those feelings and confidences that could no longer be shared at home. He was speaking of marriages in general, not of his own in particular. "In nine-tenths of our marriages," he wrote, "the love is all on the man's side. The women marry for a position, a subsistence, a protector: the man marries for a wife ... Woman marries from fear of never having another chance ... Now the young husband being in love with *his* wife, while a wife has capitulated only to *a* husband, would not always

be a loving husband if this were admitted. But he is awkward—
constrained—a novice . . . He would fain evince devotion, sentiment, idolatry; but she repulses or ridicules his maladroit demon-
strations, and bids him (in substance) not make a fool of himself.
And a few rebuffs usually tame him down into a faithful, decorous,
conscientious, un-lover-like husband."

Outwardly, though, the marriage set out with appearances of
happiness. The couple entertained frequently in their new house
in Greenwich Street, and Sister Esther was surprised to see Horace
get up and dance a quadrille at a lively party on Christmas Eve.
Soon, however, there were nervous explosions on Mary Greeley's
part. "Did Mary ever tell you," Greeley wrote Emma Whiting Newhall, years later, "how she once gave up home and wedded life
because her fire would not burn? I received a note [at the office] telling me she had done so, and ran home to take care of what was
left, but I think she had not gone—if she had, she soon returned.
Being then a young husband, I was somewhat startled, as now I
should not be." Then tragedy struck them: in 1838 Mary's first-born
son died, only a few months old. Mary's growing tension took the
form of obscure physical disorders. In the following winter, while
working much of the time in Albany, Greeley wrote his friend
Ransom, "My wife is in bad health and is left utterly alone in New
York through the worst part of the years—a circumstance which
pleases neither of us." Eleven months later he was telling his other
close Vermont friend, Bowe: "Mary is terribly ill and downhearted
—a miscarriage of the worst kind, and great danger of the loss of
her eyesight. She is now unable to bear the light, and must be kept
so all winter, without reading or doing anything, but I think she
will ultimately recover." Two years later, such messages had become chronic: "Mrs. Greeley is in her usual bad health," he wrote
Ransom in late 1841. Her nervous ailments multiplied until she took
to spending weeks and then months away from home, consulting
assorted doctors, healers and spiritualists in Boston. In May, 1843,
" 'Diah" Bowe wanted Greeley to meet him there. Greeley answered
that it wouldn't be "to much purpose. You see, my wife is there-
abouts; and it takes both of my hands to wait upon one woman, and
then it's hard work."

2

Thus marriage brought disappointment; but outside his home,
the very turbulence of daily life absorbed and reassured him. He

looked about the bustling country in the first year of his marriage, and found it promising and good. Summing up the state of the nation in the *New Yorker* in October, 1836, he proclaimed that "on whatever side we turn our eyes, we are greeted by the gratifying evidences of universal prosperity." In spite of "unwise legislation" and the "injudicious methods" of President Andrew Jackson's Administration, "each successive year adds many millions to the aggregate of the National wealth . . . For some fifteen years has the march of improvement in this country proceeded with a rarely checked and unexampled celerity; so that at this moment the actual valuation of property in the United States cannot be less than double and is quite as likely to be treble what it was at the commencement of the period indicated. . . ."

He went on enthusing; his optimism was unquenchable. True, there were evils in America: there was too much illiteracy, too much drinking, too much Jacksonianism, too much tobacco chewing, too much interference with business enterprise, and too much unruly squabbling between capital and labor. But otherwise the country was forging ahead. Greeley himself had emerged from two backwash areas where hopes had been frustrated and lives bent; but, far from being embittered by them, he reasoned that since he had now seen the worst of America, the rest must be better—far better. Every evidence of material progress thrilled him—every new canal, railroad line, or block of buildings in New York—and he thought that as they extended, moral progress would surely follow. He looked out West, and while wearing his rustic boots and flopping pantaloons in Nassau Street instinctively identified himself with it. He wrote about the West, about its illimitable promise, about "the irresistible might of American happiness," as Henry Clay had termed it, and in this he passionately believed.

He had come out of New England an "Adams man," but since then had made himself a disciple of the hawklike, homely prophet from Kentucky. Clay had projected his vision of a new, expanding "American system" in which government would work in partnership with private enterprise to further industry, to provide a country-wide network of internal communications and "improvements," and to help people the West, thereby creating a great, self-contained "home market." Greeley's *New Yorker* ardently echoed him. All who seemed bent on limiting the power of industry were its enemies, as were any who stood in the way of opening the West. And the worst were those who failed to agree that the American community as Henry Clay had described it was on its way toward becoming irresistibly happy.

For it was a community, and a close one, Greeley thought in his twenties, and those who kept dwelling on its antagonisms of classes and interests were shortsighted, selfish, or misguided. Only a few months before he himself had arrived in New York City in 1831, a young visiting Frenchman named Alexis de Tocqueville had landed at the Battery to roam through the country and write a book about it. On the first page of his *Democracy in America* the visitor had said, "Nothing struck me more forcibly than the general equality of condition among the people." This was as Horace Greeley saw it, too. Or at any rate, if there was not yet "general equality," it could soon be achieved. "Capital," he wrote in his *New Yorker* in 1836, "is labor already performed, while Labor is Capital now being or about to be realized." The American laborer, therefore, "however humble his station and doubtful his prospects, [should] regard himself not as a serf desperately struggling with his fetters, but as a freeman, quietly but surely threading his way from poverty to certain competence if not wealth."

Yet not everyone in the America of the 1830's accepted this hopeful thought. On the conservative side, the inheritors of tiewig Federalist thinking went on declaring that there were higher and lower orders in society, set apart by fixed moral differences, and that the two had little interest in common. As the *American Quarterly Review* put it in 1832, the "poorest orders" of society were distinguished by "sensual excess, want of intelligence and moral debasement," while the rich were marked by "knowledge, intellectual superiority, and refined, social affections"; it followed, then, that the poor were not fit to be anything but poor, and that the inherited hierarchy of class should be preserved as it was. This was not to young Greeley's way of thinking. But neither could he accept the charges made by spokesmen at the opposite extreme that it was precisely this vested doctrine that was shaping American life, and that the workingman's chances for equality, far from growing better, were now fast growing worse.

On the eve of the 1830's, spontaneous Workingman's parties had sprung up in several states to try to raise the worker's status by bringing about such reforms as free public education and the abolition of imprisonment for debt. Some of the "Workie" leaders, like Frances Wright, bold, redheaded and fiery, were frank apostles of inevitable class warfare. Seth Luther, a traveling "Workie" agitator from Rhode Island, burst out, "Our ears are constantly filled with the cry of National wealth, National glory, American system. This cry is kept up by men who are endeavoring by all the means in their power to cut down the wages of our own people . . . Fellow-citizens of New England, we have borne these evils by far too long . . . Let us awake!" And in New York, in 1833, a manifesto drawn up by left-wing Jacksonians—"Locofocos," as they were called—declared darkly that "The world has always abounded with men who . . . have combined to strip others of the fruits of their labor, either by violence and bloodshed, or by swaggering pretensions to exclusive privileges. It is . . . by the latter mode of robbery, that the working classes of modern times are kept in debasement and poverty. Aristocrats have discovered that [corporate] charters are safer weapons than swords; and that cant, falsehood and hypocrisy serve all the purposes of a highwayman's pistol . . ."

This, to Greeley, sounded revolutionary, "agrarian," and subversive of that social harmony which was now within sight. Besides, he thought, the charge was not true. For his part, he welcomed the coming of those factories whose growth and power was causing "Workie" and "Locofoco" leaders such concern. In only one decade, the number of cotton-weaving looms in New England had multiplied tenfold. The factories were coming anyway, Greeley argued, and any "radical" who fought against them was, in a sense, reactionary—that is, he was talking as futilely against the times as was the crusty James Fenimore Cooper up in Cooperstown, who went on denouncing industrialism from the fastnesses of his vast ancestral estate. True, the factories were bringing new problems with them. In Rhode Island, for instance, the average factory workday ran to thirteen hours and the prevailing wage to just two dollars a week. Moreover, as of 1831, two thousand Rhode Island factory hands working at such rates were children, fifty-nine of whom were not yet aged nine. But surely, Greeley thought, such evils would not last. The factory system was still callow and young; many of its managers had themselves been only small shopkeepers just a few years before; they had not learned their duty to share their reward fairly with others. But growth and prosperity would breed enlightenment; enlightenment would bring conscience, and conscience a new sense of mutuality. It might take time; but it would come, and all would be well.

Another young editor in New York, William Cullen Bryant of the *Evening Post*, was saying that matters were not well at all. The contrasts between the two men were striking: Greeley, homely, sprawling, countrified, noisy, disrespectful of urban forms and usages; Bryant, cultivated, poetic, with a high forehead, fine hands, a subdued manner of speech, and an air of blue-eyed, sensitive reserve. Both had come from inland New England; both were many-sided, precocious converts to New York; both were literary editors with a rising passion for politics. Of the two, it might have seemed more likely for Greeley, with his impoverished background, to go over to the insurgent, "leveling" enthusiasms of Jacksonianism. Bryant had started his literary life by composing superior little Federalist couplets. Yet it was Bryant, not Greeley, who became in the 1830's the critic and the crusader.

In 1834, the beginnings of antislavery agitation had provoked in New York City a sudden, savage outburst of Negro-hating mobs in the course of which Negro homes were burned and the churches, shops and offices of their white abolitionist friends sacked and wrecked. Bryant's *Evening Post* furiously denounced the rioters. Greeley's *New Yorker*—along with the rest of the city's press—passed by on the other side.

That same fall, bloody clashes took place on New York mayoralty election day between nativist, anti-Irish and generally conservative Whigs on one hand, and marching squads of Tammany Hall's immigrant Democrats on the other. "Down with aristocracy!" shouted the Tammany braves. Bryant's *Evening Post* was for them. Greeley was for the Whigs.

Next year, the merchants of New York were shocked to find themselves threatened with a new workingman's weapon: twenty-one journeyman tailors had boldly gone out in a body on strike. The men were promptly indicted, haled into the dock, and fined. Bryant, the poet, came out alone in defense of them:

. . . .They were condemned because they had determined not to work for the wages that were offered them! Can anything be imagined more abhorrent to every sentiment of generosity or justice than the law which arms the rich with the legal right to fix, by assize, the wages of the poor? If this is not SLAVERY, we have forgotten its definition.

But Greeley, again, stood aside:

> We are opposed . . . to all combinations, either of masters or journeymen, to regulate the compensation of labor. . . . Both parties clearly acted wrong.

Then, in the winter of 1836, spreading hunger and unrest in the city led to riots and raids on flour warehouses. Bryant's *Evening Post* tried to investigate the causes. Greeley's *New Yorker* said simply,

> We entreat the class of citizens more especially exhorted to unite in this reckless crusade to act rationally. . . . They can have no interest which is not our interest, and that of the business community in general.

Bryant and his militant editorial assistant, William Leggett, were concerned about the rash of speculation, reckless banking, franchise-grabbing and financial conspiracy that was coming over the nation. "Not a road can be opened, not a bridge can be built, not a canal can be dug," exploded Leggett, "but a charter of exclusive privileges must be granted for the purpose . . . The bargaining and trucking away of chartered privileges is the whole business of our lawmakers." Bryant had applauded President Jackson's move to break the power of the mighty private Bank of the United States, only to become disheartened when he saw banking as a result fall into the hands of small state-chartered groups that struck him as being equally venal; so he came out in the *Evening Post* against banks in general, arguing that they were simply lotteries designed by financiers in cahoots with politicians to round up the common man's hard-earned gold and issue worthless paper in exchange for it. The President himself, disturbed by the wild speculation unleashed by the new state banks and their paper money, warned Congress of trouble ahead. Yet Greeley remained confident. The boom rode on. Greeley was fascinated to learn that twenty downtown New York City lots, which had been gutted in a great fire a year ago and sold for $93,000, should have just changed hands for over $750,000. "Speculation, in its broadest sense," he wrote contentedly in the *New Yorker*, "is not an evil in itself, but the contrary, and relieves public distress far oftener than it creates it."

Then, a month later, came the crash.

3

Banks and brokerage houses, vastly overextended in western land deals, crop loans, and the underwriting of every sort of inflated paper scheme, had suddenly begun to feel panicky and to call in their money. The infection spread; one after another great business houses collapsed. "Times can hardly be worse than they are now," Greeley exclaimed on 1 April; "It is safe to trust nobody . . . Where will this end?" David Hale's pontifical *Journal of Commerce* tried to go on speaking as the *New Yorker* had a month before: "During the last three days of the week, we did not have a single [bank] failure . . . The result of the whole matter, instead of destroying confidence, ought to create it." But next week the great New York importing house of Arthur Tappan and the brokerage firm of Nevins & Co. went under. "The next step may precipitate universal disaster," declared Greeley, badly shaken. And in the week after that, when the nation's banks suspended gold payments altogether, Greeley cried out that the "horror" of the nation's condition was such that he could not "bear to dwell on it."

The condition of the *New Yorker*, too, was also becoming desperate. With many businesses at a standstill, circulation crashed and subscribers lost all thought of paying up. Greeley dunned them. It did no good. He took to publishing names of delinquents in conspicuous black lists, hoping to shame them:

H. Tuthill of the steamboat *James Kent*, which plies between Prescott and River Trent, evaded a pitiful demand of $5 made by our agent, by appointing a day on which he would pay, and then skulked off on the edge of the evening.

J. G. Seward of Watertown (Bookbinder) has been reported to us as worthless. The amount due by him—$4—we shall sue for.

He cajoled; he threatened: "We have lost about $3,000 by this species of knavery. We shall tamely endure it no longer." That did no good either. Neither did his frantic appeals: "Friends of the *New Yorker*! We appeal to you, not for charity, but for justice. Whoever among you is in our debt, no matter how small the sum, is guilty of a moral wrong in withholding the payment. . . ." The paper was now losing $100 a week. A new business manager let him down: "Burke Fisher has served me downright rascally," Greeley wrote Ransom. "He went away the last day of September to collect our western bills, which he did not begin to do, but first played away a month, then fooled away another, and next gave me over as a hopeless case . . ." He poured out his heart to Bowe: "There is now at least $8,000 due the concern, of which $3,000 might have been collected before this time with proper management. . . . I would gladly give away the whole concern tomorrow, with 5,000 subscribers and $8,000 due it, to any man who would pay its debts, amounting to $4,000. . . . Talbot has come back a bigger hog than he went, and he is draining my life-blood. I got a loan of $500 of him, to be paid in Michigan money, in such a way that it has cost me over $75. . . . I have got a paper note on $344 due on Friday, which will half kill me. . . ."

Meanwhile in the cities, general misery was spreading fast. In New York, every third workingman was out of a job. Greeley feared for the social order. Staggered by what he saw around him, he addressed the jobless:

Mechanics, artisans, laborers, you cannot with safety give heed to those who prophesy smooth things. . . . We say to the unemployed, you who are able to leave the cities should do so without delay. You have a winter in prospect of fearful, unexampled severity. Do not wait to share and increase its horrors. Fly—scatter through the land—go to the Great West. . . . The times are out of joint . . . Let all who can, betake themselves to the country. . . . Away, then, hardy adventurers, to Ohio, Michigan, Illinois, Indiana, or Wisconsin, if you have money to go so far.

This, dated 3 June, 1837, was Greeley's first pronouncement of that summons which was later to become inextricably linked with his name: "Go West!" It was written in sheer panic.

4

Young Greeley had confidently extolled the blessings of business, the virtues of thrift, and the resulting inevitability of American progress. But some element had failed in his philosophy. Unlimited self-interest had led only to general failure and the ruin of others. It had been so easy to say that the poor remained poor because they were naturally idle. But what was one to say when it was not through their own default but through that of business that they became idle? Whose was the responsibility for poverty then?

Deeply stirred, he decided in the depth of winter to find out at first hand how the poorest people of the city were living and feeling. He quit his house and moved into a room in the squalid Sixth Ward, the foul tenement area along Worth and Baxter streets behind City Hall, and there went to work with volunteer relief committees which the Ward's own dwellers had formed. He reported what he found:

I saw two families, including six or eight children, burrowing in one cellar under a stable . . . I saw men who each, somehow, supported his family on an income of $5 per week or less, yet who cheerfully gave something to mitigate the sufferings of those who were *really* poor. I saw three widows, with as many children, living in an attic on the profits of an applestand which yielded less than $3 per week. . . . But worst to bear of all was the pitiful plea of stout, resolute, single young men and young women: "We do not want alms; we are not beggars; we hate to sit here day by day idle and useless; help us to work—we want no other help! why is it that we can have nothing to do?"

Greeley was never to forget these sights. They aroused him, they changed his heart, and soon they sent him spinning across wide political spaces. He had begun life as an up-country Adams man, opposed to the popular incursion of Jacksonian Democracy. What he had seen and learned during the past year was not to change him over into a Jacksonian Democrat. It was to have an even more sweeping effect on him: it was to lead to his conversion to the new gospel of socialism.

5

Before he reached that point, though, Greeley was first to emerge as an influential Whig. This was paradoxical, to say the least; but so was the nature of Whiggism. In the mid-1830's, Whiggism was still more a name than it was a party: it was the unorganized focus of surviving remnants of those earlier conservative factions that had been blasted apart by the Jacksonians' triumph. By the end of the decade it was to become very much a party, with a mass basis and a sweeping national victory of its own in prospect—with everything, in fact, except an actual program. Whiggism was unique in American political history up to that time: it rounded up votes without even bothering to set forth ideas. Individual Whigs, like Greeley, had their own specific notions of what should be done. But as a whole the new party was a mass of contradictions, inconsistencies and lusty incoherence. Far from weakening it, this at the moment helped strengthen it. For it was the order of the day for statesmen to reverse themselves on almost every central issue: Webster, Jackson, Clay, Calhoun, all had done it. Greeley, far down in the heap, was doing so too. There was no point in looking for consistency in a day that lived under the sign of such rapid, increasing change. The main object was simply to try to keep up with it.

Ever since the death of the crusty old Federalist party in the years before 1820, conservatives had gone on making attempts to set up a new party instrument that would make their views prevail; but all their attempts had failed. In New York State, such manorial families as the Ogdens of Ogdensburg, the Platts of Plattsburg, the Lows of Lowville, and the Coopers of Cooperstown had tried to recapture their past power by setting up something they called the "People's party"—whose label had deceived no one. ("It is the one and implacable enemy under a new name," the popular Albany *Argus* had remarked.) Whiggism, however, represented a maneuver of another order. It was the name given to a scheme begun by a handful of skilled professionals to create a wide, loose-woven political basket into which all elements disaffected by the Jacksonian regime might fall. The professionals did not much care just why these elements had become disaffected or precisely what they sought; they simply wanted to provide a new home with a room for every tenant. They attracted Antimasons, since stories had been spread in upstate New York that Freemasonry was a secret, terroristic body in league with Jackson's strongmen. They attracted inland farmers of old Protestant stock, since anti-Catholic, anti-Irish bigotry had turned many of these against New York City's immigrant Tammany braves. They attracted eastern businessmen who wanted high tariffs, and they also attracted rich southern planters who wanted no tariffs at all but who feared that Jackson's Democrats had become too democratic. They attracted westerners who wanted more "internal improvements" than Jackson would give them, as well as Hudson River landlords who cared little about such improvements and nothing about the West, but who wanted to see radical "agrarianism" put down. They even drew in some radicals, too—disaffected "Workies" and "Locofocos" who thought that Jackson's politicians had not gone far enough. They attracted the haughty, reactionary Colonel Webb of the *Courier and Enquirer,* along with the doubting Horace Greeley. The ablest operator among them was Thurlow Weed, the jovial, strapping Albany politician and editor of that city's *Evening Journal*. And Thurlow Weed, in turn, was attracted to young Horace Greeley.

One day in November of the panic year that took Greeley into the slums, two strangers called at the *New Yorker*'s office—now in Ann Street—and asked to see the editor. They were men of conspicuous bearing; one of them was Weed himself. As Weed recalled the moment, "A young man with light hair and blond complexion, with coat off and sleeves rolled up, standing at the case, 'stick' in hand, replied that he was the editor, and this youth was Horace Greeley. We sat down in the composing room, [where] I informed him of the object of my visit. . . ."

Shortly before this, the New York State Whigs had surprised themselves as well as the nation by winning a string of local election victories over the Jacksonian "ins." At once the thought had blossomed in their minds that if a nationwide Whig coalition could quickly be rallied, it might capture the Congressional elections of 1838 and possibly the presidential contest of 1840. Like-minded politicians, led by the grand and glowering Daniel Webster, had come up from Washington to cheer the New Yorkers on. At a victory banquet that lasted until four in the morning—with Webster orating splendidly, but obviously awash—all had agreed on mounting a major propaganda campaign at once. "With that view," wrote Thurlow Weed, "a cheap weekly paper for extended circulation was suggested. In casting about for an editor it occurred to me that there was some person connected with the *New Yorker* . . . possessing the qualities needed for our new enterprise. . . . I felt sure that its editor was a strong tariff man and probably an equally strong Whig."

Now, seated on one of the high stools in the *New Yorker*'s composing room, Weed proposed to Greeley that he come up to Albany right away to start such a weekly for the Whig State Committee. It need not take all of his time; he could spend half of each week going on with his *New Yorker*, and for his part-time work he would be paid $1,000 over a year.

Greeley knew that the impressive visitor who sat opposite him was a bland manipulator, hard-shelled, cool-blooded, operating for power amid a vacuum of principles. Yet just that emptiness had its attractions: it opened opportunities to a young man to try to fill it with ideas of his own. Besides, there was Greeley's own immediate, personal vacuum that also needed filling. His *New Yorker*'s till was empty, and so were his pockets. He had experienced "months of perpetual horrors, which I would not live over again for a dukedom," he wrote Bowe. Weed's $1,000 might salvage both him and the *New Yorker*.

So he accepted the offer without delay. Weed's Albany *Evening Journal*, announcing the appointment, acclaimed the new Whig campaign editor as a man "whose character, principle and talents" would provide "the highest guarantees for a faithful and able discharge of the trust committed to him." The sardonic James Gordon Bennett, though, put it differently. "Weed took in Greeley when the rascal had not two pair of breeches to his legs," he wrote, "and gave him a clean shirt, a good dinner, and a new pair of boots."

IV. CAMPAIGNER

1

The Hudson was frozen solid above Poughkeepsie in January 1838, and Horace Greeley traveled to Albany by sleigh. He moved into a third-floor room in the Eagle Tavern and then went around to the *Evening Journal* office on State Street to report to Thurlow Weed and go to work.

It was agreed that the new paper was to be a cheaply printed eight-page, folio-sized weekly, packed as tightly as could be with campaign ammunition ranging from slogans to statistics, and sold to New York State Whigs at the nominal price of fifty cents for a year's subscription. Greeley, on arriving, had already picked a name for it. He suggested it be called the *Jeffersonian*. Weed was at first startled at the notion. Then he understood and accepted it. Young Greeley, it was clear, knew what he was after; he had measured the Albany chieftain's mind perfectly.

The taking of the name *Jeffersonian* for a Whig campaign sheet was a calculated piece of political strategy. It could also be called a case of outright theft. For the name of Jefferson belonged to the opposing, Democratic party, and the incumbent Jacksonians invoked it regularly as the fountainhead of their thought and policies. To business-minded Whigs, meanwhile, the name stood for radicalism, agrarianism, hostility to urban industry, and opposition to any federal undertakings designed to underwrite commercial enterprise. Neither Thurlow Weed nor his Albany associates had any perceptible Jeffersonian leanings; on the contrary, the leader's own friendships ran to the side of those business promoters who were intent on winning special privileges for themselves at the general expense. Yet, whether one liked the name of Jefferson or not, millions did. It carried magic; it won elections. And the object before the Whigs was to win elections too. The *Jeffersonian*? Why not, thought Weed. Let the Whigs sound even more Jeffersonian than Jackson, if that was what the people wanted.

To Greeley, the fact that the people did want this was something more than a challenge to party strategy. It was also an opportunity for real political change. When he reached Albany he had two purposes in mind, and sometimes he found it hard to reconcile them. The first reflected his persistent delight in the political game as such: it was the urge to help set up winning combinations for election day, no matter how artificial or opportunistic these might be. The second reflected his deepening political thinking: it was the desire to find a basis for a party that would do in America what none had yet done, namely unite the aspirations of labor, farmers and young businessmen. This he believed in, and he hoped that he could so apply his stratagems in Albany as to help realize it.

For although outwardly Greeley was a "regular" Whig in good standing with the machine Thurlow Weed was building, at heart he was a Whig with distinct Jeffersonian leanings. They were only halfway leanings, to be sure. He had no patience either with the old Virginia master's free-trade thinking or with his general suspicion of business enterprise. Yet Greeley found a kindred spirit in the Jefferson who had worked for the expansion of the West, for the advancement of the common man, for the limitation of landlordism and slavery, for the extension of education, and for the preservation of American simplicities amid growth and change. He thought he could prove in print that the Jacksonians in power, far from adhering to these principles, had thrown themselves into the hands of spoilsmen, political adventurers and southern pressure groups. The theme that Jackson had introduced "executive tyranny" and "elective monarchy" could be developed; the bossism and easy living of his successor, President Martin Van Buren, would provide another target. The name of Jefferson, in short, might be reclaimed for the opposing Whigs, partly in order to win for them a protective coloration, but partly also to make them become more Jeffersonian themselves. If the masses could be induced to come over to Whiggism, their presence in the camp would soon make Whiggism see its duty of serving the common man.

So Greeley reasoned—or, at any rate, so he tried to rationalize his political apprenticeship under Thurlow Weed. Having resolved these conflicts to his own satisfaction, he went to work in Albany enthusiastically. Moving into a corner of the *Evening Journal* office, where he could be in hourly contact with Weed, he managed to assemble, lay out and deliver to the presses downstairs the first issue of the *Jeffersonian* within less than a month—and this at a time when he was working without editorial help and was running another weekly on the side in New York City, a hundred and fifty miles away.

The first issue of the *Jeffersonian*, packed with small print and without cartoons or decoration of any sort, was dressed up deliberately in such a way as to look as if it were not campaign journalism at all. In fact, the editor went out of his way to say in his opening announcement that the *Jeffersonian* was "not a party paper in the ordinary acceptation of that term," and that it would "present the views of public men on both sides." The fact that it was subsidized by the New York State Whig Committee was concealed; so, also, was the very word "Whig," which was not even whispered in the opening number.

Yet the disguise could deceive no one for long. Some Democrats weary of the usual partisan ranting of the press may have been won over for a while by Greeley's columns of authoritative legislative summaries, election lists and speech texts. But before long they found that almost all of the speeches selected turned out to be those made by Whigs: Daniel Webster's six-hour oration against the Administration's banking policy, for instance, got thirty full columns of *Jeffersonian* fine print—enough to make any Democrat cancel his subscription. And the air of objectivity dropped entirely in Greeley's own editorials, which pounded the Jacksonians from every side. The men in power were too radical, he said; too careless with money; too corrupt in their banking; and besides, they were unkind to Indians: "The poor Cherokees are disheartened, overawed, confounded. They have no earthly resources. For years they have invoked the justice and the pity of our government in vain." They were also too conservative. The states where their party flourished most strongly showed an extraordinary lack—so he said —of popular democracy:

> It might be uncourteous to denounce the system of another state [Rhode Island] as short-sighted, narrow, absurd and aristocratic; we merely say that it is radically opposed to what we understand as True Democracy. No man is allowed to vote [in Rhode Island] who does not own a freehold within the State worth at least

$134 ... In truth the state is just as Democratic now as she ever was—that is, not at all ...

Whoever has mingled, however slightly, in Virginia society will have been struck by its aristocratic temperament and bearing. Ideas that he had thought banished from men's minds, or at least from this continent—ideas of birth, and blood, and family descent and dignity, which sound oddly to republican ears, but worse than oddly from republican lips, will have convinced him that if Virginia be the pattern of true Democracy, then it is high time we had new authorities for the meaning of language.

Fifteen thousand subscribers—no doubt almost all of them loyal Whigs—took the paper. But even for many of them young Greeley's assorted political sermons, arrays of statistics, and endless speech texts were heavy going. The paper provided them ample campaign ammunition, but it did so solemnly, without spice and color. Weed called it a success, but Greeley had learned a lesson. "There is nothing that bores people like instruction," he wrote his friend Ransom. "It implies that they do not know everything already, which is very humiliating. ... I have not done enough for effect."

2

On Tuesdays, after he had put the *Jeffersonian* to bed in Albany, Greeley would hurry down by night boat to work on his other weekly in New York. When he reached Ann Street on Wednesday morning he sat down to the task of putting together a whole *New Yorker* issue in time for an early Saturday closing. In order to divide the burden of selecting and editing the mass of essays, poems, reviews, letters and travel articles that made up half the paper, he had hired Park Benjamin, late of the *New England Magazine* and the *American Monthly*, as literary editor. But Greeley would not trust the poetic, partly crippled Benjamin with the conduct of the *New Yorker's* other half, which dealt with politics and general news. So he went to work himself assembling fresh items from Washington and foreign "exchanges," dropping in on City Hall, talking to political callers, and writing a new batch of summaries along with an editorial leader. Often he could lift items he had written earlier in the week for the *Jeffersonian*, and which he had brought down from Albany in pockets bulging with galley proofs. But generally he found himself revising and rearranging them, and then going over the whole paper at lockup time, meticulously checking layout, typography, spellings, punctuation, and faults of style. At some time he found a few hours to attend to his correspondence and to be with Mary. Then, on Saturday, he was off again to Albany.

There, after work, he often went around to Weed's house up the hill to map strategy well into the night. He sat at the comfortable fireside while the chieftain, amiable and relaxed, brought out French wines and lit a Havana cigar. Greeley drank milk and sometimes had difficulty enduring the smoke. Nevertheless, Weed at once took a warm liking for his young editor. "We became not only intimate politically but socially," he said in his memoirs; "he had no habits or tastes but for work, steady, indomitable work. Our sentiments and opinions of public measures and public men harmonized perfectly; our only difference was, that upon the temperance, slavery and labor questions he was more ardent and hopeful. In this I gave him credit for fresher and less disciplined feelings."

Sometimes a third man appeared at the fireside—another protégé of Weed's. He was the rising state senator and popular lawyer from Auburn, William H. Seward. Seward, unlike Greeley, did not refuse Weed's wine and cigars. On the contrary, he had a warm liking for both—as he had for the paternal Weed. Short and scrawny, advancing under a shock of red hair and behind a hawklike, searching beak, Seward would stalk in, abruptly throw himself down in an easy chair, toss his feet up at the hearth, puff furiously, talk, gesticulate, jump up, flop down again, pour himself another glass of wine, and go on talking. Weed enjoyed it. Greeley listened.

The two upstate men stood out in contrast: Weed, bluff, lantern-jawed and composed, as against the wiry, nervous Seward. With the hard frame and heavy hands of a man brought up on country labor, Boss Weed now wore well-groomed black clothes and a shrewdly cultivated, worldly air; State Senator Seward, however, a college man and proud of his learned attainments, stuck to wrinkled clothes and to the bantering, noisy manner of the upcountry. Both appearances, though, were calculated; both answered their owners' needs. Seward wanted office. Weed wanted power—the power, that is, of bestowing office on others and receiving a patron's and partner's rewards in return. Specifically, Seward wanted the governorship of New York. Weed was out to get it for him, knowing that if he did, he would win virtual control of state patronage, along with a perquisite for himself in the post of State Printer, which would probably net him and his *Evening Journal* together upward of $20,000 a year. The two men often broke a second and then a third bottle of wine together as they discussed these possibilities. Greeley sat by and learned.

There was another difference between Weed and Seward of which Greeley was aware. The impetuous, intellectual Seward was moved by humanitarian feelings and a vigorous dislike of special privilege and slavery; he had said so in many speeches and had even won radical "Workie" support in his first campaign for state office. Thurlow Weed, however, was largely unmoved by such appeals. Yet the bond between the two was firm. It had begun taking form as long as fourteen years ago when Seward, at the moment of recoiling against the state's Democratic leaders, had encountered Weed under unusual circumstances. A coach in which Seward had been riding through the streets of Rochester had lost a wheel and overturned. "Among a crowd, which quickly assembled" (thus Seward described the moment), "one taller and more effective, while more deferential and sympathizing, than the rest, lent the party his assistance. This was the beginning of my acquaintance with Thurlow Weed."

Deferential, sympathizing, yet authoritative and strong—that was Weed. Soon he placed himself in command of young Seward's political fortunes. Even then, sometimes, Weed remained deferential. He wrote his Auburn protégé a letter in which he congratulated himself on having "the happiness to secure your good opinions"—although he then added, with a quick, commanding twist after they had disputed some minor political favor, "I have concluded to only *half* forgive you for thinking me weak enough to grasp for a paltry office."

Greeley knew their linkage as well as their differences, and before long found himself linked to both. While running the *Jeffersonian*, he found time also to ghostwrite articles and speeches for Seward. "I pray you," Seward wrote to Weed of one of these efforts in mid-1838, "make my warmest acknowledgements to H—— G—— for that beautiful article in the Fredonia *Censor*. I have never seen anything better timed, or in better temper, or more discreet. I started from my chair as I read it and said to myself, 'No man could believe that this was written by anybody but myself.'" Evidently Greeley knew Seward's mind well, too. He enjoyed working with it: it was mobile, intense, and close to his own in range and principle—far closer, in fact, than that of the skeptical Weed. Of the two partners, Greeley wrote, Weed was "of coarser mould and fibre—tall, robust, dark-featured, shrewd, resolute and not over-scrupulous." As between them, then, one should have thought that Greeley would have altogether preferred Seward. Yet he never did. Seward had conscience and character; but it was Weed who had personality and style. Seward, speaking so often as the voice of conscience, also had overweening personal ambitions which frequently put that conscience to rout.

Seward, for his part, found a kindred spirit in the editor of the *Jeffersonian*, but at times the kinship was perhaps too close for his own comfort. The thought crossed his mind that Greeley might assert himself too strongly in the combine, and he protected himself by looking on the junior helper with a touch of condescension. His son, Frederick Seward, describing many years later the impression Greeley had made on his father in Albany days, summed up the editor as having been "singularly . . . original and decided in his political views" and "rather unmindful of forms and social usages." That was all, apparently, the Sewards cared to say.

Thurlow Weed, on the other hand, was not the man to be concerned about Horace Greeley's challenging originality or lack of manners. Amiably pursuing his own practical goal, he recognized that Greeley, on his side, had some quite different goals of his own. Nevertheless, they were fellow craftsmen, fellow propagandists, and fellow operators. Both were newspapermen and journeyman printers by trade as well. Often they stood at poles apart, yet in doing so they supplemented rather than antagonized one another. Furthermore, either man helped round out the education of the other. Weed, lacking book learning, took instruction from young Greeley. "Do oblige me by reading Carlyle's *Past and Present*," the junior one day wrote his boss; "best this century. If wearied skip Book II." And Greeley, for his part, learned a whole advanced course in practical party management from Weed. Rapidly they coalesced into a political planning and writing team. And at moments when Greeley heard unsavory stories of the leader's vote-buying and strong-arm methods at the polls, he could fall back on the thought that Thurlow, at any rate, was a good working newspaperman. In fact, Greeley thought him one of the best. Many years later, and long after their team had broken up, he paid him a unique tribute: "Writing slowly and with difficulty, [Weed] was for twenty years the most sententious and pungent writer of editorial paragraphs in the American press."

3

Greeley had never enjoyed himself so well as during these campaigning months in 1838. He went to the Young Men's Whig and state-wide Whig conventions in the spring with Weed to help put across Seward's nomination for governor. On days when Weed was away seeing politicians, he moved in on the Albany *Evening Journal*, editing copy, writing editorials in Weed's stead, and sometimes seeing the paper to bed. He threw himself into large-scale publicity and promotion efforts, hectoring his upstate friends for support: "We are going to publish 100,000 copies of Bond's speech here in an extra *Jeffersonian*," he wrote Obediah Bowe, now editor of the Herkimer *Journal*. "Just see that your Whig folks get at least 1,000 of them for distribution in the dark corners of Herkimer. Now mind that the thing is done . . . You *must* drive a new spirit into the pretenders to Whiggery throughout that region." He sat in with the campaign committee while it thought up such slogans as "Seward, the Poor Man's Friend" and "Proper Credit, Proper Commerce." He helped Seward formulate his mildly reformist views on banking and social policy, and at the same time went to work in the *Jeffersonian* labeling all Democratic Albany leaders as "Locofocos"—i.e., "radicals." He ran his *New Yorker*, and in his exuberance still found time late at night, back in his room at the Eagle Tavern, to write poetry and tell his friends about it: "I have written some rhymes this evening—signed Korner—which I shall publish either in the *Evening Journal* or the *Whig*."

The campaign boomed. Many men who until now had voted Democratic were being won over. Some gentlemen on the Whig side thought that Seward and his Albany friends were going too far in their appeals to the "mob"; Philip Hone, for instance, looked on the candidate's views as ominously unorthodox. Yet where else were men like Philip Hone to go? At the last moment, in fact, when an extra round of campaign funds was needed to swing some doubtful counties into line, the elegant Hone himself went out and helped raise it among his fellow clubmen. The Whig ticket won decisively. "God bless Thurlow Weed," exclaimed William H.

Seward, the first New York governor elected in forty years who was not a Democrat. "I owe this result to him."

For Greeley, though, the victory meant that the *Jeffersonian* had done its work and was no longer needed. Its editor was thanked, paid off, and returned to the *New Yorker*. There, next spring, he found himself in trouble again. "I am working confounded hard and existing on $12 a week," he told Bowe in May, 1939. "I am doing worse than ever with the *New Yorker*; the money all goes into the hands of such cursed subtreasurers as E. M. Griffing (damn him) who won't ever give me an account of what he *has* got!" Next month, with the *New Yorker* still unable to pull out from under its load of debt, matters were worse: "I owe $40 personal now, and must borrow $50 more to pay board, etc., tomorrow . . ."

In September he was out hunting part-time jobs again to save himself and his paper; he spoke of possibilities that the *Jeffersonian* might be revived, or that he might edit a new Whig daily "as soon as the *Whig* shall expire of its intense stupidity." Neither project materialized. By January, 1840, in desperation, he was writing on space rates for the Albany *Evening Journal*, the Harrisburg *Chronicle*, the Boston *Atlas*, the Fredonia *Censor*, the New York *Evening Signal* and the *Whig*, besides running his own faltering *New Yorker*. But the best he could report to Bowe was, "So here I am, with only $25 a week assured, and have to pay nearly that for the hatching of my own paper at home. It is wretchedly done this last week, don't you think?"

He thought that Governor Seward, knowing his need and his past service to the party, might at least have remembered him enough to put him on the state payroll. Years later, this thought was to become an obsession: "When you were dispensing offices worth $3,000 to $20,000 per year to friends and compatriots," he reminded Seward in 1854, "I returned to my garret and my crust." He thought that henceforth he would do better to steer clear of practical politics—or at least to stake out his claim for reward in advance. He went on seeing Weed, though, and doing odd jobs for him—even without reward. His passion for personal involvement would not stay down. Some day, if he pursued it long enough, it would have to be requited.

Then in the summer of 1839 the boss gave him a prophetically tough assignment. Greeley liked Weed; but he worshiped Henry Clay. He had been dreaming that all would be well if the Whigs would only run Clay as their man for President next year. Henry Clay himself shared this dream as he sat resting at Saratoga Springs that summer, waiting for a call from the people and more particularly for an endorsement from the key New York State operators in nearby Albany. Weed, however, raised objections. He said that Clay had compromised too much on the slavery issue, and therefore could not possibly carry the North. Privately, though, Weed had another reason for vetoing Clay. It had nothing to do with what Clay had said or not said on slavery; its point was simply that Clay had said too much, done too much, and become too famous in his own right to be a convenient party instrument at this moment. Forceful and renowned, Clay would no doubt try to run the rising Whig party, instead of letting it run him; and in attempting to run it, Clay might narrow it and make it simply the carrier of his personal beliefs, whereas the whole purpose of Whig organization now was to broaden the party's scope, to attract all kinds of people to it, to commit its leadership to as little as possible, and to hold out to voters a grand array of vague and harmonious hopes which each man could interpret pretty much as he chose. The Whig party, in short, did not need an outstanding personality at this time as its candidate; in fact, it might do better with an amiable nonentity. So Weed asked Greeley to go up to Saratoga for him and tell Henry Clay politely that he was waiting in vain. Greeley got as far as Albany on this distasteful mission. There he sat down and balked.

Weed was talking of putting up in place of Clay the statuesque figure of General Winfield Scott, whose brass buttons sparkled and whose parade-ground mind betrayed no presence of any political ideas. This was hardly militant Whiggism as Greeley had imagined it. Moreover, he had pacifist inclinations and mistrusted all soldiers, although he did not underrate their popular attraction. "We can run Scott, and lick 'em," he remarked sardonically to Bowe late that year. "What of it? I am learning philosophy, which we shall need in such a case." He thought of breaking off any further connection with the unrewarding Weed. But then Weed appealed again to his love of participating in the party game, and invited him out to the Whig national convention in Harrisburg in December. Greeley went. He helped on the floor when Weed, outvoted on the candidacy of General Scott, switched his New York men into line behind another imposing, innocuous general—William Henry Harrison.

Yet back in New York, and looking soberly at what had been done at Harrisburg in the name of Whiggism, Greeley once more felt an impulse to quit. Governor Seward, teeming with great campaign plans, invited him to come in for dinner and talk. The half-bankrupt editor of the *New Yorker*, then aged twenty-nine, answered him with an extraordinary, imperious note that was the precursor of some even more startling messages to come:

Wednesday, Feb. 12, 1840

GOV. SEWARD:

Your invitation to dinner on Friday is gratefully received, but I shall not tax your hospitality. I have once already enjoyed the honor you tender me, which is enough for Glory. It will enable me, if it so please me, hereafter to preface anecodotes of my brief excursion on the boiling sea of politics with "Once when I was dining at my friend the Governor's." That will suffice. For dining, as an art, I have due respect, but I am not proficient therein—I lack education —I have no taste—no time. I pray thee to have me excused.

Yours much obliged
H. GREELEY

4

Within two months, though, Horace Greeley was back working for the political firm of Weed & Seward—this time as a full partner. A new opportunity had arisen that was too good to be missed. In view of the success of the *Jeffersonian* in the last state campaign, Weed now proposed that a new, nationwide Whig weekly on a larger scale be set up for the coming presidential campaign, and that Greeley edit it. This time Greeley would be in full control as his own publisher, and Whig committees inside and outside the state would guarantee him initial backing and subscriptions. Greeley did not take long to consider. On 1 May, 1840 he published the first issue of his *Log Cabin*. Before long, this time, he found himself famous.

Candidate Harrison had avoided stating any political views on anything. The Whig party now also avoided officially stating any: its nominating convention had not even bothered to adopt a platform. Instead, it adopted slogans: "Tippecanoe and Tyler too"—"Harrison, two dollars a day, and roast beef." The scheme of attracting all kinds and classes of men to the new party reached its logical conclusion: in order to capture everyone, one had best say nothing—that is, nothing to which anyone might object. One would do best simply to cheer, sing and shout, and let the Democrats do the talking in self-defense.

The folly of saying too much appeared early in the campaign when a Democratic newspaper let go a jibe at Harrison, calling him an old crony who would be happiest in a log cabin with plenty of hard cider about. This gave the Whig campaigners a heaven-sent opportunity to come out solidly for log cabins and hard cider—"the poor man's lodging and the poor man's drink." The more the Democrats talked back and tried to raise serious issues, the more the Whigs raised monster log cabins, passed out hard cider, and composed choruses making fun of President Van Buren and his circle of jaded aristocrats who preferred champagne. As organized by men like Weed, this was sheer masquerade. Yet it was picked up and carried on by men all over the country who sincerely believed that "aristocrats," wherever they were found, must be unseated. The popular, leveling enthusiasms which Jacksonianism 'tself had unleashed transplanted themselves into the Whig party—and to an extent that sometimes surprised its own leaders. Daniel Webster had already found it necessary to apologize publicly for not having been born in a log cabin. A rising young insurgent in Pennsylvania named Thaddeus Stevens was speaking in such fiery language of the common people's rights that the ruling Democrats denounced him as a reckless radical—and Stevens was a Whig. Hearing such language, Philip Hone complained in New York about "the Locofocos in my own party." But Governor Seward, running for relection, found his popularity rising when he attacked corrupt bankers and feudal Hudson Valley landlords. And in his *Log Cabin*, Horace Greeley—partly out of campaign exuberance, but partly also in earnest—proclaimed an "Uprising of the People."

This year, Greeley did not attempt to produce simply an enlarged, sober *Jeffersonian*. He caught the spirit of the moment and designed an entirely new kind of paper for it—big, handsome, bold-faced and arresting, with woodcuts, cartoons, and catch lines splashed across its four pages. At its head the teetotaling editor placed an emblem showing "Tippecanoe" Harrison's fictitious log cabin, with barrels of hard cider ready at the door. In place of lengthy editorials sedately discussing currency or sound banking, he hit upon simple themes such as that of Harrison, the People's Soldier, and rang endless changes on them. He ran illustrated narratives of Harrison's

Indian battles and skirmishes almost forty years before; homely testimonials by aged militiamen who had served with him; pictures of Harrison dressed up as a farmer, as an Indian Chief, and as Cincinnatus in a flowing toga; eye-catching panoramas such as "Harrison's Humanity in War," in which the great man was shown ordering his soldiers to spare womenfolk and children; jingles and choruses such as "Old Tippecanoe; or, the Working Man's Election Song":

> The President boasts of his Palace and "chink,"
> And says a Log Cabin won't do,
> And sticks up his nose when Hard Cider we drink
> To the health of good Old Tippecanoe . . .

Then, as the lilting enthusiasm caught on, Greeley ran announcements of parades, jollifications, outings and fireworks displays. In order to commemorate the "Great Victory at Fort Meigs," for instance (a minor skirmish the general had fought in 1813), all freedom-loving New Yorkers were called upon to assemble upon a salute of one hundred guns at noon in Tompkins Square and march with bands playing to Niblo's Garden to hear Whig speeches. Upstate and out West, according to the *Log Cabin,* the fever was spreading:

The Harrison boys of Chenango have raised their second or third Log Cabin . . .

The Whigs of Albany have erected a noble Cabin, and their friends abroad will always find the latchstring on the outside of the door.

In Kalamazoo, a Free Dinner for 4000 is in preparation.

Such is the spirit and such its manifestations throughout the whole country . . . The "Log Cabin fooleries," which so disgust the exquisite sensibilities of Locofocoism, have a significance to the People which the Office Holders are slow to comprehend. They imply organized and energetic resistance to Misgovernment—they herald a return to the stern simplicity and economy of better days—they bespeak a union of all classes and interests in the great work of National Regeneration.

It did no good for Democratic editors to try to challenge Whigs in general and the *Log Cabin* in particular to say what their plans were for the control of banking and the currency. "Tippecanoe and Tyler too," "Van, Van is a Used-up Man!" the Whig marching columns roared back, smothering all debate. The *Log Cabin* ran more songs:

Oh! where, tell me where, was your Buckeye Cabin made?
Oh! where, tell me where, was your Buckeye Cabin made?
'Twas made among the merry boys that wield the plough and spade
Where the Log Cabins stand in the bonnie Buckeye shade.

"Our songs are doing more good than anything else," Greeley reported to Weed; "I know the music is not worth much, but it attracts the attention of even those who do not know a note." Then some of President Van Buren's harried followers, losing their tempers, took to sneering at the Whig bully boys as "coons" and "cider-suckers." This only added to the uproar. The *Log Cabin* helped spread wildly exaggerated stories about the President's "golden spoons," "maroon coach," and "silken tassels." "Liberty in Log Cabins rather than Slavery in Palaces" proclaimed nightly torch-lit signs in the streets. "O.K.—back to Kinderhook!" the Whig rallies jeered at the unhappy "Van."

Within only a few issues, the *Log Cabin* had become the liveliest voice in America's liveliest national campaign. Its circulation bounded to forty, fifty, sixty thousand copies. Without steam presses and an adequate mailing staff, Greeley could not keep up with the soaring nationwide demand for it. Visitors to his Ann Street office found him submerged under floods of manuscripts, news items, letters, cartoons, subscriptions, bulk orders and printing bills. He was disheveled, hopelessly overworked, but obviously happy. And when not buried under the *Log Cabin* (with the *New Yorker*, now delegated to assistants, running at its side) he made time to hurry to Albany to confer with Weed, to sit on the central Whig campaign committee, and to make speeches. "I am a wretched speaker, lacking voice, confidence and command of language," he had written a manager early in the campaign, trying to avoid a platform engagement; "I am astonished and vexed at myself that I cannot say what rises so clearly to my mind, and what I can write so readily." Nevertheless he was drafted into service, and orated in the approved fashion:

. . . .We will not detain you here, Fellow Citizens, to speak of the innumerable and flagrant abuses of Federal Power which the last four years have developed. . . . No, Fellow Citizens, we turn from this gloomy but transient cloud upon our National character to a

brighter and more alluring picture ... to that Farmer's Cabin by
the margin of the placid Ohio, where dwells the veteran Soldier
and Statesman ...

He traveled to Philadelphia, Syracuse and Buffalo, speaking, cajoling, gathering news, listening to politicians, and shaking hands.
He even found time to sit down and write a campaign song of his
own, which he published in the *Log Cabin* ("with music composed
especially by E. Ives, Jr."):

> Hark! an Earthquake's deep roar o'er our Country is booming;
> But no ruin behind it is seen;
> With joy each heart swelling, each visage illumined,
> Earth brightens where'er it has been.
> The West's gallant spirits first thrilled to its pealing,
> As onward it rolled to the sea:
> Now the North, South and Centre the impulse are feeling,
> 'Tis the Rising and March of the Free! ...

Until the early morning hours on closing nights, he was to be
found in the downstairs composing room making up *Log Cabin*
heads of his own at the type case and fitting them into the forms.
The heads, as the weeks advanced toward election day, became
steadily bigger. Bold caps, exclamation points, eagles, bullets, stars,
thick rules and other devices were pulled out to serve him. Early
state elections in October helped him proclaim a rising groundswell.
One week, the *Log Cabin* trumpeted, "CONNECTICUT FOREVER!"; next came, "RHODE ISLAND IS TRUE!"; then,
"GEORGIA FALLS INTO LINE!"; thereupon, "SOUTH CAROLINA UNFOLDS THE HARRISON BANNER" ("After years of
dreary and sluggish submission to the rod of Calhoun and his
devotees, South Carolina's Freemen have determined to strike a
blow for Independence"); next, "ALL HAIL LOUISIANA!" (whose
election of several Whig Congressmen "ensures the State for Harrison beyond contingency—LONG LIVE THE REPUBLIC!"). When
the editor's home state of Vermont showed a rising Harrison current, his enthusiasm burst all bounds:

VERMONT TO THE RESCUE!

The Freemen of Vermont—the upright, the unconquered, the incorruptible—the Switzerland of America—the cherished home of
true Republican principles and feeling—came together at Burlington last Thursday ...

Then early returns from the Middle West came in, and Greeley broke out all he had to produce a sensational display head:

VOICE OF THE MIGHTY WEST!
The Harrison Tornado Is Sweeping Over
Kentucky and Indiana!
BIGGER ELECTED GOVERNOR OF INDIANA BY OVER 10,000 MAJORITY!
Harrison Majority on other Tickets is still larger!
LETCHER ELECTED GOVERNOR OF KENTUCKY BY 10,000 to 15,000! LT. GOVERNOR, LEGISLATURE
and PEOPLE, *Whig by Acres!*

The *Log Cabin's* circulation passed seventy, then eighty thousand, with huge piles of orders lying unfilled as presses and mail-room clerks fell behind. "NEW JERSEY AVENGED!" the editor proclaimed in October; *"Her Star is Restored to the National Firmament! Her Sovereignty is Vindicated by Her Freemen!"* Then, in November, came triumph: Harrison and Tyler were elected.

Elected with Greeley's help; there was no doubt about that. "I judge that there were not many who had done more effective work in the canvass than I had." He began to think of a coming reward. "Two or three papers have named me for *Postmaster General*," he wrote Bowe, underlining the words; "and several have started me for Postmaster of this city! Of course, I am at liberty to look down with contempt on all smaller places, which I do devoutly. I want none of their dirty spoils . . ." But he did want spoils. He had let hints to this effect fall in Thurlow Weed's camp. Hints, however, were not enough. And Weed, for his part, may well have felt that Greeley was best just where he was—as a crack Whig editor who was now recognized as a force up and down the nation. As for General Harrison, lumbering into the Presidency, he neither knew Greeley nor cared about him; the old soldier, it seemed, read very little.

Years later, Greeley voiced to Seward (who was reelected governor, although he ran behind the national ticket) his chagrin at having been left out in the distribution of the spoils. He recalled the post-election "scramble of the swell mob of coon minstrels and cider-suckers at Washington—I not being counted in. Several regiments of them went from this city; but no one of the whole crowd—though I say it who should not—had done so much toward General Harrison's nomination and election as yours respectfully. I asked nothing, expected nothing; but you, Governor Seward, ought to have asked that I be postmaster of New York...."

But this was Greeley writing in later days of embitterment. At the moment, he was buoyant enough to pocket the rebuff. He went back to his "poor old *Yorker*," as he called it. The paper was neglected and impoverished, and after his recent splurge on the national stage he was inclined to be impatient with it: "The hand of death is upon it," he told Bowe. He kept the *Log Cabin* going on a reduced scale on the side, although after election day that was not satisfactory either. Restless and bursting with energy, he began to think of a new, far more ambitious journalistic plan. In the meantime he kept on mending his personal and political fences: "I have written a heap of letters today," he wrote Bowe on 25 December, 1840. Mary Greeley, who had not seen much of her husband this past year, saw little of him even on this Christmas Day.

V. TRIBUNE

1

While Greeley was busy helping to elect General Harrison, an extraordinary intramural fracas had broken out in the daily press of New York. The man who had provoked the outburst was the squint-eyed James Gordon Bennett of the *Herald*. Few newspapermen liked him; no gentleman, Philip Hone told his diary, could like him. Within five years Bennett had made his raucous paper the most formidable one in New York, and the most feared. His methods were revolutionary; their results, to many sound citizens, seemed simply scandalous. He himself said that he "disclaimed all principle, as it is called," in running a newspaper, and his *Herald* showed it. He covered every side of the news as no editor before him had done, but with a special eye on dredging up crime stories, gossip and chitchat. He ran columns about Wall Street and the city's churches, but with intent to insult both bankers and Presbyterians. He had invented the interview, but the first time he used it was in reporting a long talk he had held with one Rosina Townshend, madam of a bordello in which a murder had just been committed.

The man had no morals, yet his paper was hugely interesting. Philip Hone dismissed him as a "serpent," but went on reading his *Herald* nevertheless. That was the worst of it: far more people were now taking the *Herald* than were following such veteran "blanket sheets" as Colonel Webb's grandiloquent *Courier and Enquirer* or David Hale's silk-stocking *Journal of Commerce*, and almost as many had succumbed to it as to that gutter sheet, the *Sun*. The town's other daily editors agreed that something must be done to stop Bennett. With the knightly Webb leading them, the editors of the *Journal of Commerce*, the *News*, the *Express*, the *Evening*

Star, the *Evening Signal* and even the *Sun* decided on a "moral war" that would drive him out of business. Park Benjamin, formerly of the *New Yorker* and now of the *Evening Signal*, fired away first, publicly denouncing Bennett as a "liar" and "poltroon" who was "notorious for daily habits of blasphemy, obscenity and falsehood." Then the pack closed in. Bennett, they shouted in chorus, was an "obscene vagabond"; a "polluted wretch"; a "daring infidel"; a "common bandit"; a "Prince of Darkness"; an "infamous profligate"; a "pestilential scoundrel." They called for a readers' boycott against the *Herald*. The *Herald*, outwardly unperturbed, hit back with sneers. The assault by the high-minded, Bennett laughed, was "the War of the Holy Alliance"; his antagonists were "penny mosquitoes"; the *Evening Star*'s undersized Mordecai Noah was "half Jew, half infidel, with a touch of the monster"; and—still more venomously—Park Benjamin's physical handicaps were "a curse by the Almighty."

The pack could not equal such snarling vulgarities and soon called off their "war," leaving Bennett, the pariah, gloating at his old stand. Greeley had watched the proceedings with rapt interest. It was clear to him that for all his bad morals and worse manners James Gordon Bennett as a newspaperman stood head and shoulders above the "mosquitoes" who were trying to prick him. Insatiably curious, Bennett found news every day where others editors saw nothing, since they were too busy pontificating. He saw it in a small street-corner accident; in the story of a lost child; in the names present at a glittering ball and the gowns worn there; in the feelings of an immigrant on first setting foot in New York. This was to the good, said Greeley the journalist: never before had the human scene really been reported. What was evil in Bennett—and here spoke up Greeley the moralist—was that he had misapplied his gift to the uses of mere sensation. There was no reason why information should not be spiced with showmanship: Greeley himself had learned and enjoyed the art on the *Log Cabin*. But information should also be so chosen as to enlighten and lead the public, rather than merely divert and possibly seduce it. An editor, then, as Greeley saw it, should be by trade both an entertainer and an inspirer. In order to succeed, he must be adventurous and resourceful; but the more he did succeed, the more he fell under moral obligation to the community as a whole, for his duty was to serve it on weekdays almost as a pastor did on Sundays.

The problem was to make the two sides or qualities of an editor's role work together in harmony. Bennett, who was not the least interested in harmony (or, said Bryant of the *Evening Post*, in anything other than "selling papers"), had never even considered the problem. Greeley, though, had encountered it acutely, especially in his relations with Thurlow Weed. He had sought quick success and political adventure at the boss' side, only to be seized at times with qualms of conscience. During the exuberant, campaigning months of the *Log Cabin* he had managed to suspend his deeper questions. But they would not stay down for long. Both sides in him clamored for expression. He had now to find some effective means for uniting his whole being—the journalist, the practical politician, and the moralist. He must speak his mind more fully, more honestly, and more persistently than he had ever done. He must be independent. And he must make himself heard.

It was this line of thinking that led him in the winter of 1840-41 to decide to launch his own penny daily in New York. It would be called the *Tribune*.

2

He had no money to speak of. The fading *New Yorker* was consuming most of what he had earned during the campaign, and the surviving *Log Cabin* was but a shadow of its former self. In ready cash he had little more than $1,000 in hand with which to launch the New York *Tribune*—most of which starting capital was lent him by a Whig political friend, James Coggeshall. As for himself, Greeley possessed an office, two uncertain weeklies, several cases of type, some make-up stones with their furniture, and a slow job press or two, not fast enough to run off a daily. But beyond that he possessed two ideas. The first—which echoed Bennett's—was that people liked to read about themselves. Years later, after having applied it in the *Tribune,* he stated the principle in classic form to a friend who wanted to start a country paper:

Begin with a clear conception that the subject of deepest interest to an average human being is himself; next to that he is most concerned about his neighbors. Asia and the Tongo Islands stand a long way off after these in his regard. . . . Do not let a new church be organized, a mill set in motion, a store opened, nor anything of interest to a dozen families occur, without having the fact duly, though briefly, chronicled in your columns. If a farmer cuts a big tree, or grows a mammoth beet, or harvests a bounteous yield of wheat or corn, set forth the fact as concisely and unexceptionally as possible.

The second idea went beyond this and held that the same people who wanted simply to read about themselves were also for the most part drifting, morally irresolute people who both wanted and needed all the daily good advice they could get. The world they lived in was sadly imperfect; evil abounded; oppression was accepted; yet most men sought freedom and a rough justice even as they sought happiness, and it might be the function of a great newspaper to help lead them toward it. One of Greeley's youngest and most perceptive assistants, John Russell Young, was thus to paraphrase the *Tribune* founder's thinking:

This was an atrocious world—that he knew well. It was permeated with Democrats, and free traders, and idle folks given to drink. These were evil men and evil women; but there was no reason for giving it over to the fire. It should be converted. . . . Greeley labored with the world to better it, to give men moderate wages and wholesome food, and to teach women to earn their living . . .

And, apart from these general incentives, there was the specific one that the Whig party, although victorious in state and nation, was still without a mass-appeal newspaper of its own in the city of New York. Both the popular *Sun* and *Herald* leaned toward Democrats; and as for the Whiggish Colonel Webb of the *Courier* and Davy Hale of the *Journal of Commerce*, Greeley knew they could never appeal to the mass. To be the independent, popular spokesman of Whiggism in America's biggest city would not only greatly enhance his own standing with the Weed-Seward combine, Greeley knew, but it might some day make him their equal in political power. And, having been rebuffed, so he thought, he resolved to work hard for that power. For power and for morals: preferably for both at once.

The *Tribune*'s prospectus, published at the start of April in the *Log Cabin*, announced it as "a New Morning Journal of Politics, Literature and General Intelligence" designed to "advance the interests of the people, and to promote their Moral, Political and Social well-being." Slapping at Bennett and the *Sun*, Greeley went on to say that "the immoral and degrading Police Reports, Advertisements, and other matter which have been allowed to disgrace the columns of our leading Penny Papers, will be carefully excluded from this, and no exertion spared to render it worthy of the virtuous and refined, and a welcome visitant at the family fireside." He declared the new paper's support of the Whig cause and its belief "that the political revolution that called William Henry Harrison to the Chief Magistracy of the Nation was a triumph of Right, Reason and Public Good over Error and Sinister Ambition." And he wound up by telling readers that they could subscribe to the *Tribune* for only four dollars a year, and that "it will contain the news by the morning Southern Mail, which is contained in no other Penny Paper."

By 1 April Greeley had rounded up a staff of ten, bought some paper on credit, arranged for the use of a steam press down the street, and was ready to start. On the evening of the 9th, light shone late in the second-floor office in the rear of 30 Ann Street while the four large-sized pages of the first issue of the New York *Tribune* were being made up, with Greeley helping foreman Thomas Rooker at the stone. Then the locked type pages were trundled down the cobbled street to press. The print order read 5,000 copies.

Next day broke snowy and sleety—an ill omen that could not help reminding Greeley of the foul weather that had confronted and promptly buried Shepard's *Morning Post* eight years before. Meanwhile an event had occurred that also made the moment unpropitious for launching a new Whig newspaper: President Harrison, after only a month in office, had suddenly fallen ill and died, and the city's Whigs were at the moment preoccupied with absorbing stately essays and orations that mourned his passing. Greeley, in the haste of organizing his paper and getting it on the street, had not even found time to deliver himself of the appropriate elevated sentiments. Instead, the first issue of the *Tribune* appeared with a front page given over entirely to a verbatim text of the learned opinion of Willis Hall, state attorney general, "on the legality of the conduct of Robert H. Morris, Recorder of the City of New York." What Attorney Hall had to say, in the course of half a dozen columns of unbroken six-point type studded with citations from Coke, Camden, and "10 George I, c. 10, §13," was that Recorder Morris' conduct had been unlawful. Inside the paper was spread a miscellany of local and Washington news, much of it sketchy, most of it late, and some of it picked up from other newspapers of the day before. The first issue of Bennett's *Herald* had been a good deal more promising. Of the 5,000 copies of the *Tribune* printed, most of them—apart from the 500 which had been subscribed for in advance—had to be given away.

The paper on the second day was not much better. Opening with a summary of press comment on the President's death, the front page then gave itself over to a historical essay called "The Horrors of War" (which set out to show, citing many examples, that war was indeed horrible), followed by a travel piece called "The Dyaks in the Island of Borneo," which described the natives' fierce looks and regretted that they had not yet been Christianized. Inside, there was an editorial voicing tentative friendliness toward Harrison's successor, President Tyler, followed by a detailed list of candidates for an imminent local city election, a handful of local police-news items (featuring stories of arrest for drunkenness, under the head "Victims of Intemperance"), and a half page of advertisements (the biggest of these being a display for "Beals' Hair Restorative: All humbug or Quackery in this Matter is Utterly Disclaimed"). The back page took up more of Attorney General Hall's interminable legal argument against Recorder Morris.

At the end of his first week Greeley could chalk up total receipts so far of only $92 as against current outlays of $525. At this rate the New York *Tribune* might last another two weeks at most.

Greeley had started recklessly, without giving enough thought to the amount of good copy he would have to produce every day—not just every week—in order to compete with Bennett. He had in his shop only four editorial hands, of whom the best was a beginner. Of the older men, the only one who lasted at the *Tribune* was George Snow, its soft-spoken, knowing financial editor and writer. The beginner, meanwhile, served as Greeley's lieutenant, and later was to move on to greater things. He was Henry J. Raymond, aged twenty, an upstate New Yorker fresh from the University of Vermont, where he had met the footloose litterateur, Rufus W. Griswold, who had introduced him to Greeley. A recommendation from Griswold was not necessarily an asset in the newspaper world; for the amiable "Gris," as dozens of editors knew him, was a fly-by-night, flamboyant liar and faker who between editorial jobs drifted into odd operations on the fringe of the literary world, and one day was to be found forging compliments to himself in letters from Edgar Allan Poe. But young Raymond, short, dark-eyed, coolly self-possessed, and intensely ambitious, stood at the opposite pole from the bohemian Griswold. Greeley had taken him in for a tryout on the *New Yorker.* "I decided to keep him," Greeley wrote "Gris," "because I believe I can train him in the way he should go." The editor trained Raymond well enough to make him his right-hand man on the *Tribune* at eight dollars a week.

This first product of what was later to become Greeley's editorial school and college soon proved himself to be a meticulous reporter and a thorough desk man, insistent upon speed, accurate facts, and on pursuing a story through all its ramifications. He handled most of the flow of news while Greeley was busy writing his editorial; he clapped on his hat and went out after local stories himself. From Greeley's point of view Raymond had only one shortcoming: his instinct for caution was coupled with an immovable conservatism. "He doesn't feel the grave importance of our vocation," Greeley soon complained to Griswold. "I am afraid he has hurt me by the ultra-Federalism of his remarks on Hamilton this week, though I have softened them and qualified them." Yet many years later, after dozens of other crack men had been trained in his shop, Greeley remarked of his first pupil, "A cleverer, readier, more generally efficient journalist, I never saw." This was the Henry J. Raymond who ten years after he started with Greeley on the *Tribune* was to found the New York *Times* and become his teacher's most skillful and bitter rival.

3

Greeley had not even found himself a business manager when he launched the *Tribune*—a glaring omission, since in spite of all his learned editorials on finance Greeley had not the slightest idea of how to handle larger business transactions or keep his books straight. In his impatience to begin, he appears to have thought that the business end of the paper would virtually run itself when placed in the hands of a clerk or two, prodded now and then by Greeley. All the five or six successive business partners whom he had taken into the *New Yorker,* he remembered, had turned out to be flat failures. The result of his one-man operation, however, was sheer chaos. He still had hanging about his neck the improvident *New Yorker,* with its $9,000 of uncollected subscribers' bills. He also had the *Log Cabin,* bogged down by inefficient distribution and another load of subscribers' debts. The books of these two enterprises became hopelessly confused with those of the *Tribune.*

Some readers who had ordered the *Tribune* found themselves getting the *New Yorker* instead, and vice versa. Although in its third week the paper's circulation began to pick up, growing to three and then four thousand copies, the paper's till was empty and Greeley had set up no organization for replenishing it. "There was no system in the pressroom," observed the lawyer and former New York bookseller, Thomas McElrath, who came in to look around, "and the accounts of sales of papers delivered to the carriers were kept on loose pieces of paper; and when the papers were paid for the money was put into the pocket of the delivery clerk, who once a week made returns without vouchers or checks." By July, although the *Tribune* was now selling eight or nine thousand copies daily, Greeley was reduced to such straits that he tried to borrow cash from the crooked Griswold. "Where's them funds you were going to send me?" he dunned him. ". . . I am poor as a church mouse and not half so saucy."

In the meantime, though, Thomas McElrath, a genial, perceptive man, had been watching the *Tribune* climb, and he decided that in spite of its unbusinesslike confusion it might be well worth investing in. He had known Greeley since *Jeffersonian* days, and felt that the wild-haired young editor's diffuse talents might yet lead to a winning result if only he could get the benefit of good business advice and a little more working capital. So McElrath agreed to put up $2,000 and come in with Greeley as full partner. He settled into the business office as publisher and cleaned up its disorder. Then, shrewdly realizing that Greeley was spreading himself too thin between his daily and his two weeklies, he proposed that the *New Yorker* and the *Log Cabin* be merged with the newspaper to form the core of a weekly *Tribune* edition, in which leading news stories and editorials would be picked up from the daily, along with literary and miscellaneous features. The weekly *Tribune*, as McElrath saw it, would be designed for out-of-town subscribers—and especially for the rural upstate and western audience that lay beyond reach of good eastern dailies and lacked competent newspapers nearer home.

McElrath's idea was an inspiration. It salvaged Greeley's sprawling properties and cheaply projected the *Tribune* far beyond the city's boundaries—into that western area, in fact, where Greeley's heart and understanding lay. It was this new far-flung weekly *Tribune*, far more than the local daily, that was to make Greeley famous and McElrath rich. Greeley was always to remember gratefully McElrath's one big idea—especially since the amiable partner made no attempt to look into editorial matters, but kept his mind strictly on business. "During the ten years or over that the *Tribune* was issued by Greeley & McElrath," Greeley wrote in his *Recollections,* "my partner never once even indicated that my anti-Slavery, anti-Hanging, Socialist, and other frequent aberrations from the straight and narrow path of Whig partisanship, were injurious to our common interest, though he must often have sorely felt that they were so."

4

Understaffed and insecure, the *Tribune* pushed ahead in its first months largely by bluster and bluff. When news matter was thin and his product looked meager, Greeley took to staging crusading attacks against rival editors, hoping that they would hit back and thereby attract attention to him. They invariably did. He lambasted the "loathsome" kinds of advertising run by the *Sun* and *Herald*—an assault that was safe for him, since the *Tribune* itself was carrying very little advertising. The *Sun*'s displays, Greeley said, showed "every species of depravity." Bennett's, he charged, were such as to make the *Herald* appear designed to circulate chiefly "in houses of infamy . . . and drinking saloons of the lowest order." Both the *Sun* and the *Herald* raged, variously calling Greeley a "miscreant," a "blockhead" and "a large New England squash."

All this helped. Furthermore, having asserted itself as the popular guardian of civic virtue, the *Tribune* could now go to businessmen and persuade them that an advertisement placed in the *Tribune* rather than in the *Sun* or *Herald* would show that their product was reputable, too—as reputable as the *Tribune* itself. Accordingly, McElrath's office soon signed up advertisements for "Dr. Allen's Balsam: Surprising Cure of Consumption"; "Pectoral Honey of Liverwort"; "Gouraud's Depilatory Powders" (for the "intellectual development and personal beauty of ladies"); "Harvey's Relief for Ladies"; and, in the entertainment world, the "American Museum" on Broadway, which at the moment was featuring "Winchell!—the laughable, droll and original delineator of Scotch, Irish, Dutch, French, Yankee and other characters," along with "Dr. Collyer—the scientific experimenter on Animal Magnetism" and "Mons. and Madame Canderbek, who will appear and execute a beautiful adanta [sic] German Air, imitating the English Bugle and Scotch Bagpipes!" By early fall, the *Tribune*'s advertising columns were doing so well that McElrath raised the rate from four to six cents a line.

Having goaded the *Sun* and *Herald,* Greeley went to work on Mordecai Noah of the *Union,* too: "Major Noah! Why won't you tell the truth once in a century, for the variety of it?" He assaulted the earnest, cultivated Bryant of the *Evening Post*: "You lie, you old villain! . . ." Then he learned that crass abuse was far less appealing and effective than comic mockery. Late in the year, James Fenimore Cooper, whose fame had made him irascible, sued several editors—among them Weed and Colonel Webb—for libeling his new book, *Home As Found*. (The editors had said that Cooper's book, a sharp criticism of American life written upon his return from a long stay in Europe, was itself a libel against the country.) Greeley published a sardonic story of the court proceedings held in an upstate town, and was at once himself sued by Cooper for another libel. In December, the other libelers having been judged against, Greeley traveled upstate to defend himself against the crabbed Cooper, too. But by now Cooper's rages were becoming a public joke, and Greeley delighted his audience by sending back from the courtroom in Ballston Spa a burlesque hour-by-hour account that ran to eleven columns in the *Tribune*. The judgment went against Greeley for $200, and the editor, still in high humor, scribbled on for the *Tribune*, "Yes, Fenimore shall have his $200 . . . We rather like the idea of being so munificent a patron of American Literature . . ." The final twist to the story was that Cooper, after seeing Greeley's comic *Tribune* account, sued him all over again. "But, Fenimore," Greeley thereupon wrote in the *Tribune*, "*do* hear reason a minute. . . . You push a very good quill of your own except when you attempt to be funny—there you break down . . . Why not settle the difference at the point of a pen? We hereby tender you a column a day of the *Tribune* for ten days, promising to publish verbatim whatever you may write. . . . You may cut us up to your heart's content. We will further agree not to write over two columns in reply to the whole. . . ."

Finally Cooper came to his senses and decided neither to press his new suit nor answer Greeley's challenge. By that time the *Tribune* had the whole town laughing.

Greeley was feeling his strength now; his paper, by midwinter was selling almost 10,000 of the daily edition and 13,000 copies of the weekly. He could suspend gratuitous attacks on others, and let them vent their spleen on him. Colonel Webb of the waning *Courier and Enquirer* obliged, in a manner that played perfectly into Greeley's hand. "The editor of the *Tribune*," Webb wrote from his aristocratic perch, "seeks for notoriety by the strangeness of his theories and practices; we, on the contrary, are content with following in the beaten path and accomplishing what good we can in the old-fashioned way. He lays claim to greatness by wandering through the streets with a hat double the size of his head, a coat after the fashion of Jacob's of old, with one leg of his pantaloons inside and the other outside of his boot, and with boots all bespattered with mud . . . We, on the contrary, eschew all such affectation as weak and silly . . . we recognize the social obligation to act and dress according to our station in life; and we look upon cleanliness of person as inseparable from purity of thought. . . ."

Greeley's reply was self-possessed and sure. "The Editor of the *Tribune*," scrawled the attic pen, "is the son of a poor and humble farmer; came to New York a minor, without a friend within two hundred miles, less than ten dollars in his pocket, and precious little besides; he has never had a dollar from a relative, and, has, for years, labored under a load of debt . . . Henceforth he may be able to make a better show, if deemed essential by his friends; for himself he has not much time or thought to bestow on the matter."

5

To beat the starched Colonel Webb was easy; but to beat James Gordon Bennett meant beating the *Herald* with the news, which was hard. Throughout his first year, Greeley still received most of his out-of-town news in the form of "exchanges"—that is, items clipped from papers from other cities. If Blair's *Globe* arrived late, his Washington news was late. If no fresh European gazettes arrived on board a packet docking from Liverpool or Antwerp, the *Tribune* next morning had no European news. On some days, apart from local items, market reports, legal notices, and Albany summaries, the paper carried no news at all; on those days its columns were padded with poems, "Literary Intelligence," travel accounts or serials. Installments of Charles Dickens' new *Barnaby Rudge* took up most of Greeley's front page for days on end.

When the exchanges did arrive, much of what they reported had happened many weeks ago. Thus on 30 April, 1841, the *Tribune* picked up this item from a Memphis paper:

A son of Mrs. Sarah Jackson of Memphis, Tenn., who was bitten in the hand by a dog on the 4th of February, died of hydrophobia on the 1st inst. in terrible agonies.

Mrs. Sarah Jackson was ex-President Andrew Jackson's daughter-in-law; the death of her son had occurred just twenty-nine days before the *Tribune* reported it. Newspaper readers were accustomed to such long delays. But those who read Bennett's *Herald*—and there were more of them each month—were finding that news could move much faster when the editor had enterprise and placed his own man at the spot.

Bennett in 1841 was sending his own reporters hundreds of miles out of New York to cover trials, conventions, disasters, and more especially to gather their own news in Washington. This had led him into collision with capital dailies that had heretofore held exclusive rights on Capitol Hill, along with rich government printing contracts—the *Globe* and *National Intelligencer*. With Henry Clay's aid, Bennett had broken this monopoly and won the right to get his own men admitted to the Senate chamber. The reports which they then sent back direct inevitably beat all the papers that received theirs at second hand. Greeley did not yet have money enough to set up his own rival Washington staff. What he did do was to extend his old *New Yorker* method of getting individual senators and congressmen to rush him advance texts of their own bills and speeches, thereby often winning the edge on Bennett in completeness and accuracy. Then he went on to get newspapermen in other cities, and especially in the West, to send him special articles, short items, private letters and tips on local matters: in mid-1842, for instance, he was asking Schuyler Colfax, the promising editor of the South Bend, Indiana, *St. Joseph Valley Register,* to keep him up to date regularly on Indiana political developments. The *Tribune* thereupon wrote with such a familiar, authoritative air about the Hoosier State that readers along the Wabash took in the weekly as their own.

Greeley could not yet compete with Bennett everywhere; but he could try to steal a news beat from him every now and then— and publicize the victory. In 1843 he sent Raymond to Boston to report a speech of Daniel Webster. A *Tribune* man, Augustus Maverick, who became Raymond's friend and biographer, recorded the result:

Rival city journals also dispatched their reporters, each selecting for the purpose two of their best short-hand operators to work against Mr. Raymond. The speech was delivered . . . The several New York reporters took the night-boat to return to New York, and all, save Mr. Raymond, gave themselves up to such enjoyment during the evening as the boat afforded. Mr. Raymond sat quietly in the back cabin, and was observed to be writing furiously. Presently one of the reporters had his suspicions aroused, and setting forth on an exploring expedition, found that Mr. Raymond had on board a small printing-office, fully equipped. His manuscript was taken page by page to the compositors, set up immediately, and on the arrival of the boat in New York, at five o'clock in the morning, Mr. Raymond's report, making several columns of the *Tribune*, was all in type. These columns were put into the forms at once, and the readers of that journal were, at six a.m., served with a full report of Daniel Webster's speech delivered in Boston on the previous afternoon. This, at that time, was one of the greatest journalistic feats on record, and so completely astonished and astounded the *Tribune's* rivals that they never published the reports furnished by their short-hand writers, but acknowledged themselves fairly beaten.

The *Tribune* crowed. It patted itself again when it brought the rush text of Governor Seward's annual legislative message from Albany to New York by means of three riders and ten relays of horses in twenty-two hours (a feat "almost—if not quite—unparalleled in this country," it declared). It bestowed public praise on one of its hired postriders or "expresses," Enoch Ward, for rushing the returns of a Connecticut state election to the *Tribune* office through storm and danger:

[Mr. Ward] left New Haven Monday evening in a light sulky, at twenty minutes before ten o'clock, having been detained thirty-five minutes by the nonarrival of the Express locomotive from Hartford. He reached Stamford—forty miles from New Haven—in three hours. Here it commenced snowing, and the night was so exceedingly dark that he could not travel without much risk. He kept on, however, with commendable zeal, determined not to be conquered by any ordinary obstacles. Just this side of New Rochelle, and while descending a hill, he had the misfortune to run upon a horse which was apparently standing still in the road . . . The effect of the concussion was to break the wheel of the sulky. . . . The night was so dark that nothing whatever could be seen . . . Mr. Ward then took the harness from his horse, mounted him without a saddle, and came on to this city, a distance of seventeen miles, arriving at five o'clock on Tuesday morning.

But the achievement which delighted Greeley most was the trick played by a *Tribune* reporter on his *Herald* rival one day in western New York. The *Tribune* man, Maverick recorded, "quietly gathered up the details of some important news . . . and then sped with it to New York on an engine which was in waiting, under a full head of steam, for the use of the representative of the *Herald*. Of course, the *Tribune* had the news exclusively; and Bennett, very naturally, uttered blasphemies."

Those were the days when enterprising editors also ran private "pigeon expresses" to beat their rivals—which in turn led their rivals to hire marksmen to shoot the pigeons down. Several editors—Greeley among them—ganged up on Bennett by chartering a pilot boat to rush some European diplomatic news all the way across the Atlantic and thereby beat the regular Cunard Line packet; but Bennett, hearing of this, bribed the Cunarder's skipper to lay on more steam and thereby beat the pilot boat. Bennett beat all rivals again in his use of the newly invented telegraph: his biographer, Oliver Carlson, describes how he scooped the New York press one day in 1846, when Henry Clay was to give a speech on the Mexican War, by sending expert stenographers all the way out to Lexington, Kentucky, to take down Clay's words, rush them by pony express to Cincinnati, and in Cincinnati put them on the wire to New York. But soon the race grew costly. In order to outdo Bennett, the *Tribune* was forced to pool its resources with other rivals: thus it teamed with the *Sun* and the *Journal of Commerce* to set up a combination horseback, locomotive and steamer "express" to rush news from European packets that touched the American continent first at Halifax. "We pay no less than $1800 for a single trip of our steamer on the Bay of Fundy!" exclaimed the *Tribune*. This was the kind of pooling that led within a few years to the formation of the Associated Press, in which Greeley and the *Sun* were principal movers.

"We're doing middling well in the *Tribune* now," Greeley had written his old friend Bowe in March, 1842, "though money comes awful hard from the country and there is no currency beyond

Buffalo and Lancaster, Pa." Three years later the *Tribune* was
doing very well, with its own steam presses, a mechanical and
editorial staff of about thirty, and earnings running to $500 a week.
The *Herald* was still a much bigger enterprise, with a staff of over
fifty and earnings sometimes reaching $1,500 a week. But when
Greeley's old quarters in Ann Street were burned out that year, he
and McElrath felt so sure of their paper's future that they contracted at once for a new five-story building to house the *Tribune*
at the corner of Nassau and Spruce Streets, across from City Hall.
By 1847 the *Tribune* and the *Herald* were running neck and neck,
both selling close to 30,000 copies of their daily and weekly editions.
By January, 1849, Greeley was claiming a total circulation (with
a semiweekly edition included) of over 45,000—which put him in
the lead—and by January, 1850, of almost 50,000. That January
saw Greeley ordering a new $12,000 press, increasing his total staff
(including part-time correspondents and space writers) to 125,
and proudly writing Schuyler Colfax, "We thrashed the *United
States* this morning in a column of news from California, made up
for us in San Francisco by Bayard Taylor and telegraphed direct
from New Orleans . . . We came through from New Orleans in a
day, getting our whole dispatch ahead of even a hint of the arrival
of the steamer. . . . The whole town rings with it."

6

In 1841, with more than a touch of self-dramatization, Greeley had
described himself as "tow-headed, and half-bald at that . . . slouching
in dress; goes bent like a hoop, and so rocking in his gait that he
walks down both sides of the street at once." (Walt Whitman, then
a young Brooklyn printer and somewhat effete editorial hack, had
not yet discovered the advantages of a similar turnout for himself.)
But five years later, when the *Tribune* was about to take on the
dignity of a five-story building of its own, it was expected that the
successful young editor would subdue his manner, spruce up his
clothing, and acquire at least the appearance of a gentleman. Those
who looked for this totally misunderstood Greeley and what he was
after. For he did nothing of the kind.

He did the very opposite. His clothes, if anything, became even
more wayward: one trouser leg usually hung inside his country
boots, while the other flopped down over it; his collar and string
necktie had a way of slipping around to one side; his worn jacket

pockets bulged with clippings, letters and manuscripts; and over all this he wore in warm weather a bleached white duster, while in winter he bundled himself in a shapeless overcoat that was distended with still more papers. Somewhere he had picked up a wide-brimmed, low-crowned country hat, and this in all weathers now completed his habit. He pushed down Ann Street or up Park Row, hatbrim flopping, spectacles drooping, wads of paper or possibly a market basket for Mary swinging in his hand, and his legs moving more in a shuffle than a walk. If he stopped acquaintances or they stopped him, he broke into his high, squeaky, nasal voice, bantering, asking insistent questions, throwing out brisk, jocular replies, and then moving unceremoniously on. Hat pushed back on head, he reached his office, stopped for a joke with foreman Tom Rooker or for an outburst of sputtering profanities if he had spotted a typo in the morning's *Tribune,* lurched upstairs, and there at his desk addressed himself to a scene of utter disorder.

How much of this was ingrown eccentricity, how much of it was calculated showmanship, and how much of it was simply casual disregard of conventions, no man could tell—perhaps least of all Greeley himself. His natural leanings had told him to remain his bluff, careless, frugal rural self even in the city; and his instinct for dramatizing himself told him to remain so just because he was in the city. His very hat, standing out among the high-crowned beavers of the gentlemen on Park Row, was a walking advertisement of the *Tribune.* Some men said that he looked like a country preacher, others that he looked like a Quaker farmer who had just blown in from the West. That suited him entirely, and it made more people turn curiously to his *Tribune.* He swore; his language was rough, vigorous, direct; so was the *Tribune's*. And his third-floor office, with its sprawling confusion, was again the embodiment of the *Tribune*: anyone with something to say could come in and have it out.

In the old shop on Ann Street, Greeley had never even had a room for himself: "My office is everybody's rendezvous," he once remarked to his Indiana correspondent, Schuyler Colfax, "and I write and publish leaders with a din in my ears like Babel's." Now, in the new building, he was able to shut himself off from staff men and visitors in a cubicle overlooking City Hall Park; but he rarely did so for long, and never successfully. A third-floor sign read "Editorial Rooms: Ring the Bell." Sometimes the bell was out of order. Most callers simply walked in.

When the caller entered Greeley's office he found himself in a slatternly, dusty room furnished with several cane-bottomed, creaking chairs, a thin green carpet, a sofa that was usually piled high with old newspapers, a bookcase crammed with directories and almanacs, a lopsided engraving on the wall called "The Landing of the Pilgrim Fathers," and, by the window, a high-topped desk buried under geologic layers of clippings, pamphlets, "exchanges," and correspondence. At this desk, hunched nearsightedly with his face only a few inches above the topmost strata, sat the whiskered editor, usually scratching away with a swift, spattering pen over manuscript or proof sheets. Without looking up, he would reach out his writing hand at quick intervals to stab into an inkwell half-buried somewhere amid the litter. Almost above his head, at the end of a unique block-and-tackle arrangement suspended from the ceiling, dangled a large pair of shears which he could pull down when needed. Beside it hung a bellpull to summon a copy boy or messenger. To one side, rising unsteadily from the floor, stood a brass speaking tube that connected the editor directly with partner McElrath, two stories below. A huge paste pot, a box of crackers, and an empty milk glass or two often added to the jumble on the desk. All that was missing were ashtrays and a spittoon: these Greeley banned.

Usually the visitor had no trouble getting in; the problem was to attract Greeley's attention. One had to speak up first, while he went on scratching; and often one got no reply until he had finished another page, or until one had spoken one's piece twice over. Then the answers were likely to come fast. A political visitor from across the river who wanted a favor from Thurlow Weed talked at great length one day while the editor obliviously scrawled on, only to find himself suddenly interrupted with one sentence: "I'll be damned if I'm going to spend my time getting New York offices for Jerseymen"—which ended the conversation. On another occasion a New York City political leader whom the *Tribune* had opposed barged into the room and began abusing Greeley, calling him a traitor to the party. The editor went on serenely writing. The visitor talked louder, repeating his accusations, jumped up, brandished his arms, and shouted—to no effect. Finally, furious and frustrated, he stalked to the door, only to have Greeley at last look up, his face wreathed in innocent smiles, and say, "Don't go! Don't go! Come back and free your mind!"

On still another occasion a middle-aged man of important bearing pushed in, sat down, cleared his throat, and began, "I am Cornelius Vanderbilt." No recognition: the editor was working. The multimillionaire had come in to take Greeley to task for having befriended his own wayward, epileptic son, Cornelius Jeremiah, whom the Commodore had thrown out of the family fold in shame and disgrace. "Greeley, I hear yer lending Corneel money," said Vanderbilt, raising his voice. "I give you fair warning that you needn't look to me; I won't pay you one cent."

There was a pause while the editor went on writing. "Who the hell asked you to?" Greeley said suddenly, without looking up.

7

Settling into his office shortly after noon, Greeley would begin the day's work by spreading out his marked-up copy of the morning's *Tribune* before him for a post-mortem with the chief men of the staff. His searching eye relentlessly hunted down stylistic flaws, unsupported generalizations, wrong-font letters and incorrect middle initials. If the error was heinous—and a misspelling was that, in his eyes—there was sure to be an explosion. He would "scold like a drab," remembered his most famous assistant, Charles A. Dana. He looked on blunders in his paper as if they were moral offenses; he seemed as set on making the *Tribune* accurate as he was on making America virtuous. Good proofreading—a neglected craft—became to him a sort of sacrament. He described a *Tribune* proofreader's qualifications one day in a letter to an applicant:

I think a *first-rate* proof-reader could always find a place in our concern. But the place requires . . . immense knowledge of facts, names and spellings. Do you happen to know offhand that Stephens of Georgia spells his name with a *ph* and Stevens of Michigan with a *v* in the middle? Do you know that Eliot of Mass. has but one *l* in his name, while Elliot (lately in the House from Kentucky) has two? Do you know the politics and prejudices of Oliver of Missouri and Oliver of N. Y. respectively so well that when your proof says "Mr. Oliver" said so-and-so in the House, you know whether to insert "of Mo." or "of N. Y." after his name? Would you dare to strike out "of Mo." and put in "of N. Y." if you perceived the speech taking a particular direction respecting Slavery which shows that it must be wrongly attributed in the telegram?

Then, having delivered admonition and reproof, he sat down with the managing editor—first Raymond, and then Dana—to hear what news stories and features were scheduled for next day's page. By midafternoon he was usually at work on his editorial, rummaging around for clippings, statistics and quotations that would start him off. When the idea became firm in his mind, he pulled out a handful of copy paper and began writing almost as fast as his hand could move his pen, rarely pausing, seldom correcting, and dropping finished sheet after sheet in rapid succession on the floor until a whole column or two of "brevier" was completed. The ink-splotched sheets, when picked up and sent downstairs to the compositor, presented an extraordinary sight: the jiggling, scratching handwriting ran uphill and down so fast and with strokes so torn and tortuous as to be virtually indecipherable at first. Some called Greeley's a "worm-fence" hand. Others likened it to "the tracks of a drunken hen." Tom Rooker downstairs—himself a perfect Spencerian penman—detailed one journeyman to master the Greeley hieroglyphics and then hoped for the best.

After finishing his editorial and perhaps dashing off a short political story or two Greeley set to work on his correspondence, which was mountainous. It began with brief, peremptory notes to correspondents and contributors around the country, demanding answers to questions, energizing them and calling for copy: "What goes in Chicago? . . . Is it decided that Edward Bates will preside at the River and Harbors Convention? . . . How long must I wait to know?" Then came letters to politicians, trying out views, making recommendations, proposing appointments, or warning of the *Tribune*'s displeasure. Sometimes these became peremptory, too: "Alex H. Wells is (I understand) before the Senate as a candidate for a South American Consulship. You know his worthlessness, baseness, knavery and blackguardism. Can't you contrive to have him rejected? . . ." And later, to Schuyler Colfax when a leading Congressman: "You are mad. You talk about division of the spoils as coolly as if we had them in our vest pockets . . . Now look here. This is not a matter of whom we choose [for Speaker of the House], but of whom we can get . . . Mind what I tell you . . . " And on top of these, Greeley made time to write rambling chronicles to personal friends about his latest travels, activities, and family problems. Thus, in 1842, to "'Diah" Bowe, recounting a trip to Connecticut and Albany:

I took the Bridgeport boat (7 a.m.), the Housatonic R.R. (1 p.m.), the Albany stage at Canaan (7 p.m.) and next morning at half past five I rolled into [Albany] thoroughly fumigated by infernal tobacco-smokers . . . I went 'round to four hotels, to get in, but couldn't, there was such a perfect gouge of Loco-Foco office-seekers, who are here in stacks, as voracious as Pharoah's lean kine . . . At last I got liberty, through much persuasion, to get my trunk into a barroom, and started off to find [George] Jones' house, which I found a little past six, penetrated the interior, and laid myself down on a sofa, and when I awoke he was sitting down to breakfast. Next day I moved here to Thurlow's, where I have the run of the parlor, to say nothing of the kitchen, and am busy part of the time in concocting a lecture which I am to spout before the Young Men's Association . . . You know about my and Molly's bad luck again (fourth time) in the baby line. Molly is fairly discouraged, and wants to die. . . ."

Then, at some time in the evening—the hour could never be predetermined—Greeley would discover that he was hungry. (A legend had it that he was so absent-minded a copy boy had standing orders to remind him each day when he had eaten last.) Extraordinary things happened when the editor went out to eat. His principles were frugal and vegetarian; but his appetite, when he yielded to it, was now more voracious than ever. Bowls of milk filled with Sylvester Graham's crackers, hurriedly consumed around the corner, were his staple fare; but sometimes he consumed four or five of them. Beman Brockway, inviting Greeley to his house one day, watched the editor abstractedly devour an entire platter of gingerbread that had been laid out for company. On another occasion, after a lecture in Chautauqua, Greeley made away with a whole tray of doughnuts and cheese without feeling the worse for it. In his vegetarian absent-mindedness he was also observed one day bolting a fat slab of roast beef, without making any sign that he knew what it was. And Bayard Taylor, one of the *Tribune*'s brightest stars, recorded that one morning his teetotaling chief dropped in at the Taylor home at breakfast time and, being thirsty, began to pour himself amber liquid from a carafe—which turned out to be wine. Greeley contentedly gulped several glasses of it and never admitted that this was a queer-tasting kind of water indeed.

After dinner, or what passed for it, the editor usually came back to the shop for several more hours' work—although not to supervise the actual assembling of the paper. That he now delegated to Raymond or Dana or whoever was sitting at the main desk in the outer editorial room. He did not even demand to see proofs of what was going into it. So long as he knew in general what the paper would carry, he was satisfied; from that point on the other editors must take responsibility. In this he was wholly different from the dictatorial Bennett over at the *Herald*, who saw everything and ran everything himself. The peremptory, commanding manner which Greeley cultivated was largely for show; actually, he steered the *Tribune* with relaxed, easy reins, and enjoyed giving his men their head.

His method was unique in a day of newspapers owned and ruled by one man and served by anonymous inferiors without standing. It reflected his own earnest respect for the profession of journalism, which had led him also to respect journalists. It embodied, also, his growing wish to build a *Tribune* team and make his paper a central proving ground for talent. He voiced this instinct to one of his most talented acquisitions, Bayard Taylor, in a letter congratulating him on a piece he had just written:

I wish you would resolve henceforth to write one such article per week, and sign your own initials or some distinctive mark at the bottom. I want everybody connected with the *Tribune* to become known to the public (in some unobtrusive way) as doing what he does, so that in case of my death or incapacity it may not be feared that the paper is to die or essentially suffer.

There must be no slovenly writing on the *Tribune*, said Greeley to his men, and no misstatements of fact and no technical blunders; but there might be opinions galore. Sometimes the opinions published ran directly counter to his own. In the *Tribune's* second year, for instance, when the public was aroused by the revelation of a mutiny on board the United States warship *Somers*, Raymond wrote an editorial approving of the captain's summary hanging of Midshipman Spencer, one of the mutineers. Greeley was away at the time and Raymond knew that one of the editor's many "causes" was the abolition of capital punishment. When Greeley returned and saw the editorial in print, he told Raymond he wholly disagreed with it. But, having let Raymond have his say in public, he stuck by him and declined to reverse the *Tribune's* stand.

Three years later he found matters getting out of hand again. "I am away a good deal . . . and often abstracted from my paper for days," he wrote Colfax; "Articles creep into my paper, in my absence or otherwise, that I don't begin to like, but I let them go." Later, when Raymond's successor, the strong-willed, vigorous Dana, ran articles that again conflicted with his own point of view, Greeley sometimes lost patience to the extent of informing his readers that they had been published in spite of his disapproval; yet he kept Dana on. The readers, although at times bewildered by the range of the *Tribune*'s opinions, enjoyed the show. The editors, whetting their pens, did so too. It was this condition that led E. L. Godkin of the *Nation*—on most matters no admirer of Greeley—to remark years after, "The [*Tribune*] writers were all, as it were, partners in a common enterprise, and Greeley, though all-powerful, was simply looked on as *primus inter pares*."

In the end, Greeley's loose-hung, cooperative plan triumphed: it drew a whole new generation of writers into journalism, and a new generation of journalists to the *Tribune*. The editor had a sure instinct for finding the best of them, and then for training them and helping them unfold. He had begun with Raymond; then he hit upon Charles A. Dana at the time when the young New Hampshireman was still a Brook Farm utopian. From Brook Farm he also got George Ripley, who was to become for many years America's leading literary editor; he won over Margaret Fuller to journalism; he hired the romantic, poetizing Bayard Taylor and helped make him in a few years America's favorite globe-trotter; he spotted for his editorial page the serious, solid Richard Hildreth, later famous as a historian; he started Theodore Tilton, subsequently the brilliant editor of the *Independent*; and, as the *Tribune* talent procession swelled, it was to include names like Solon Robinson, Greeley's immensely popular farm editor; Charles T. Congdon, his deft editorial satirist; James S. Pike, George W. Smalley and Albert D. Richardson, all reporters celebrated in their day; George William Curtis, John Russell Young, Amos J. Cummings and Joseph Bucklin Bishop, editors who later rose to top positions in the American press; the poet E. C. Stedman; the dramatic critic William Winter; for a brief period, Henry Villard and Carl Schurz; and in later days, John Hay and Whitelaw Reid, the founder of the later *Tribune* dynasty.

8

Greeley, said the highly superior E. L. Godkin, "is self-educated, and very imperfectly educated at that—has no great grasp of mind, no great political insight, and has his brain crammed with half-truths and odds and ends of ideas." Greeley's ways, Godkin added fastidiously, "are disagreeable . . . to everybody who hates vulgarity in public life." But the *Nation*'s editor went on to admit that Greeley "has an English style which, for vigor, terseness and simplicity, has never been surpassed, except, perhaps by Cobbett." Greeley himself, far from apologizing for his lack of higher learning, prided himself publicly on having missed it. He entertained *Tribune* readers who had come no nearer than he to Harvard or Yale by remarking that "of all horned cattle the most helpless in a printing office is a college graduate." He showed off his smartness, but never his book knowledge. He expected sound study and general information of his writers and reporters, but never a college degree. To the end of his days he thought that a man with a degree had no place in the rough-and-tumble of his city room.

As for his style, he once remarked that "I can write better slang than any editor in America." He learned to write as he talked: in brisk, astringent phrases, without decoration and without ceremony. It took him many years to achieve this and to rid his written speech of the wordy conventions of the time. In the first year of the *Tribune* he was still writing such lumbering stuff as this:

We need not waste words to prove to you that Loco-Focoism is hostile to the prosecution of Internal Improvement . . . For two years our City has presented the disgraceful spectacle of a Commercial Emporium voting against the extension of our own Commerce—voting the surrender of her own precious advantages to her more sensible rivals!

Electors of New York! Will you so vote, can you wish, to be so represented again? Never! Never! Rally, then, in your might for the Whig ticket and the prosperity of your City!

His private letters, garrulous and relaxed, gave a better indication of the Greeley style that was to come, even when they were as casual as this one to his crony Obediah Bowe of Herkimer, New York, referring to mutual friends whom he had lately seen in the Midwest:

Mary Ann Cook has been married to Hansha, Bates' partner, in Detroit. It is a fair match. Hansha is about her age, or a little older—neither more of an old bachelor than she is an old maid—a slight, small, insignificant, well-meaning fellow, steady as a clock, and worth from $500 to $1000 which, whatever it may be, he will never diminish or increase by $100. He will treat Mary Ann well, after his fashion . . . At Pittsburgh I found Burke in his glory, surrounded by his family and doing a heavy business . . . Burke is trying to marry a rich girl, which is the cause of his branching out so. I don't know whether he will get ahead or swamp; it depends pretty much on his getting the girl aforesaid—or rather, her fortune—pretty soon.

He worked toward the short word, the tart epithet, the quick, homely twist of thought. One day the persistence of reactionary men in the Whig party aroused him. He ticked them off in two sentences: "The stubborn conservative is like a horse on a ferryboat. The horse may back, but the boat moves on, and the animal with it." On another day the *Express* had dismissed a weighty Greeley argument with the brief comment, "Bah!" Greeley came back and dismissed the *Express*: "We are quite willing that every animal shall express its emotions in the language natural to it." In the fall of the presidential-campaign year 1844 it seemed to him that his Whig friends were growing overconfident of their ability to elect Henry Clay without trouble. He offered them a parable:

There is an old legend that once on a time all the folks in the world entered into an agreement that at a specified moment they would give one unanimous shout, just to see what a noise they could make, and what tremendous effects it would produce. The moment came—everybody was expecting to see trees, if not houses, thrown down by the mighty concussion; when lo! the only sound was made by a dumb old woman, whose tongue was loosed by the excitement of the occasion. The rest had all stood with mouths and ears wide open to *hear* the great noise, and so forgot to make any.

When occasion demanded, though, he pulled out all the verbal organ stops, and then one read such outbursts as these:

By the midnight mail, we have the astounding intelligence of the passage of annexation [of Texas] through the Senate by a vote of 27 to 25; every Locofoco voting in the affirmative, with just the three necessary Whigs: Johnson of Louisiana, Henderson of Mississippi, and Merrick, the purchased traitor of Maryland . . .

Yes, the mischief is done and we are now involved in war! We have adopted a war ready-made, and taken upon ourselves its prosecution to the end. We are to furnish the bodies to fill trenches and the cash to defray its enormous expense. Mexico, despoiled of her fairest province by our rapacity and hypocrisy, has no choice but to resist, however ineffectively, the consummation of our design. . . . By our proceedings in getting possession of Texas, we have declared ourselves to be the enemies of the civilized world, and are only constrained from becoming such by the lowest considerations of self-interest. . . . Surely there must come a reckoning for this.

He demolished a certain Dr. Potts, a fashionable Episcopalian rector who had denounced the *Tribune* as being subversive of the social order, by quoting Jesus against rich men and citing Potts' own fat salary. Then he calmed down into amiable rural essays on crop prospects, only to warm up again and lay into New York's dirty streets and lack of adequate parks. He insisted on reforms ranging from sound currency to faster horse-car service. He became interested in spiritualism, utopianism, women's rights, the abolition of sweatshops, improved farm machinery, and inventions of every sort. ("I do want inventions treated just like other occurrences," he instructed Dana. "If a man should invent a new locomotive that could be readily and profitably used in cornfields or on common roads, I would wish to see it announced in a leader on the very day after it was patented; whereas by your present method it would probably appear the next month in a supplement, buried up under new raspberries and improved beehives . . .")

All this, in turn, represented only part of his range and activity. While writing two and sometimes three columns for next day's paper, he also turned out temperance tracts, Whig campaign booklets, occasional doggerel, and articles for other newspapers and magazines. He went for a while into general publishing with McElrath, printing a magazine called the *American Laborer* along with a miscellany of books and pamphlets. He took on the job of completing Epes Sargent's lengthy life of Henry Clay, and later wrote his own book-length history of the slavery controversy. He served as adviser and agent to writers seeking publishers: he read and criticized the work of Alice and Phoebe Cary, the fragile, poetic sisters of Cincinnati, and he marketed a series of articles which Henry D. Thoreau had written after coming out of Walden Woods. ("My friend," Thoreau wrote Greeley in 1848, "how can I thank you for your kindness? . . . Here I have been sitting idle, as it were, while you have been busy in my cause, and have done so much for me.") And he traveled—endlessly, it seemed to him. He lectured. He took to the road and made himself one of the favorite performers on the country's lyceum lecture circuits.

Announcing one of his first platform appearances, in 1843, Greeley wrote of himself in the *Tribune,*

Horace Greeley will lecture before the New York Lyceum at the Tabernacle, this evening. Subject, "Human Life." The lecture will commence at half past 7, precisely. If those who care to hear it will sit near the desk, they will favor the lecturer's weak and husky voice.

His voice remained "weak and husky"—and squeaky, too—no matter how much he tried to train it for the platform; yet he kept on. His whole bearing before an audience, in fact, was inauspicious and odd. A *Herald* man who watched Greeley in action in a New Jersey hall reported that "Mr. Greeley then rose, and was speechless for a few moments, looking around the audience in a kind of vacant stare. At last he broke silence in a low, indistinct tone of voice, and with a furious motion of his body, swaying backwards and forwards, as if it were impossible for him to stand perpendicular and erect." This shuffling presence was a strange sight in a day when public speaking meant "classic" oratory, and when the public flocked into the Lyceum to see and hear performers like Edward Everett and Daniel Webster go through stylized routines—the rolling period, the noble gesture, and the grand peroration. Greeley, totally unable to declaim or strike a Roman pose, was once asked by Henry Ward Beecher, a paragon among platform artists, what he meant by a "successful" lecture. Greeley answered, "When more folks stay in than go out." Yet he kept on. He stuck to his own ways and to his own message. Soon, in spite of his inadequacies, he was filling the halls.

In New York, in 1843, he was billed as the first speaker on the affirmative side in a public debate on the question, "Resolved, That a Protective Tariff is Conducive to our National Prosperity"—the opposing speakers being Samuel J. Tilden and Parke Godwin. But when he took to annual lecture circuits he picked far more general subjects as vehicles for his intention. He spoke throughout New England and the Middle West on "True Democracy"; on "Self-Made Men"; on "Human Life"; on "The Nation"; and, most persistently of all, on "Temperance." When he arose to exhort listeners to "Temperance," he held in his hands a sheaf of slips of paper bearing notes such as these:

Intemperance has no advocates.
Yet many abettors.
Fair women proffer the sparkling glass.

Every drunkard was once a temperate drinker.
Many believe themselves still such.
The Queens County case.

Yet the drunkard's son does not take warning.
The drunkard dies and is forgotten.
Our lying tombstones.

What is temperance? What is intemperance?
The moderate use of things essentially hurtful is intemperate.
Opium. Chloroform. Arsenic.

How liquor affects the human constitution.
Incipient inflammation of the stomach.
Dr. Sewell's plates.

Old men who drink.
I once heard of one who died 108 years old.
The adulteration of liquors. All but universal.

The manufacture of Burgundy.
My experience of champagne.
More champagne drunk in New York City than is made from grapes in the world.

Strychnine whiskey.
An Ohio distiller.
"Seven other devils worse than the first."

The cost of crime.
Pauperism a frightful and growing evil.
Rum the main cause.
"I have been young and now I am old," &c.

He sometimes said that he went off lecturing because of the money in it—which was not the truth. Often he found himself out in small towns speaking for nothing, and not even being paid his expenses; he complained to Colfax that an address in out-of-the-way Warren, Ohio, had cost him three day's time and $15, "of which I had to pay $8 in that village for a horse and carriage to take me out of it." He lectured because he had to; because a demon for work pursued him; because the need for continuous, strenuous self-expression never left him; because the role of the popular lecturer combined those of the entertainer and the missionary, and he always saw himself cast as both; and because, in going out to face the people at first hand, he also wanted them to face him, to talk to him in hundreds of towns and villages, and tell him what he needed to know about them in order to steer the *Tribune* closer to their needs and aspirations.

He had to be on the move. At home, there was not enough to hold him. Of Mary he had written to Bowe on one occasion in 1842, "Molly has never been so disconsolate as now, and I was almost sorry to leave her for a week"; but several years later he was writing another friend, "Mrs. Greeley's life is all absorbed in the pettiest, meanest cares"—and going off for months. He clapped on his wide hat, wrapped himself in his ulster, picked up his red-and-blue blanket roll, and set forth in midwinter on the swaying "steam cars" to outlying northern towns and western villages, riding all night and often arriving in the chill hours before dawn. If no house was open to him at that hour, he would curl up in his blankets on the depot's wooden benches until the time came for him to get up, wolf several portions of griddle cakes, and emerge as the *"Try-bune's"* traveling mentor to the people at large. One winter took him out to Wisconsin; another, into northern Michigan; another, through Maine—where he moved from town to town giving temperance lectures, "speaking three times in Bangor, twice in Gardiner, and once each in Waterville, Augusta, Bath and Portland. I had to keep traveling most of the days and writing for the *Tribune* between meals, but I contrived to get tanned by March winds, soaked in March storms, and thoroughly shaken up by the snowdrifts and mud of March roads. My health is greatly better for the journey."

VI. UTOPIAN

1

A curious destiny kept involving Horace Greeley with men who hailed from upstate New York. Some time after Thurlow Weed of Albany and Henry J. Raymond of the village of Lima had variously introduced themselves to him—and some time also after he had taken up campaigning for William H. Seward of Auburn—there entered into his life a frail, bookish dreamer from the Genesee valley named Albert Brisbane.

According to Redelia Brisbane, who wrote a life of her famous husband, their first meeting took place as early as 1839, when Brisbane had just finished his socialist reform tract, *The Social Destiny of Man*, and taken it around to Park Benjamin in Ann Street to ask him what he thought of it.

"There's Horace Greeley," said Benjamin, "just damned fool enough to believe such nonsense."

"Who is Greeley?" asked Brisbane.

"Oh, he's a young man upstairs editing the *New Yorker*."

So, said Redelia, Brisbane tucked his book under his arm and took it upstairs to Greeley, who read it and at once became converted to the revolutionary principles of Brisbane and Charles Fourier.

Actually, Greeley did not meet the young socialist from Batavia until the following year, after his book was published. The *New Yorker* noticed it only briefly. But in the months during which he was planning his own *Tribune*, the attraction of Brisbane's thought began working powerfully on Greeley. Shortly before he launched his own paper, he undertook to print for Brisbane in his Ann Street shop a new magazine named *The Future, Devoted to the Cause of Association and a Reorganization of Society*. In the first issues of the *Tribune*, Horace Greeley & Company advertised *The Future* to "the friends of Association and Social Progress." Then, in October, reporting briefly that Brisbane had given a lecture "on Social Christianity and Fourierism," the *Tribune* went on to say:

> Mr. Brisbane will lecture hereafter on the practical details of the system of *Fourier*, of whom he is a zealous disciple, and we shall then endeavor to give a more clear and full account of his doctrines.

And on 1 March, 1842, readers of the paper were astonished to find the left-hand column of the front page given over to a special feature introduced as follows:

ASSOCIATION;
OR, PRINCIPLES OF A TRUE ORGANIZATION OF SOCIETY.
General View . . . No. 1.

The advocates of the Social Principles discovered by CHARLES FOURIER, have made arrangements to purchase from the Proprietor a column of the Daily *Tribune*, the matter of which will be transferred to the Weekly *Tribune*. Through this medium they intend to lay before the Public the practical means which that great Mind has proposed for alleviating the vast amount of misery which exists in Society, and for elevating the social Condition of Man, and securing ultimately his happiness.

Therewith Horace Greeley publicly entered the lists of reform, and specifically of that reform which in the 1840's passed as Socialist. He did it in his own way, by making Brisbane and his group pay him to be heard, rather than by paying them himself for their contributions. This unique arrangement, designed to combine insurgency and revenue, also had the advantage of enabling Greeley at any time to disavow Brisbane's column as being merely paid advertising matter, in case it went too far. Yet in practice, instead of playing safe, Greeley did his best to help put Brisbane's ideas into effect and build utopias throughout America.

The new enthusiasm in which Greeley had become swept up was only one of many that seized the America of the expansive early 1840's. It was the great day of conventions, causes, mass movements and conversions, all going on simultaneously, and all inspired by the pervasive belief that progress was here to stay—or at all events must be made so. In 1835 the members of the Mechanics' and Workingmen's Temperance Society of Philadelphia had risen in a body at a pioneer prohibitionist convention to sing:

> Now let us rise united
> And the great monster crush,
> By water draughts excited,
> We to the rescue rush.

But if one did not agree that the barring of strong drink was the prerequisite for a better world, one could attach one's self to half a dozen other causes just now beginning to flower. The year 1838 saw American pacifists holding an inaugural congress and drawing up resolutions calling for universal disarmament, nonresistance, and nonallegiance to any government. ("Such a mass of free mind as was brought together I have never seen before in any one assembly," Josiah Quincy had remarked of the proceedings; "there was so much talent and a great deal of *soul*.") Next came agitations for causes ranging from prison reform and women's rights to the abolition of flogging in the United States Navy and the propagation of the wearing of bloomers—and all this in addition to the deeper, angrier, irrepressible agitation to end black slavery.

If Greeley during the summer of 1840 had not been entirely taken up with helping to elect General Harrison, he might have found it stimulating to attend in Boston a convention of men and women who wanted to bring about so many changes in America that they called themselves The Friends of Universal Reform. At this convention, as Ralph Waldo Emerson somewhat worriedly put it, "madmen, madwomen, men with beards, Dunkers, Muggletonians, Come-outers, Groaners, Agrarians, Seventh-Day Baptists, Quakers, Abolitionists, Calvinists, Unitarians, and Philosophers—all came successively to the top, and seized their moment, if not their hour, wherein to chide, or pray, or preach, or protest."

Emerson, of course, was there himself. So were Bronson Alcott, the most garrulous and irrepressible dreamer in all New England; blue-eyed Henry Thoreau, not yet gone into seclusion at Walden Pond; Dr. William Ellery Channing, the learned inspirer of Unitarianism, now bent but unquenchable at sixty; his pupil Theodore Parker, the deep-browed young Unitarian minister at West Roxbury; James Russell Lowell, the high-spirited, socially impeccable belles-lettrist; William Lloyd Garrison, a flinty, Cromwellian man, poised for battle or for martyrdom; and still another Unitarian minister, the radiant and ever-hopeful George Ripley, aglow with a desire to read everything and regenerate the world—and fated to become, after he had tried to regenerate it, the literary editor of the New York *Tribune*.

Many of these men were to become Greeley's friends; all of them, in one way or another, became his co-workers for reform. But just what did the word "reform" mean? At the start of the 1840's, the very concept was exciting but bewildering: it took forms ranging from literary self-culture and polite hunanitarianism to mystical communion and the creation of utopian retreats—sometimes all these forms in one person. If one found the Concord philosophers' doctrine of transcendentalism too heady to take, or if one felt one's self unready for the semisocialist rigors of New Harmony, Brook Farm, or the Mormons' Nauvoo, there was always spiritualism, Adventism, vegetarianism, and phrenology, along with such riskier gospels as Frances Wright's "free love." Even Greeley's new friend, the red-faced, Rabelaisian showman Phineas T. Barnum—who had just taken over Scudder's American Museum on Broadway in order to exhibit there such monstrosities as his embalmed "Feejee Mermaid," flanked by his "Great Model of Niagara Falls, with Real Water" and the sensational midget, Tom Thumb—responded to the general reformist spirit when he also ran on his premises a "Moral Lecture Room," in which daily temperance dramas were performed. Religious enthusiasm flourished: Barnum liked especially to go to Dr. Chapin's Universalist church to sing hymns standing side by side with Horace Greeley. For those who needed dramatic evidence of the existence of a life after death, there was soon to be the rage of "spirit-rappings" (at which Horace and Mary Greeley's protégés, the remarkable Fox sisters of Rochester, became amazingly adept); and for those swept up by new popular teachings of the wonders of the human mind, there were establishments such as Fowler and Wells' Phrenological Cabinet on Nassau Street in New York—not far from the *Tribune* office—where they could have the "bumps" on their heads examined.

The America of the dawning 1840's had reason to be self-critical, expectant, romantic and exuberant—all at once. Three years before, it had been seized by business paralysis; now it seemed restored to full, bursting vigor. There was a belief that in the decade now opening, the time for great actions, great changes, and great American ideas was near at hand. All were borne along by the dream of a "manifest destiny"—physical or spiritual or both. American man seemed cut out for illimitable possibilities; he was not only good (as the politicians congratulated him on being) but he was far better than were many of his inherited institutions (so the reformers, from Emerson down, added). In this man, so abounding in moral worth as his energies unfolded, lay the chances of full fraternity, and—what was more, for those who could face the shimmery prospect—of true perfectibility, and therewith the achievement of a millennium on earth.

2

But there were also certain realities to be considered; and it was on these, primarily, that Greeley's less exalted mind became fixed. He was by no means unique in this. Even the seraphic Emerson, who had managed to declare that "Uplifted into infinite space ... I become a transparent eyeball," came down to earth long enough to survey the prospects. Emerson touched upon them when he wrote that he felt it his mission "to celebrate the spiritual powers in their infinite contrast to the mechanical powers and the mechanical philosophy of this time." There was the problem: man was like a God, but he was also a wage slave. And these "mechanical powers" —meaning the factory system and the emerging large business corporation—were now threatening to engulf those same sturdy artisans and small independent producers whom Emerson's own essays were calling upon to be always self-reliant. Self-reliance did not amount to much when one's pay was three dollars a week; Greeley had seen that for himself in 1837 in the slums. Progress was a splendid thing, but to sensitive men there was something fearful about the smoking factories and the mill-hand drudgery that were bringing it. Progress was inevitable; but what about the kind of progress recorded by eleven textile mills in Lowell, Massachusetts, which trebled their aggregate dividends from 1844 to 1845, but in the same period slashed their weekly wages from $2 to $1.75? What were Americans to do to guide and control this new industrial system of theirs before it got out of hand and controlled them?

Militants like the fiery John Windt in New York—a veteran of the earlier Workingman's Party agitation—had one answer: Organize the wage-earners! Demand higher pay and a ten-hour day! Fight! But middle-class men like Horace Greeley were by no means that militant; and they knew, in turn, that leaders like Windt at this point had everything but a following. For the depression of 1837-38 had not only broken wage levels but their union treasuries as well, thereby leaving America's young labor movement demoralized. Ten years were to pass until even the elder craft unions began effectively to reassemble themselves: the once-vigorous New York Printers' Union, for instance, did not pull itself together again until the very end of the 1840's (at which time the first new president whom it elected was an employer—Horace Greeley). Urban Democratic Locofocos, upstate antirent farmers, and scattered political inheritors of the Jacksonian tradition could be heard speaking out, but rarely in unison. For a few years, therefore, leadership in the cause of general reform fell into the hands of a curious assortment of middle-class intellectuals. Perhaps these were not the best people to undertake the task. Still, they tried.

"Who shall apply for us Christianity to social life?" This was the question the strong-minded young Unitarian, Theodore Parker, tossed out from his pulpit in West Roxbury. It was the central question of the reformers' day, and it was to become the theme of dozens of *Tribune* editorials. Perhaps self-culture, universal education, and a resulting glow of general enlightenment would lead to it: this appeared to be the teaching of the ethereal Dr. Channing, who also hoped that by simply appealing to the inborn goodness of New England factory employers he could prevail upon them to raise workers' wages. (The answer was that, good or not, the employers did not raise them.) Sensing such results, other aroused spirits—even such persistent individualists as Greeley—declared that the cult of self and self-culture was not enough. People working alone, they said, were not going to be able to improve society—either through pressure or through isolated example. Unbridled individualism, as they saw it, had led merely to savage business competition, which in turn was now leading to social anarchy. Men, high and low, must therefore cooperate and pool their energies for social purposes. How? There was much fuzziness on this. But there was no lack of determination to experiment.

At this point—the fall of 1840—two future key editors of Greeley's New York *Tribune* expressed themselves in words prophetic of their next step. First, the Reverend George Ripley, addressing his Boston congregation on the occasion of resigning his pulpit:

I have never attempted to play the priest in your churches . . . I have had no faith in the mock solemnity which is sometimes assumed for effect . . . I cannot behold the degradation, the ignorance, the poverty, the vice, the ruin of the soul, which is everywhere displayed in the very bosom of Christian society in our own city, while men look idly on, without a shudder. I cannot witness the glaring inequalities of condition . . . and the burning zeal with which men run the race of competition . . . without the sad conviction that the spirit of Christ has well-nigh disappeared from our churches . . .

Second, an earnest student from New Hampshire named Charles A. Dana, then at Harvard, writing a western friend:

Apropos of Mr. Ripley, he leaves his church on the 1st of January, as I am informed. He is to be one of a society who design to establish themselves at Concord, or elsewhere in the vicinity, and introduce, among themselves at least, a new order of things. Their object is social reformation, but of the precise nature of their plans, I am ignorant . . . The leaders of this movement are Mr. Emerson and Mr. Alcott, and those who are usually called Transcendentalists.

Very soon young Dana learned just what their plans were, and put up $1,500 of his patrimony to buy shares in Ripley's colony, where he settled down to wait on communal tables, teach Latin, and help Nathaniel Hawthorne with the haying.

3

Albert Brisbane, the dreamer from Batavia, New York, had returned in 1834 from a six-year intellectual grand tour of Europe (paid for out of his father's canal-country real-estate profits) during which he had studied under Friedrich Hegel in Berlin, introduced himself to the aged Goethe in Weimar, taken private lessons from Charles Fourier in Paris, befriended the rebellious Heinrich Heine, visited the Middle East, and learned Turkish (this because Fourier thought that Constantinople might one day become the capital of the world). With his tall forehead, pointed nose, long hair, and petulant, low-slung chin, he looked in profile like a cross between a less handsome Byron and an unrealized young Richard Wagner; he was, in fact, the very model of the American romantic rebel, even down to studying language reform and animal magnetism.

Troubled by the coming of an industrial society and looking for some philosopher's stone that might bring order out of competitive chaos, Brisbane thought he had found it in Fourier's attic. There this extraordinary Frenchman, dry, aquiline, mathematical, rationalistic, and yet capable of surging human sympathies, preached that amid the confusion and neglect of modern national states, what humanity now needed was organization into smaller, compact social cells—each of them to number, for mysterious reasons, just 1,620 souls. In these cells or "phalanxes," work and rewards were to be divided according to an elaborate, preordained system under which the oppressiveness and monotony of industrial labor would be overcome by harmonious teamwork of all classes. The earnings of a phalanx, after subsistence needs had been met, would be split up between labor, capital, and scientific or managerial talent—in that order. Unpleasant, menial labor would be ennobled by special rewards or assigned to adolescents; labor in general would be dignified by being located in ideal, colonnaded tabernacles surrounded by orchards and fountains; mass education would "refine the passions" and give each of them a productive place. Since the beehive's manual workers were to get just a little less than half of all communal profits, this added up to a little less than halfway socialism—but still it was a good deal more than they had been getting. All would be happy. "Eureka!" cried Brisbane, bringing the gospel home.

In buying this doctrine for the *Tribune* in 1842—or rather, in selling Brisbane the space in which to propagate it—Greeley appears to have missed one of its implicit points. The New England intellectuals around Parker and Emerson spotted it when they criticized Fourier's mechanical scheme as submerging the individual. This was true: as far as Fourier had been able to see from his European experience, the individual had already become submerged by feudalism and was doomed to become more so by industrialism. And since he frankly accepted industrialism (something the Brook Farmers could not quite persuade themselves to do) he thought less of liberating the individual than of simply making the masses happier at the side of their machines—a program that included band music, a hierarchy of titles and parades. Greeley's eye, too, was on improving industry rather than on escaping it. It was all very well to buy your way into a Brook Farm retreat if you had $1,000 (as Hawthorne had—although he later sued to get it back), but what if you didn't? What if your fate was to work for wages?

So Greeley encouraged Brisbane to go ahead with his unique *Tribune* demonstration. Just what the guest columnist paid for the privilege, no one knows for certain. Brisbane himself said that he paid Greeley $500 for the space for one year. Greeley's business partner, McElrath, however, insisted that no payment had ever been made. But, whatever money may or may not have changed hands, the *Tribune* threw itself wholeheartedly behind Brisbane, and soon found itself building up news interest, discussion and circulation at an extraordinary rate as it helped him popularize his cause. Later, in fact, Brisbane thought that Greeley had helped him almost too well—or, at any rate, too quickly.

For in August of their first year's association, when Brisbane had announced in the *Tribune* his plan of setting up a large-scale Fourierist colony to be called the "North American Phalanx," he had also specified that work should not begin until an ambitious stock issue had been fully subscribed. But by this time his *Tribune* column was being picked up by papers as far away as Indiana and Illinois, and Greeley's editorial enthusiasm had helped cause the formation of local Fourierist clubs which were talking of setting up little runaway "phalansteries" of their own. By October the *Tribune* reported that at least forty newspapers were reprinting or sympathetically discussing the column; and now Greeley himself joined the camp of those who were too keen for immediate action to be able to wait for the formation of Brisbane's large-scale establishment. He put perhaps $3,000—the bulk of his *Tribune* profits for that year—into a scheme concocted by some New York artisans, with the help of a landscape painter, of setting up their own "Sylvania Phalanx" in a mountainous section in northern Pennsylvania. But that picturesque tract, Greeley might have told them, was just as unpromising as the Erie County backwoods to the west of it which his father, Zac, had settled. The colony promptly collapsed. Within the next few years, helped by the *Tribune*'s enthusiasm, almost forty more small "phalansteries" were attempted—one of them near Abraham Lincoln's home in Sangamon County, Illinois. None of them thrived; few survived even the first winter. Meanwhile Brisbane himself, in order not to be left totally behind as his movement mushroomed, hurried his "North American Phalanx" prematurely into existence in 1843 on 700 acres of fair farmland near Red Bank, New Jersey. Instead of thereby starting a model community with several hundred families, comfortably quartered, he broke ground with only a few dozen, living in shacks and squalor while they prepared communal dwellings for the others—who never came. The North American Phalanx cost Greeley another $4,300 of his early *Tribune* earnings. Finally he got about half of this back—long after the settlement was abandoned in 1854.

By that time it was no longer news to him that Utopia—under whatever American name or guise or capital structure—was a failure. The attempts to outwit industrialism by cooperative harmony, "refined passions" and a devotion to frugal living were doomed by lack of harmony, a continuance of unrefined passions, and a very natural suspicion on the part of those who were being frugal that their lustier neighbors were getting too much. Brook Farm was, at bottom, simply a writers' cooperative which wanted to avoid urban life while preserving the urbanities. Brisbane's laborious North American Phalanx, meanwhile, with its schematic blueprint for total security for workers and investors alike, was an attempt at a small corporate state. Both talked socialism without being actually socialist. Hawthorne, pitching Brook Farm hay in yellow pantaloons while the genteel Sophia Ripley scrubbed floors and young Dana milked cows and served as headwaiter, was in effect one of America's first intellectual escapists. Greeley, visiting the gaunt, communal building at Phalanx, New Jersey, where a leaning porch substituted for the intended Fourierist grand colonnade and where dedicated men wore long beards while their elderly women took to bloomers, was one of America's persistent romantics—and then, when he returned to his office, he went to work for the highly realistic Thurlow Weed and Henry Clay. Both Brisbane's and the Brook Farmers' reformist schemes could be dismissed as the confused product of social mysticism, misty-eyed sentiment and the afterglow of the Enlightment. Either one evaded more issues than it faced. And certainly neither became large enough to threaten remotely the established order.

Then why all the excitement? Why did Webb's *Courier and Enquirer,* for instance, try to read Greeley out of the Whig party, charging the *Tribune* with "overrating entirely the suffering of the poor" and declaring that "there can be no peace in Whig ranks" so long as the paper was permitted to call itself Whig? And why did Greeley's own conservative associates—his managing editor, Henry J. Raymond, and his business manager, McElrath—make a point of suppressing Brisbane's columns from the paper whenever its editor was out of town?

4

Confused or not, the bundle of new ideas at which Greeley was grasping were in fact a threat—even though it was not at first clear to whom, or to what extent. Primarily they were a menace to the traditional simplicity and political orthodoxy of those who had been seized with them. The ideas did not embody anywhere near as formidable a revolt as had at first been expected. Yet they went on providing a leaven that might produce strange stirrings.

Greeley, in taking up his new discovery, had not gone "Locofoco." Far from it. His best friends were Whigs. He remained suspicious of doctrines advancing principles of class antagonism or even of women's rights. "We repudiate the doctrines advanced by Frances Wright and her co-workers . . . of the rightful equality of the sexes in political privileges and in social conditions," he had stiffly declared in his *New Yorker*; "not disputing the mental capacity of women, we yet insist that . . . [the wife] should yield a general and cordial though not servile deference to the husband." He stuck to that. He held also to the point of view he had voiced originally in reviewing the visiting Harriet Martineau's *Society in America*, namely that anyone who started from the thesis that class conflicts were central to American life was making a basic mistake. And as for the idea that the government might have the right to regulate such matters as the hours of factory labor, he had said— and still believed—that these things should be left to private agreement: "What have governments and Presidents got to do with it?"

Yet here was Greeley finding himself swept up in company with such firebrands as Parke Godwin of Bryant's Democratic *Evening Post*, who was trumpeting that "Blind competition tends to the formation of gigantic monopolies . . . While the few rich are becoming more and more rich, the unnumbered many are becoming poorer . . . Our modern world of industry is a veritable Hell, where disorder, discord, and wretchedness reign." He had discovered for himself the paradox of want and degradation in a country of such promising plenty. The protective tariff was a fine thing for building up industry, but alone it was apparently not enough. "We spend half our energies in building fences and providing safeguards against each other's roguery," he now took to arguing, "while our labor is rendered inefficient and inadequately productive by bad management, imperfect implements. . . . It is quite within the truth to estimate the annual product of our National Industry at less than one half what it might be if better applied and directed."

This he felt to be an explosive fact. It might be comfortable to go on arguing, as he had in the *New Yorker,* that the American laborer, "however humble his station," should "regard himself not as a serf desperately struggling with his fetters, but as a freeman, quietly but surely threading his way from poverty and toil to certain competence if not wealth." But at the present rate of uncertain production and faulty distribution, the laborer might never be able to gain wealth—or even a competence. It was all very well to laugh off the Locofoco theory of acute class conflict in the America of the moment; but what about the future? Wasn't the present scheme of things leading inevitably toward just such conflict? Then how, for America's general happiness, could this conflict be avoided?

This was the issue which Greeley pondered as he traveled, asked questions, looked in on factories, scribbled editorials, and made his regular trips by night boat to talk practical politics with Weed and Seward in Albany. He turned up again and again at Brook Farm to see what answer the intellectuals had. He arrived there—as one of the colonists, Amelia Russell, described him—in a habit designed to outdo even their unworldly garb: "His hair was so light that it seemed white; his face was entirely colorless, even his eye not adding much to save it from its ghastly hue; his coat was a very light drab, almost white, and his nether garments were the same." But he always found their highly individual minds set simply on restoring what the elder Henry James called "the divine life in man," or—as their nominal leader, Ripley, put it—preparing "a society of liberal, intelligent, and cultivated persons, whose relations with each other would permit a more wholesome life than can be led amidst the pressure of our competitive institutions."

Fine words; but what would they amount to without practical organization? Clearly, the answer lay in "Association or Cooperation, or whatever name may be given to the combination of many heads and hands to achieve a beneficent result. . . . I shall be sorely disappointed if this Nineteenth Century does not witness its very general adoption as a means of reducing the cost and increasing the comfort of the poor man's living." So he went to work with Brisbane to try to convert the Brook Farm individualists (whom he called "lazy") into a tight-knit, Fourierist cell.

This did not work. It was fantastic to think that it might. Greeley himself had already complained to his new friend Dana that Brisbane was so "exclusive" as a reformer as to be a "curse": "He won't consent to let his great Reform progress in harmony with other Reforms, even as the complement of them all, but it must be pitted against them all—something diverse, original, antagonistic." The Brook Farmers, rather than submit to disciplined, "associated" living, drifted away. The North American Phalanx, as drab in appearance as it was ambitious in design, never attracted more than ninety families, and Greeley blamed its "crotchety, selfish, played-out, idle" tenants for its failure; but others blamed poor sanitation, bloomers, lack of privacy, regimentation, and the dismal food.

It was at this time, in 1846, that an extrordinary opportunity presented itself to Greeley's sometime assistant, Henry J. Raymond—who in the meantime had moved over to the more sympathetic surroundings of Colonel Webb's *Courier and Enquirer*—to score a number of points off his former chief. For Greeley had expansively proposed that the two papers debate in public the whole subject of Fourierist "association." Editor Webb gave Raymond all the space he wanted to let go. The resultant discussion ran to a total of twenty-four articles—twelve by Greeley, defending the "association" principle, and twelve by Raymond, seizing the initiative and knocking it down—and it soon became apparent, amid Raymond's unexpected display of virtuosity, that a struggle not only between beliefs but between newspapers and personalities was at hand.

Greeley, with all organ stops out, opened on the theme that "the earth, the air, the waters, the sunshine, with their natural products, were divinely intended . . . for the sustenance and enjoyment of the whole human family. But the present *fact* is, that a very large majority of mankind are landless. . . . Those whom society has divested of their natural right to a share of the soil, are entitled to *Compensation*, i.e. to continuous opportunity to earn a subsistence by Labor. . . . But, as society is now organized, this is not, and cannot be, done. 'Work, work! give us something to do! anything that will secure us honest bread,' is at this moment the prayer of not less than thirty thousand human beings within the sound of the City-Hall bell. Here is an enormous waste and loss. We must devise a remedy, and that remedy, I propose to show, is found in Association."

But Raymond, a sharp-eyed, foxlike figure behind his thickening mustache, was not to be maneuvered into a defense of social exploitation as such. Instead, he cunningly countered that Greeley's idea about the right of all men to land was shared by Fanny Wright, the notorious radical, who was for free love too—curious company indeed for an editor who went around calling himself a sound and moral Whig. In vain did Greeley keep repeating that all he had in mind was the setting up a type of association "which shall take the place of the present township, to be composed of some hundreds or some thousands of persons, who shall be united together in interest and industry," et cetera. Such "association," Raymond kept hitting back (being well-informed about what was going on at the North American Phalanx), would lead only to greater social friction than before: the more successful it became, the more its skillful members would grumble at the lazy and awkward, who for their part would do little work while demanding their full share of the return. And besides (here Raymond drove home) hadn't Parke Godwin, Greeley's new-found partner, written that under socialism, "Reason and Passion will be in perfect accord; duty and pleasure will have the same meaning?" Didn't that clearly mean that under Greeley's system, rank self-indulgence would be enthroned, and that religion, morality, and marital constancy would give way to every conceivable vice?

Greeley—who himself had once criticized Raymond for his lack of moral earnestness—recoiled from this assault in horror. It was true—although he had tried to skirt the fact—that Fourier and at least some of his followers had peculiar ideas about marriage. (Greeley himself had remained a staunch champion of strict lifelong fidelity, and a lofty enemy of divorce.) It was a dreadful thing for the *Tribune,* a paper designed to be a "welcome visitor at the family fireside," to find itself placed in company with men and women whose doctrines might lead to uprooting the family. For a man whose personal religion was intense and orthodox, it was shattering to find himself pilloried as an enemy of Christianity. For a while Greeley had felt himself able to throw off such accusations: "Don't bother yourself about the stories told of me," he had written Colfax in 1845; "they must have their day. . . . I am not afraid of such stuff, and shall publish some things soon for Robert Owen, who is very thick-headed in his theology, but a more Christ-like man than any fat parson in New York." But this attack by the man whom he called "the little viper," coming on top of so much disappointment at the hands of the utopians themselves, was too much for Greeley. It came at a moment when his own doubts about the whole Fourier-Brisbane idea were growing intense. It was not that he had gone too far; but the more he thought about it, the more he felt he had gone off in the wrong direction. He did not admit the fact in the *Tribune,* but privately he said farewell to utopias. The next step would have to be closer to the earth.

5

He lost a faith, and yet he felt he was on the road toward finding one. The ferment, the earnestness, the turmoil of Reform had entered him; he would never again—with a clear conscience, that is—be able to renounce it. It was exciting to sit at the raised table at a banquet given in New York in 1844 honoring Fourier's birthday and to hear himself toasted by Brisbane as the man who had "done for us what we never could have done. He has created the cause on this continent. He has done the work of a century. Well, then, I will give a toast: 'One Continent, One Man!'" It was exciting, too, to travel in May, 1845, as a delegate to the first meeting of the New England Workingmen's Association—a political-action group set up by resurgent labor unions, land reformers, Brook Farmers, abolitionists, and tough city bosses like Manhattan's Mike Walsh— and there to find himself in a vortex of enthusiasm beside men like Dana, Ripley, Brisbane, Garrison, the strident young Wendell Phillips, and the eloquent William H. Channing. New ideas swirled through the hall. There were better ideas than Fourierism, he felt—by far.

"All agree that society is sick—very sick—but few can agree as to the nature of the complaint," declared one of the speakers at a "World Convention" of reformers held that fall in New York. Greeley, of course, was there. The revered Robert Owen presided. Owenite Socialists and Associationists headed the list of groups and cults that crowded the sessions in Clinton Hall. An obscure editorial writer named Walt Whitman watched the curious proceedings. A delegate arose to propose as a slogan, "Let's All Be Unhappy Together."

Greeley let go an editorial laugh, and thought of striking out on his own. For himself, out of his first experience and disappointment, he had rescued two principles—both of them new in his time. The first was, There is no excuse for anything less than full production. The second was, Every man has the inherent right to a job and then to a wage on which he can not only subsist decently but contribute to the advancement of society. He stood on these. But he did not yet know where they would lead him. As a result, in the mid-forties his language took on a new vehemence—as when he wrote, for instance, in response to an invitation to attend an antislavery meeting in Cincinnati in June, 1845, "if I am less troubled concerning the slavery prevalent in Charleston or New Orleans, it is because I see so much slavery in New York . . . Wherever opportunity to labor is obtained with difficulty and is so deficient that the employing class may virtually prescribe their own terms and pay the laborer only such share as they choose of the product, there is a very strong tendency to slavery." In that year Moses Y. Beach, publisher of the New York *Sun*, published a directory of wealthy New Yorkers that ran to thirty-two pages of fine print, listing A. T. Stewart, the merchant, as worth $400,000, Commodore Vanderbilt as worth $1,200,000, and John Jacob Astor as worth $25,000,000; but in that same year it was reported that one fifth of the city's population—or some 80,000 people—were in need of private charity or public relief. Greeley's *Tribune* studied the facts and pointed its warning finger:

Our city of New York is now enjoying an unusual degree of thrift and prosperity, growing and expanding on all sides . . . Her working classes are probably as well employed as ever before . . . And yet it is our deliberate estimate, the result of much inquiry, that the average earnings of those who live by simple labor in our city—embracing at least two-thirds of our population—scarcely, if at all, exceed one dollar per week.

Then Greeley lost patience, laying into ministers, politicians, businessmen: "Never have I heard such a mockery of Heaven as a clergyman rising before a wealthy and fashionable congregation on Thanksgiving Day to express gratitude that, in this favored land, everyone who chooses may earn a comfortable subsistence! . . . Where were his eyes!" What was the answer? So far, Greeley had not found it. But he began to have some inklings as to where to look. No wonder conservative Whigs took to attacking him—as he himself reported—for "attempting incessantly to incite the prejudices of the poor against the rich."

What a thing to say about Horace Greeley, the admirer of Henry

Clay! In 1844, Clay had run on the Whig ticket for President against the reviving Democrats' dark horse, James K. Polk, and Greeley had campaigned heavily for him. In fact, Greeley had worked so hard that summer and fall that "very often I crept to my lodging near the office at 2 or 3 a.m. with my head so heated by fourteen or sixteen hours of incessant reading and writing, that I could only win sleep by means of copious affusions of a shower-bath; and these . . . brought out such a myriad of boils that I was covered by them for the six months ensuing, often fifty or sixty at once, so that I could contrive no position in which to rest, but passed night after night in an easy-chair." And during all that year there had not been a better campaign booklet than *Whig Songs for 1844*, published by Greeley & McElrath. Not only had Greeley put into it such rousing choruses as "Ye Jolly Young Whigs of Ohio" (to the tune of "Rosin the Bow")—

> Ye jolly young Whigs of Ohio,
>   And all ye sick Democrats too,
> Come out from among the foul party,
>   And vote for great Harry the true . . .
>
> And if we should get at all thirsty,
>   As in time of Old Tippecanoe,
> We will tap a large keg of hard cider,
>   And drink to great Harry the true.

—but he had also contributed to it a thumping Whig lyric of his own composing:

> THE GATHERING SONG
> They're rousing, they're rousing, in valley and glen,
>   The noble in soul, and the fearless in heart;
> At Freedom's stern call, to the contest again,
>   They rush with a zeal she alone can impart . . .

VII. LOVER

1

Apart from an unresolved adventure in ideas, Greeley got three things out of his years in utopia: Charles A. Dana, whom he hired in 1847 as *Tribune* city editor at $8 a week, soon raising him to $14; George Ripley, whom he hired in 1849, after Brook Farm's collapse, as a part-time "literary assistant" at $5 a week, later raising him to literary editor at $25; and Margaret Fuller, who brought a unique talent to his paper, a troubling presence into his house, and a new emotion into his life.

In his *Recollections,* Greeley is reticent as to where and when he met this formidable and somewhat frightening exemplar of self-emancipated womanhood. He is also silent upon much else that may have passed between them. But since her admirer was one of the most relentless letter writers of the age, at least fragments of a correspondence between them survive. The fragments, in turn, suggest more than they say. For Margaret Fuller moved into Horace Greeley's house in New York, witnessing each day much of what passed between him and his wife, and many things that may have been understood are only implied in the scrawls that Greeley later addressed to Margaret in Europe from his office.

One cannot be certain just what that understanding was. There may very well have been none at all. But there were stirrings and yearnings on his side, even if they were deflected underground. And on Margaret Fuller's side, although her emotions never appeared to be directly engaged, there was a visible reaction which led her into the very opposite direction—toward her personal emancipation.

When Greeley met her she was not, for all her ardent feminism, a holder of "free" views resembling Fanny Wright's. Later she broke through society's central moral conventions. But while this led to her being called an American imitator of George Sand— which in fact she was—Horace Greeley did not take after George Sand's Frederic Chopin. He stuck to the *Tribune*—and to the lyceum lecture circuit, when he could bear home no longer.

Apparently they met during mutual visits to Brook Farm, when Margaret Fuller was meeting everybody. Of the Greeleys, it was not Horace but Mary who first cultivated her, hurrying to Boston to attend those lectures or "conversations" on intellectual subjects which Margaret was giving to culture-hungry ladies on Saturdays at Dr. Peabody's. It was Mary, not Horace, who first fell under her singular, rhapsodic spell—and it was Mary who proposed that she bring her brilliance to New York and live under the Greeley roof, sustaining herself by a job on the *Tribune*. All that Greeley himself did—so he says—was to fall in with the idea. He needed a literary critic on the paper.

Margaret Fuller, the eldest child of a harsh, dogmatic small-town Massachusetts lawyer who was obsessed with teaching his offspring Latin, was as precocious, as talkative, as encyclopedic and as homely as Horace Greeley, and a year older. Like Mary Greeley, she had also been a schoolteacher, although her experience in Bronson Alcott's experimental school in Boston had been far different from Mary's in North Carolina. When the editor of the New York *Tribune* met her, she had also been an editor on her own at thirty, in command of the lofty transcendentalist house organ, the *Dial*, with Emerson and Ripley standing as advisers at her side. But therewith any similarity between the Greeleys and this extraordinary apparition ceased. Horace Greeley knew every county vote and the background of every senator; Mary Cheney Greeley knew a great deal about poetry, much about raising children (at least, so she insisted), and nothing about running households; but Margaret Fuller, a fluent Latinist at eight and a phenomenal metaphysician at twenty, was reputed to know everything—or, at any rate, far too much for anyone of her age and certainly of her sex.

What was worse, she exulted in it. Even before her father had died and left her the acting head of his family (her mother simply being ignored) she had adopted from him those mannish, masterful airs that appalled many men and overwhelmed many women. Not only had she mastered Oriental scripture, German epic poetry, Icelandic saga, Greek, Italian, Middle English, and the obscurities of

Immanuel Kant, but she hurled all this cultural heritage at you with intent to inspire you with it if you were sympathetic or stagger you with it if you were not. Most men, at first, were not; so she pursued them by outtalking them, and reduced even the great Emerson to the status of an audience. She used a lorgnette with surprising effectiveness at twenty-six. She strode in before her lady subscribers at Dr. Peabody's, a short, dumpy figure in a costly, rustling dress, with books under her arm and flowers at her breast, craning her stringy, preening neck as she prepared to hold forth on "The Ideal" or "Persons Who Never Awaken to Life"; and then, as she carefully shut her nearsighted gray eyes as if invoking mystical assistance and let loose an avalanche of words, listeners began to forget her nasal voice and florid face and to feel her exerting upon themselves a force like some divining priestess, converting the lecture into a séance. She was, in fact, a priestess—so women like Mary Greeley soon decided—and her message went to their heads.

She preached—as who did not, in that Emersonian circle—a gospel of self-fulfillment through self-culture. But she gave it an edge by turning her appeal to women, in whom she saw the voiceless handmaidens of a crass commercialism imposed by men. It was high time, she proclaimed, for these women to realize their own latent powers, to aspire through education to equality, and by following the "inner light" that illumined each unshackled soul to break through the money-grubbing crust that had so chilled and darkened their New England. She intoxicated herself as well as her apostles when she described herself frankly as the greatest American intellect of the age: "I feel chosen among women; I have mystic feelings in myself and intimations from elsewhere." She was vague and precious when she taught women from on high that their liberation could come through literature rather than through laws. But this very loftiness of hers made her something more than America's first professional woman talker. She was a romantic woman talker. And, lorgnettes or not, she was first and last a romantic woman, even as she had been a romantic girl—describing, for instance, how like another Juliet she had dreamed of mighty steeds coming to trample her.

Horace Greeley shrewdly sensed the troubles of her maturity when he remarked that "two or three bouncing babies would have emancipated her from a good deal of cant and nonsense." Some years later, mating with Count Ossoli in Italy, she got her baby.

Difficult as she was as a woman, Margaret was not a full-time feminist. Mastering men's ideas, she kept looking for men who might master her; and when very few appeared, she at least kept moving among ideas. Emerson said of his dear friend Margaret that "All the art, the thought and the nobleness in New England . . . seemed related to her, and she to it." And Horace Greeley, who complained of her preciousness at work as well as of her airs at breakfast, eventually found in her a graphic reporter of New York prison conditions and a brilliant correspondent covering the republican uprisings in Rome in 1848-49.

2

The Greeley household, when Margaret Fuller was invited in late 1844 to join it, had just moved uptown to the very outskirts of New York. Throughout the past thirteen years, for all his countryman's air and predilections, Greeley had made his home in the city's built-up downtown areas and close to the *Tribune* office. He said this had to be because the late working hours he kept would otherwise prevent his getting home at night. But Mary had never been deceived by this explanation; for even when they lived in Greenwich Street, barely four minutes' walk crosstown from Ann and Nassau, he had often failed to get home, preferring to stay in bachelor lodgings he had taken just around the corner from the shop. For weeks on end, during the busy 1844 campaign, he had stayed apart from Mary, pleading later hours than usual. The next step was either to stay away altogether, or to make some attempt to pull the marriage together before it was too late.

Greeley had faced the alternatives; but formal separation or divorce was inconceivable to him if his moral universe was not to be sent crashing. So he had decided to transplant the family upon fresh and more wholesome ground—country ground, under the trees and by the river—and to try to make the place so appealing to himself that he would keep coming home to it. It was in part a self-disciplinary move: for the place he found, an old farmhouse surrounded by seven acres at Turtle Bay along the East River, could be reached only by a forty-minute ride on the hourly Harlem stage, followed by a walk down a long country lane. But there was also new life stirring there to attract him. The Greeley's first child had died in 1838. Their second, a boy, had died similarly in infancy in 1842. Two miscarriages had added to their despair. But now they had the newborn, rollicking Arthur, blue-eyed and golden-haired. They called him "Pickie" and prayed that at least he might live.

Almost as soon as the Greeleys moved into the old rambling, clapboard Turtle Bay farm, bringing with them their frugal furniture, Margaret Fuller arrived, with her boxes full of dresses, from Fishkill, where she had been in retreat while finishing her tract, *Woman in the Nineteenth Century*, which Greeley & McElrath were to publish as a book next year. With her headaches, her need for quiet while she read and wrote, her calls for strong tea late at night, and her desire to have New York ladies call on her in numbers, she was a demanding guest. But Mary Greeley was entranced by the brilliance of this sister schoolmarm whom she had brought into her house. She humored her, doted on her for having risen so high above mundane concerns, shared breathlessly her interest in mystical symbols, omens, and phrenology—and meanwhile let her own household lapse deeper into disorder. Soon Margaret spoke of Mary Greeley as keeping house in "Castle Rackrent fashion." But for the moment, absorbed by her own entry into a new world of hopes and challenges, she concentrated on the landscape. "The place is, to me," she wrote of the Greeley farm, "entirely country, and all around is so bold and free. It is two miles or more from the thickly settled parts of New York . . . and I can command time and retirement. Stopping on the Harlem Road, you enter a lane nearly a quarter of a mile long, and, going by a small brook and pond that locks in the place, and ascending a slightly rising ground, get sight of the house, which, old-fashioned and of mellow tint, fronts on a flower-garden filled with shrubs, large vines, and trim box borders . . . Passing through a wide hall, you come out upon a piazza stretching the whole length of the house, where one can walk in all weathers; and thence, by a step or two, on a lawn, with picturesque masses of rocks, shrubs and trees, overlooking the East River. . . . The beauty here, seen by moonlight, is truly transporting. I enjoy it greatly, and the *genius loci* receives me as to a home."

The *genius loci* was Horace Greeley—who, except at breakfast, was rarely there. And breakfasts—like other meals—were sometimes trying occasions. Running a strictly Grahamite household, Mary Greeley frowned on tea and coffee as well as meat in any form, and usually had her meals consist (as Greeley reported) of "beans and potatoes, boiled rice, puddings, bread and butter, with no condiment but salt, and never a pickle." Greeley approved. But

Margaret definitely did not. Appearing one morning at breakfast with a bad headache, she was told by her host that her trouble lay in having drunk so much strong tea the night before. "I decline to be lectured on the food or beverage I see fit to take," Margaret snapped back.

Then Greeley, in turn, became irritated by Margaret's nervous complaints, her malingering, and her slowness about her work at the *Tribune*. "I could easily write two columns to her one," he remarked; "indeed, she would only write at all when in the vein, and her headaches and other infirmities often precluded all labor for days." And not only was she drawing salary while she fussed and dreamed at Turtle Bay, but she seemed to him to have an inordinate love of luxury. She dressed elaborately; she had to have flowers about; while as for himself, Greeley said, he "delighted in bare walls and rugged fare." She needed also to be the center of an admiring coterie; and Greeley, coming home when a flock of elegant ladies were paying court to her, objected to this "Oriental adoration." He told himself that Margaret was his wife's friend, not his, and that he would deal with her only at the office.

Then she came home. As she sat in the run-down, barren Greeley parlor after late hours of work, drinking cup after cup of tea, she poured forth that illuminated discourse that had bewitched Emerson and apparently upset Hawthorne at the other Farm. Greeley cared little about her earnest metaphysics, while she cared less about his practical politics and his concern with such matters as land reform; yet their spirits, expansive, lucid, optimistic and sometimes extravagant, had much in common. Although they squabbled, they seemed to have learned at some point not to try to outtalk one another. Both liked to stay up late. Mary did not.

Besides, Margaret was lonely in New York. Her ladies came to call, but after hearing her spend teatime discoursing on the nature of the soul (and being Manhattan ladies rather than Bostonian ones) many did not call again. Mary Greeley, for her part, was obviously unequal to her flights, as well as to her energy. It was left to Horace Greeley to try to harness that energy—and when he did so, he found himself being struck by its sparks.

Margaret Fuller, late of the *précieuses* of Boston, sat down to a third-floor desk in the grubby, noisy *Tribune* building, hustled to get her copy in on time, and then saw it attacked by the spluttering front-office pen of an editor whose short temper and harried look made any last-minute discussion of fine points impossible. Margaret said she hated going there. To the end, her letters to others concerning Greeley breathed condescension: "Mr. Greeley is in many ways very interesting for me to know. He teaches me things which my own influence on those who have hitherto approached me has prevented me from learning." She did learn. And before long she rose to the head of Greeley's class.

In effect, he was instructing her in practicalities. Heretofore she had lived in a private realm of introspection and disembodied ideas. No other man so far had thrown her into the world's daily stream. Sniffing a bit at first, she plunged into it. It was not pleasant for her to have Greeley tell her that the trouble with her writing was that she had been reading too much grandiose German and that as a result her *Tribune* copy was ponderous and fuzzy. But after he had blue-penciled her, she went back and rewrote until, within a few months, her language had become transformed into terse, vivid English—somewhat like Greeley's own, in fact. She tackled current books of many sorts. She rewrote items from the foreign press. She went out on special stories. She wrote a series exposing prison conditions on Blackwell's Island. Margaret Fuller, the finest flower of the Emersonian hothouse, spent Christmas interviewing convicts at Sing Sing.

Her main *Tribune* contributions, signed with an asterisk, were book reviews; but even into these, as Greeley watched over her, she threw a verve and dash that surprised her "Oriental" devotees and staggered many a victim. Thus she disposed of the inflated Henry Wadsworth Longfellow, when his *Poems* appeared in 1845:

Mr. Longfellow has been accused of plagiarism. We have been surprised that anyone should have been anxious to fasten special charges of this kind upon him, when we had supposed it so obvious that the greater part of his mental stores were derived from the work of others. He has no style of his own, growing out of his own experiences and observation of nature. Nature with him, whether human or external, is always seen through the windows of literature.

This want of the free breath of nature, this perpetual borrowing of imagery, this excessive culture which he has derived from an acquaintance with the elegant literature of many nations and men, out of proportion to the experience of life within himself, prevent Mr. Longfellow's verses from ever being a true refreshment to ourselves.

Mr. Longfellow presents us not with a new product . . . but rather with a tastefully arranged Museum, between whose glass cases are interspersed neatly potted rose trees, geraniums, and hyacinths, grown by himself with the aid of indoor heat. Twenty years hence, when he stands upon his own merits, he will rank as a writer of elegant, if not always accurate taste, of great initiative power, and occasional felicity in an original way, where his feelings are really stirred.

She aimed shrewd shots at the fashionable James Russell Lowell as well; she challenged some of Poe's more lugubrious ballads; she acclaimed the newest works of Hawthorne, but to Greeley's intense pleasure ticked off Bryant; she was even ready to drop a quietly withering comment about her adored Emerson, writing that he had "raised himself too early to the perpendicular, and did not lie along the ground long enough to hear the secret whispers of our parent life." All told, she conducted a book column whose critical standards and style stood well above any other in America.

In this she especially delighted Greeley, who could now point out that his *Tribune* was not only elevating the masses but setting a pace for intellectuals as well. Her presence on his paper as the ablest interpreter of new writing talent testified to his own astuteness in having spotted one of those new talents—and a woman, too—and training her in his own editorial school. He praised her work for its "truthfulness, directness and practicality." He liked being seen with her at the Saturday literary soirees given by the romantic poetess, Anne Lynch—effusive gatherings at which friends of his such as Poe, Emerson, Bayard Taylor and Henry Ward Beecher often appeared, along with rivals like Bryant and Henry Raymond. There poems were read, Goethe was debated, and on one occasion "a series of tableaux" was "presented by notable artists." Back at the office, Greeley made sure that Margaret's columns were being given front-page or top-of-column play in the paper. She was, he felt, a fine journalist and a richly endowed woman. She was more than that: she was, he concluded, "the most remarkable, and in some respects the greatest woman whom America has yet known."

At home, after work, they went on sparring. Margaret liked to hold forth on her favorite subject—equal rights for women—and Greeley liked to break into her speeches by throwing back at her sardonically a sentence he had lifted from her own tract: "Let them be sea-captains if they will!" But Greeley found that he was not as strongly against Woman's Rights as he had been. He was also talking freely to Margaret about his personal life—something that he had done before only to a very few intimate men. She was an ideal confidante, for she talked first. "She probably knew the cherished secrets of more hearts than any one else," Greeley later wrote, "because she freely imparted her own." She had criticized the cheerless way he lived at Turtle Bay; now he began echoing her. Although he had prided himself on his "bare walls" and "rugged fare," he took to speaking of his house as "our old, desolate rookery." The phrase "Castle Doleful" appeared frequently in his letters. On one occasion he burst out to a guest that he wished he could offer a home "not so desolate and barren as ours is—one where they habitually serve breakfast, at least." And one of his few surviving letters to Mary Greeley—dated February, 1846, from Washington—begins with a paragraph addressed to his son, Pickie, saying that "your sore, sick father" will return home at the end of the week "to his own crazy house and his boy's bright smiles." Then the husband turns to his wife, briefly: "My piles are ugly, especially a great new one, and my general health is not good . . . I see nobody you would care for—and hear nothing to interest you." And at the close, shaking off other subjects and underscoring, he adds, "Ask *Margaret* to be home on Saturday if she can."

3

At home, there was Pickie; and Pickie, the golden-haired youngster tumbling amid the shadows of Castle Doleful, was the embodiment of what home might be. He lived; he survived; therein lay a fulfillment that made up for much that had been denied. He lived with immediate impact on Margaret, too, as she felt herself at thirty-five advancing into inevitable spinsterhood. He cast a spell upon three adult people in their loneliness. The emotions of all three in that mansion became fixed on him. Their loves, displaced from other channels or unable to enter them, converged on him. It was as if they found in him both a realization of their needs and a substitute for their wants. He served as their link with living, their common hope, and, as a result, their battleground. Mary Greeley, the mother of the dead, claimed the living Pickie fiercely for herself. She "looked upon his birth in the light of a miracle," recalled her sister-in-law, Esther Greeley, "as if no other child had ever before been born." Horace, for his part, became obsessed with the unique promise of his boy, whose light complexion, flaxen hair, and brittle energy seemed to resemble his own. At the same time he grew alarmed at Pickie's increasing tempestuousness, and this he ascribed to Mary's controlling influence. Margaret, for her part, watching the parents struggle, moved in to try to delight and enchant the child, calling upon her skill as a story teller and mimic to enact nightly tales for him; and in return she received from him a devotion that made her once declare, with great earnestness, that she preferred Pickie's company to that of almost any adult.

Margaret's own emotion toward Pickie, in the meantime, had grown possessive too. On one occasion, shortly before she left for Italy—as Greeley narrates the incident—Mary Greeley had brought Pickie to the *Tribune* office and left him asleep on the editor's couch while she went shopping. "He rolled off and hurt himself in the fall," Greeley writes, "just before Margaret, hearing of his arrival, rushed into the office to find him. I was vainly attempting to soothe him as she entered. . . . She hastened to him, in perfect confidence that her endearments would calm the current of his feelings—that the sound of her well-remembered voice would banish all thought of his pain—and that another moment would see him restored to gentleness . . . But, half-wakened, he did not heed her. . . . At last she desisted in despair; and, with bitter tears streaming down her face, observed, 'Pickie, many friends have treated me unkindly, but no one had ever the power to cut me to the heart as you have!'"

But Mary, increasingly suspicious and resentful, insisted at least on being in full physical charge of Pickie. Her plan was to protect, isolate, and wall him in from any outside contact or from any influence that she feared might harm him. She could not prevent Margaret Fuller, whom she had invited into her household, from assuming a role which Horace described as that of "teacher, playmate, and monitor" of the boy. But she could keep Pickie locked like a child hermit behind the Greeley homestead gate. She could —and did—order that no other children were ever to come and play with him. She could see to it that he was raised as a solitary vegetarian; so she denied to her treasured Pickie any meat or sweets whatever. She knew about children, she said; she was a schoolteacher.

Fought over by opposites, and placed under such a regimen, Pickie rapidly developed traits that reflected the tension and took advantage of it. "He was selfish and violent at times," Greeley later wrote Margaret, adding, "you know whether he had good reason to be." Horace and she were drawn together in their common anger at Mary Greeley's management. They talked about Pickie's problems as if talking about one another. In the meantime Mary, receiving only a diminishing affection from her boy, had become interested in keeping Horace and Margaret apart. Not that they had been anywhere near as close together as she may have feared. In fact, at some time early in 1845 Margaret had confessed to Mary that, for the first time in her life, she had fallen in love—with a New York businessman named James Nathan. Nathan was cultured, poised, well-to-do, exactly Greeley's age, and, unlike Greeley, found time to see Margaret at all hours of the day.

That spring, Greeley was away for a while, lecturing. While he was out of town, Mary Greeley agreed to having Nathan come out to the farm to entertain Margaret with an evening of music on the guitar. Horace, when he returned, sensed that something was amiss and said that Margaret was neglecting her work at the paper. Mary, for her part—according to Margaret's biographer, Mason Wade—"plagued her with well-meant advice." Some of that advice may well have been in the direction of making a match. But then in summertime Nathan left for Europe, without having proposed to Margaret. Now the friendship between Mary and Margaret perceptibly cooled. That fall, Margaret moved away from Turtle Bay and into a boardinghouse.

Next spring, however, when she had begun forgetting about Nathan (who had already forgotten entirely about her) she was back at the "rookery" again. Horace's spirits rose. He was especially glad to find, he said, that her work at the paper was improving; she was no longer being distracted. Yet soon Mary's tensions reached the point where Horace decided he had better leave home awhile. He took again to boarding downtown—sometimes in Bayard Street in the house of his sister Esther, who by now was married to a *Tribune* staff member, John F. Cleveland, and at whose home as a result Greeley could find a double refuge.

In the meantime, amid his conflicting desires, he had made Mary pregnant again. In this sense he remained faithful to her in Margaret's presence. There was for him no possible alternative. "Sexual love was implanted in Man by his creator expressly that the Race should be perpetuated," he was to write several years later in a *Tribune* debate with the elder Henry James, in which he rigidly opposed divorce; "all Sexual Relations that do not contemplate this end are sinful . . . The commandment from Sinai, 'Thou shalt not commit Adultery,' is a part of the natural or moral law, contemplating and forbidding every form of Sexual Relation except the union for life of one man with one woman."

That summer, in hot July, Greeley spent much of his time in Albany, where delegates were meeting to draft a revised constitution for the State of New York, and where he tried to prevail upon them to adopt his new radical discovery, land reform. Margaret moved away again, this time to lodgings in Brooklyn. The moment —if actually it was a moment—passed. Margaret's mind became set on going to Europe, where Nathan had gone. An opportunity to travel opened in August, when some wealthy friends proposed taking her there. Greeley, when consulted as her employer, raised no objections and thought that she might act as the *Tribune's* roving European correspondent. Pickie made a scene when she boarded the packet, while Horace and Mary together stood on the dock watching her leave.

Five months later, Mary Greeley gave birth to a daughter. Pickie, by turns spoiled and overdisciplined, became so jealous as to be almost unmanageable. Writing to Margaret in February, 1847, Horace spoke of the boy's "terrible propensity for mischief." Mary, who was having servant trouble, he said, "was nearly worn out when I returned from Washington, and Pickie was almost sick of hope deferred." Next summer, turning to his old friend Obediah Bowe, he was complaining that while his wife was "middling well for her," his son was "not very; he is subject to terrible fits of savage crying that seem like delirium."

Then there happened again what had occurred before. "You will have heard, probably, of the death of our little daughter," he wrote Margaret in July. "Alas for us! Neither Pickie nor Mother realized her worth till called to part with her. Pickie regarded her as a rival and an obstacle to his enjoyments, urging that she should be given away; while Mother often said she wished her dead, on account of the labor and anxiety she caused." As for Pickie, "it is impossible to be stern with him, yet I feel that he is running to weeds. His mother whips him often but never rules him; and I have no voice in his management and never can have without fighting for it—probably not with it."

Mary Greeley's condition was now such, Greeley decided, that some new third person must come in and help. Mere servants would not do; besides, hired girls had been finding the household so impossible that they usually quit after a few weeks. What was needed—now that Margaret had left him helplessly behind while she stayed on in Europe—was a mediator, a new ally who might take over. Soon he wrote Margaret that he had found one in the person of Miss Emma Whiting of Chicago, a Fourierist convert, phrenology enthusiast and admirer of Margaret's, who was to join the household nominally as governess. And to the new confederate, Emma Whiting, he wrote before her arrival, in warning her of Pickie's "terrible" temper, "You will find all the virtues and vices of both his parents condensed into his little person. . . . He is affectionate, gentle, vivacious, versatile, sweet and wonderfully fascinating, except when he is furious, phrenzied, delirious, diabolic. If he would only be satisfied with breaking one dish per day and the crystal of my watch once a week, I should regard him, not with more affection, but with less apprehension and terror. *You can civilize*—no, Associatize—him if his mother will only surrender him entirely to you, and she says she will if persuaded that it is *surely* for the best. . . ."

There was a delay in Emma Whiting's arrival. Mary Greeley became increasingly distracted. "We are . . . all out of sorts up at Castle Doleful," Greeley wrote the expected Emma; "Mrs. G. thinks she can accomplish nothing toward putting her house in order till you come." Then Emma came, but Mary Greeley took such a dislike to her that within six weeks she had to leave. "Mother could not like her quick motions, abundant talk, her weak and diseased eyes, etc., and complained of 'bad magnetism,'" Greeley confided to Margaret abroad. After Emma left, many wished her back. Horace fled, too. "I have taken dinner at home but two days since I saw you," he told Margaret.

"Pick is glorious," Greeley wrote in one letter to Margaret. But then, in the next, "Pickie's mind is much poisoned with supernatural terrors." Greeley was intrigued by the curious, unworldly language his boy of four spoke after having been shut off from all outside human contact, but he was also alarmed at Pickie's "paroxysms of passion." Then to Margaret, in April, 1848: "Pickie . . . is addicted to secrecy. 'Don't tell Mother' is quite a common request with him." "Why should you linger in Europe in such miserable health?" Greeley went on . . . "Do come home, where you can have nursing and air and repose . . . Why should you stay?" Again, in June, discussing Pickie's increasing aversion to his mother: "When beaten, as he was when we rode out last Saturday, he looks her in the eye with an aspect of indignation and grief, 'O you ugly creature.'" The little boy, Horace told Margaret, "becomes more and more of a Locofoco daily. He is governed, and restricted, and cramped till he hates all law and authority." Greeley himself was now staying downtown at Esther's every night—"though I go up about every other morning for an hour or so." He was sad, he said, to be away from Pickie so much: "He has often threatened to leave his Mother, but never to leave me. He and I are very needful to each other."

In July, Greeley was happier:"Pickie grows in grace and in his father's good opinion." But in the following winter, this from Washington: "Poor Mother gets along badly . . . She rejoiced at my coming to Washington, hoping that she would do better with Pickie in my absence, but it proved otherwise." And in the same letter to Margaret: "When are you coming home? You have already outstayed all expectation."

But by that time Margaret, having toured Britain, France and Italy with the reportorial eyes that Greeley had trained in her, had gone on to entirely new sights and experiences. She had found both a lover and a revolution—and thus, in her new-found fulfillment, swum far out of Horace Greeley's ken. He had printed (paying ten dollars each for them) the weekly letters to the *Tribune* in which she described European cultural life, art collections and popular stirrings in the capitals where she had met George Sand, Chopin, Mazzini and the papal entourage. Then the tenor of her letters deepened as the stirrings of 1848 burst into revolt. She wrote a shining set piece for the paper on the Roman people's joyous demonstration when Pius IX granted them partial self-rule, and an equally vivid story of the people's anger when the Pope later turned back from his position. Her copy became fiercely partisan and republican; she described from her window the civil fighting in the streets of Rome. And while her *Tribune* audience grew and Greeley wrote her congratulatory letters (still keeping to his price of ten dollars a piece, however), she was finding another release in the arms of the republican Roman marquis, Giovanni Angelo Ossoli, by whom she conceived a child.

By late 1848, after having secretly married Ossoli, she was deeply involved with the insurrectionists of the *risorgimento*. Meanwhile her child was born. And the next April saw Margaret Fuller, the *Tribune's* Rome correspondent, tending republican wounded when the rebel city was placed under siege by that ill-starred interventionist, Louis Napoleon of France. Greeley was thrilled with what she wrote. In return—striking a key that was now remote from hers—he wrote her, "You ought to see Pickie before he is wholly spoiled. The attitude and manner of his saying to Mother, 'Don't you *dare* to shut me up in a room!—Ain't you *ashamed* to strike me, you ugly creature!' would be a study for a tragedy queen." Margaret was concerned at this moment about preserving her own child amid Italian cholera epidemics.

And then came a horrifying letter. "Ah, Margaret! The world grows dark with us. You grieve, for Rome has fallen; I mourn, for Pickie is dead! The one sunburst of joy that has gladdened my rugged pathway has departed. . . . I have never had an intimate friend—my life has been too intensely busy and my aims not entirely common; but this one dear being already promised to be my friend in every trial, my solace in every care. . . . He was selfish and violent at times—you know whether he had good reason to be—but he was generous and tender-hearted . . . O he was a dear child . . .

"We had not the least premonition of this blow. I last saw him in health at 10 a.m. on the 11th, when I went downtown leaving him as hearty and joyous as ever in the world. His mother went down too; he, on account of the heat, was persuaded to stay at home. . . . I came home and went to bed at 11—still no complaint or alarm. At 2 he had a call, and his mother got up with him—still no alarm. At 3, he was called up again by violent purging; now his mother came up and called me. Very soon he was vomiting as well as purging . . . We doctored incessantly, but not efficiently; it was 7 o'clock before we got a physician . . . [But] at 2 he was hopelessly sinking, and for the first time became conscious of it himself . . . exclaiming at intervals, 'O it's no use trying to do anything for me!—I am afraid!—I am afraid!—I am sinking—I am sinking—I am dying!' . . . The next day I carried the new coffin down into our vault and laid it beside the other—the mother going down into the narrow house and directing, with a burning heart but a tearless face. Ah me! Ah me! ..."

Still another child had been born to Horace and Mary in the meantime—their fifth attempt—but the new arrival was, Horace told Margaret, only a "good-natured, commonplace daughter." "My Pickie! My Pickie!" was his refrain; "how sad is this world without him!"

Margaret, receiving the news in Italy, wept bitterly. Almost a whole year passed. Then, in the summer of 1850, she and her husband and her child Angelo took ship for home, and perished by shipwreck just outside the harbor of New York.

4

Time passed. The Greeleys entered their forties. The wonderment that had surrounded the presence of Pickie lingered with them, and some of the anger was forgotten. There was no alternative now. There was no third person who would entrance, deflect, challenge and unsettle them. They would go on—or try to—as they had before. They sat together at night talking of their lost boy's life, and dreaming that perhaps his spirit was not beyond recapture. It was just then that America had become entranced by a new, mystifying pursuit—the attempt, through "table rappings" and the like, to establish communication with the dead. Greeley was later inclined to say that it was Mary rather than he himself, who had been swept up in the current belief in "spiritual manifestations." At all events their Turtle Bay home became a meeting ground for mediums and clairvoyants, and Greeley joined in the seances. The famous Fox sisters, who had gone through western New York State supposedly receiving signals or "raps" from the dead, were invited to stay at the Greeley farm to establish communication with Pickie. Jenny Lind, the devotional Swedish soprano whom Greeley's friend P. T. Barnum had just brought to America, attended a seance held by Katy Fox in the Greeley house.

"All were soon seated around a table," Greeley recorded, "and the 'rappings' were soon audible and abundant. 'Take your hands from under the table!' Mademoiselle Jenny called across to me in the tone and manner of an indifferently bold archduchess. 'What?' I asked, not distinctly comprehending her. 'Take your hands from under the table!' she imperiously repeated; and I now understood that she suspected me of causing, by some legerdemain, the puzzling concussions. I instantly clasped my hands over my head, and there kept them until the sitting closed, as it did very soon. I need hardly add that this made not the smallest difference with the 'rappings . . .'"

He was sometimes highly inclined to doubt such "raps," he said, yet "I am sure they cannot be accounted for by merely human agency." The churches were denouncing them; but Greeley—who had already found himself revulsed by the social views of many ministers—rather hoped that the manifestations would be proven genuine if only "to confound and mortify their priestly enemies." Probing on, he wrote in an unpublished manuscript that it was his "earnest hope that, even though the so-called 'spiritual manifestations' of our day should all be proved brainsick phantasies or blasphemous juggles, it will nevertheless be deemed possible . . . that some further, fresher evidence of the verity and individuality of our friends' existence in the Spirit World should yet be vouchsafed to Man. Faith needs the assurance, sorrow the consolation, that such evidence would give. . . ."

And, in fact, he wrote to Emma Whiting, Mary persisted in telling him that she had "talked daily with dear Pickie for weeks when Catherine Fox was with her." Then he tried to correspond with his dead child himself. His surviving notes describe one such mysterious interview:

"H. G. said: 'Well, now, Pickie, tell the story of that last day that you were well—how you came up to my room where I was writing and kept trying to pull my pen from me—how about that?'

"Answer by rapping: 'You put me out.' (As was the fact . . .)

"Here . . . Mother said, 'I do not see why you should bring up that disagreeable, melancholy reminiscence.'

"Pickie, answering: 'No, Mother, it is *not* melancholy. I *disturbed* Father.' (This was as much like his habitual talk with her in my defense when in the body as I could well imagine.)"

In the end, though, Greeley was disappointed even in this attempt to dream his way out of present life and to recapture a remote echo of what had gone before. In his *Recollections* he dismissed the whole subject of "spirit rapping" with the brusque remark, "To sit for two dreary, mortal hours in a darkened room, in a mixed company, waiting for some one's disembodied grandfather or aunt to tip a table or rap on a door, is dull music at best;

but so to sit *in vain* is disgusting." Then he added, "Those who discharge promptly and faithfully all their duties to those who 'still live' in the flesh can have little time for poking and peering into the life beyond the grave. Better attend to each world in its proper order."

The point was well taken. But there were some duties to the living that he himself had failed to discharge—duties of attendance upon his wife and of responsible daily guardianship over his son. He had fled the one person and merely intoxicated himself on the other. And as for the third person, Margaret, who had become so involved in his imaginings, he had skirted her challenge too and reverted safely to the lecture circuit, to Thurlow Weed's smoky evenings, and to the daily and weekly *Tribune* (total circulation, in 1852, approaching 75,000).

"Wednesday morning," he wrote to Schuyler Colfax of one of his multiplying speaking tours, "I started at eight and went to Nashua, N. H. (240 miles) over five or six different railroads, changing cars repeatedly, lectured to 1,200, visited my relations, slept and started next morning for Albany (some 200 miles of crooked riding), lectured there, and sat up talking politics till 1 a.m. Started next morning for Rochester (250 miles), lectured, caught the cars at 8½ evening, came through during the night to Albany (horrid cold) and so on to the City, arriving at 2 p.m., having been absent 3½ days, lectured three times, and travelled 1,090 miles. I call that industrious." It was. The date was January, 1852; he was virtually homeless now, and constantly on the move. Another child—this time a boy—was born, begotten during sporadic visits home. He tried to muster up new love, but, as he wrote still another woman friend, Georgiana Kirby, in December, "You know that all our children you ever saw are dead, and that we have two born since you left, Ida and Raffael. . . . They are fair children, but not equal to the son you saw, but did not know."

Next year, upon Mary's bidding, he bought a new farm—this time a tract of 75 low-grade acres, part swampy, part stump-ridden, part sour, but all picturesque, outside the Westchester County village of Chappaqua, about an hour's distance due north by rail from New York. He planned to spend time with his children and become an intensive farmer. He managed to visit the new homestead for at least all the daylight hours on Saturdays. Sometimes he managed to stay a bit longer. There was one duty he did not always escape. In the summer of 1856 he wrote Emma Whiting—whom he now called "my friend from Pickie's time"—that Mary Greeley was "thinner and feebler even than when she landed" from a trip to Europe, and that she was "in the saddest mental condition." But almost exactly nine months later he wrote Emma Whiting again, this time to say that Mary had just given birth to another daughter. This was his wife's seventh effort. The boy Raffael—her sixth—in the meantime had died. "Mother has stood up gloriously," reported Horace Greeley.

VIII. TRIUMVIR

1

Whether or not Horace Greeley actually loved Margaret Fuller, he "profoundly loved"—so he records—Henry Clay. This passion was one he could more nearly understand. It was political. It was, he liked to think, realistic. But it was also unrequited. For the great Harry of the West, deprived of the presidential nomination by the Whig managers of 1840, had won the nomination in 1844 only to lose the election, and in 1848 lost the Whig nomination again, after which there was nothing left for him to do but to write another grand Compromise between American sections and die.

During those years Greeley was never an intimate of his idol. The "Great Commoner," aging and aloof, left no record of just what he thought of the bustling, half-bald gnome from the *Tribune* who went about insatiably promoting Clay for President, perhaps hoping someday to land himself a Cabinet post thereby. Greeley, for his part, watching Clay from the press chairs in the Senate chamber, described the Kentuckian as "by nature genial, cordial, courteous, gracious, magnetic, winning," although he had some reservations about the man's haughty ways and his fondness for whisky. Clay, he said with admiration, was "a true conservative." This tribute came from a man whose own views in the later 1840's became increasingly radical, even "agrarian," as the ever-vengeful Henry Raymond of the *Courier and Enquirer* charged. And tributes kept coming from Greeley even after he had abandoned many of Clay's principles and broken from his Whig party. Thus in 1852, after the statesman's death, the busy *Tribune* editor found time to edit and complete a lugubriously partisan biography of Clay, written originally by one Epes Sargent, and to leave in the text an obituary on Clay's 1844 election defeat which ran, "You would have thought some stupendous public calamity had occurred . . . A profound sigh seemed to be wrung from the nation's heart. Tears, such as Cato might have wept, were shed from many eyes; and many of its truest friends began to despair of the republic."

Greeley meant it. For him, Clay was Whiggism at its best. Failing Clay as President, Greeley had to deal with Whiggism at its second best—in the persons of boss Thurlow Weed and Governor (later Senator) William H. Seward. When these men and their friends, in turn, put up their own candidates for President—the fumbling General Zachary Taylor in 1848, and the even more fatuous General Winfield Scott in 1852—Greeley had to deal with Whiggism at its third best, or possibly its worst. This led to crises between Greeley and the party leaders. But Greeley's personal crises had a way of generating political ones. The revolts and excursions of the editor of the "agrarian" *Tribune* were instrumental in speeding the creation of that new, insurgent body, the Republican party.

Much had to happen in Greeley's own mind, however, before he could arrive at this particular solution. He had already unlearned much of his initial predilection for stock, traditional ideas. Now he had to overcome his instinct for party regularity—a loyalty with which his voyages into utopia had not seriously interfered. This took time. His close alliance with Weed and Seward had carried him to extraordinary heights of national influence for a man not yet out of his thirties. There were inviting possibilities in that influence. One was the reward of public office.

A political place and title—was that the chief thing he wanted? The editor E. L. Godkin thought so, when he later remarked of Greeley that he was "as time-serving and ambitious and scheming an old fellow as any of them." But Weed and Seward, partners in the triumvirate, never could be sure. They might handle Greeley on that basis only to find that some new outburst of what sounded like principle on his part would make him threaten to walk off the reservation. During the 1840's, to be sure, these threats were never carried out. Weed wrote that while "Mr. Greeley's sympathy with and friendship for the 'toiling millions' led him to favor 'associations' and 'unions' of laborers and journeymen—organizations which, countenanced by the widely circulating *Tribune*, became as formidable as they were mischievous," still Greeley's "peculiarities in this respect never turned him away from or impaired his consistent and hearty efforts in the Whig cause." Nevertheless, shrewd as Weed was in assessing other men's motives, he remained uncertain just what it was that his press ally was really after. "I shall never comprehend Greeley," he remarked to Seward, "for I can never discern the personal considerations which sway and govern him."

If it was merely a job that he wanted, they would give him one —not as big a job as he had dreamed of, but a small, temporary one, as a tryout. Greeley had been agitating for one for a long time, although protesting in the same breath that he didn't really want it. In 1846, for instance, there was held in Albany a specially elected convention to revise the New York State Constitution. Greeley, realizing its importance as a forum where reform ideas would be presented, had been eager to go as a delegate. But he had not wished to sound too eager. Proudly he had remarked to Weed of his standing as a citizen, "I say what I please every day, and have a sufficient audience"; therefore Weed must not place his desire for a convention seat on a level with that of those other Whigs "to whom it is an *object* to go—who very rarely have an opportunity to say what they think . . . so that the public will hear it." Weed had taken him at his word, and left him out of the running. ("I begin to suspect I ought to have tried to go to the Convention," Greeley later told Colfax, somewhat archly.)

That same year Greeley had also become struck with the idea of succeeding to the governorship of New York. He wrote Weed that an intermediary in Albany had "talked with several (I can't imagine who) and had gone home resolved to defy my entreaties and propose my name for *Governor*!" (The word was underscored, as if Greeley had been amazed at the very thought.) He went on to say that he had told this man, Sanford, that "this would be the maddest foolery ever started. . . . I told him finally that if he would let me off on the Governor, he might use my name for Lieutenant Governor . . ." But Weed appears to have seen through this play, too. Greeley was not encouraged to try even for Lieutenant Governor.

Then, two years after, the idea that struck Greeley was that of being a United States senator. But here the difficulty was that Seward, with the prestige of two terms as governor behind him, was set on becoming New York's new senator that year himself. Weed cast about for some other office that might satisfy Greeley and keep the political family happy. Here it was: an interim place in Congress, to fill out the last months of a seat that had become vacant when its holder, a New York City Democrat, had been ousted for election fraud. The post would be purely temporary, since the Whig who was to inherit that seat in the subsequent Congress had already been picked. Nevertheless Greeley rose to the bait. So, in late 1848 he ran, won, and became, for ninety days, "the Honorable" —to serve until the new Congress convened in March.

Weed no doubt thought that he had paid off a political debt cheaply. Yet Greeley planned to make the most he could out of it, and as a result he managed to convert his brief stay in Washington into something approaching a political explosion. There were sacrosanct Congressional customs about the behavior of freshman members, especially when they arrived late in the session. But Greeley, taking his seat in December among such representatives as Horace Mann, Joshua Giddings, Alexander Stephens, Robert Toombs, Andrew Johnson, and the one-term Whig from downstate Illinois, Abraham Lincoln, at once began throwing his and his newspaper's weight about—forgetting that as a legislator, in addition to being a lame duck, he had never yet flown. With only ninety days in which to operate, he decided to soar and to reform the whole Congress, if not the country.

He scoured the House for "abuses," and soon hit upon the members' prevalent habit of pocketing some ready money by charging the government for more mileage than they actually covered between their homes and Washington—since a loophole in the law enabled them to collect on the basis of circuitous routes. This evil, said the round-faced newcomer from New York, must go. What was more, he said so also in the *Tribune*, splashing across his front page the names of all his colleagues and the amounts they had pocketed during the session. For instance, take the case of Congressman Lincoln of Illinois. It appeared, said the *Tribune*, that Lincoln had charged the government for travel by a route of over 1,600 miles, whereas the shortest mail route from Washington to his home in Springfield was less than half that distance. Lincoln had, therefore, collected $676.80 "in excess of mileage over what it would have been if the distance had been computed by the most direct mail route." And Congressman Greeley added editorially, "The usually travelled route for a great many Members of the last Congress was an exceedingly crooked one, even for politicians."

No wonder that Greeley wrote Margaret Fuller that within a few weeks he had made himself "the most detested man who ever sat in

Congress, enveloped by a crowd who long and pray for a chance to extirpate me." He was, of course, exaggerating. He was far less detested than looked upon as an extraordinary nuisance. "I drill from day to day in favor of longer sessions, previous question, stopping debate in Committee, etc., etc.," he told Colfax, boasting of his prowess on the floor. He could not be still, and he simply would not sit down. Hunting for more reforms, he put through by main effort a committee resolution to abolish the issuance of grog in the Navy. Later the resolution was defeated on the floor; but at any rate Greeley had what he called his "first flush of delusive thiumph," recalling incidentally of the moment that "a member sitting near me, who had voted to stop the grog ration, said to a friend who, I believe, had voted the same way, 'Giddings, that was a glorious vote we have just taken,' 'Yes, glorious,' was the ready response. 'Gid,' resumed the elated reformer, 'let us go and take a drink on the strength of it.' 'Agreed,' was the willing echo; and they went."

Next, Greeley was on the point of introducing a resolution that the United States change its name to "Columbia" when a fist fight over floor rules broke out, with the result that his speech calling for this particular reform was indefinitely postponed. In the meantime, however, he found time to propose a reform that really mattered. While the House sat listlessly by, he introduced the startling innovation of his Homestead Bill—a measure providing for the granting of 160-acre tracts on the public domain to bona fide settlers, with no immediate payment whatever to be required of them, the provision reading that after seven years of occupancy they could take formal title to the land at the nominal government price of $1.25 an acre. The bill was "not so radical as I would prefer," he told his confidant, Colfax, "but as strong as the people were ready for." Whether or not the people were ready for it, though, Congress was not. The House buried it—while Greeley made good copy with it in the *Tribune*.

That, again, was precisely the trouble, as both Greeley's friends and enemies pointed out. Even while trying to be a party officeholder he could not cease being a newspaper editor, always on the hunt for hot stories, exposures and crusades. Greeley, to be sure, enjoyed Washington, even if it did not enjoy him. The ninety-day experience, far from satisfying his political ambition, merely whetted it. But Weed, while highly valuing his press partner, had seen enough. And Weed had in his hand a letter from Seward, the newly elected senator, who had looked in on Greeley's performance in the House and reported, "He won't let them adjourn until three o'clock, and martyrizes himself five or six times a day by voting against the whole House. I am sorry, but who can reason with him?"

Obviously not Seward. Then perhaps Greeley's own wiser self? there seemed hope of this when Greeley remarked, during the first weeks of talk of distributing the political spoils of Zachary Taylor's presidential victory, "As for myself, I want nothing." But then he quickly added to Colfax, "I would just as soon be talked about for Postmaster General as not." And in case he couldn't be Postmaster General? Well, he asked, what about a diplomatic mission abroad?

2

He did not get the Postmastership under Taylor. He did not get a foreign mission. Thereby tension grew between him and the twin New York dispensers of patronage, Weed and Seward. Yet the source of the conflict, for all of Greeley's importunate job-seeking, lay further back than that. His annual problem, in continuing as a Whig adviser and confederate, had been that of reconciling his own changing principles with the party's increasing lack of any. His annual hope had been that this very vacuum in the party would enable him to impose his own ideas on it. His frustration came when he saw that the party, intent on simply winning the next election in the face of gathering crisis, decided it could get along best without ideas at all. The game worked, for a while, but he correctly predicted the hour of its doom.

Back in 1840, he had played the game himself. But there had been no air of urgency then; there had not even been a readily apparent issue. In the following presidential campaign, though, when his hero, Harry Clay, bore the Whig banner, Greeley had felt that a true issue had emerged, and that he himself was no longer playing a game. What had overcast the otherwise bland early forties was an ominous change in the make-up and direction of the opposing, Democratic party. Within a few brief years all those vivid, clashing hues which the unruly Jacksonian host of the 1830's had lent it had been overcome by one dominant color— the deep dye of the southern slaveholders' faction. This proud and skillful group, led by the intransigent Calhoun, had won new wealth and power as they expanded their holdings clear across the Gulf States, and now stood ready to challenge the entire North. Their eyes had become fixed on two absorbing objects: first, still further extension of their slaveholding dominion (this time through annexation of the Republic of Texas, and possibly of the entire Mexican Southwest), and, second, the abolition of any tariffs designed to protect at their expense the industries of the rival North. The North, they said, must compromise; the only question was, how far, and on one issue or both?

Greeley at first had been willing to compromise—on slavery expansion. Reformer or not, he had never adhered to that small advance guard of northern abolitionists who took their voice from Garrison. Greeley's insistent advice in 1844 had been that the Whigs, while avoiding a frontal collision on expansion, should run their campaign on the issue of the tariff—a far less explosive question than the other, he thought, and a more basic one. For he still believed ardently in the "home-market" idea, with its vision of a self-contained, tariff-walled America expanding with the help of ambitious internal undertakings, and he felt that with a certain shift of emphasis (to be supplied by himself) this doctrine could be so applied as to increase not only the profits of industry, but the wages and profits of workers as well. Wouldn't a prospering, cooperative industrial system, with fair play all around, of itself doom the antique slave order? He thought so.

Yet the campaign of 1844 had gone wrong. The tariff issue had not proved itself to be the magnet Greeley had hoped it would. Neither had the old Whig log-cabin word magic, revived for the occasion, succeeded; Thurlow Weed had lamented of the campaign songs and slogans poured out by Greeley & McElrath's presses that "they don't warm up the masses as they did in '40." In vain had Greeley hammered in the *Tribune* at the fact that the Democrats, for the first time in their history, had failed to reaffirm in their campaign platform their devotion to the principles of the Declaration of Independence. What, after all, were the principles of the Whigs? Some northern antislave Democrats had indeed bolted the Polk ticket, but some northern antislave Whigs had bolted their own ticket too, uniting with the others to vote for a third-party candidate, James Birney, who had declared himself for the extinction of slavery. Their numbers had not been large, but they were large enough to upset Greeley's pre-election boast of a safe Whig majority in the state ("I am a good deal about, and do not see how I can be mistaken") and enough to throw the state's electoral vote over into the Democrats' column, thereby deciding the outcome of the whole election.

There was a lesson in this confused campaign, and it was not lost on Greeley. It was that if one was going to have to compromise on the slavery question—something he himself was still ready to do—one must at least have another central issue on which one could seize the liberal initiative with compelling force. If one did so, one would be able to cut right across America's growing sectional schism—and, if not overcome it, then at least blanket and soften it. If one did not—that is, if one took the current need for hedging on the slavery issue as the excuse for hedging on every other, in the interest of some vague national harmony—one would find oneself simply losing extremists at either end without attaching to oneself a decisive bloc of adherents in the middle. The tariff issue, apparently, was not good enough: it had not prevented a minority of extreme antislave New Yorkers from drifting off on their own and thereby paradoxically throwing the whole nation under the command of the slave power. But there were other issues. They must be seized upon quickly. If one hung back, one would soon find oneself resorting in desperation to the kind of strategy which Cassius M. Clay, a Kentuckian turned abolitionist, had just advocated to Greeley: "When the South unites in despotism, the North ought to unite for their own salvation. And you have the power of numbers and wealth." And what would that mean? Obviously, disunion and probably war—and thereby an end to every other prospect of improvement.

Greeley, meanwhile, had found his "other issue." His next task was to sell it to the leaders of the Whig party—and, especially, to the two other members of the New York triumvirate. He knew he stood in a minority with this issue—and an ill-organized one at that—but the late election had dramatically shown the power of minorities. So, in early 1846, when the unseated Whigs were at the nadir of their strength, he began campaigning with it. He was, he declared in the *Tribune*, bent on reforming the whole system of land tenure and settlement in the United States.

"Good God," Weed is reported to have said, on learning of Greeley's new crusade; "again?"

3

Fifteen years before, when the journeyman printer Horace Greeley descended the Hudson on his way to find work in New York, he had passed near Albany a part of the river frontage of that immeasurable manor of the Van Rensselaer dynasty on which upward of 50,000 persons lived in perpetual tenantry to a feudal lord. The reigning Van Rensselaer, at that time, had been called the "Good Patroon" for having let many poorer farmers go without paying him their annual tribute; but upon his death several years thereafter his heirs had demanded prompt payment of all back rents and thereby aroused the whole countryside. Villagers on the old demesne had taken to arms to resist the rent collectors. Governor Seward, fearing a large-scale outbreak, had called a truce, marched his militia through the hills, and invited the farmers to present their grievances before the state legislature. Yet Albany had temporized, and when Seward's Democratic successor appeared to favor the landlords' side, the revolt had flared up again.

Greeley had not been sure, at first, that he approved of the demonstrating bands of "down-renters," with their secret drills, hooded Indian disguises, and horns blowing in the Helderberg hills to summon comrades against rent collectors and the sheriff's posses. But by the fall of 1845 he was writing Schuyler Colfax that while some of the farmers were no doubt "reckless and criminal," they had "a good deal of right on their side." Thurlow Weed, at that time, thought they did not; at all events, they were disturbing law and order. Greeley pondered the issue further. He had backed some reformers before, but they had been abstract and ineffective. These upcountry men were of another sort. With their pitchforks and antique muskets, they were talking the language, not of the benign George Ripley or the cloudy Brisbane, but of the embattled farmers who once had followed Daniel Shays in rebellion. They were talking class grievance, and their leaders were beginning to suggest class war. Greeley was one of those who had bridled at the very thought of class war. His conclusion now was simply, Well, then, remove the grievance.

Antirentism was a local issue, but grievances concerning the tenure of American land were not. At this moment a small group of New York radicals sprang up with the intention of seizing control of the first in order to exploit the second. And while attempting this they would enlist the interest of organized labor as well, in order to build—as in Jackson's day—a farmer-labor coalition with which to face the creaking, artificial parties of the hour. For this purpose they needed the help of a newspaper of liberal name and wide circulation. Why not try Greeley, then flirting with all manner of reforms? They did, and he became their man.

This group numbered among its members such men as John Windt, whom Greeley already knew as the tough, agnostic first president of the New York Printers' Union who had befriended Frances Wright and in early 1837 had incited a streetful of hungry New Yorkers to break into a warehouse filled with speculators' flour. With him was Lewis Masquerier, an itinerant Owenite socialist who had recently been lecturing on his subject at Tammany Hall. Next there was an impoverished young upstate law student and college teacher named Alvan Bovay—a man who had been reared as a Whig. More colorful than these was the redheaded, bushy-browed, cantankerous Thomas A. Devyr—a fighting Irishman who lately had fled England to avoid imprisonment on charges of sedition for having helped launch the Chartist revolt, and who, almost the moment he settled in New York, had gone into battle as the Jacksonian editor of a small Brooklyn weekly. But the firebrand of the group was the veteran George Henry Evans of the *Working Man's Advocate*—a perennial apostle of Tom Paine who had now come forth, after several years of rural retirement in New Jersey, with the gospel which he popularized under the slogan, "Vote yourself a farm."

In earlier "Workie" times Evans had preached inevitable class conflict. Now he argued that the conflict was not inevitable, but that what had caused it primarily was the unequal distribution of land. Grant free acreages to every settler willing and able to work them, he proclaimed—something that America, with its vast western domain, could readily do—and the struggle would eventually be resolved. It was land pre-emption by speculators and large investors, he argued, that was having the effect of bottling up surplus labor in the eastern cities, thereby depressing wages and nullifying all other efforts at advancement and reform. What was the use of going out on strike for better conditions and pay when the urban employer knew all the time that the steady influx of new workers from abroad would force them in the end to accept his terms?

Every word of this appealed powerfully to Greeley, whose heart was bent on class harmony, whose instinct was against strikes, and whose feeling for western space had led him to argue as far back as 1837 that jobless city workers seeking better chances ought to try moving out there. And when Evans and his group fortified their teaching by declaring that all men, of whatever condition, had a natural, inalienable right to the soil, this adaptation of natural-rights doctrine completed his conversion. He had never been a Jeffersonian, but he was strongly inclined to be a romantic. His own memories of rural homestead life were chiefly those of grim family failure and stultifying isolation, but he turned inland nevertheless to find new hope. His pioneer blood stirred in him. The illimitable West might, after all, relieve and readjust the distracted East—and, at the same time, bring popular pressure on such ensconced figures as Weed.

So, when he came out for Evans' land reform in the *Tribune* on 23 January, 1846, he proclaimed:

This system . . . would rapidly cover the yet unappropriated Public Domain with an independent, substantial yeomanry, enjoying a degree of Equality in Opportunities and advantages such as the world has not seen. . . . Shame on the laws which send an able, willing man to the Alms-House or to any form of beggary when the Soil on which he would gladly work and produce is barred against Poverty and accorded by this Government of Freemen to those alone who have the money to pay for it.

Then, having thrown himself into the fray, he warmed up. "The right of owning land is one thing," he wrote; "the right to own thousands and even millions of acres of land is another . . . I condemn a system of Land Monopoly which robs the producer of one-half to seven-eights of the fruits of his toil, and often dooms him to absolute starvation on the soil he has faithfully and effectively tilled!" What, after all, was the test of the validity of a man's ownership of land? The possession of legal title to it? No, said Greeley, warming up still further, that was not enough: "use and improvement alone can vest in any individual a right to call some spot of earth his own." It followed, then, that absentee ownership must vanish and that land must be subdivided into small, individual holdings. But what if the settler, in time of hardship, ran afoul of his creditors, with the result that banks or other absentees might take his land away from him again? Greeley had seen just this happen to his father in New Hampshire. It must not happen again, he said. Hadn't most men by now agreed that it was both unjust and futile to imprison a fellow citizen for debt? Just so they should agree that it was wrong to take a settler's roof from over his head. The settler had built the roof; they hadn't. He had done the work of hacking a home out of the forest; they had merely sat by, waiting for its increment. The homestead remained his by right; and if readers had difficulty accepting this (so Greeley argued in a parting thrust in his tract collection, *Hints toward Reforms*), they should at least remember that "in our diseased and unstable social condition, the banker of today may himself be the bankrupt of tomorrow. Let us all in prosperity remember the teachings of adversity and be merciful."

This was "agrarianism"—a red-flag word in the 1840's. And it was in fact far removed from the Horace Greeley who back in 1838 had stiffly declared in his *New Yorker* that only such settlers should be admitted upon the public lands as could pay a good price for acreages in advance. (For, he had argued, "the price of public lands is the barometer which regulates the general value of landed property . . . Reduce the price of public lands and you reduce the value of all lands in the country.") Now he was talking about free homesteads and about keeping the price of public lands not up but down. He was beginning to talk about large-scale labor organization, too—sometimes rather cloudily, to be sure, since he held to a preference for high-minded "cooperation" between manager and worker as against strikes and federal laws to bring about better conditions, but still bluntly enough to write in the *Tribune* in 1847:

To talk of Freedom of Labor, the policy of leaving it to make its own bargains, etc., when the fact is that a man who has a family to support and a house hired for the year is told, "If you will work thirteen hours per day, or as many as we see fit, you can stay; if not, you can have your walking papers; and well you know that no one else hereabouts will hire you"—is it not the most egregious flummery?

This was no longer the airy language of a utopian. But was it proper language for a Whig? Henry J. Raymond, Colonel Webb, and the New York Whig press in general thought not, and went to work to read him out of the fold. Greeley, for his part, thought the party had better accept this language, or face a new third-party revolt. And to enforce his point, he let it be known that he was tinkering with revolt himself.

4

As early as 1842, the fiery Tom Devyr had gone up into the Helderberg highlands west of Albany and there prevailed upon the simple antirent farmers to make him their propaganda agent—with the ulterior purpose of radicalizing them as a nucleus for a general land-reform movement. Two years later Devyr and Evans and their group, now calling themselves the National Reform Association, had started moving in on workingmen's congresses of every sort and planning their own national convention. The spring of 1846 had seen Greeley and Evans in Boston, trying to steer a new "Industrial Congress" whose purpose was to link up the agitations for land reform and the ten-hour day, while Devyr and Alvan Bovay toured the still rebellious New York highlands to talk up the idea of a new party to unite all progressive groups. And in that year Thurlow Weed, sitting among his Whigs in Albany while Democrats ran the nation, became earnestly concerned.

Greeley had told Devyr privately that he was in favor of starting a reform party. Meanwhile he went on working with Weed on day-to-day Whig maneuverings—reporting to him, for instance, of the fall gubernatorial campaign that "We might make a heavy inroad into the Adopted Citizens [i.e., New York City Irish] this fall if we were not obliged to coax the Natives to vote with us. It is very difficult to gain both ways. We will do our best." But how long would his party loyalty last? Weed realized that the Whig management must make concessions to the reformers and once again reestablish contact with the masses. That was why he had already called upon the state constitutional convention to bring about sweeping electoral reforms—much to the annoyance of stalwarts like Philip Hone. He had even sought to appease antirent sentiment by coming out bodily for abolishing feudal holdings such as the Van Rensselaers'. This had brought many rebels back into line. But some of them had broken away nevertheless to put up Lewis Masquerier as their own man for governor. This could become uncomfortable. Which way would Greeley turn?

Luckily for the regular Whigs who feared a possible split in their ranks, an actual split was occurring at the very same moment in the opposing camp of the Democrats. Its occasion was the nation's advance into the Mexican Southwest by annexation and conquest. All territories so acquired, said the party's dominant southerners, must of course be opened to slavery. But to this principle many northern Democrats could not agree. One of their number, David Wilmot of Pennsylvania, rose in the House to introduce a resolution excluding slavery from the new lands; and at once the whole party divided along North-South lines. Now Thurlow Weed and his lieutenants could feel relieved: with the Democrats so divided, the coming national election was pretty sure to fall into the Whigs' laps in any case. For the moment, then, the Whigs could forget about the kind of reforms Greeley wanted to press upon them. And as for Greeley himself, hadn't he better return to the fold while he could? There would be a reward waiting for him, whispered Weed.

The spectacle of Greeley backtracking was a disheartening one—to himself as well as to his new friends outside of Albany. For it was a voyage back into a now aging vacuum. His gorge had risen at the discovery that the man whom Weed and Seward were grooming for the next Whig presidential candidacy was the brassbound, slaveholding General Taylor of Virginia—a figure distinguished in war, but utterly fatuous in politics. Greeley, for his part, had sent them warning messages: "The more I see of Taylorism, the more I don't like it." The man they obviously should pick was—once again—Henry Clay. But there was hollow laughter at this in Albany. "Confidential!" Greeley scribbled on, pressing his case upon Weed; "Clay is for Free Territory and none other . . . He is anxious that the Wilmot question shall be pressed . . ." Albany was not interested. Albany had another idea, namely that of installing a President so pliant and dependent that he would let Albany itself run the administration for him—with Seward (who was sure to go to Washington as Senator) acting as Weed's emissary on the spot. What did this mean? Greeley asked. Weed and Seward, professed liberals, maneuvering a slaveholding figurehead into power? Where was there chance now for a forthright Whig social program? "We *cannot*, with any decency, support General Taylor," he blurted to Colfax in April, 1848. And in the same letter, prophetically: "If we nominate Taylor, we may elect him, but we destroy the Whig party . . . I wash my hands of the business."

He did—almost. June seventh saw him in Philadelphia at the Whig National Convention, trying somehow to stop the Taylor boom. There was not a chance: with Weed steering, Taylor was swept in, along with the vain, ineffectual Millard Fillmore for Vice-President. Furiously Greeley stalked out of the hall. Alexander McClure of the Philadelphia *Times* described him as he went: "It was evident he was mad clear through. His low-crowned, broad-brimmed, fuzzy hat set at an angle of forty-five degrees on the back of his head, his profusion of shirt collar protected from wandering over his shoulders by an immense black silk handkerchief that he used as a necktie . . . and his immense baggy, black swallow-tail coat and the carpetbag he held by one handle—all this did not contribute to genteel appearance!" And another newspaperman, who encountered him hurrying away, carpetbag in hand, stopped to ask, "Where are you going, Mr. Greeley?"

"I'm going home!" he snorted.

"But there's no train tonight."

"I don't want any train," Greeley snapped. "I'm going across New Jersey afoot and alone!" And away he went.

He still had a chance, that summer, to make good his threat of desertion. For many others were bolting either party—and this time in formidable numbers. "Conscience" Whigs, repelled by their party's evasiveness on slavery expansion, were streaming out and joining with northern antislave and radical Democrats to set up a third ticket, which under the slogan of "Free soil, free speech, free labor and free men!" in August nominated Martin Van Buren for President. Greeley flirted with them awhile, advising them privately on nominations "for the sake of some leading Independents here who want to set the ball rolling right away." But it remained a flirtation only. Greeley's own revolt collapsed; grudgingly and angrily, after having first denounced the Whig's choice at Philadelphia, the *Tribune* fell back into line. And the nadir of its editor's self-respect was reached when in August he ghostwrote a speech for Weed, presenting "arguments to the anti-slavery Whigs in favor of supporting Taylor, and the best I can think of. I don't care how much stronger you make it. . . ." But, he added, "Don't let it be seen in my hand."

How was he to explain this relapse to others, let alone to himself? He tried in a letter to Colfax: "I am going to vote for Taylor—at least I think I am—and I am not clear that this is right. If I could make Van Buren President tomorrow, I would. I don't like the man, but I do like the principles he now embodies—Free Soil and Land Reform. And, very properly, the Free Soil party is

the only live party around us . . . I could have been the oracle of
the Free Soil party, with any extent of circulation, had I chosen.
Party fidelity—or rather, fidelity to men I love who still cling to
the putrid corpse of the party butchered at Philadelphia—has
withheld me. So I cling to a party which never loved me and am
helping elect a President who will curse me. I could shake the
whole rotten fabric by a bugle-blast, yet will not do it, because
some good men I love would be crushed beneath its ruins . . ."

"Men I love": did he still mean Weed and Seward? There was
little enough love left there. Then whom was he deceiving?

5

But at least he could say to himself, when mid-century came,
that his on-and-off agitation for reform had not been entirely in
vain. Even Whigs did move: he had the comfort of seeing the
aged Daniel Webster, standing in the Senate with coal-black eyes
whose fire still glowed, introduce a free-homestead bill that resembled his own. And there was no question but that the general
reformist spirit which he had helped spread during the 1840's, no
matter how confusedly, had left its effect. State constitutions had
been rewritten; masses of new voters had been admitted to the
ballot; labor organization along with land reform had won aggressive footholds; prisons (at least some of them) had been cleaned
up; imprisonment for debt had just about disappeared. Even the
realists had listened to the utopians. Sometimes, in the optimism
of the hour, Greeley rose into sweeping flights: "Let us take courage from the evidences of Progress around us . . . We have yet
Doctors of Divinity who justify laws which authorize the buying
and selling of mothers from their children; but this is widely dying
out; and, in a few years, Sermons proving Slavery a Bible institution
will be advertised as antique curiosities. So of Privateering, War,
and the traffic in intoxicating Liquors."

He was sure of the early attainment of Prohibition. But the
progress being made against slavery left a good deal to be desired.
He himself—so he told his constituents in early 1845—had
"shunned and deplored any needless agitation against slavery." The
issue, he had felt, must not be allowed to dominate all others and
lead to irrevocable clash. For years he had echoed Henry Clay's
standing arguments for compromise; national harmony was possible
through concessions between sections, just as class harmony could

be achieved through cooperation and "association" between high and low. But this was the year 1850. The issue raised by Wilmot's Proviso had not been solved. How long must the country remain in suspense?

Here was Clay, in Washington, proposing another compromise. Here also was Seward—senator, innermost counselor to the President, and now also controller of the New York patronage—who suddenly, almost overnight, had struck fire. There must be no more compromise, Seward was declaring; the proposed deal meant abject surrender to the slave power. Greeley thought awhile, and then came around to agree with Seward. No compromise! echoed the *Tribune*; better that the Union be "a thousand times shivered" than that the North submit to those who would "plant Slavery on Free Soil."

Greeley went to Washington to join Dana in the Senate press seats and judge for himself the high debate at which Clay, Webster and Calhoun, three haggard, shrunken giants of a day now dying, contended for their last and greatest time. There, as the old Romans rose into their perorations, he saw the men of a new, more strident senatorial generation stirring in their seats—the caustic, superior Charles Sumner of Massachusetts; the six-foot, lantern-jawed, Biblical Salmon Chase of Ohio; tousled Seward, pacing the floor with sudden, sweeping gestures as he spoke; and, on the southern side, the portly and deceptively amiable Judah P. Benjamin of Louisiana, seated not far from the flinty Jefferson Davis. "The Union!" was the substance of Clay's hoarse, two-day appeal: "I consider our country is in danger . . ." But there was a "higher law," answered Seward—higher than the Constitution—that condemned slavery and all its works. Calhoun, wrapped in flannels and near death, sat staring at Seward with relentless, blazing eyes. The iron entered Greeley's soul. "We agree to no compromise that perils or looks toward perilling freedom in New Mexico!" thundered the *Tribune*.

But in the end, of course, there would have to be a compromise. Greeley came to see that as the explosive months wore on. He thought that Clay's proposals—under which California would come in as a free state, while the New Mexico and Utah territories might also be admitted on that basis—might serve as a stopgap, so long as it was clearly understood that they were a stopgap only; steadily, gradually, with increasing vigor, the North must assert its moral claim. The storm showed signs of abating. The *Tribune*, now tacking downwind, counseled patience. But it had no patience with the new law providing for the return of fugitive slaves to southern owners, and declared flatly that northerners would simply refuse to obey it. This was the year in which the *Tribune*'s circulation topped 100,000.

It appeared amid all this that the old alliance between Greeley and Seward had been reestablished. "If [Seward] can only maintain that position," Greeley had enthused to Colfax after hearing the "higher law" speech, "he is our hope for 1856." Weed, backstage, applauded. And it looked as though Seward now had the bemused soldier-President, Taylor, safely in tow. But then Taylor died. Seward's star dimmed. With President Fillmore, a time of further evasion and appeasement returned. The partners again drifted apart. There was a curious interlude when Seward, appointed to arbitrate one of the many libel suits in which the *Tribune* was involved, rapped the editor's knuckles with a decision which Greeley thought "needlessly humiliating . . . cruel and mortifying . . . I think you exalted your own judicial sternness unduly at my expense." And later he could not help adding bitterly to Seward, "If I am not mistaken, this judgment is the only speech, letter or document, addressed to the public, in which you ever recognized my existence. I hope I may not go down to posterity as embalmed therein."

The disappointments, the twistings and turnings, had been too much for him. A wave of acute depression swept over him. He was going off to Europe, he told Colfax, in order "to cool my fevered brain." What was the use of continuing on as he had? "The times are unpropitious; the people are lazy; the Administration excites no enthusiasm; the Whigs are distracted." Politics? "I suppose we must run General Scott for President [in 1852], but I hate it. He is . . . an aristocrat by long habit—and anything else than wise or winning . . . I see it all, and don't much care whether we win or lose with old Feathers—either is disastrous."

For the next four months, Greeley "rested." That is, he toured Europe at reportorial speed to write for the *Tribune* from England, Scotland, Ireland, France, Italy, Switzerland and the Rhineland, in addition to finding time to serve as chairman of a prize-awarding jury at the London Crystal Palace Exposition. It was his first organized recreation in almost twenty years, as well as his first effort as a foreign correspondent. The *Tribune* had maintained its own correspondents abroad before: Bayard Taylor had written his popular color stories from the hillsides of the Rhine and Savoy, and Dana had shared with Margaret Fuller the assignment of covering the revolutionary uprisings of 1848. But this trip was on another scale: the Yankee editor was staging his own grand tour.

He conducted it precisely as his readers hoped he would. Instead of bowing low before the wonders of European culture, as the glowing Margaret Fuller had, he looked around quizzically, squinted at the size of buildings or the handling of express trains, and wrote home that Americans weren't doing so badly, after all. He thought the Louvre "deficient in height." British railroad trains were "not to be relied on for punctuality"; and as for the running time of the famed London-Edinburgh express, "We should easily beat this in America with anything like equal facilities, and without charging the British price." French railway porters, of course, were grossly incompetent: in unloading baggage at Dijon "they consumed the better part of half an hour, though half as many Yankees fussing over it would have had it all distributed in ten minutes."

In Rome, surrounded by the splendors of antiquity, he looked into the matter of newspaper circulation, and reported to his readers that "Lynn or Poughkeepsie probably, Newark or New Haven certainly, buys and reads more newspapers than the entire three million people who inhabit the Papal States." In Florence he did take time to look at fine art—particularly that of the resident American sculptor, Hiram Powers. "I defy Antiquity to surpass—I doubt its ability to rival—his 'Proserpine' and his 'Psyche' with any models of the female head that have come down," he at once notified the *Tribune*. In Paris, he relaxed, while his readers took in every word. He saw the ballet and confessed that "I am, though no practitioner, a lover of the Dance. Restricted to proper hours and fit associates, I wish it were far more general than it is. Health, grace, muscular energy, even beauty might be promoted by it." But he hastened to add that the kind of dancing he had seen that night had repelled him:

What grace, what sense, what witchery, there can be for instance in a young girl's standing on one great toe and raising the other foot to the altitude of her head, I cannot imagine. Such a medley of drinking, dancing, idol-worshipping and Delilah craft I have never before encountered. I came away after the second of five acts.

Paris, he went on to report, "is a Paradise of the Senses; a town of Enjoyment, not of Happiness. . . . Paris has tens of thousands who would eagerly pour out their heart's blood for Liberty and Human Progress, but no class or clan who ever thought of denying themselves Wine and kindred stimulants in order that the Masses should be rendered worthier of Liberty and thus better fitted to preserve and enjoy it." He found the same difficulty in Scotland: "I am afraid the good cause of Total Abstinence is making no headway here."

Yet he enjoyed himself abroad, and he saw to it that his readers would do so too at home. Writing from London, he made fun of the trappings of royalty at the Crystal Palace Exposition: "What have Gentlemen Ushers of Sword and State, Ladies in Waiting, Master of the Horse, Groom of the Stole, and such fossils to do with an exhibition of the fruits of industry? . . . The Mistress of the Robes would be in place if she ever fashioned any robes." He gloated in the triumph of Cyrus McCormick's new American reaper, and wrote home about it:

Several machines for cutting grain were exhibited and tested, including two from America, and an English one which was declared on all hands a mere imitation. . . . [McCormick's] is the same lately ridiculed by one of the great London journals as "a cross between an Astley's chariot, a treadmill and a flying machine," and its uncouth appearance has been a standing butt for London reporters at the Exhibition. . . . It came into the field, therefore, to confront a tribunal . . . already prepared for its condemnation. Before it stood John Bull, burly, dogged and determined not to be humbugged—his judgment made up and his sentence ready to be recorded. Nothing disconcerted, the brown, rough, homespun Yankee in charge jumped on the box, started the team at a smart walk, setting the blades of the machine in lively operation, and commenced raking off the grain in sheaf-piles ready for binding, cutting a breadth of nine or ten feet cleanly and carefully. . . . There was a moment, and but a moment, of suspense; human prejudice could hold out no longer; and burst after burst of involuntary cheers from the whole crowd proclaimed the triumph of the Yankee "treadmill."

He came home happily from his whirlwind tour, rested—so he said—and restored to American self-confidence and pride. Seward, on his return, praised his *Tribune* correspondence from abroad:

"I never saw a man who did not read all the letters if they came his way, nor a man who did not praise them." There was only one piece of upsetting news that met him. During his absence, plans had gone forward for the launching of a new Whig daily in New York City, in direct competition with his *Tribune*. The editor was to be Henry Raymond, and the publisher, George Jones of East Poultney, Vermont—both old *Tribune* hands. It was to be called the New York *Times*. Weed and Seward, his friends, had apparently both given their blessing to it.

IX. MOVER

1

Except for the fact that Henry Raymond was present on both occasions writing copy, there was little resemblance between the launching of the New York *Times* in September, 1851, and that of the New York *Tribune* ten years earlier. Greeley had started out in an attic with only ten men to help him and little over $1,000 in hand; the firm of Raymond, Jones & Co. began with $100,000 capital, a six-story building on Nassau Street, a city-room staff complete with rewrite men and copy boys, and a pressroom force of eighteen. The type pages of the first *Tribune* had been trundled down the street to a neighboring print shop to be put on the press there; but the first issue of the New York *Times* came rolling off a Hoe steam cylinder press of the latest model that had been set up in the *Times'* own building at a cost of $20,000, and was capable of turning out 10,000 copies an hour.

Thereby still another day dawned in American journalism. The *Times* was the first newspaper in the country that was a major business venture from its outset. Its biggest single stockholder, George Jones, had gone far since the days when he and young Horace Greeley had ambled together across East Poultney's shaded green: he had risen through various merchant enterprises to become a leading Albany banker and a friend of Thurlow Weed. The *Times'* other backers were also for the most part upstate businessmen looking for a sound investment. Raymond, as editor, did try to preserve the simplicities of an earlier time by giving himself only $50 a week as a starting salary (Greeley had given himself just $15) but he also held almost $20,000 worth of the firm's capital stock. Greeley had been thirty when he launched the *Tribune*, and Raymond was only thirty-two now; yet there was little in common between the boisterous enthusiasms and ramshackle look which Greeley still carried about with him and the air of solidity which Raymond was already cultivating, even down to carrying a gold-headed walking stick and raising sideburns.

If Augustus Maverick, a *Tribune* man who went over to Raymond and became his biographer, is to be believed, the New York *Times* was conceived on the Hudson River ice one winter day at Albany, when Raymond and George Jones were making their way across the still-unbridged stream to the railroad station on the eastern shore to catch a train to New York. The two men had first met years before on the *Tribune*—where all aspiring newspapermen seemed to meet—while Jones was doing a brief stint in Greeley's business office during Raymond's time as editorial lieutenant there. Later, in 1848, while Raymond was on the *Courier and Enquirer*, there had been some talk between them about taking over the Albany *Evening Journal* from Weed, who was thinking of selling. Nothing had come of that, but the banker and the reporter had gone on meeting every now and then—especially during Raymond's visits to Albany as a state assemblyman—to talk about starting a new Whig daily on their own in New York. Both felt that Horace Greeley was not the right man to speak for Whiggism there: he was obstreperous, he was radical, and there must be many readers of sound background and beliefs who by now were repelled by his *Tribune*. Raymond and Jones knew, though, that he would run them a fierce competition. So they hesitated, wondering whether in this game they could really win and make money.

"I hear the *Tribune* made a profit of $60,000 in the past year," said Jones suddenly to the muffled-up Raymond, as they crossed the ice that January, 1851.

The figure hit Raymond with a mighty impact. Right there, in mid-river, he decided that if such earnings were possible, they ought to go ahead at once and invade the *Tribune*'s territory. He pledged his own full participation on the spot, and urged Jones to go ahead and round up other investors.

Actually, the *Tribune* in 1850 had earned no more than $40,000. But no matter. Now the firm of Raymond, Jones & Co. was under way. Raymond moved secretly, hiring men away from other papers but ordering them to stay put at their current jobs without a word to anyone until the last moment. He staged an especially successful raid on the *Tribune*, rounding up several junior editors and a dozen printers, including two assistant foremen. When this crowd walked out of the *Tribune* in a body on the eve of the *Times*' appearance, Greeley blew up. Next, Greeley learned that Raymond and Jones were planning to upset his circulation network too by persuading the *Tribune*'s carriers to handle the *Times* as well. He blew up again. This warning went up on the *Tribune* bulletin board:

NOTICE TO THE CARRIERS

A new daily paper is to be issued in a few days, and any carrier of the *Tribune* who interests himself in said paper, in getting up routes, etc., prejudicial to the interests of the *Tribune*, will forfeit his right of property in the *Tribune* route. We give this notice now, that all who do so may know that they do it at the peril of losing their route on the *Tribune*.

Then the *Times* appeared, sober, well printed, edited with an accurate eye for news, and proclaiming itself as being safely "upon the side of Morality, of Industry, of Education and Religion." "There are very few things in the world which it is worth while to get angry about," added Raymond in his opening statement.

Not for Raymond, perhaps. But for Greeley there was at least one thing worth getting angry about, and that was "the little viper"—Raymond. The new arrival aroused him not so much because he was a competing newspaperman—Greeley felt sure he could handle that—as because he was a rival, rising political force. Raymond, enjoying practical politics no less than Greeley, had gotten himself elected to the state assembly and after only one term had been elevated to the speakership—a post which lent him power in the state and brought him close to Thurlow Weed. It was clear to Greeley that Raymond was not only out to force his way into the ruling Weed-Seward-Greeley combination, but to push Greeley out of it. That, Greeley felt, was the whole purpose of the *Times*. And why hadn't Weed, knowing of Raymond's plan all along, tried to dissuade the newcomer from it? That was the worst part: people were now saying that the *Times* had been started against the *Tribune* with Thurlow Weed's private blessing.

To be the newspaper member of the firm of Weed & Seward meant obtaining inside party news, political preferment, and official state advertising. On each count the *Tribune* was now threatened. Part of its statewide prestige came from its ability to print texts of speeches by Seward and other Whig chieftains in advance of any other paper; and speeches, in those days—no matter how long—were the very substance of the news. In March, 1852, Senator Seward was still notifying Greeley, in accordance with their standing arrangement, "I am to have the floor tomorrow at one o'clock. I send you my speech which I mean to deliver. You will please give it in your paper if it is worth the trouble, only be sure to give it to the *Times, Sun, Courier* and *Herald* if they want it, or such of them as do." This, of course, gave Greeley the privilege of carrying it first. But before many months Greeley found Seward welshing on this comfortable arrangement, and letting the New York *Times* man get his speeches first. Again, Greeley blew up. Seward answered coolly, "You *are* rather ugly tho," and remarked that all that had happened was that the *Times* man in Washington was quicker on his toes than the *Tribune*'s, and was coming around sooner to his office to get the text.

Here was Seward telling Greeley that his staff was sluggish. That was something Greeley would not stand for. He blasted back, declaring that the senator's favoritism toward Weed's paper tended to show that "the *Times* is your special organ and its filibustering editorials and general negation of principle [are] especially agreeable to you. . . . I do not dispute your right to *make* it your organ. . . . I only ask for such treatment as you would cheerfully accord to your bitterest enemy . . ."

Greeley had seen the truth, although his words distorted it: Seward, watching the emerging *Times*, had already decided that Raymond would be a more amenable and reliable partner of his own ambitions than the headstrong Greeley. But how did Thurlow Weed feel in Albany? Soon Greeley found out. The state legislature had just passed a law requiring that New York City banks insert each week in one city newspaper a paid announcement summarizing their week's transactions. The official empowered to select the lucky paper to carry this valuable advertising was the state banking superintendent, D. B. St. John, who happened to be a friend of Raymond and, for a while, an investor in the *Times*. In fact, it appeared that Speaker Raymond himself had engineered the law, knowing all along that the *Times* would get the business. When the *Times* did get it, rather than the bigger *Tribune*, Raymond thereby gained also prior access to city financial news. "I cannot bear everything," Greeley exploded to Weed, charging that Raymond had "fixed" the State Banking Commission. After the bill's passage,

Greeley said to Weed, "I wrote St. John about it. . . . I asked for no favor, no advantage to my own paper, but simply that whatever paper should be selected for the service should, as a matter of common justice, furnish slips [i.e., copies] of the returns to *all* the other papers. . . . Well: St. John hesitated and prevaricated and pretended to misunderstand . . . and I soon heard that he had reported that I had offered to do the Advertising for nothing in order to get it from the *Times*." To make matters worse, Greeley said, Raymond had offered to send him copies of the bank texts if the *Tribune* should prove itself "worthy" of the privilege. He enclosed Raymond's note with his own to Weed. "Just see the insolence with which the little viper talks to me of his 'benevolence,' 'favors,' etc., to those who prove worthy of them! . . . Ought I to bear this?"

But Weed did nothing to set matters right. And then, in 1854, came the final humiliation. It was the year of another New York gubernatorial election. "Mr. Greeley called on me at the Astor House," recorded Thurlow Weed, "and asked if I did not think that the time and circumstances were favorable to his nomination for Governor? I replied that I did think the time and circumstances favorable to his election, if nominated, but that my friends had lost the control of the state convention. This answer perplexed him . . ."

Weed, at the moment, was somewhat perplexed too. His Whig party in New York was in immediate danger of falling apart, as disgusted antislavery men continued their exodus and were replaced in its ranks by nativist, anti-immigrant or "Know-Nothing" bigots—who in turn repelled other men. Now, to add to Weed's troubles, Prohibitionist fanatics were making inroads on the party too, threatening to pull their followers out of it unless the Whigs declared themselves bone dry. This was clearly not the moment for the party to take on the additional hazard of running Greeley for governor. Patiently Weed explained that he had already picked a prominent Prohibitionist for that post.

"Is there any objection to my running for lieutenant-governor?" asked Greeley.

Patiently Weed explained to him that it wouldn't do to have Prohibitionists at both ends of the ticket. "After a little more conversation," Weed recorded, "Mr. Greeley became convinced that a nomination for lieutenant-governor was undesirable, and left me in good spirits." Upon whom would the choice fall then? Greeley could not imagine. His spirits fell, though, when he found that

Weed's choice for lieutenant governor was none other than Henry J. Raymond—a great fancier of wine. The worst of it was that Raymond was elected.

2

During their first year in business, Raymond and Jones spent all of $100,000 to build up *Times* operations and drive the *Tribune* to the wall. It was an unprecedented outlay, piling up a huge deficit; but their stockholders could afford it, and at the end of the year they had 25,000 circulation to show for it. The *Tribune*, however, had not been caught wholly by surprise. Instead of letting his own stockholders pocket their record 1850 profits, Greeley had insisted on plowing a great part of them back into the paper, improving the plant, adding staff, increasing the amount of telegraph news, and fighting Bennett's *Herald* for circulation. "We spend $500 more per week (I think) on our Daily than the *Herald* does," he had told Schuyler Colfax that December, "yet it sells the most. I don't see why—can you? Its editorials are very stupid and empty, while its correspondence certainly does not surpass ours."

Next year he pushed even harder. New writers were added; a new, bigger format was considered. Top salaries were kept down during the period of costly physical expansion: Greeley took only fifty dollars a week, while Dana got twenty-five and Bayard Taylor twenty. The last was a small sum indeed for the *Tribune*'s crack travel reporter, whose high, Byronic profile and richly flavored prose had become known across the land, especially after he had entertained the nation by telegraph with pioneer descriptions of the mining camps and gambling hells and bad men of gold-rush California. Dana, that year, was functioning at his very best in the limited compass which eight pages allowed him. Now he had fourteen staff reporters as well as ten "writing editors" feeding their work to him, along with almost forty regular outside correspondents or "stringers." He presided over the nightly fight for space, his eye always out for human news, balance, variety and impact. Greeley, of course, had to have all the room he wanted—or almost all. Then there was George Ripley, the literary editor, who on one occasion persuaded Dana to give him almost the entire front page for a review of a new volume of George Bancroft's *History of the United States*. The new city editor, F. J. Otterson ("the most industrious and efficient man for outdoor news we could have," Bayard Taylor said of him to Greeley), was on hand to try to get top play for local crime and political and shipping stories. The paper's new Washington correspondent, James S. Pike, was sending up daily interpretive copy that was attracting attention all through the North and rated as a "must" with Greeley. Dana himself, in making decisions, was "an uncommonly ready man," said Beman Brockway, who did time on the staff; he never showed "the least hesitation" but "acted intuitively and decided on the merits of an article after the first six lines."

Varied and brisk as the *Tribune* was, so much copy crowded it that it sometimes burst at the seams. Extra folded-in pages or supplements had to be added at great cost to carry the news which Greeley thought essential. Thus, one day late in 1850, when a flood of government reports had swamped the paper, Greeley had complained to Colfax, "These left us, on going to press at 5 a.m., with twenty columns still standing over. This morning we print another Supplement, though half our subscribers have not yet got the last; their papers tomorrow morning will contain *two* supplements, and still we shall have twelve columns or so left over . . . I don't know what to do. I must make a move in some direction soon. . . . I don't get in half the Editorials I would like to."

Yet, hoping to stand off both the *Times* and *Herald*, the paper crowded itself even more. As agricultural columnist it hired Solon Robinson, already famous among farm readers as a country editor, land reformer, town planner and practical farmer, whose homely articles demonstrating scientific techniques and the use of better tools now raised *Tribune* circulation in rural areas. Meanwhile Dana, on the hunt for obtaining better correspondence from Europe, had taken on as a twice-weekly contributor from London a caustic economist and socialist pamphleteer named Karl Marx.

Dana had met the author of the *Communist Manifesto* in Cologne in 1848 while covering that year's rash of European republican uprisings for the *Tribune*. The virulent young Dr. Marx, setting up his revolutionary *Neue Rheinische Zeitung* in defiance of the Prussian police, had at once attracted the admiration of the American ex-Brook Farmer, who himself at that moment was sending home to the *Tribune* such ardent declarations as "The Right to Labor is the Right to Live . . . Unless [society] assures to all the opportunity of living by their labor, it leaves thousands upon thousands . . . without any escape for their miseries other than the destruction of themselves or society." Another visitor to Cologne that year—Carl Schurz, soon to come to America and much later to work for the *Tribune*, too—had reacted differently to the bearded, savagely brilliant publicist: Marx's manners, Schurz remembered, had been "provoking and intolerable." But Dana was not then concerned about manners. Three years later, from a hovel in Soho, Marx began writing weekly letters to the *Tribune* on European politics, economics and wars; and the money he earned from this—ten dollars a week, and later only five dollars, when the *Tribune* cut down his space—was for a long time his only regular source of income. During this period he was also working on *Das Kapital*, and his well-to-do collaborator, Friedrich Engels, apart from helping him out financially also sometimes ghostwrote his *Tribune* pieces for him. Dana did not know about this. But Marx and Engels knew—at least, so Marx's biographer, Franz Mehring, charges—that Dana in turn lifted whole sections of articles sent in by the pair and ran them as *Tribune* editorials. "The lousiest petty-bourgeois cheating!" Engels called this.

Still the *Times* gained on the *Tribune*. Advertisers who had been estranged by Greeley's involvements with socialism and land reform moved over to the orthodox Raymond. As a dramatic gesture Greeley now enlarged the size of his sheet, knowing that the additional cost might run to $70,000 a year. "We *had* to enlarge," he told Colfax; "The *Times* was crowding us too hard. . . . It is conducted with the most policy and the least principle of any paper ever started. It is ever watching for the popular side of any question that turns up, and has made lots of friends by ultra abuse of Abolitionists, Women's Rights, Spirit Rappers, etc., which I cannot do. Besides, it has had the most room for reading matter the past winter, and so too, the crowd who like Literature and gossip . . ." And again, seven months later: "You are wrong about our Enlargement—it will keep us poor for a year or two, but make us rich in the long run. We now get in our Foreign Letters when they *belong* in, and can generally squeeze in an Editorial the day it ought to appear . . . There is no use in printing any newspaper that isn't a *real* one, and ours *is*. There are enough troubles and mortifications in an Editor's lot without having to get beaten on news every day in the week . . ."

"Now let anyone print as good a two-cent paper if he can," Greeley boasted after the expansion. His daily had touched 25,000 circulation and his weekly was running well above 60,000. "If I can

only keep down the fatal attempt to raise our price for one year or
more, all will go on swimmingly," he told his confidant, Colfax. But
Tom McElrath, his partner and business manager, was insisting on
three cents as a safeguard—and the difficulty was that McElrath
now held a greater financial interest in the paper than he. This had
happened as a result of Greeley's move, several years before, of converting the original Greeley-McElrath partnership into a profit-
sharing corporation in which Greeley had parted with half of his
interest in order to let employees in on stock participation, while
McElrath, on the other hand, had held on tight to most of his.
McElrath, with other stockholders behind him, forced the issue.
Greeley for the first time faced defeat at the hands of his own
Tribune family. But here, ironically, it was his enemy, Raymond,
who bailed him out. For Greeley had finally agreed to a price rise
to three cents only on condition that the *Times* and *Herald* would
raise theirs too. This Raymond refused to do. "One explanation of his
ability to refuse," writes Professor Jeter A. Isely, a careful student
of the record, "possibly lies in the fact that Weed was at this time
lending him money."

3

The year 1854 broke. It looked at its outset as if it would be
prosperous, expansive and contented. On every side one could see
signs of American enrichment. Two million bales of cotton had been
harvested in 1850, and at the present rate of growth, annual production might reach four million by 1860. Two thousand miles of new
railroad trackage had been laid in just one year. A dozen new banks
had opened their doors in 1851 in New York City alone. The political
storm over slavery expansion in 1850 had subsided; men hoped it
would not arise again.

New York City was growing so quickly that Broadway was now
four miles long, while Fifth Avenue was being built out into the
open country above 34th Street. The palatial St. Nicholas Hotel was
soon to open for business with plush-lined marble halls and seven
hundred beds. Downtown, at his American Museum, P. T. Barnum
had followed up his triumphal presentation of Jenny Lind by importing ten elephants from India, which he paraded up Broadway in his
"Great Asiatic Caravan and Menagerie." And across the river in
fast-growing Brooklyn one could see another new sight in the shape
of the blatant, garishly garbed Reverend Henry Ward Beecher,

recently arrived from Indiana, who was packing crowds into Plymouth Church with his lurid sermons on young men's temptations, on the dangers of the *National Police Gazette*, on "animal passions" in general, and on the "fornication and concubinage" of southern slaveholders in particular—for which he was paid the unprecedented salary of $10,000 a year.

The preacher's sister, Harriet, not long ago had aroused America with her searing indictment of the slavery system, *Uncle Tom's Cabin*. Her dramatic effects were phenomenal, but brother Henry Ward knew how to improve on them. One day, from his pulpit, he went through the motions of auctioning off a handsome slave girl before his congregation, thereby combining lusty excitement with spine-chilling oratory. His competitor across the way in Manhattan, the formerly crass and cynical P. T. Barnum, had taken to morals just as Beecher had taken to showmanship. After hearing several years' worth of temperance lessons propounded in the highly profitable "Moral Lecture Room" of his circus establishment, Barnum had finally foresworn liquor himself and gone downstairs into the cellar of his Bridgeport mansion to smash up his entire store of champagne. The press was duly informed. Morals and materialism seemed now, in fact, to have found the way of going hand in hand. Another Brooklynite—a bardic follower of Emerson and the socialist reformers, and at the moment at work on *Leaves of Grass*—stood up to exult, "I hail with joy the . . . intense, practical energy, the demand for facts, even the business materialism of the current age, our States." And Horace Greeley, a friend of Whitman as well as Beecher, expanded especially in the company of the reformed P. T. Barnum, whom he visited frequently in the Moorish palace which he had built for himself in Bridgeport, complete with minarets and a deer park, out of the fortune earned from exhibiting General Tom Thumb.

All would be well, it was thought—if only the dread issue of slavery extension would not rear up again. Perhaps it would not have to, thought a gaudy, splurging age. Meanwhile its favorite performers went through their accustomed acts. Weed and Seward, with Horace Greeley still outwardly attached to them, were one popular team. Beecher and Barnum and Greeley, in turn, were thought of as another. All three of the latter were New York's special celebrities. All were showmen; all, in their separate ways, were moralists; all three were Yankee countrymen who had come to town. The first had been a backwoods revivalist preacher; the second had begun as a traveling rural entertainer; the third had started life as an upcountry printer; all had made good in the city, but all had instinctively preserved on Broadway their rustic ways and country shrewdness—a winning fact in a sprawling metropolis that was all growth with few roots, and whose urban life was far from urbane. Beecher's antislavery sermons echoed Greeley's editorials. Greeley, in turn, heavily publicized Barnum's Jenny Lind. Barnum sang hymns with Greeley and dined with him around the corner from the *Tribune* office on vegetables and graham crackers.

The *Tribune*, in the fallow time verging upon 1854, had gone on crusading—it would not have been Greeley's *Tribune* if it had stopped—but the issues that occupied it had not aroused it to anything like the high-pitched excitement of earlier years. On one occasion, in mid-1851, Greeley had in fact touched a central nerve when he had his newspaper do a pioneer statistical survey of the effect of rising living costs on the condition of the New York working class. Retail prices of staple foods had risen by 50 per cent in just seven years, reported the *Tribune*; the minimum weekly budget of a family of five, as well as it could figure it, could now not be placed lower than $10.37 (including $3 for rent, 40 cents for fuel, 20 cents for bed clothes, and—as the family's only luxury—12 cents for newspapers). But then the *Tribune* went on to report that only a small percentage of skilled workers were earning anything like this minimum amount. In most trades the prevailing wage varied between four and six dollars a week, while cotton mills and garment shops were paying the semiskilled as little as two and three dollars. "I ask, have I made the workingman's budget too high?" wrote Greeley; "Where is the money to pay for amusements, for ice-creams . . . for trips on Sunday up and down the river in order to get some fresh air, to pay the doctor or the apothecary?"

But there he had let the matter drop. For the time being his fighting mood had left him. His mind drifted off to other reforms—such as "abolishing the Army, which is an absurd nuisance, unworthy of the Nineteenth Century, reducing the Navy to six frigates and a few sloops, and cutting down all [government] salaries to what the work is worth." His *Tribune* editorials called for cleaner streets, better conditions on immigrant ships, an end to child labor and prostitution, and for more New York parks: "Buildings multiply like rolling snowballs . . . A few years will block out

every chance for obtaining the least bit of salubrious verdure . . ."
The presidential campaign of 1852 had bored and repelled him.
General Winfield Scott, the Mexican War hero whom the Whigs had
picked as their candidate because he seemed nonpolitical and
"safe," struck him as "an aristocratic, arbitrary ass." Reluctantly he
had gone through the motions of supporting Scott, but at the same
time he had published an independent *Tribune* platform of his own
that called for measures Scott had no idea of carrying through—
above all, western homesteads and repeal of the fugitive slave
law. His dislike of the candidate had increased the coolness between
himself and the Weed-Seward organization. Raymond's *Times* and
half a dozen other Whig papers had branded him as disloyal.
Greeley had merely shrugged. When Scott lost the election, Greeley
had dismissed the Whig party as "annihilated." "As to Politics," he
wrote Colfax in the following year, "you are all blockheads, but how
can I help that?" He said he was going to abandon politics and take
up farming in Chappaqua, New York: "I mean to spend most of
my time there, reading and writing, leaving Dana to take care for
the paper." He did that—for a week or two.

4

On the fourth day of January, 1854, the squat, bouncing, bull-like
chairman of the Senate Committee on Territories, Stephen A.
Douglas (Democrat) of Illinois, reported to the floor the first draft
of a highly important bill. Senator Douglas, a vivid and precocious
man in every respect, possessed the glowering look of a younger
Daniel Webster along with the sleek method of a new Henry Clay:
he liked to thunder, but he preferred to compromise. His bill concerned the still-unsettled plains of faraway Kansas and Nebraska,
which were now to be organized into territories as the first step
toward statehood. Free-soil and slavery rivalries were immediately
involved. Under the first compromise which Henry Clay himself had wrought—the famed Missouri Compromise of 1820—
there should have been no dispute at all: all this region was to be
exempted from slavery forever. The second compromise, also engineered by Clay thirty years later, had left the matter in abeyance.
Now Douglas, a westerner, was coming forth with a new theorem
that reopened those compromises and suggested a further one—
and one that appeared to be slanted toward the South. For Douglas
was proposing in his bill that slavery was or was not to be admitted

into the Kansas-Nebraska territories, depending on how its settlers chose. With one stroke a new, vast area of the West was to be opened again to a naked struggle for power between North and South—the stake being possible supremacy in the nation.

Greeley had been writing placidly in the *Tribune* about farms. Privately he was busy worrying about Henry Raymond, about the need of a three-cent price for his paper, about the position of his stockholders, about the gradual dissolution of his friendships with Weed and Seward, and about where to go next politically. Now he read the first news of Douglas' bill. It mobilized him at once. Here, under the guise of an amiable new compromise, was a frontal challenge. All that had been done to stem the spread of slavery was threatened. The false four-year calm had been broken overnight. Did the slaveholders and their Douglases in the West want to stage another showdown? Very well! This was the *Tribune*'s meat. The paper's leading pen scratched far into the night. Next morning, when its subscribers turned to the editorial page, they read this:

. . . . Freedom's battle was fought and lost in 1850, and the cowards and traitors have all run to the winning side. But although antislavery is weak in political circles, it was never stronger with the masses of the people. The great heart of the country is sound. Thousands and millions of true men all over the North await but the occasion for a practical demonstration of their power, to show how firm is their attachment to the principles of freedom . . .

We expect to see Slavery go on pressing and pushing the advantages it derived from the adjustment of 1850, till a reaction is created that will again convulse the country. . . . Slavery is imperious, encroaching, truculent, belligerent. Its own conduct will thus ultimately generate an explosive force that must blow it to atoms . . .

We denounce every attempt to remove the salutary restriction upon the introduction of slavery into the Northwest . . . [as] a breach of solemn compact between the North and the South. Let the Country take notice that this convulsion is not commenced on the side of Freedom.

The *Tribune*'s opening shot in the new battle reverberated across the nation. Then Greeley laid down a rolling barrage: "If Slavery may encroach upon the domain of freemen, freemen may encroach upon the domain of Slavery," he threatened on 11 January; "if Slavery thinks this is a safe game to play at, let it be pursued as it has been begun." By the end of the month he was in full swing:

the backers of the Kansas-Nebraska bill were "traitorous scamps . . . deliberate violaters of solemn compacts . . . vagabond repudiators of obligations the most sacred," while Douglas himself was the "executioner" who had "mounted the scaffold and called down the infamy of murdering liberty upon his head." Douglas might go around piously peddling his doctrine of "popular sovereignty," but the whole thing was a fraud—a device to invite slaveholders to move in and take over:

The pretense of Douglas & Co. that not even Kansas is to be made a slave state by his bill is a gag of the first water. Ask any Missourian what he thinks about it. The Kansas Territory . . . is bounded in its entire length by Missouri, with a whole tier of slave counties leaning against it. Won't be a slave State! What liars there are in the world! Ask Mr. Atchison. He lives on the boundary line of Kansas and owns eighty or a hundred Negroes. How anxious he has been from the start to get the Missouri restriction repealed! He has watched Douglas' bill like a cat watching a mouse, and has had all the little details of it fixed exactly to suit him . . . Slavery won't go into Kansas! Gentlemen! Don't lie any more!

Almost every morning, now, Greeley led the paper with a fiery blast. New readers by thousands and ten thousands, dismayed and bewildered by the sudden turn of events, took to picking up the *Tribune* to see the fireworks—and then stayed with it as they found it formulating their own thoughts. With each week, its circulation and influence soared; print orders of its weekly edition alone now ran to eighty, ninety thousand copies. Senator Douglas, at first so confident that he could steer his bill handily through a Democratic Congress, grew alarmed at the sentiment Greeley was arousing against him right in his own Middle West. What was the *Tribune* becoming so wrought up about? he protested. All he wanted to do in his Nebraska bill was to help open the West to settlement and growth—the very thing Greeley himself had championed all along. But at this, Greeley hit back all the harder. Western growth, yes, he declaimed; but it must be a growth that led to free soil, free homesteads and free men. Better no expansion at all than one under the slavers' lash!

He threw his whole news staff into action as propagandists. *Tribune* editors and correspondents promoted and helped organize protest meetings against the Nebraska bill in a dozen northern cities. Then they reported them under the standing head, "THE VOICE

OF THE NORTH: No Extension of Slavery!" Whole antislavery speeches by men like Garrison and Theodore Parker went into their pages. Letters were produced from the deep South to show that many southerners, too, were repelled by slavery: "O! that the Northern people would awake to what is right," ran one message allegedly received from New Orleans; "do not let the friends of slavery out-general you in Washington." Advertisements of slave auctions were picked up and reprinted from southern newspapers as daily object lessons. One day the *Tribune* spotted in a Texas paper an announcement by a local slave catcher named Devreux, who was offering his bloodhound pack at $25 a day for "catching runaways." This Greeley reproduced on several days with all its detail, letting its repulsiveness sink in. "Northern Freemen!" he added below it; "shall the vast territory of the Northwest, once solemnly consecrated to FREEDOM FOREVER, be converted into a new range for the bloodhounds of future monsters like this John Devreux?"

"Abolitionism! . . . Niggerism!" roared Stephen A. Douglas in reply, as he pushed his bill onward toward passage. (The weekly *Tribune*, meanwhile, had climbed to well above 100,000 circulation, and the combined figure of the paper's daily, semiweekly, weekly and Pacific Coast editions was fast approaching 150,000.) Greeley lunged on in his crusade. This was campaigning as it suited him. It had high moral dedication—something that his first fighting campaign, back in *Log Cabin* days, had lacked. It had an immediate, political goal—a far change from old utopian days, when in the end he had found himself preaching into thin air. Now his tested skills and his pent-up fervor could work together as never before. Conservative Whigs and southern proslave Democrats alike denounced him; but the more they did so, the better he liked it. He struck back with slogans, sarcasm, exhibits, and rousing diatribes that were read aloud in country stores and around family tables from Maine to California. He ran up the Stars and Stripes over the *Tribune* building, vowing to keep the banner there unless the legislators of the North capitulated and let the Kansas bill go through. Then the bill did go through the Democratic House. Next morning Greeley pinned to his paper's masthead a black-bordered "Roll of Infamy," blazoning the names of the northern "traitors" who had voted for it.

He thought he could still help fight it down in the Senate; he kept his flag flying. Now he tried divisive tactics in the South itself: he leveled his attacks on the "little oligarchy of slaveholders" who ruled the great mass of slaveless southern whites and left them poor and neglected. He tore into the inequities of Virginia, "where the struggle of thirty years has been to enable a slaveholding minority east of the Alleghenies to rule a Free Labor majority west of those mountains." Next, South Carolina—"where two freemen in the slave-peopled rice swamps along the coast are constitutionally equal to five or six freemen in the Free Labor mountain districts." This, he snorted, was what Douglas' southern senatorial friends meant when they talked of "popular sovereignty." He charged the planter politicians with ruthless greed, with moral depravity, and with secret ambitions to extend their empire not only into the West but into Central America and Cuba as well. And did the slave lords threaten, in case their wild dreams were cut short, to secede from the Union? Very well! exclaimed the *Tribune*. Go ahead! Let them try it! Their threat was a bluff; their economy was neither strong nor balanced enough to stand alone; they needed for their own survival the commerce and credit of the North. "The South plainly cannot *afford* to dissolve the Union," Greeley concluded—with statistics. He exhorted slaveless white southerners to cut loose from the perverted thinking of their masters. And he called upon all northerners to stand firm.

But at this point the question arose, Stand firm with whom? Around what leaders? Under what party banner? The Whig party, that shrewd contrivance for rounding up great numbers with a minimum of ideas, was now trying to get along without any ideas at all. The Democratic party, on the other hand, had several sets of ideas—one for southern slaveholders, another for Ohio valley farmers, and still another for immigrant masses in eastern seaboard cities—but since the slaveholders were now in command of the party, it was only their ideas that finally counted. One could take one's choice between the two organizations—that is, if one saw any. But for those who could no longer stomach either, there was the question of where else to go. Greeley had called the Whig party "bankrupt," which indeed it was. The Democratic party at the moment was triumphant, yet many antislavery men who had been Democrats as long as they could remember were leaving it in disgust. Among these were figures like the veteran Jacksonian chieftain of the Midwest, the stormy Senator Thomas Hart Benton of Missouri. There was Benton's eastern comrade-in-arms of Jacksonian days, the sharp, wizened Francis Preston Blair—Washington

editor and Maryland country gentleman. There were Blair's
brilliant political sons, Frank, Jr., and Montgomery, and the rising
party moralist in Ohio, the magisterial Salmon P. Chase. All these
men were jumping Democratic traces to band together with northern
free-soil spokesmen wherever they could find them. And many of
these spokesmen, in turn, were functioning now as independents.
One of the most effective was Senator Charles Sumner of Massachusetts—learned, strident, relentless, a radical product of Harvard
education and Boston conscience. Spontaneous groups were forming
around them in North and West. But they still lacked national cohesion as well as newspaper support.

Greeley had been carefully watching each dissident move. Now
he thought he saw his chance. His ties to Weed and Seward were
strained to the breaking point; there was nothing further to hold
him back. On 20 May, at the height of the Senate fight over the
Nebraska bill, he threw out in the *Tribune* an ominous warning:

> From the moment that the Nebraska bill passes . . . the politics
> of the country will be placed upon a new footing. The interposing
> partition of compromise being removed, Slavery and Freedom, in
> other words, Despotism and Democracy, will stand face to face
> for a desperate and deadly struggle. . . . The passage of the bill
> can then be regarded in no other light than a declaration of war
> by the slaveholders against the North . . . Let those who have
> chosen to commence this war take the responsibility for it . . .

Moderate Whigs and appeasing politicians were generally affrighted
by such words as these. Meanwhile Douglas and his Democrats
drove their bill through the Senate and to enactment. The *Tribune*
hauled down its flag in shame. The North sat looking at the wreckage of its hopes. Then, on 16 June, in an editorial read in every
corner of the North and West, Greeley stood up to call for a new
national party organization to speak for all free-soil men:

> We should not care much whether those united were designated
> Whig, Free Soil Democrats or something else; though we think some
> simple name like *Republican* would more fitly designate those who
> had united to restore our Union to its true mission of champion and
> promulgator of Liberty rather than propagandist of slavery.

5

He was not the first to issue such a call. Eight years before, the
veteran insurgent, George Henry Evans, had predicted a time

when there would be in America "but two parties, the Great Republican Party of Progress and the Little Tory Party of Holdbacks." Greeley at that time had dreamed of the same thing, but had remained safely a Whig. Early in 1854 his old antirent friend and fellow land-reformer, Alvan E. Bovay—since resettled in Ripon, Wisconsin—had told him about his own efforts to organize a "Republican" party out West, and Greeley had dodged Bovay's requests for support by answering, "I am a beaten, broken-down, used-up politician, and have the soreness of many defeats in my bones. However, I am ready to follow any lead that promises to hasten the day of Northern emancipation. Your plan is all right if the people are ripe for it. . . . But remember that editors can only follow where the people's heart is already prepared to go with them."

Even after having made his manifesto, he found it hard to break entirely from the allegiances he had built up through two decades. Seward was running for relection that fall on the Whig ticket, and—whatever else Greeley might think of him—there was no doubt that the man's personal record against slavery extension was good. This did not seem to be the moment to scuttle Seward. Perhaps, thought Greeley, the senator could be weaned away from his boss in Albany and allied to the insurgent "anti-Nebraska" or "Republican" elements. The editor turned up at a summertime state convention of these party bolters, arriving at fashionable Saratoga with his hanging spectacles, flopping white hat, duster and worn carpetbag, and advised them to stick with Seward. He tried to discredit Weed for his deals with bigoted, nativist "Know-Nothings" for votes. ("You knew from the first," he said to Colfax, "that Nativism is our traditional, implacable enemy, and that it will cut Seward's throat the moment it can get hold of it.") He explained all this to Seward, hoping to cause a breach between him and Albany: "I have tried to talk to Weed, but with only partial success. Weed likes me, and always did—I don't think he ever had a dog about his house that he liked better—but he thinks I know nothing about politics . . ."

No use. Weed and Seward were inseparable. The pair stuck to their Whiggism and stayed aloof from the emerging Republicans. On the eve of the election Greeley lost patience and publicly attacked them for having blocked the formation of a new, winning combination in the state. The Whig party, the *Tribune* had already said, was "a thing of the past." Yet Seward won the election, with

Weed's well-oiled help. The *Tribune* called the victory hollow and shabby, and arraigned Seward as a lost leader who, instead of "taking the position which circumstances and his own antecedents seemed to require," had adhered to "the vacant shell of Whiggery [and] stood aside allowed the great movement of the Free States to go forward without a word of bold and hearty encouragement or sympathy." Greeley was sorry he had tried to help Seward at all. "This is just the most scoundrelly canvass I was ever engaged in," he blurted to the receptive Colfax; "I feel a crawling all over on account of it."

Now the new movement must go forward on its own—without Weed and Seward, the "holdbacks." Directly after the election, on Saturday night, Greeley sat down to write Seward a long, embittered, excited letter. "It seems to me a fitting time," he began, "to announce to you the dissolution of the political firm of Seward, Weed and Greeley, by the withdrawal of the junior partner . . ." He went on to retrace the whole history of their political relationship since 1838, recounting all the times when the senior partners had used the younger's skills and then deprived him of any share in the rewards of victory. He led up to the late campaign, and gave his own version of how Weed had done him out of a chance to run for governor or even lieutenant governor:

> I think I never hinted to any human being that I would have liked to be put forward for any place. . . . But this last spring, after the Nebraska question had created a new state of things at the North, one or two personal friends suggested my name as a candidate for Governor. . . . I said nothing, did nothing. A hundred people asked me who should be run for Governor . . . I never hinted at my own name. But by and by Weed came down and called me to him, to tell me why he could not support me for Governor. . . .
>
> I am sure Weed did not mean to humiliate me, but he did it. The upshot of his discourse (very cautiously stated) was this: If I were a candidate for Governor, I should beat not myself only, but you. . . . It was in vain that I urged that I had in no manner asked a nomination. At length, I was nettled by his language—well intended, but *very* cutting, as addressed by him to me—to say, in substance, "Well, then, make Patterson Governor, and try my name for Lieutenant. To lose this place is a matter of no importance, and we can see whether I am really so odious."
>
> I should have hated to serve as Lieutenant-Governor, but I should have gloried in running for the post. . . . It was thought best

to let the matter take another course. No other name could have been put upon the ticket so bitterly humbling to as that which was selected. The nomination was given to Raymond—the fight left to me . . .

And so on and on. Weed, he said, had virtually read him out of the Whig party. And what had been his crime? Simply "that of doing today what more politic persons will not be ready to do till tomorrow." Very well, he went on; from now on Greeley and the *Tribune* were going to be on their own. "I trust I shall never be found in opposition to you," he added to Seward. Then, as he closed, a spell of gloom came over him: "I have no wish but to glide out of the newspaper world as quietly and as speedily as possible, join my family in Europe, and, if possible, stay there quite a time—long enough to cool my fevered brain."

"My political life is ended," he blurted again several days later to the surprised Seward. Then he added, with a curious pang of memory, "I do not think I could have stood so long and so steadily before the cannon's mouth by your side as by Weed's, for Weed, with all his faults and all his unintended harshness toward me . . . is still in my judgment *the* man of New York."

"It is bad to see him so unhappy," said Seward to Weed of their former partner. The Senator went to see Greeley at the *Tribune* office, hoping to patch matters up. It would have been shrewder if Weed had gone instead. For Greeley could always understand and share Weed's frank pleasure in political juggling. What estranged him was Seward's persistent assertion of high moral aims while joining in that same juggling. (Some people had also been estranged by Greeley's own way of doing both at once.) Seward, the forceful free-soil leader, was now finding it safer to cling to the narrow ladder of equivocal Whiggism as the nearest way up to higher office. Greeley himself had known that same passion for advancement, and had given in to it. But he thought that now, fully enlisted in a moral cause, he had overcome it—or that, at least, he would put the cause first. Seward, he was equally sure, could never be expected to do that. So Greeley turned away from the amiable, long-beaked, senator from Auburn as if from his own past. He might never be able to banish his own weaknesses entirely. But he might someday be able to banish Seward, the ever-present, shifty reminder of them.

6

No, in spite of what he had told Seward, he was not going to "glide out of the arena." His political life was by no means "ended." Mary Greeley and the children, Ida and Raffael, had left for a lengthy stay in Europe in the fall; but, setting aside what he had written in an hour of excitement, Greeley did not join them there until the spring of 1855. In the meantime there was work to do. He pulled himself together. The loosely aligned, leaderless mass of free-soil, "anti-Nebraska," and "Republican" men who were emerging from both the old Whig and Democratic parties needed backing and a major editorial voice. They needed advice, political planning, and protection—or at least forewarning—against the footloose demagogues and opportunists who were trying to move into their midst. This was not going to be an easy job to do. If it failed, the new Republican party would simply be the old Whig party under another name—a political grab bag, with emphasis on getting your private reward first. Greeley thought he had learned his lesson. This was the moment, he thought, to do some teaching on his own.

The newly forming party was to be dedicated to resisting any further extension of the slavery system into America's western domain. So far, so good. But the men gravitating to it through their hatred of southern slavery were driven by a diversity of motives; and there its difficulties began. At one end stood humanitarians and reformers like Theodore Parker, anxious to eradicate slavery as an institution. At the other stood hard-headed manufacturers from cotton-spinning New England and the booming coal-and-iron country of Pennsylvania, whose main anger seemed to be leveled at the South's current power to dictate low tariffs. Greeley—in his own mind, at least—was able to rationalize these differences by arguing that low tariffs were almost as immoral as slavery: they held back the industrial development of the country. Furthermore, his old belief in all-American cooperation told him that enlightened, prospering businessmen would make natural allies of social reformers. Republicanism, indeed, would teach businessmen how to think and act socially. Those who could not be taught would remain benighted Whigs—or Democrats. Republicanism, therefore, must embrace all classes. It must draw the line only at ingrown, unsocial prejudices.

Here the second problem arose. The obscurantist Know-Nothings, mushrooming as the "American party" in a time of party disintegration and moral confusion, had managed to elect over one hundred members to the new Congress. Some of these were sincere antislavery men who had merely made use of the most convenient current label. Others were blatant flag wavers and racists of whom no good could be expected: "Their bases are bigotry and proscription," Greeley lectured Colfax (who was flirting with them himself): "their object, office." Some Republicans wanted to take in all the Know-Nothings in order to gain voting strength. Some purists, on the other hand, wanted to have nothing to do with any of them. Greeley, in the middle, set himself up as a moderator, trying to win "good" Know-Nothing elements away from the "bad," thereby strengthening the Republicans and withering the nativist mushroom. It was a difficult and complex maneuver. The test of a man's Republicanism, he argued, should simply be his devotion to the cause against slavery expansion. Any man who stood firm on that, said Greeley, was morally right or soon could be made so. It followed, then, that in order to round up "good" elements, Republicanism must become the moral instrument of a continuing warfare against the one, immediate evil.

Continuing warfare, in turn, meant that all men of good will were to go on disputing with the victorious South its self-assumed right to take over the West. The *Tribune* admitted frankly that this might lead to an ultimate clash of arms. Nevertheless, the issue had to be faced; and the basis for judging a Republican was whether or not he did face it. Bloody fights, in fact, had already broken out on the plains of Kansas, where free-soil settlers backed by the money and arms of northern abolitionists were contesting the ground against proslavery men hurried out from the South. The New York *Tribune* was not an abolitionist organ. Its editor went on voicing his personal horror of extremism and violence. Yet he was now appearing on platforms beside the most explosive of the antislavery radicals, the furious Wendell Phillips of Boston. And he proudly told the worried Thurlow Weed that he was serving on a citizens' committee to provide rifles for free-soil fighting men in Kansas.

He dramatized the fight on the Kansas plain with all the devices he knew—highly colored dispatches from the scene, agitational "letters" from outsiders that echoed the *Tribune*'s line, sober-sounding statistics, rousing editorials, calls for mass meetings, for money raising, for mass emigration to Kansas, and then more editorials, slogans and reports describing the same. The fire in the West spread. Its heat had just the effect which Greeley and men like him had planned: it began to fuse many diverse elements in the new retort called Republicanism.

Free-soilers like Charles Sumner gave strength to the amalgam. Among the Whigs who joined it was the Illinois ex-congressman, Abraham Lincoln, who had just stepped forth from obscurity with a ringing speech at Peoria: "Nearly eighty years ago we began by declaring that all men are created equal; but now from that beginning we have run down to the other declaration, that for some men to enslave others is a sacred right of self-government. These principles cannot stand together. They are as opposite as God and Mammon; and whoever holds to the one must despise the other." Many antislavery Democrats like the Blairs came over; William Cullen Bryant, long New York's leading Democratic editor, was now found joining forces with his old enemy, Greeley of the *Tribune*. Know-Nothings, catching the new drift, moved in, although Greeley kept attacking the nativist side of their program and Theodore Parker remarked, "There has a deal of bad stuff come over to the Republican Party." And in New York the stalwart Thurlow Weed now thought he had better get in too with his cohorts before they found themselves stranded outside.

A presidential campaign was to come up in 1856—the first major test of the new coalition's strength. But before that, work had to be done speeding the "fusion" process in state conventions and local elections. In late summer, 1855, Greeley threw himself into intense political operations. By careful prearrangement, Weed's New York Whigs met in convention at Syracuse at the very moment when the new Republicans were gathering in the same town a few blocks away. Greeley was on hand to serve as a bridge between the two parties, and helped draw up a platform that was accepted by both. Then, at a climactic moment, Weed's Whigs marched down the street to the neighboring hall filled with Republicans, and joined forces with them there amid songs and speeches.

The joint New York party platform called for an absolute halt to slavery extension; at the same time it attacked the bigotry of the Know-Nothing chieftains. Bennett of the *Herald* attacked it as a "niggerizing" program. His slaveowning friends in the South tried to make out that the Republicans were bent on freeing all Negroes and making them the political equals of whites. Greeley answered vigorously that this was not so—at any rate, not for the present. The process of emancipation must be gradual. The immediate issue was not abolition of slavery, but resistance to its further growth. He hoped in this way to attract to the party many men whose leanings were conservative, although their sentiments were moral. Thereby he made firebrands like Garrison, Wendell Phillips and Theodore Parker impatient at himself. But he persisted in his course. Voting size and strength, he thought, would tell.

He went down to Washington in December, 1855, to watch and report the new session of Congress, leaving Dana in charge of the paper. A crucial fight was in the making. Due to the number of assorted Republican, Know-Nothing and Whig members who had taken their seats, the Democrats had lost their controlling majority in the House, and no one could tell in advance which group or combination of groups would succeed in "organizing" the Congress—that is, electing its Speaker and dominating its committees. The fight for control took all of nine weeks, during which no other business could be transacted. Greeley, nominally a *Tribune* correspondent, was busy every day in the cloakrooms as a Republican manager, trying to pull together a "fusion" bloc that would win. Scribbled notes, written on *Tribune* notepaper, of which he kept large wads inside his hat or stuffed pockets, descended in peremptory gusts and showers on the men on the floor. Other notes followed up Greeley's nightly telegraphed stories to Dana, telling him how to play this or that item, whom to attack, and when to hold back. Greeley was promoting Nathaniel P. Banks, Jr., an antislavery or "good" Know-Nothing, as his compromise candidate for Speaker. Republicans who endorsed Banks won the *Tribune*'s praise. "Holdbacks" who did not incurred its savage displeasure.

"I hate this hole, but am glad to have come," Greeley scrawled to Dana; "It does me good to see those who hate the *Tribune* fear it yet more." He was being attacked heavily by administration men on the floor for his cloakroom activity. "Every traitor and self-seeker hates me with a demoniac hatred," he wrote again to Dana, exulting in the fight. But then, as the tense weeks wore on, there were moments when he and Dana got their editorial signals mixed, and irascible outbursts flew back from the editor on the firing line to his deputy in New York. "You have terribly weakened our power to hold these villains in check or punish their misdeeds," Greeley reprimanded Dana one night over a minor slip; "I wish you had made an editorial correction." Next day he was even more upset:

DANA: I shall have to quit here or die, unless you stop attacking people without consulting me . . . Now comes the awful attack on old Brenton, who has been voting steadily for Banks . . . Do send someone here and kill me if you cannot stop this, for I can bear it no longer . . .

Greeley's enemies on the floor were losing their patience too. One of them, Congressman A. J. Rust (Democrat) of Arkansas, decided that the insurgent editor needed physical chastising. Rust was "a stout, athletic man, whom I did not know," Greeley afterward remarked. One afternoon in late January, 1856, the man from Arkansas confronted Greeley as he was walking down Capitol Hill to his room at the National Hotel.

"Would you resent an insult?" said Rust.

"That depends on circumstances," squeaked Greeley, taking in the man through his spectacles.

According to Greeley's account, Rust at once let go with his fists, landing "a powerful blow, that I neither saw or anticipated," and which "temporarily stunned and staggered me." Greeley brought up against the wooden railing of the walk through the public grounds. "Dozens of all parties were around, but no one interposed; and Rust, whirling on his heel, proceeded on his way. Soon recovering my consciousness, I followed; and just before reaching my hotel, overtook Rust and his party, who were probably awaiting me. He turned, with three or four friends flanking him, and again assaulted me. . . . I repaired to my room in the hotel, which I was obliged to keep for some days thereafter."

Greeley did not give up, though, although badly shaken and warned by friends that other slaveholders' men were waiting to assault him. "Drunken Bowie of Maryland was threatening me in the bar-rooms last night, and several others," he scribbled to Dana; "But we are making up a fighting party of northern men that will ultimately do good. Several pistols will be bought today." Later that night, in another posthaste note, he was apprehensive:

"I am too sick to be out of bed, too crazy to sleep, and am surrounded by horrors." Yet, a week after, he was enthusiastically carrying on: "Although this is to me the most detestable spot on earth," he blurted to Dana, "I want to stay here through the Reeder fight, if you will let me. I will stand any chances to be horsewhipped and pistolled, if you will keep me clear of being knocked down by the *Tribune*. But bear gently on the Know-Nothings while I have to operate with them here. . . ."

The long battle paid off. Greeley's man, Nathaniel Banks, was elected Speaker, and the new coalition which he had helped fortify with Republican antislavery men took over control of the House. Greeley telegraphed the news to the *Tribune* in high excitement. This time there were no crossed signals between himself and Dana. Next morning the paper broke out its boldest type to proclaim the triumph of Freedom over Slavery.

X. SHAKER

1

Greeley stayed on happily in Washington after the Congressional victory and flooded Dana's columns with nightly copy. Sometimes, when other news pressed for space, Dana cut it. This in turn added to Greeley's outpouring of words—to Dana personally. "I wish you would humor my prejudices a little," he blurted in a scratchy protest in March, "and when I send two or more dispatches, not make them into one . . . I would stay here forever and work like a slave if I could get my letters printed as I send them, but the *Tribune* is doomed to be a second-rate paper, and I am tired."

The *Tribune* at this moment was not second-rate, nor was Greeley perceptibly tired. Both, on the contrary, were at the height of their powers. By the start of summer, 1856, the paper was boasting of a nationwide circulation, daily and weekly, of better than 220,000. "Greeley does the thinking for the whole West at $2 per year for his paper," wrote Ralph Waldo Emerson during a lecture tour. In Washington, meanwhile, Greeley was doing a great deal of the daily thinking for his new party, too. Commanding messages kept on issuing from under the worn white hat in the cloakroom. "Adjourn at the earliest moment, that's all I have to say," he instructed Congressman Schuyler Colfax; "if the Appropriation bills should fail, why should we cry? Be sure to have all sorts of amendments to amendments in readiness, to be offered when such inequities occur."

This was presidential-election year, and Greeley's eye was on big prospects and results. Yet there were *Tribune* balance sheets and stockholders to be considered. On this he exploded to Dana (who was also a stockholder), "The infernal picayune spirit in which [the *Tribune*] is published has broken my heart. . . . McElrath is an excellent businessman in a certain style, but, if he had his way, the

Tribune would have been just half-way between the *Commercial* and the *Mirror* in circulation, character and profits." He called for extra pages, extra supplements—no matter what the cost—to carry the inexhaustible news files he sent up: "I know you do your best, but you have never seconded me as you ought in defense of the great principle that a daily newspaper should print everything as fast as it is ready, though this should oblige it to issue two supplements a day. If you can't do this, better give up the ghost at once."

No, he was not tired at all. He was merely eruptive at times, and at others exhausted. As if he were not busy enough running the *Tribune* and trying to run the House Republicans on the side, he went on taking time for his annual lecture circuits, for magazine articles, for occasional pamphleteering (at the moment he was at work on a survey history of the slavery contest) and now, in addition, for an experiment in practical farming in Chappaqua, New York. He was going past forty-five. His trip to Europe in 1855 had not rested him. But then, no rest was to be expected from any Greeley expedition. The bigger the trip, the more copy it produced. His latest had at least delighted his readers.

He had gone to meet Mary and the children in London and then had moved over to Paris with them, hoping to relax for a month in a house he had rented there. He had hardly settled in, though, when four French officers of the law one day arrived at his door, armed with an order for his arrest as a debt defaulter, and hauled him off to the Clichy prison. Far from being loudly outraged, Greeley saw a farce in the proceedings—and the chance for some good *Tribune* copy. What had happened was that two years before, Greeley had let his friend P. T. Barnum inveigle him into serving as a director of a company organized to imitate the London Crystal Palace Exposition of 1851 with an equally grandiose show in New York. This New York fair, set up in an iron-and-glass hall especially built for it on Reservoir Square at Sixth Avenue between Fortieth and Forty-Second Streets, had turned out to be a fiasco ("It was located much too far uptown," Greeley wrote), and one of its angriest creditors had been a Paris sculptor named Lechesne, who had been left unpaid for some figures he had executed for it.

The arrival in Paris of Horace Greeley, a participating director of the unfortunate exposition, had given sculptor Lechesne his chance. Either *M. le directeur* would himself pay over the demanded $2,500 or go to jail. Greeley went to jail. His progress through Paris in a police wagon was in itself ludicrous enough: his four guards were apparently afraid that the whiskered, benign-looking American would try to escape. "Crossing the Avenue Champs Elysees, densely thronged at that hour, our carriage came into violent collision with another, and was disabled; when a very superfluous display of vigilance and pistols was made by my keepers, who could not be persuaded that I was intent on sticking to them like a brother." Then Greeley was escorted through "several gigantic iron doors, with gloomy crypts between them," and locked in a cell. There he lost little time in sitting down to write for his American audience a first-hand description of a Parisian hoosegow:

... By 10 o'clock, each of us lodgers had retired to our separate apartments (each eight feet by five) and an obliging functionary came around and locked out all rascally intruders. I don't think I ever before slept in a place so perfectly secure ... We uniformly keep good hours here in Clichy, which is a virtue that not many large hotels in Paris can boast of.

The bedroom appointments are not of a high order, as is reasonable, since we are only charged for them four sous (cents) per night—washing extra.... I have two chairs, two little tables (probably one of them extra, through some mistake), and a cupboard which may once have been clean. The pint wash-bowl, half-pint pitcher, &c., I have ordered, and am to pay extra for. I am a little ashamed to own that my repose has been indifferent; but then I never *do* sleep well in a strange place.

Further pieces in this vein followed, under his Clichy dateline, describing the obvious bewilderment of his bearded keepers at the strange Yankee in their midst, and then detailing his own efforts to convince the vast, creaking machinery of French justice that he really was not responsible for Lechesne's failure to get paid for his plaster nudes. While he lay in the lockup, leading Frenchmen called at his house. Hector Bossange, the publisher, arrived there one day. "Have you seen Mr. Greeley?" Mary Greeley asked him. "Seen him?" Bossange answered in astonishment; "I do not understand you; have I not called to see him?" "Then you have not heard that he is in prison?" "In prison?" Bossange exclaimed; "what can that mean?" "I do not well understand it myself," Mary replied; "but it has some connection with our New York Crystal Palace." "Oh, it is *money*, is it?" Bossange said with relief; "then we will soon have him out. I feared it was politics!"

It was all a mistake. Greeley was freed. Now he was anxious to get back home. He was distressed that even after her long vacation abroad, Mary Greeley was still in feeble health. Little Ida and Raffael, too, were "much sick." He left them in Lausanne, "tired of Europe," and Mary decided to spend the winter with the children in Dresden, Germany.

Coming home alone to New York, he settled into one corner of the three-story town house at 35 East Nineteenth Street which he had bought several years before. The family had rarely occupied it together. His own occupancy—according to a next-door neighbor, William Allen Butler—was somewhat picturesque. "He kept a goat in his backyard and appealed, when necessity required, to his neighbors to aid him in looking after his gas meter when the lights went out. As the houses in our row were identical in appearance, it was not strange that Mr. Greeley, with his mind on great affairs, should mistake one or the others for his own. Returning home one time carrying a box of tea, he made an ineffectual attempt to enter our house. My wife, hearing someone at the front door, opened it rather suddenly and the founder of the New York *Tribune* was precipitated, tea chest and all, into our front hall."

On Saturdays, when time allowed, he went out on the Harlem Railroad to his farm in Chappaqua—"Greeley's Bog," as some of his friends called it. He found it "cold and forlorn" this fall. "I should have been a farmer," he remarked later in his *Recollections*. But the seventy-five acres he had bought in hilly, wooded Chappaqua were a very poor place for a man to attempt to be one. The choice of land had not been his own. It was Mary who had specified that the tract must have on it: "1. A peerless spring of pure, soft, living water; 2. A cascade or brawling brook; 3. Woods largely composed of evergreens." He had found all these things for her. But for himself, he had wanted to find a farm.

"Living water" and "brawling brooks" were present on the place, but in such profusion that the flow regularly flooded the land's lower half and turned it into marsh and swamp. It had so many trees and thickets that Greeley had to spend most of his week-end working hours cutting out swamp alders, chokecherry, witch hazel and encroaching cedar. A steep slope gave it scenic attraction, but the slope pitched off to the north, thereby shutting out southern warmth in the cool, wet months. And on this hanging ground, at the point where dense woods made it especially damp and dark, stood the family cottage.

Nevertheless Greeley went to work to try to make the place a model farm. He designed a network of ditches to carry water off the bottom land. He burned off the rank bog grasses. He put in over $5,000 to build a spacious, three-floor, concrete barn. He built a catch basin at the upper end of his tract and drew water off from it to irrigate the scrubby little fields he had laid out on the slope. He dragged off stumps and boulders, plowed, drained, fertilized, and put his young fields under flax and corn. He hired a farmer, kept elaborate books, put in improved strains of beets and turnips, raised chickens—and wrote articles about what he was doing. Then he entered his produce at agricultural fairs. As set down in the record of the New York State Fair of late 1854, these were his first results:

Turnips. H. Greeley, Chappaqua, Westchester County.
Second prize—two dollars.

Twelve ears of white seed corn. H. Greeley.
Second prize—two dollars.

Each year there were troubles with the unlikely land. One spring flood swept away $3,000 worth of new dams, along with poultry, fences, walls and part of a wagon house. Next spring he was writing Schuyler Colfax, "See my barn as you go home this summer. It is very nearly drowned out now, and looked most drearily yesterday, but a week of sunshine will greatly improve it." And in May of the year after that he was saying to Emma Whiting that although most of his land was "hopelessly water-soaked and impracticable," the farm nevertheless was "beginning to look thrifty and lovely." It looked thrifty; yet it was not. His farm account book for fifteen months beginning in 1857 showed outlays for current expenses running to a total of $2,100—a sum easily twice as great as what his produce brought in at the market during that same time. He complained that Chappaqua was "devouring" his *Tribune* earnings. Yet he kept on with it. Years later he wrote a pamphlet called *What I Know About Farming.* By that time he had lost a small fortune at Chappaqua, but still he felt that he had proved himself as a countryman. His father Zac, he remembered, had not.

2

He missed Mary during the long fall and winter she spent in Switzerland and Germany. "My wife . . . was very thin when I left her and has been wasting ever since," he wrote apprehensively to Obediah Bowe after returning from Paris. And in the following spring, while Mary and the children were still abroad, he confided to Emma Whiting, "Mother is thin and feeble . . . and thinks she has but a short time to live . . ." When she returned to the farm in mid-1856 she appeared physically stronger; it was clear that her disturbance was mental. She spent days and even weeks in bed, and suddenly rose from it to launch into a distracted rush of household chores that only left her more exhausted and the home in worse turmoil than before. At night she desperately feared burglars. She kept asking for a pistol, and Greeley finally obliged her by sending to the Colt factory in Hartford for one—taking the opportunity to write the company that "though her pistol will never be loaded, I know that it will be flourished a great deal in the sight of all who come near the house." Even when so protected, she was "terribly frightened" one night when Greeley himself rapped on the door after midnight, returning from a lecture he had given at nearby Sing Sing on the river. "I think we are not so badly situated," he told Emma Whiting at that time, "If Mother could be made to think so." He could not comprehend the root of her trouble. "Six weeks ago, she had fully made up her mind to die of rather a quick consumption," he told Emma that September, "and came down [to New York] to have Dr. Curtis second the motion; but he was obstinately, perversely, concertedly, dogmatically hostile to it, and after determined struggle she was obliged to give it up."

He usually came out to the farm only on Saturday, to give one day of the week to his family at most. Some weeks he did not come at all. Emma Whiting, whom he had invited to come out one week end, waited all day Saturday with Mary for him and then learned that he would be out only on Sunday—bringing Lucy Stone with him. "Mrs. Greeley was in a peck of troubles," Emma remembered: "her washing and ironing all went wrong. She got greatly excited and I thought [my sister] and I had better make ourselves scarce though I wanted to stay a little over the week on purpose to see him." And Greeley's remoteness from his wife took him away from his children, too, whom he could not help comparing to his beloved Pickie—to their disadvantage: "Ida is reserved and shy . . . She has good qualities but they are latent . . . [She] is clever in her way, but never intimate with me . . . Raffy has more vivacity than Pickie, but less elevation. I can hardly guess what he will be good for, should he live."

Raffy did not live long. Although in December, 1856, Greeley was telling Colfax that "My boy and I monopolize the health and vivacity of the entire family," within a few months the boy was dead. This time, it was said, the cause was "malignant croup." Now, although Greeley granted that "Ida is a pretty good girl in her cold, still way," he burst out that "I miss my brave and beautiful, loving and joyous boys." Then spring came, and with it still another birth. It was a daughter, and they named her Gabrielle. "The little one is the paragon of good babies," he told Emma; "And though I love no more, I greatly admire her."

The mother, although wasted and feeble, recovered from childbirth with surprising rapidity, and in midsummer was busy running the "Bog" in a state of tempestuous confusion. On one August Saturday Greeley brought along his long-standing friend Beman Brockway—now a member of the *Tribune* staff—to stay the week end. Brockway set down this description of what he saw and heard:

"Arriving at the [Chappaqua] station, I was somewhat surprised to hear him say, 'I guess we had better register at the hotel; you may want to stay the night. . . .' We then proceeded to the Greeley mansion, a plain story-and-a-half or two-story wood dwelling, standing in a pretty dense forest . . . A little girl was standing on the piazza.

"' I am dreadful glad to see you, Ida,' said Mr. Greeley.

"The child made no response—did not smile—and seemed to regard with entire indifference her father . . .

"The piazza led into a sitting-room, in which were two domestics, one of them nursing an infant [i.e., Gabrielle] three months old. Mr. G. spoke caressingly to the infant in the nurse's arms and then disappeared . . . In a few moments he returned accompanied by Mrs. Greeley.

"'Mr. Brockway,' said Mr. Greeley, when I gave her my hand which she received solemnly, and, I believe, without speaking.

"Mrs. Greeley was a woman rather below the medium size, thin, with dark hair and eyes. She had thin lips, irregular and somewhat defective teeth. There was little expression in her face, but that little was rather against her. She spoke quickly—not peevishly, nor angrily, as a rule, but her words had a kind of crack like the report of a rifle . . .

"'Things have gone on very well on the farm, mother, since I went away,' said Mr. G., addressing his wife.

"'They haven't gone well in the house, Mr. Greeley. The roof has leaked; it has rained down all over the house . . . and everything is being ruined and spoiled.'

"These words and many others of the same purport came . . . like so many electric discharges. A lull ensued, when Mr. Greeley calmly and good-naturedly replied, 'No, mother, I don't think everything will be spoiled. I have tried to find Mr. C., whom you desire to fix the house, but he has gone west. When he returns I will see him at once. . . . We shall want supper, mother. I haven't had anything to eat since morning, and I am beginning to feel hungry . . .'

"By the time supper was over—if a meal composed of bread and and butter and milk, applesauce, custard and cocoa can be called a supper—it was nearly dark . . . Still, there was no light for at least fifteen minutes after supper was over. When a tallow candle was finally produced, Mr. Greeley complained that he could see nothing by it, and inquired of 'Mother' whether she could not furnish a better one.

"The reply was, that the light was 'good enough.'

"At length we drew back from the table, and uncovering the basket he had brought with him from the city . . . Mr. G. drew up at the side of his wife, with the view of disclosing to her its contents. He said he thought it contained articles that would please her. The first thing taken out was a calfskin nicely rolled up, which was handed to Mrs. Greeley.

"She looked at the roll, smelled of it, condemned it as good for nothing, unrolled it, smelled of it again, declared it 'horrid . . .' and then finally threw it under the table in evident disgust . . .

"Another package was taken from the basket, which appeared to be a pair of shoes which Mrs. Greeley had ordered made for herself in the city.

"'Have you paid for them?' was the first interrogatory.

"Being answered in the affirmative, 'What did you pay?' was the next inquiry.

"'I paid two dollars.'

"'Why did you pay for them? How did you know they would fit? . . . Why, these will never do. They won't fit at all.'

"'How do you know, Mother? You haven't tried them on. You had better try them on.'

"'I don't want to try them. Haven't I got eyes, and can't I tell whether a shoe will fit me? . . . You can carry them straight back.'

"This ended the argument touching the shoes, and a third package was taken from the basket.

"'Here is a pair of rubbers for Ida,' said Mr. G. . . .

"'What horrible things, Mr. Greeley!' said the sweet wife; 'why, they are too heavy. . . . Here you have gone and got a great, heavy pair of shoes, heavy enough for a man. . . .'

"'Can't we have a better light, mother? Let us have a better light, and I will read a little. Wouldn't you like that, mother?'

"'I don't want to hear any reading, and the light is good enough. . . .'

"At length I concluded to return to the hotel where lodging had been secured.

"'I guess you had better decide to remain all night, and we will look over the farm in more detail in the morning,' said Mr. G.

"'He can't stay here!' interposed Mrs. G. . . .

"Here I took my departure from the house, to the relief of my hostess, probably—most certainly to my own."

3

In the city, meanwhile—so Greeley told his "Friend Emma"— "I keep bachelor's quarters and get on very well with it." He relaxed with friends like Bayard Taylor, P. T. Barnum, and the aspiring poetic sisters, Alice and Phoebe Cary, whom he had persuaded to come east from Cincinnati. The talkative, vivacious Carys, busy writing sentimental verses for popular magazines, were a striking pair, eager to meet celebrities and entertain them in their 20th Street apartment, and with Greeley's help they soon became famous for their Sunday literary teas. He first met them in their Ohio cottage ("one of the greenest oases in my recollection," he called it) and now he was to be seen steering other famous editors and writers to their crowded little flat, where he sat beaming in the central armchair while he consumed glasses of milk sweetened with sugar. It was a happy place for him; it combined, he said, "one of the best private libraries with the sunniest drawing room (even by gaslight) to be found between King's Bridge and the Battery."

Another close friend now was Lucy Stone Blackwell—or rather, Lucy Stone, since her feminist precepts kept her from adopting her husband's name—who on occasion visited Greeley at Chappaqua with her sister while Mary Greeley was away. The formidable Elizabeth Cady Stanton, another reforming heroine, appealed to him and took to mothering him. "More than once, before a public appearance," the biographer Don C. Seitz recorded, "she adjusted his unruly necktie and forced his wandering trousers-leg down to his instep." Emma Whiting, patient, humble and understanding, remained his special confidante; over and over he confessed to her his marital unhappiness, along with Mary Greeley's "inability to accomplish anything." Later, in need of still further outlet, he entered into frequent correspondence with Mrs. Rebekah Whipple, a childhood friend from Westhaven. And at about the same time he met, at the Barnums', a highly perceptive and religious woman named Margaret Allen, of Jamestown, New York, to whom he soon began pouring out his heart.

"Of my few friends most are women," Greeley wrote Margaret Allen when confessing; "Some of them were schoolmates, and know all that may be truly said in my dispraise. I wish to hold you permanently enrolled among them, because ... I need you as the one woman who can understand and appreciate my reveries concerning the Unseen World." But many of the letters that he wrote her, far from being concerned with the Unseen World, dwelt on the details of his domestic life. Mary Greeley, moving into town for the winter, sometimes refused to open the Nineteenth Street house, preferring to take rooms in Everett House over on Union Square. So Greeley wrote Margaret Allen, "I stay with them [i.e., the family] very little. Every Saturday evening, when in the city, I dine with them at 5½, stop all night and to breakfast; take away any to church who will go with me, leave them at the door or in the car when the service is over and come down to work. I may not see them again till the next Saturday; for I have a den of my own at our house, where I sleep when I choose and write most of the day ..."

Greeley's friendships with women grew and multiplied, but they all stayed platonic. Of his rival across the way down on Newspaper Row, Henry J. Raymond, there were rumors of another sort. The prospering editor of the New York *Times*, who liked to drive up Fifth Avenue with his family in a spacious carriage, elegantly turned out and proud of his groomed side whiskers, was understood also to be carrying on an affair with an actress named Rose Eytinge. The very thought of anything like that remained inconceivable to Greeley. A few women may have tempted him— he kept in his files a letter from one Kate Warrenton of Monroetown, Bradford County, Pennsylvania, who wrote him to say that she was in the market for a husband ("I am only eighteen years of age and considered good-looking")—but his escape from Mary Greeley was never to take any form such as that. He found refuge in talk—and work. He went away on travels. He lectured. His family being in town, he spent Christmas, 1857, in Buffalo—on tour. His elder daughter, Ida, was then going on eight. "She is reserved and sullen," he remarked, "and has a habit of stuttering, which, being scolded for, is perpetually growing worse."

4

"I *have* to go off lecturing some in the winter," he had told Colfax in December, 1853; "it can't be helped." He meant by this that he needed the money. Three winters later it was still the same story: "I am so horrid poor that I am going off lecturing tomorrow and shall be away half this winter." He went West annually at the harshest time of the year. Simply to get from New York to Chicago was an adventure in itself, for one had to change trains five times on the way—at Albany, Buffalo, Erie, Cleveland and Toledo, with waits and river crossings in between. Then Greeley's route, in the winter of 1856-57, took him on out to Madison, Wisconsin, and Davenport, Iowa, in January sleet and snow, after which he made his way back southward by buggy across muddy, thawing Illinois prairies to meet a lecture engagement at Galesburg. The plains, he reported to the *Tribune* of this particular swing, were "covered in good part with water and not pretty wheeling." In a washout in Warren County his team overturned, ditching him and his blanketroll in a sea of mud; but he pushed on through pounding rain and reached the lecture platform sopping, but on time. He got off a story of his day's trip to the paper that same night, and next morning again pushed on. At Laporte, Indiana, "the weather was horrible and the mud unfathomable." He rode the cars to Terre Haute. To an Illinoisian who wanted him to stay over for still further lectures he objected, "I have a sick family with many weighty cares, and must not be long away." This time he had already stayed away for a month and a half.

He was truthful when he said that he needed the money. But this did not explain how he had ever gotten himself into such a scrape for cash. The *Tribune* Association in the 1850's had been distributing annual profits ranging between $25,000 and $50,000. Had he held on to his original half interest in the concern, he would have been earning, in addition to his salary, lecture fees, magazine payments, and pamphlet royalties, a yearly average of about $20,000. The answer was that he had parted with much of his stock, and then in addition had let the greater part of what he earned from the rest slip through his fingers, without knowing just how.

He had started out as the owner of fifty of the *Tribune*'s hundred capital shares. In 1848 he had sold a few to raise personal cash. When the *Tribune* Association was formed, he had turned over about twenty shares to employees like Dana, Bayard Taylor, George Snow, Thomas Rooker, and young Samuel Sinclair (then a bookkeeper), letting them pay for them out of dividends rather than with cash. By mid-1857 he was telling Colfax, "My stock is sold down to nineteen shares, and the money all spent, or lent, or given away—I couldn't well say where." And there was no stopping this process of financial erosion: by 1860 his interest was to be down to fifteen shares, and eight years after that it was to be found that he possessed only nine.

But what happened to all the money he did make? He invested. He speculated. He showered it variously on men and women with get-rich-quick schemes, supposedly revolutionary inventions, idealistic reform projects, and simple hard-luck stories. As his protégé and *Tribune* heir, Whitelaw Reid, put it, he "bought wild lands destined never to be anything else, copper mining shares, desiccated egg companies, patent looms, photolithograph companies . . ." He found himself involved in northern Michigan mining speculation; he took over "for a slow debt" some 2,400 acres of rough land in Pike County, Pennsylvania; he sank $2,500 into something called the "Fertilizer Company"—and then wrote its promoter in 1857, "I need money (as I always do) . . . You know I only went into the Fertilizer Company for your sake. I shall be obliged to you to get me so soon and so well out of it." He let himself be victimized by his one-time *New Yorker* partner, the slippery Jonas Winchester, who had gravitated from cheap book and juvenile magazine publishing into fly-by-night schemes to exploit Tennessee lead deposits. "I promise," Winchester wrote Greeley in 1856, asking for further backing, "to make you cease to regret or feel the ill effects of your kindnesses to me." Next year, Winchester was after him for another $1,000, writing, "But you look on me as an 'evil genius' for misfortune or 'ill luck,' which in each instance it is in my power to show was not through *my* fault, except in too *confiding* a temperament in re to associates." And so on. Winchester gulled him again.

In addition, Greeley years before had put sums approaching $10,000 into his favorite Fourierist colonies, of which he eventually got back only a fraction. But these outlays, in turn, were small when compared to his personal handouts and charities. He had begun helping out fellow printers with advances in his earliest time as a New York apprentice—and had rarely gotten the money back. Later, when money began flowing in, he had taken to pressing it on his friends. "If you should want another gob of cash any time along soon, I can fork it over," he had written his improvident crony, Obediah Bowe, in 1849; "don't be bashful, and don't scrimp yourself, for there's no use in it." And again to Bowe, in the following year: "Won't you have some money? I earn a good deal and two-thirds of it goes every way to all manner of loafers—why not you?"

The word of Greeley's free hand with money got around, until his *Tribune* office was besieged by applicants and mendicants of every sort. Charles T. Congdon, his urbane and witty editorial writer, watched them come and go: "There were people with machines of perpetual motion; with theories about Spiritualism . . . with new religions; with schemes for the abolition of every religion whatever; with mining stocks sure to pay a thousand percent; with stories of personal destitution harrowing to listen to, and yet only requiring the loan of a few shillings to enable the petitioner to go to his friends; widows whose sole claim upon him or upon anybody was that they were widows; orphans, sometimes suspiciously well grown, who had nothing to plead but their orphanage; Irishmen who had lost everything in an attempt to give the green island a better government . . ." Among Greeley's borrowers was the perennially impoverished Edgar Allan Poe—a fact that came to light when an autograph collector wrote in to ask Greeley whether he didn't have some letters from the poet which he would be willing to part with. Greeley answered:

DEAR SIR: I happen to have in my possession but one autograph of the late distinguished poet, Edgar Allan Poe. It consists of an I.O.U. with my name on the back of it. It cost me just $51.50, and you can have it for half price.

Few borrowers ever paid him back—and he seemed not to expect it. One man who did aroused his astonishment: "Once, when I was exceedingly poor and needy, in a season of commercial revulsion or 'panic,' I opened a letter from Utica and found therein five dollars, which the writer asked me to receive in satisfaction of a loan of that sum which I had made to him . . . Perplexed by so unusual a message, and especially by receiving it at such a time, when everyone was seeking to borrow,—no one condescending to pay,—I scanned the letter more closely, and at length achieved a solution of the problem. The writer was a patient in the State lunatic asylum."

He made over thousands of dollars to his father, Zac; hundreds to his brother, Barnes; occasional round sums to his niece, Margaret Bush; and fragmentary surviving records show that he handed out to a nephew, Horace Greeley, 2nd, $900 in a three-month period in one year. He lent $300 to Count Adam Gurowski, a stormy Polish republican exile who worked for the *Tribune* and later became a household friend of President Lincoln—and in return got numerous letters regretting the Count's inability to pay back. He staked the spacious, alcoholic, T. F. Meagher, publisher of the New York *Irish News*, to $500, who also sent regrets. He advanced $2,500 to Albert Brisbane and $5,000 to Dr. Edward Bayard, neither of which sums were made good during his lifetime. He hoped that the sick, unstable Cornelius J. Vanderbilt, whom he had helped out when the mighty Commodore had cut off the vagrant younger son, would pay him back. Instead, he got incoherent letters from "Corneel," asking for more money amid his dissipations and promising "before God" to go straight: "In the midst of my dissipation, Sir, I did deceive you . . . I shall in a few days after this Bankruptcy is settled, get all the notes together, compute carefully the interest and present you with legal notes therefor . . ."

Not even lengthy lecture tours could enable him to recoup against such continuing handouts as these—especially since Greeley seemed much more interested in the chance to travel and talk than he was in the money he got for it. Bayard Taylor, handsome and gifted with a splendid speaking voice, was going off on lecture circuits too to tell about his travels, and was bringing back over $5,000 per season. But Greeley, far from looking for high fees, often cut down what was offered or good-naturedly spoke for nothing. Even many years later, as a figure of national renown, he was still to be found notifying a lyceum manager, "You must only charge fifty cents for a ticket. . . . I do not lecture well enough to charge a higher price."

As a result he found himself in serious financial trouble early in 1857, and went to the length of asking Colfax whether there weren't some businessmen whom he knew for whom Greeley could do some paid lobbying on the side. He said he had to raise $5,000 quickly. "Don't consider me temptation-proof till I am tried," he wrote; "I shall very likely break down." This was at a time when Greeley was the head of the biggest and most prosperous newspaper in America. There is no record that he yielded to that "temptation." He simply sold more of his *Tribune* stock. He worked even harder at his writing and lecturing. Reporters would see him coming in to the *Tribune* office at eleven or twelve at night, weary after a lecture in Brooklyn or Jersey, and settling down for several hours' work supervising copy and answering his correspondence. He made each moment count. One evening at a public dinner, learning that several speakers were scheduled to precede him, he bolted his dessert and hurried down to the *Tribune* to write an editorial, finishing it in time to get back and be found sitting amiably in his chair when his turn came to speak.

Dana ran all the daily routine at the paper now, while Greeley from his cubicle showered him daily with little blue chits bearing staff orders, ukases and scribbled ideas for editorials. Greeley himself made it his business to keep on ferreting out new writers, to read most of the correspondence that came in and all the poetry, and to find new causes to pursue—sometimes a new one every week, Bayard Taylor complained. The young poet Edmund C. Stedman cornered Greeley one day while he was having his muddy Chappaqua boots shined downstairs and stated at length his qualifications for a job, finally asking if there was an opening. After a long while Greeley looked up from behind his newspaper and dismissed him with just one word: "None." But within a year Stedman was writing regularly for the paper and then joining the staff. Greeley even approved of this mildly alcoholic effort which the young man turned in:

The Ballad of Lager Beer

On winter evenings, cold and blowing,
   'Tis good to order 'Alf-and-alf;
To watch the firelit pewter glowing
   And laugh a hearty English laugh.

Here comes our drink, froth-crowned and sunlit,
   In goblets with high-curving arms,
Drawn from a newly opened runlet,
   As beer must be, to have its charms . . .

Charles Congdon, Greeley's favorite editorial writer, thought it "remarkable" that his chief should have passed this, especially since "he probably did not know the taste, if even the smell, of beer." Greeley's tastes were obviously broadening. He let all manner of men have their head in the *Tribune*. Next to such doggerel, he printed a learned essay by Henry James the elder on the philosophy of Auguste Comte. Edwin L. Godkin of the *Times* remarked of these years that "To get admission to the columns of the *Tribune* almost gave the young writer a patent of literary nobility."

Meanwhile articles on farming, travel, monetary policy and Christian morals poured from Greeley. In the space of one week the editorial subjects he touched on ranged all the way from the overall outlines of the Republican program to the foul conditions aboard immigrant ships and the need of an earlier milk train from Westchester County. Sardonic, flashing letters hurried from his desk to Washington party leaders. Thus Colfax was subjected to this typical bombardment:

Now as to that good-natured, good-for-nothing, indolent, useless piece of ornamental furniture, Jack Hale [Senator from New Hampshire]. He ought *not* to be reelected—you and I know it—but I presume he will be. . . . I know that Geo. G. Fogg or Amos Tuck would be worth any two of him—or we'll say, for instance, him, his wife and daughter all in a hump—to the Republican cause in Washington, but I expect to go on dissembling and choking down my convictions and let him be reelected. And then if he kicks our dish over by another of his blundering, thoughtless, brainless concessions, I only ask the privilege of saying, "I told you so."

And if there were any among the army of *Tribune* readers who thought that possibly, with advancing years, the editor's far-ranging enthusiasms would become toned down, Greeley emphatically disabused them:

> Doubtless many of our readers have heard of the *Isms of the Tribune*, its disorganizing doctrines, its numerous hobbies, and its frequent changes from one of these to another. And yet, as one mind has presided over its issues from the outset, so one golden thread of purpose may be traced through them all, under every variety of circumstance and condition. That purpose is the elevation of the masses through the diffusion and inculcation of intellectual freedom, industry, skill and virtue, and the consequent abolition or limitation of ignorance, slavery, idleness, pauperism and vice.

He exulted in this work—and he stayed away from home. One day a caller from Washington rang the Greeley doorbell on East Nineteenth Street, not sure whom he would find in, and found himself confronted by a lady "with sleeves tucked briskly under her arm, and her hair twisted to a knot on top of her head."

"Is Mr. Greeley in?" he asked.

"He is not."

"Do you know where he is?"

"I do not. He is not stopping here now."

"Can I see Mrs. Greeley?"

"You can; I am Mrs. Greeley."

"Do—was—is—does Mr. Greeley come home sometimes?"

"Occasionally. He has not come home this week."

"Do you know where he is stopping?"

"I do not. He stopped at the Everett House last week."

5

Horace Greeley was also busy trying to steer the new Republican party to national victory. Not that he had any personal political ambitions, he said. "Having defied all solicitations," he told Colfax in late 1856, he was "cured" of being an office seeker—so much so that now he had come to "despise the breed" and hoped earnestly that "there is not in store for me the ordeal of ever again being a candidate for any office."

The earthy Colfax did not believe this for a moment. Neither did Greeley—except perhaps at the moment he wrote it. Nevertheless, Greeley behaved politically for at least the next three years in a manner that showed independent dedication to a cause. His own line of thought was neither easy nor always consistent. In fact, it sometimes struck others as so tortuous that Theodore Parker exploded angrily one day to Abraham Lincoln's law partner, William H. Herndon, "Greeley is not fit for a leader. He is capricious, crotchety, full of whims, and wrong-headed as a pig." Yet he had a central, governing idea, and he meant to see it through.

At bottom the idea was that the institution of slavery was doomed anyway in a day of physical and social progress, and that the main object now must be to keep up the pressure against its beneficiaries by political firmness coupled with social generosity. By this he meant a program of isolating the slaveholder in American society and of holding out to all others—especially to all non-slaveholders in the South—the prospect of well-being and national harmony under the principles of free labor, free soil, and benevolent protection of industry. His premise—and he was not alone in stating it—was that the slavemasters were not only in a minority, undeserving of the enormous political power they held, but that they were also a minority that was feared and disliked inside the South itself. In this argument he was supported by the bristling tract of Hinton R. Helper, himself a southerner, who reported in his *Impending Crisis of the South* that slaveholders actually numbered only one twentieth of the total southern white population. It followed, then—at least as Greeley saw it—that slaveholding did not actually represent the South. Then why shouldn't Republicanism try to represent it? It was essential that the new party be something more than the voice of certain northern militants. It should move in on the South and appeal to the region's great mass of slaveless small farmers, artisans and workers. While doing this, it should also try to carry with it the great bulk of northern merchants and manufacturers who were seeking security and protection too. Meanwhile it should go on attracting free-soilers in the West and men of high moral principle everywhere. Could it do all these things at once? Greeley thought so. No one could talk down his inborn optimism.

He had not worked for nothing for so long with that master of political combination, Thurlow Weed. Even while attacking the boss for his "corruption" and "public plunder," Greeley had carried away some lessons from the bland master of the Albany school. He had learned that because of the unique size and diversity of America, a political party that wished to succeed here must be not so much the bearer of one political idea as a broker in several. The failure of the Whig party, he recognized, was that it had failed to recognize the force of any ideas at all. This had made it in the end a bad broker. Here was Weed's error; and here Greeley saw his own mission. He hoped that under the newly erected moral roof of Republicanism, the differing ideas of industrialists, free farmers and workers could safely be reconciled, since all were at one in their dislike of the cruelty and imperiousness of black slavery.

"Moral" was the key word here. He was anxious to exclude from this new fold such crass elements as the more cynical Know-Nothings. But otherwise he wanted to let the new net be cast wide, hoping that it would uplift those whom it gathered. He called for moderation, "harmony," and a willingness to compromise for the moment on every issue except the irreducible one of slavery extension. "This country ought to be and yet will be cleared of slavery," he wrote in 1856; "but the first practicable step is to stop the progress and extension of the evil. In this step, all true conservatives, all believers in the doctrines of our Revolutionary Fathers, ought to unite. When this has been successfully taken, other steps will naturally follow from which some conservatives will probably recoil."

Republicanism, in short, must not be a class party. Neither should it be a sectional party. Its program could be so devised, Greeley argued, as to prevent it from becoming either and thereby endangering the nation's fabric. What the urban worker needed above all in order to raise his status was to be enabled to move out of the overcrowded eastern cities and on to free western land; there he could write his own ticket, economically speaking, and become the creator of new American growth. What the eastern capitalist needed, in turn, was just such an expanding home market as that which this great movement to new homesteads would provide; and as the capitalist found his labor becoming more mobile and independent, a protective tariff would enable him to raise wages. Thirdly, what the South needed—so Greeley argued—was free land, industrialization and high wages too. It needed to balance its lopsided economy by throwing new, varied production into the scales against the monopoly of cotton. The South needed factories, general commerce and white immigration—all three of which were now being discouraged there. It could profit from the blessing of a tariff too—no matter what its cotton oligarchy said. In short, it stood in need of liberal Republicanism.

All told, Greeley's argument was reasonable and powerful. Economically, as far as the South was concerned, it made prophetic sense. There was only one immediate flaw in it: it failed to recognize the uniquely closed, collective mind that was already forming in the South and making the whole region impervious to argument or change.

Men like Garrison and Theodore Parker, convinced that the South's whole heart had hardened, called Greeley's call for harmony between sections "soft." A few others, like the surviving radical of antirent days, Tom Devyr, at the same time denounced his call for harmony between classes as downright fraudulent. Yet Greeley persisted in his belief in both. He staked his accumulated experience on the hope that Republicanism, rooted both in working-class aspirations and moral businessmen's drives, would provide the bridge between both. Here again, the operative word was "moral." And he knew that even though he counseled friendly understanding with the South, he was resolutely set against any further submission to an arrogant plantation minority. He had figures to prove how small this "minority" was.

He backed for President in 1856 the unlikely figure of John C. Frémont, the romantic, somewhat windy, and politically inexperienced western explorer. This was another attempt at "harmony," colored by Greeley's belief in the mighty leaven of the West. In part his desire to put Frémont in had also been based on an impulse to keep William H. Seward out. For Seward, jumping at the last moment from the sinking Whig ship onto the fast-sailing bark of Republicanism, had wanted at once to be made its captain. No, said Greeley, one of its builders and managers; you can just wait. ("Greeley has struck hands with enemies of mine and sacrificed me for the good of the cause," Seward bitterly wrote his wife after the Republican convention that year.)

Frémont—the "Pathfinder"—was not of great help as a candidate. Publicly Greeley proclaimed him as having "a singular force of character and a distinguished ability in every undertaking to which he has applied himself"; but privately he admitted to Colfax, "I grow more and more afraid about Frémont. I am afraid he lacks the stamina for President, or even for a Canvass. I am afraid several volumes might be filled with what he don't know about the first elements of politics. I am afraid we shall all be sorry if we get him elected. And I'm afraid we can't elect him." That was it, exactly: at this moment of party youth—and especially

with a third, Know-Nothing ticket in the field—there was no
chance of electing a Republican. Seward could at least be thankful that he had not been thrown away on a fruitless campaign.
The Democrats were returned to office under the musty, proslavery Buchanan. But a number of key northern states had gone
solidly for the new party. "We have made a great beginning,"
exclaimed Horace Greeley.

6

It was enough of a beginning to worry the ruling southern Democrats and put them on their mettle. Only two days after Buchanan's inauguration they hurled back their answer. Their captive
agency, the Supreme Court, had been reviewing the case of Dred
Scott, a Negro slave who had claimed his freedom because he
had been transported from a slave state into a free one. Now the
learned judges declared not only that Dred Scott must remain a
slave but that slavery must be allowed to follow wherever the
United States flag went. Any compromise on this matter, apparently, was unconstitutional. If there was to be national harmony,
such as Greeley had hoped for, it must follow the southern tune.
Many northern men now lost their patience. Greeley did not. He
had let go his explosive anger back in the Kansas-Nebraska heat of
a few years back, and now he steeled himself to control and
direct his fire. Of course, he said, the Dred Scott judgment was
"iniquitous"; "it brings us face to face with the great issue in the
right shape." But he kept on counseling that the best way to
face the southern rulers was not by a desperate sectional challenge at the present moment, but by the careful, considered
building of a mass organization all over the country that soon
would be strong enough to strangle them—peaceably. He talked
with Republicans, advising patience as well as firmness. He met
with northern and western Democrats, hoping to win them away
from their southern chieftains. He called particularly on Senator
Stephen A. Douglas, whom he had attacked so bitterly over the
Nebraska bill, trying to create a split between the "Little Giant"
of Illinois and the plantation fire-eaters who were running away
with the leadership of his party. He moved up and down Capitol
Hill "like a Methodist exhorter from the interior of Vermont," as
one eyewitness described him, buttonholing senators and congressmen. And always he went back to Douglas, the outstanding

Democrat on the Senate floor. There he confronted the swarthy, orotund westerner with the argument that his own call for "popular sovereignty" in the territories had now been repudiated by his betters: the Buchanan administration was insisting upon slavery everywhere in the West. Was this what Douglas had really had in mind? No, Douglas admitted frankly, it wasn't; he had hoped for a compromise. Well, Greeley showed, the slaveholders' crowd were shutting off all compromise. Where would Douglas go now? Greeley offered his recent enemy the support of the *Tribune* if he would make a clean break with the administration. Douglas listened carefully. He had already been thinking of doing such a thing. Meanwhile he was up for reelection in Illinois. His opponent was a shambling, homely, downstate Republican named Abraham Lincoln.

7

One reason why Douglas was popular in the West, even among many who disliked his equivocal stand on slavery, was that he was an ardent champion of "internal improvements" on the grandest scale—which now meant the building of a railroad line clear across the still-unsettled reaches of the continent to the Pacific. Greeley, too, had been fighting for the idea with all his fervor: such a railroad would open and revolutionize a vast, waiting domain. The *Tribune*'s editor had only one qualm about the project. Douglas and his fellow promoters, he knew, while talking of the vast national benefits of a Pacific railroad, had first made sure that they would reap a benefit for themselves out of it in the form of a boom in the western land and securities they had bought. "Can't we have a Pacific railroad bill that don't stink of land-jobbing?" Greeley sharply asked Colfax in Washington. "I have got to go for any Pacific bill, but I hate to go for one that smells of corruption."

He had to go for any Pacific bill because of what he himself had been telling America all along—"Go West":

> If any young man is about to commence in the world, with little in his circumstances to prepossess him in favor of one section above another, we say to him publicly and privately, Go to the West; there your capacities are sure to be appreciated and your industry and energy rewarded.

All America had heard this exhortation in one form or another. At some point it became reduced to a slogan: "Go West, young man, go West"! Everyone knew the words were Greeley's, although no one could remember just when he had first uttered them. Neither, for that matter, could Greeley. In thousands of minds the legend was formed of the white-whiskered editor peering over his specs one day at some young wanderer and directing him with upraised quill to go far out there and "open up the country." Many who had followed the advice claimed the honor of having been that particular young man. (Another legend, less pious, had it that Greeley uttered the famous words in the middle of Eureka Street in the bonanza mining town of Central City, Colorado, after he had been charged the round sum of five dollars for a haircut by the stylish barber of Gilpin County, who called himself "Count Murat.") The truth of the matter was that Greeley had either said it or written it in substance to hundreds of people who had come to him for advice. He voiced it in 1854, for instance, to a young New Englander named William H. Verity, who had written him in great trouble to say that he had fallen deeply in love but had just learned from his doctor that he was ill with tuberculosis (or rather, "consumption"). What should he do about the girl? Marry her and go West, answered Greeley—which Verity did, settling in Illinois and living there until 1930, when he died at ninety-seven.

Actually, Greeley had been busy promoting emigration to the West ever since *New Yorker* days in the 1830's. Now, in 1859, he decided it was time that he travel all the way out across the country and see the future for himself. He wanted to look over and report on possible western railroad routes, on the new mining towns, on life in the faraway oasis of Utah, on the growing wonders of California. He wanted to get away for a while from political turmoil. He may have thought that it would be a good thing to get his readers' minds off it too. The West was America's greatest adventure. It might also prove now to be its place of self-renewal and salvation.

He was in high spirits when he set out by rail in May, carrying his rumpled white duster, his old glazed traveling bag, his blanket roll and a faded blue umbrella. Once out on the familiar ground of Illinois, he began sending expansive "letters" back to the paper: "Doubtless the child is born who will see here a State of Ten Millions of People, One Million of them inhabiting her commercial emporium. . . ." Then he described reaching the western railhead at St. Joseph on the Missouri River, dropping down the swollen stream by barge to grubby Atchison, Kansas, and there beginning the long overland journey by stagecoach.

He was anxious to push on out beyond the fringe of settlement, but here, in fought-over Kansas, there were several speeches to be made. He lectured in Ossawatomie, which still bore the scars of the pitched battle John Brown and his men had put up there against proslavery "border ruffians." Then he headed over the rain-soaked, dark plains for Topeka, and found this particular frontier not to his liking. He had fought for a free Kansas; but here he saw land sharks and idlers "squatting on a quarter-section in a cabin which would make a fair hog-pen . . . living from hand to mouth . . . with hardly an acre of prairie broken (sometimes without a fence up) . . . waiting for someone to come along and buy their 'claim.'" Privately he wrote Dana: "Rain—mud most profound—flooded rivers and streams—glorious soil—worthless politicians—lazy people —such is Kansas in a nutshell. Goodnight."

But he felt cheered when he reached the lonely outposts of Fort Riley and Junction City in brightening spring weather, and predicted for Kansas a great future and possibly a gold-mining boom. He was keeping a meticulous record of the disappearance of amenities along the way, one by one:

May 12th, Chicago.—Chocolate and morning journals last seen on the hotel breakfast-table.

23rd, Leavenworth.—Room-bells and bath-tubs make their final appearance.

24th, Topeka.—Beef-steaks and wash-bowls (other than tin) last visible. Barber ditto.

25th, Manhattan [Kansas Territory].—Potatoes and eggs last recognized as blessings that "brighten as they take their flight." Chairs ditto.

27th, Junction City.—Last visitation of a boot-black, with dissolving views of a board bedroom. Beds bid us goodbye.

28th, Pipe Creek.—Benches for seats at meals disappeared, giving place to bags and boxes.

Now the overland express took him out upon the short-grass country, due west along the middle fork of the Kansas river, where the only living things he saw were frightened antelopes, pounding herds of buffaloes, and occasional coyotes ("a mean sort of stunted or foreshortened fox," he called them). At length, passing within sight of Pike's Peak, he reached the isolated mining town of Denver, then just six months old.

The Denver of 1859 consisted of about one hundred cottonwood log huts and a "hotel" called Denver House, which had no flooring, only canvas roofing, and just two rooms, one of which was a bar. There Greeley put up, together with his traveling companion, Albert D. Richardson of the Boston *Journal*—a crack reporter and experienced westerner whom Greeley was eyeing as a *Tribune* possibility. Both men had arrived there in a shaken condition, for their stagecoach had been attacked the day before on the plains and overturned by stampeding buffaloes, leaving them with severe cuts and bruises. They needed rest. But there was no chance of getting it on the board bedsteads which had been set up around the dormitory room, separated by only a low partition from the mobs of gold seekers who gambled and brawled at the bar all night. Greeley, nursing his wounds, watched these goings on with disapproval. He was annoyed especially at the "blacklegs" who, he said, "had rented opposite corners of the public room and were steadily swindling greenhorns at three-card monte; one stage driver, who was paid off with $207 at noon, having lost the last cent of it to one of these harpies by 2 p.m." Nor did he like the show of guns and the occasional bursts of shooting out front. "I soon tired," he summed up "of hotel life in Denver."

But before his injuries had mended enough to enable him to move on, there came across his path at Denver House a stocky young man with a drooping mustache and a pronounced German accent who introduced himself as Henry Villard, correspondent of the Cincinnati *Commercial*. Several years ago, when freshly arrived from Germany, Villard had tried to get Dana to give him a job on the *Tribune*—without success. Villard's meeting with Greeley in Denver was destined one day to change all that. Now the young reporter was out here as one of the first to cover the gold strikes that were making Colorado boom overnight. He had just been up looking at the new Gregory diggings in the mountains above Denver, and he wanted Greeley to come along and see them for himself.

First, though, Greeley had to get some sleep. Villard watched the editor operate on the raucous customers of Denver House:

His benign countenance, indeed, usually wore an expression typical of resignation and forbearance. But, what with the pain of his wound and the endless racket in the place . . . those Christian virtues gradually lost their control over him. . . . His wrath culminated on the third night of his tortures. I was fortunate enough to be with him, and became an eye-and-ear witness of what happened. About ten o'clock he got up, and insisted upon limping to the bar-room. His appearance, though his presence in the building was generally known, created surprise and instant silence. He begged for a chair, and, "Friends," said he, "I have been in pain and without sleep for almost a week, and I am well-nigh worn out. Now I am a guest at this hotel, I pay a high price for my board and lodging, and I am entitled to rest during the night. But how can I get it with all this noise going on in this place?" Then he addressed one of the most pathetic appeals I ever heard to those around him to abandon their vicious ways and become sober and industrious. He spoke for nearly an hour, and was listened to with rapt interest and the most perfect respect. He succeeded, too, in his object. The gambling stopped, and the bar was closed at eleven o'clock as long as he remained.

Then, when he felt cured, he set off with Villard and Richardson on an overnight expedition up mountainous Clear Creek to the month-old Gregory mine at what was to become Central City. He had not ridden a mule in twenty-five years, he said. Yet he hoisted himself on one and stumbled along behind Villard up the rocky chasm. High up, they had to cross the swollen creek. "Greeley was a sight to behold," said Villard. "Alarmed by the sudden immersion of his mule, he had first raised his legs in order to avoid getting wet. This movement made him lose his balance, and, to steady himself, he threw his arms around the animal's neck. The mule did not like the embrace, and commenced struggling against it and taking his rider down-stream. I took in the situation on reaching the other side, galloped down the creek, and, reentering it, managed to seize Greeley's bridle and pull him along the bank. The rider's face bore an indescribable expression of fear mingled with mirth at himself. As he came up the bank, dripping all over, a number of gold-seekers who had watched us gave him three rousing cheers . . ."

Then Greeley saw the glittering veins of gold-bearing quartz and the rich powder that men were panning in the stream. At once he wrote the *Tribune* about it. With Villard and Richardson he also sat down to draw up a joint public statement describing the new gold country in such exuberant terms that Bennett of the *Herald,* back home, snarled that he had been taken in by swindlers. Then he pushed on, first northward to remote Fort Laramie in Wyoming, then across the main chain of the Rockies at South Pass, and so on across hundreds of miles of empty alkali desert to the Mormon oasis at Salt Lake.

Here he enthused again. Descriptions of fertile fields, irrigation, blossoming fruit trees and joint, dedicated effort went off by the next stage to the East. In Brigham Young and his flock Greeley saw apostles of his own ideal of cooperation and frugality. He disapproved of their polygamy; but so, he reported after several interviews, did their women.

Onward, then, along the Pony Express route across parched, western Utah. At Camp Floyd, the loneliest spot of all, he spent an evening with the post commander, Colonel Albert Sidney Johnston—"a grave, deep, able man, with a head scarcely inferior to Daniel Webster's"—who before long would be heard from in the role of a leading Confederate general. Then into central Nevada: across the dry basin lands to the headwaters of the Humboldt and the Carson River valley, where at this moment the rush to the newfound Comstock Lode was just beginning. Five days and four nights out of Utah, the stagecoach party stopped to eat and sleep at rudimentary Genoa—"for Virginia City was then nothing," Greeley recalled—and then made the climb into the Sierras.

At last, in early August, Greeley reached the Coast Range valleys. Great receptions awaited him in Sacramento and San Francisco. He came as a prophet and celebrity, arriving out of the mountains sun-bleached and freckled, with a hat that had now become dun-colored and an umbrella that had lost all its blue. Somebody had clipped the buttons off his duster as a souvenir. People along the way in California picked up his words. He lectured. He enthused. He cruised up and down the state, examining its soils, minerals, timber stands, clear water, people, burgeoning youth, and politics, and found them all good. He rushed the story home to New York by pony express and telegraph.

He admitted that he deplored the "chilly August fogs and winds" of San Francisco, but otherwise he loved the city and predicted a population of one millon for it. He rose into apostrophes:

May Intelligence and Virtue keep even step with her material progress! May the great-grandchildren of her adventurous pioneers rejoice in the knowledge that her stormy, irregular youth has given place to a sober, respected, beneficent maturity! May her influence on the side of Freedom, Knowledge, Righteousness, be evermore greatly felt and greatly blest throughout the awaking, wondering, plastic Western world!

The White Hat went everywhere and saw everything. One day he had an appointment to speak in Placerville. The stagecoach driver who took him there told a story of the trip that became famous. Other drivers retold it. One of their most frequent passengers, Mark Twain, heard it in this form:

I can tell you a most laughable thing indeed, if you would like to listen to it. Horace Greeley went over this road once. When he was leaving Carson City he told the driver, Hank Monk, that he had an engagement to lecture at Placerville and was very anxious to go through quick. Hank Monk cracked his whip and started off at an awful pace. The coach bounced up and down in such a terrific way that it jolted the buttons all off Horace's coat, and finally shot his head clean through the roof of the stage, and then he yelled at Hank Monk and begged him to go easier—said he warn't in as much of a hurry as he was awhile ago. But Hank Monk said, "Keep your seat, Horace, and I'll get you there on time"—and you bet you he did, too, what was left of him!

It was not a very good story, thought Mark Twain, but stage drivers, conductors, chance passengers and even Chinamen and vagrant Indians repeated it wherever he went. In fact, he wrote in *Roughing It*, "Within a period of six years I crossed and recrossed the Sierras between Nevada and California thirteen times by stage, and listened to that deathless incident four hundred and eighty-one or eighty-two times."

XI. PRESIDENT MAKER

1

The wide-eyed, beaming Greeley who made his appearance on the West Coast in the summer of 1859 was a disarming personality, but also a somewhat deceptive one. Wherever he went, he bore with him an air of benevolence and simplicity. Yet for the past twelve months he had also been engaged on a political maneuver of extraordinary sophistication. Some men who knew what he was up to thought him devious. Others called him plain dishonest. Two of those whose political fortunes became most involved with his operations—Stephen A. Douglas and Abraham Lincoln, both of Illinois—were not always sure that they understood the editor's motives at all.

Actually, his purpose was plain. It was to prepare the way for a Republican sweep in the national elections of 1860. And there was nothing obscure in his general thinking about the problem. He reasoned that, first, the present popular base of the Republican party was too narrow; therefore it must be broadened. Secondly, the base of the opposing, Democratic party was stretched so wide between divergent elements as to show signs of strain in the middle; therefore there was a chance of cracking it in two. The strategy Greeley proposed was simply, Attach to yourself the maximum number of allies; then divide and conquer.

What was complex was the tactics he applied to this end. He was functioning now as an independent, serving no party chieftain or central committee, and recognized as a political power in his own right. So it did not matter to him whether he injured this or that entrenched Republican leader or ruling faction in demanding that the party's base be broadened. In fact, he took special pleasure in doing so—in shaking up the party organization and sidetracking those who thought they had the tightest hold on it. And on the other hand, he saw no harm whatever in dealing privately with certain Democrats, in the hope of dividing their own party. What upset many leading Republicans most of all, though, was the fact that he dealt especially with the opponent whose attraction they feared most of all—Senator Stephen A. Douglas.

Douglas had broken publicly with the dominant southern wing of his party over the issue which his own famous bill had raised—"popular sovereignty" in Kansas. The growing antislavery sentiment among his Midwest constituents had disturbed him, after he had let himself be identified with letting slavery loose in Kansas. Then, in the turmoil between free-soil and proslave factions in the territory, a rump convention of southern men had met at Lecompton to write an extreme proslave constitution for the forthcoming state, and it was this document which the Buchanan administration had wished to accept as valid. But Douglas, bridling, had demanded that the paper be resubmitted to the entire people of Kansas. There the free-soil majority had at once rejected it. Afterward, Horace Greeley had chuckled to Colfax, "Douglas has broken the back of the Democratic Party. It will hold Douglas responsible for the loss of Kansas, and will never forgive him—never!"

Ever since this breach had opened, Greeley's plan had been to exploit and widen it. His object was thereby to sunder and collapse the Democratic party in crucial 1860. For this purpose he had to encourage Douglas, the leading Democrat of the West, and do everything he could to advance the "Little Giant" against the ruling southerners who were now out for his scalp. Greeley knew that by the very act of lending Douglas the *Tribune*'s support, he would divide Democrats against themselves: "Everything I have done to favor Douglas since 1857," he told Colfax, "is treasured up [in the South] and used to diffuse and deepen the impression that he is a disguised Abolitionist and virtual ally of the Black Republicans." Privately Greeley had no illusions about the massive, growling "Little Giant," with his bulldog look, his sardonic wit, his rumbling oratory, his whisky and cigars. He called him "a low and dangerous demagogue," and felt therefore that it was fair game to bestow the political kiss of death upon him. But in public Greeley's dealings with Douglas looked more like an overt flirtation. To some Republican chieftains it seemed shameless and indecent. Could it be that Horace had been taken in by the man's belated halfway conversion, and that he was possibly thinking of promoting Douglas, the Democrat, for President?

For a while it almost looked as if he was. In early 1858 he had launched his pro-Douglas operation by trying to make sure that Douglas would be reelected as Senator from pivotal Illinois—a post from which he might move on to greater things. The southern Democrats, meanwhile, were all down on Douglas. "I know how to humor the Douglas rebellion without weakening his Democratic standing," Greeley had told Colfax, who fell in with the scheme. "You must form a party of young men to call on Douglas every week or so. Bring in some Democrats if possible . . . The danger now is that Douglas may feel isolated." Then Greeley had turned to the Illinois Republicans and advised them not to put up anyone at all against Douglas. He gave them his long-range reason why. But the Illinois party leaders had already picked their man—the shambling, storytelling, rustic Springfield lawyer, Abraham Lincoln. Keep your man Lincoln on the shelf, the New York *Tribune* went on arguing— and the *Tribune* had many thousands of subscribers up and down Illinois. Lincoln's downstate backers became aroused, as did rising men like Joseph Medill of Chicago; all of them resented this easterner's interference in their own state politics. After all, said Medill, he himself was part owner of a *Tribune*, too—even if it was only Chicago's. Lincoln's law partner, Bill Herndon—a frowsy, long-gaited man, who carried the air of a country revivalist about with him, and often a load of liquor—had called on Greeley to ask him whether he was set on pursuing his Douglas strategy at Lincoln's expense. "Douglas is a brave man" was the laconic answer; "forget the past and sustain the righteous." Of course there would be strong objections to this among the Illinois party faithful, Herndon made clear. "The Republican standard is too high," snorted Greeley; "we want something practical."

Herndon went home to report this. From that moment mutual suspicion and misunderstanding began between Lincoln's camp and Greeley. Greeley declared later that at their meeting in New York, Herndon had "perfectly agreed" with his own argument for letting Douglas win, but that, on arriving back in Springfield, Herndon had "found his partner nominated *against* Douglas and immediately commenced writing me to turn about as he had done." This statement was untrue. Herndon had made no turnabout at all; drunk or sober, he had been advancing Lincoln's cause all along.

The letters with which Herndon now bombarded Greeley had a force that could not be overlooked. On 8 April he opened up:

> The Republicans at first justified you *in full*, as to your compliments of Douglas; they thought that this was policy, and I suppose it was; but they now *think* they see a disposition up on your part ... to *sell us out* in Illinois without our Consent to accomplish some *national* political purpose. ... To accomplish this ... purpose, *it is said* that Mr. Douglas must be Elevated over the heads of long and well-tried Republicans—men who have toiled and battled for us a quarter of a century; and *who have never flinched.*
>
> This is wrong, if it is so. The politicians of New York may chaffer and banter as to their own local offices and *local* men ... but we in Illinois had rather do our own trading "in our own way." We want the man *that we want*; and it is not for New York—Seward—Massachusetts—Banks or any other State or man to say when—what or who we *shall* have. We want to be our own masters; and if any *politician* wants our respect, confidence or support now or heareafter, let him stand aloof and let us alone. ...

The Illinois Republicans were set on running Lincoln, no matter what the New York *Tribune* might say. Would Greeley therefore please suspend at once his "Eulogiums on Douglas"? ("Do you know Douglas?" ran another Herndon exhortation; "did Douglas ever give an inch in his whole political life? He is the most impervious and selfish man in America. He is the greatest liar in the world ...") "Greeley is not doing me right," Lincoln himself complained. At the start of June, the Republican candidate was bitter: "I have believed—I do believe now—that Greeley ... would be rather pleased to see Douglas reelected over me."

Greeley's embarrassment at this point was great. He had not counted on the Illinois leaders' determined enthusiasm for Lincoln. It was becoming more and more difficult each week to stay on Douglas' side in the face of this. The *Tribune* sought refuge in a safe middle ground: "We *know* that Mr. Lincoln will prove an excellent Senator if elected; we *believe* Mr. Douglas cannot henceforth be otherwise." Soon Herndon grew hopeful that the *Tribune* would come over all the way, and told Lincoln, "Horace is with us and soon will be *heart* and *hand.*" But Greeley was still grumbling at what seemed to him the clumsy undermining of his grand strategy by self-centered Illinoisans. To Joseph Medill he addressed this final shot:

You have repelled Douglas, who might have been conciliated and attached to our side . . . You have thrown a load upon us that may probably break us down. . . . What I have said in the *Tribune* since the fight was resolved on has been in good faith, intended to help you through . . . If Lincoln dare not stand on broad Republican ground, he cannot stand at all. That, however, is *his* business . . . I shall stand on the broad anti-slavery ground which I have occupied for years—I cannot change it to help you fight; I should only damage you if I did. You have got your elephant—you would have him— now shoulder him! He is not very heavy after all. . . .

Medill, in Chicago, forwarded this letter to Lincoln, asking for its return. Lincoln found it so interesting that he made a copy of it in his own hand. He did this although he was at that moment a very busy man, traveling up and down the state to face Douglas and debate with him before tens of thousands who came to listen.

2

The *Tribune* had its reporter on hand to cover the Lincoln-Douglas encounters on sun-baked courthouse squares amid a circle of farmers' buggies, galluses, and stovepipe hats. "Mr. Lincoln's style is colloquial, affable," the reporter wrote; "he states the case at issue with so much easy good humor and fairness that his opponents are almost persuaded he is not an opponent at all . . . If Douglas were equally careful to take his positions rightly and espouse only a good cause, he would be a stronger man."

Even so, Greeley could not bring himself to come out wholeheartedly for Lincoln. Toward the end of the campaign, Herndon burst out to his friend, Theodore Parker, that Greeley was "lowering the Republican flag." In November, Douglas was elected. On lecture tour through Illinois that winter Greeley visited the county seat at Bloomington at a time when Lincoln was there. They met in passing. "I understood him to say he would call on me at my hotel," Greeley remarked later, "but he didn't."

It might have been an interesting interview, if Lincoln had been able to swallow the treatment he had received at Greeley's hands and come on downtown. There were many things to talk about. Greeley could have presented his argument that Lincoln's own defeat at the hand of Douglas, far from harming the Republicans, actually was aiding them: for now Douglas sat in the Senate as the public hero of northern and western Democrats, and his very presence there as such was already widening the rift within his own party. Furthermore, outside of Illinois the Republicans had done very well last November, making sweeping election gains throughout the free states. What was essential now for ultimate triumph was to keep on broadening the Republican base. As Greeley had just put it in the *Tribune*:

> We do not regard the Republican as essentially a sectional party—we are not willing that it shall continue even to seem such. We believe that its objects and principles, fairly expounded and understood, must commend themselves to a large proportion of the best citizens of the Slave States, even as they did in the days of Washington and Jefferson.
>
> To this end, we propose to fight the next Presidential battle on the platform of essential and genuine conservatism. . . . Whoever is anti-Fillibuster, anti-Cuba-stealing, anti-Slavery-extending, is a good enough Republican for us. . . . If the Sham Democracy are beaten in 1860, the struggle against slavery extension will be virtually concluded. We shall have Kansas, Nebraska, Dakota, New Mexico and Arizona added to the number of free states during the ensuing Presidential term . . . We shall have a hook in the jaw of the pro-slavery Leviathan from which he will not easily free himself.

It followed, then—at least, so Greeley was privately arguing—that in order to round up this wide, "conservative" support, the party should pick as its presidential standard-bearer some man who was not identified with radical appeals that might be mistaken for downright abolitionism. Then also—and here Greeley had learned his lesson from the Lincoln campaign in Illinois—it would do well to avoid picking a man who represented the dominant eastern leadership of the party, and who would therefore be suspect in the West as well as the South. In short, it stood the best chances for victory if it chose a moderate, a westerner, and a new face.

This description precisely fitted the man whom Greeley had invited to call on him at the hotel in Bloomington. Conceivably, the editor might have recognized this if they had sat down to talk that day. Instead, Greeley now spent a whole year looking for some man other than Lincoln who might fill the specifications.

3

A moderate, above all things. This meant that the man who was being mentioned throughout the East as the leading Republican contender, Senator William H. Seward, would not do. The processes

in Greeley's mind concerning his former partner were obscure but
decisive. He respected Seward, he sometimes praised him, he went
on meeting him with outward cordiality after their private break
in 1854, but at heart he resented him and sought his political
destruction; there could be no doubt of that. Seward, knowing
Greeley well, sensed this, and sometimes wished that he had not
provoked the editor so carelessly to wrath. Thus he wrote a friend
in 1858, intending that the message be conveyed to Greeley,

> I know how hard it is for Greeley to bear with me. Only one
> thing in all this matter has given me any concern, namely that
> persons who don't like the *Tribune* nor love Greeley as I do—and
> who wish to undermine that great paper—seek by sympathies with
> me in a matter upon which I differ from him to excite prejudices
> between us. I regret this and it gives me anxiety. Though I never
> have pretended to agree with Greeley nor he with me in all things,
> yet I regard his paper as a great and reliable agency of this great
> revolution. . . . I have supposed that we should go on together
> while I continue differing where we must differ as friends, and so
> rather making the common cause stronger.

But within the same week Greeley was writing his ever-present
listener, Colfax, that Seward "has great qualities, but an enormous
self-conceit and a sanguine disposition that are apt to try his friends.
I like him very much as a man; I have ceased to follow his lead as
a politician." And he added, "Seward is a good fellow at heart, only
he is a bad one to *belong* to. I have been there."

The spindly, long-beaked senator from New York, with his bouncing air and irrepressible talk, had become the outstanding
Republican presence on the floor—a fact which made Greeley's
effort to sidetrack him far more difficult. His manner in debate was
greatly admired: his hoarse voice could be both brusque and
cordial, hearty and confidential. Ideas, phrases, repartee, darted
out of him with quick, original gestures. Body and brain moved
fast together; he became a hero to the galleries. Murat Halstead,
reporting for the Cincinnati *Commercial*, described him in action:

> Seward's is the most singular head in all the [Senate] assort-
> ment . . . It rises above the ears like a dome, and looks not unlike
> a straw stack in shape and color . . . This head is perched upon a
> body that is active and restless . . . It walks with a slashing swagger.
> It strikes off with a rollicking gait from one point to another, and
> is in and out of the Chamber by turns. . . . He sits down, takes a

pinch of snuff, and presently you hear a vociferous sneezing, and the high-headed, straw-thatched gentleman is engaged upon his beak with a yellow silk handkerchief. . . . In the Republican corner of the Senate Chamber is [another] familiar face and form—you recognize the portly person and massive intellectual development, the thin frizzly hair and the oval brow of Salmon P. Chase . . . Seward comes up . . . they laugh violently but quietly, and Seward rubs his oaken breeches with his hands and then gives his nose a tremendous tweak with the yellow handkerchief. He is wonderfully affable. He acts as though he would kiss a strange baby. Ah, he is a candidate for the Presidency.

Seward was famous—perhaps too famous. Therein lay Greeley's argument against him as a choice. The Senator had thrilled many antislave crusaders when he faced southern legalists with the outcry that there was a "higher law," even above the Constitution, to which moral men owed obedience. But with those same words he had also affrighted many moderates. Then Seward again had rallied the militant with a blast proclaiming an "irrepressible conflict" between the free states and slavery. But this slogan again served to embitter against him all those who read into it the threat of a northern crusade against the South. Greeley, in the heat of the contest, had generally agreed with Seward's sentiments; but he thought them injudicious in a candidate. No, Seward would not do. He could not carry the middle-of-the-roaders, the moderates, the waverers, the border states.

Now Abraham Lincoln, campaigning in 1858, had expressed almost the same thought as Seward's about an approaching "irrepressible conflict"—and, in fact, he had advanced it earlier. "This government cannot endure permanently half slave and half free," he had declared in his "house divided" speech in Springfield. But Lincoln's way of putting it had been less strident than Seward's, and more circumspect and philosophical; and besides, he was nowhere near as famous as Seward. He had stepped forth in his debates with Douglas as a man who was utterly opposed to any further extension of slavery and who personally detested the slave system on moral grounds; but at the same time he also opposed any agitation to bear down on the South and forcibly root out the slave system where it already existed, believing that the death of slavery must and would come gradually. In this he was a "conservative" of the sort Greeley now wished to see come to the fore. Lincoln's own political friends—most of them also conservatives, in this sense —began to think that in spite of his Illinois defeat, Lincoln had already come forward enough to be just the right Republican candidate for President. One of these men, James Fell, buttonholed Lincoln one day on the Bloomington courthouse steps to say that he thought his chances were good. Lincoln (according to Carl Sandburg's account) objected that men like Seward and Salmon P. Chase of Ohio were far better known than he, and had given far more service to the party. That was just why they were handicapped, said Fell: "They have rendered *too much* service, have made long records and said radical things which, however just and true, would seriously damage them, if nominated . . . What the Republican party wants, to insure success in 1860, is a man of popular origin, of acknowledged ability, committed against slavery aggressions, who has no record to defend and no radicalism of an offensive character."

This might have been Greeley speaking. But Greeley, at this point, was not addressing himself to Lincoln. And Lincoln, for his part, had learned not to count on any support from Greeley. The two men passed by each other in the America of the eve of 1860 as if they were either total strangers or sworn enemies. Yet they were neither. They had known each other ever since the summer of 1847, when as young Whig promoters of "internal improvements" and western development, they had met amid the speechmaking of a "River and Harbors Convention" in rough-hewn Chicago. Later, Greeley and Lincoln had sat together briefly in Congress, Greeley remembering his Illinois fellow Whig simply as "a quiet, good-natured man, who did not aspire to leadership . . . noticeably tall, and the only Whig from Illionis—not remarkable, otherwise, to my recollection." Lincoln, for his part, remembered Congressman Greeley as the author of a willful attack on himself over the matter of just how much mileage money he was collecting for travel between his home and Washington—a blast that had not hurt Lincoln much, and that had helped Greeley not at all.

In Washington either man had encountered the other at a disadvantage: Greeley had seen only the drifting, indecisive side of Lincoln, while Lincoln had watched Greeley at his most strident and impulsive. Then they had drawn apart—Greeley to soar to ebullient fame, while Lincoln in middle years emerged slowly from his wrappings of doubt. But their first mutual impressions had stuck. It was not that they actively disliked one another. It was that either man failed to account for the other's growth. As a result, when the crucial days of the eve of 1860 were upon them, neither could quite bring himself to take the other seriously.

They differed in many things, but above all in temperament and in their ways of handling men. Greeley was the public oracle who wanted to be a ruling politician; Lincoln was the politician who instinctively avoided sounding oracular. Greeley, always strenuous, looked at Lincoln's amiable, shrugging moods and thought that he was too easygoing for leadership. Lincoln watched Greeley's brittle, hortatory air and thought that he was too tense. In this, either man mistook one characteristic of the other for the whole person. Greeley, as his own friends knew, could be supple and compromising when he was sure of the goal ahead. And Lincoln, America was soon to know, could be hard as flint when he was also sure. The differences between them, in fact, were often simply those of timing, of public address, of choice of words. But these differences were enough. Lincoln could be imperious; but he never—or very rarely—let himself go in the vein which Greeley cultivated, for instance, when writing his Washington ally, Schuyler Colfax, when Colfax in 1859 was helping organize the new Congress: "I'm not particular how it is organized, so that the thing be done. It *can* be done; it *must* be done; if it isn't, I'll hold you and two or three more responsible."

In spite of all divergences, though, Greeley and Lincoln had much in common—more, in fact, than any two other Republican leaders of comparable position. They shared a point of view on the slavery issue that avoided the extremes of both abolitionism and appeasement. They were alike in their suspicion of the party's entrenched eastern chieftains—Lincoln's opposition to Weed and Seward being general and regional, while Greeley's was immediate and personal. They spoke a common party language of plain people's aspiration —which on their tongues had a different ring than it did on Weed's, who had now deeply involved himself with corrupt New York traction rings and with lobbying for the slatternly Erie Railroad. They talked of free homesteads, of the open land, of drawing labor to the further West—issues that did not move the hearts of the established New York–New England men who now looked to Seward as their spokesman.

Moreover, they had in common their impoverished back-country origins; their history of torn and distracted families; their own struggles upward in the professions; their dismally unhappy marriages; their reputations for being odd, quizzical, rustic characters far out of conformity with the urban East; their homespun, familiar jocularity; their improvidence; their recurrent plunges into lonely, abysmal despair; their yearnings toward poetry; their insatiable reading; their accumulation of vast stores of folklore, legend, and citation; their love of the just use of words; and then, when mastering the practical employment of daily prose, their emergence as unique craftsmen of language, writing and speaking with sure rhythms of their own the terse, unvarnished common speech.

They thought so much alike and they often wrote so much alike that at some moments, to an ear unable to detect their differences in mood and cadence, their words sounded almost interchangeable. The two men themselves, in fact, may have sensed this. At some point when their ideas were marching in agreement while their temperaments were not, they may each have detected in the other the image of many of his own thoughts and hopes and doubts—a reverse picture, no doubt, but still an uncomfortably close one, and one that could best be banished by looking the other way. This, at all events, was what they mutually did. They had a way of repeatedly repelling one another, especially at moments when they seemed most in danger of reaching political or intellectual concord. They retired to opposite corners. Yet, before long, one or the other of them felt bound to look back, to come over and make a new approach. Intermediaries were called in to help. When they met again, they did so with reserve: "I knew him more than sixteen years," Greeley was to write of Lincoln in his *Recollections*, "met him often, talked with him familiarly; yet . . . I cannot remember that I ever heard him tell an anecdote or story." This made Greeley unique among those who knew Lincoln. Still, the two communicated. In fact, Lincoln kept a special pigeonhole in his desk for letters from Horace Greeley—some cordial and helpful, others imperative and crusty, and still others downright angry. And, if Lincoln was not inclined to tell Greeley stories, he at least was always ready to hear him out. One day, for instance, Greeley went down to Washington to lecture at the Smithsonian Institute on the topic, "The Nation," and there, listening to him on the platform, sat the President of the United States, Abraham Lincoln, flanked by two members of his Cabinet.

4

While Greeley had been out in California looking at the future, a prophetic event had occurred nearer home—only thirty miles, in fact, from his own parents' homestead in northwestern Pennsylvania. There a former New Haven railroad conductor named Edwin Drake, making the novel experiment of boring an artesian well to bring up "rock oil" of the sort that had already been found on the scummy surface of Oil Creek at Titusville, struck petroleum in what seemed to be limitless quantities.

The promoters of Drake's venture kept their discovery secret until they had bought out their unwitting fellow stockholders and thus made sure of harvesting all the coming profits for themselves. Therefore the *Tribune* had not been able in this case to follow Greeley's injunction to report every significant scientific development at once and in full. While Greeley went on discussing California fruits and slavery expansion, the age of John D. Rockefeller dawned over America silently.

Not far south of Titusville, another sign of a new age was just appearing. The ironmongers of Pittsburgh, who up to now had depended for their supply of pig iron on little upcountry furnaces and bloomeries scattered throughout the Allegheny highlands, had just decided to build their own blast furnaces on a large scale. Thereby the day of the small village iron producer, converting his bog ores for the local smithy, wagon shop or mill, was at an end. Big industry had begun. Greeley, however, like every other editor, was absorbed in the coming national election.

There was other news, too, that year, of startling physical developments—most of them in the North. Twenty-five hundred miles of new railroad trackage had been laid in just six months. By far the greater part of it had been spun out in the North and West, and now the two regions were firmly tied together by bands of steel. The South was too busy with its cotton fields to catch up. Now it was too late: the main lines were drawn.

In the same year 1859, the *Tribune* reported the showing of the new Fawkes steam plow at the Illinois State Fair. Here was something Greeley could fully appreciate: within a few months he was out calling on the Chicago farm-machinery man, Cyrus McCormick, to advise him to buy up the patent. ("I unfolded to him the merits of steam plowing," Greeley wrote, "and told him that we wanted to plow all the prairies.") And there was still another piece of news from Illinois which had its special meaning for readers in the South. The home state of Abraham Lincoln had just climbed to first place in the nation in terms of the money value of annual agricultural production, leaving rich Mississippi and Alabama far behind. Next summer, an observer with a spyglass reported that from one point on the Illinois prairie he had been able to see 146 mechanical reapers working simultaneously through the wheat. Most people South of the Ohio had never seen a reaper—let alone a steam plow.

Such pieces of news meant that no matter how powerful the South might be politically, the economic scales were now definitely tilted against it. Some men recognized this. Others, on either side, could not quite believe it. Many plantation southerners, when they came face to face with it, talked of desperate remedies. That language was heard in the North while the machines hummed, and it brought forth answers in kind. Abraham Lincoln, for instance, a man known for his moderation, came east to give a speech at Cooper Union in New York City, and addressed himself to the South in words like these:

> You [say] you will not abide the election of a Republican President. In that supposed event, you say, you will destroy the Union; and then, you say, the great crime of having destroyed it will be upon us! That is cool. A highwayman holds a pistol to my ear, and mutters through his teeth, "Stand and deliver, or I shall kill you, and then you will be a murderer!"

Greeley was there that night in February, 1860, at the Union. Lincoln's speech, as it unfolded before the crowded, gaslit hall, thrilled the audience. A new star had risen from the West—and thereby a new contender for the Presidency. In the chair on the platform sat the bearded William Cullen Bryant, Greeley's old Jacksonian foe, who had headed the move of several anti-Weed and anti-Seward Republicans to exhibit the Illinois speaker in New York. Greeley, listening to the gathering force of Lincoln's words, had reason to ask himself why it was Bryant, and not he himself, who had first seen this star. An ex-Democrat—and the editor of an evening paper, too—had beaten him. But at least Greeley would try to beat the rest of the press with the story. He advanced on Lincoln the moment his speech was finished, asking for the manuscript of his address. He got it and hurried back to the office, ordering that it be run in full.

The other morning papers would now have to wait for their full texts until the *Tribune* released it. Later that evening, at Greeley's request, Lincoln came around to the *Tribune* office to check the rush galleys of the speech. Amos Cummings, then a young proofreader, remembered the lanky westerner appearing over his shoulder amid the noise of the pressroom at midnight, drawing up a chair, adjusting his spectacles, and in the glare of the gaslight reading each galley with scrupulous care and then rechecking his corrections, oblivious to his surroundings.

That January Greeley had written his good friend, Margaret Allen, to say that he was intent on doing "a great year's work this year—I hope to do my best toward securing a Republican President." In April, to his other close woman correspondent, Mrs. Whipple of Westhaven, Vermont, he laid bare his campaign plan:

Now about the Presidency: I want to succeed this time, yet I *know* the country is not Anti-Slavery. It will only swallow a little Anti-Slavery in a great deal of sweetening. An Anti-Slavery man *per se* cannot be elected; but a Tariff, River-and-Harbor, Pacific-Railroad, Free-Homestead man, *may* succeed *although* he is Anti-Slavery; so I'll try to get a candidate who will fairly and readily unite votes to win.

By this time he thought he had already found his man—or at least a man. It was not Lincoln. "As to President," he wrote in a letter, "my present judgment is Edward Bates; but I am willing to go anything that looks stronger. I don't wish to load the team heavier than it can pull through." The man to whom he wrote that was Bill Herndon, who shared Abraham Lincoln's office and much of his life.

5

Who in Heaven's name, many people asked in early 1860, was Edward Bates? And, once they found out, they kept on asking themselves, why should Horace Greeley have hit on him, of all people? For Edward Bates, an eminent, white-bearded, St. Louis lawyer and Missouri patriarch, was more of a relic than a fighting leader. He had indeed fought—in the War of 1812. Shortly thereafter he had moved out from his native Virginia to the West, siring seventeen children there and living the life of a transplanted Jeffersonian gentleman of the old school. He had read his Tacitus, made money, become a Whig, freed his slaves, emerged as a gracious, warmhearted champion of western growth—but he had retired from national politics as far back as 1836. Free-soil Missourians revered him. But most Republicans further off had never heard of him. "A fossil of the Silurian age," Medill of the Chicago *Tribune* called him. Even Greeley admitted that Bates was "old-fogyish." In fact, he had not yet gotten around even to joining the Republican party. Quietly ensconced among his books and horses, Edward Bates was one of the nation's few vestigial Whigs.

To many an antislavery radical, such a choice was preposterous. Yet Greeley had his reasons for it, if one could follow them. Objectors asked, how could a figure so elderly, so innocuous, and so conditioned by southern border origins as Bates be expected to lead the nation in a time of frontal crisis over slavery? To this there were three answers. In the first place, it was the object of Greeley and men who thought as he did to try to avoid just such a frontal crisis over slavery—or, in any case, to alleviate it. Secondly, it was part of their strategy to concentrate on just those wavering and divided border states which men like Bates, the Missourian, represented, and by offering preferment to their leaders to try to swing them safely into the free-soil camp. Thirdly, men who had lived as long and as closely with American politics as Greeley had were not inclined to believe that Presidents really did lead the nation, after all. Their experience made them feel that it was the Congress and the forces behind it that led the President. They had not seen a strong figure in the White House since Andrew Jackson's time, and they did not count on seeing one again. Instead of electing a Daniel Webster or a Henry Clay, the nation had willingly received a Taylor, a Fillmore, a Pierce and a Buchanan. The golden age of the Presidency seemed beyond recall; and while little leadership was to be expected of Edward Bates, that made him all the more safe. Venerable and humane, he could at least be placed before the people as a symbol of American continuity and stability; and it was therefore to his credit that he had been born in Washington's administration and had met Jefferson in Virginia as a youth.

In this argument for Bates, Greeley by no means stood alone. The powerful Blair family clan—all of them also border-state men, reared as Jacksonian Democrats and now become free-soilers and Republicans—was with him. To many shrewd political operators, the candidacy of Bates was not unlikely as it had first seemed. Meanwhile to certain men in Springfield, the boom for Bates was not wholly quixotic either: it at least expressed a dissatisfaction with the established eastern leaders of the party. Who knew what this might lead to, once the revolt gathered force? But to William H. Seward, moving between Washington, Auburn, Albany and New York, the talk of Bates for President—or of Lincoln, too—was simply mischievous. Seward was the outstanding politician of the party. Thurlow Weed stood behind him. The national convention at Chicago would surely nominate him. Then what was Horace Greeley up to?

6

Some weeks before the convention met, Senator Seward and Boss Weed—neither of whom were ardent churchgoers—were moved simultaneously one Sunday morning to attend the service at Dr. Chapin's Universalist Church in New York. This, as most New Yorkers knew, was the place where Horace Greeley worshiped, and where he could be seen every Sunday in his pew. Seward and Weed, in due course, met Greeley there, for they had taken the precaution of moving right into his pew. There was something they very much wanted to talk about with him. But this was a church service, and besides, Greeley was not just then in a mood to talk with Weed and Seward.

"Well, what did they say?" the *Tribune*'s city editor, F. J. Otterson, asked him, when Greeley told him at the office of their encounter.

"Nothing," muttered Greeley.

"What did you say?"

"Nothing."

"What was the text of the sermon?"

"The text?" Greeley's eyes lit up shrewdly. "Let me see. It was in Isaiah:—'My thoughts are not your thoughts, neither are your ways my ways.'" He burst out with a cackling peal of laughter that was heard throughout the outer office.

Keeping his own counsel, Greeley went off to Chicago in mid-May, itching to do battle with the New York leaders on the convention floor. With the fate of their party and possibly of their nation at stake, the Republicans met there in the setting of a carnival. The mushrooming prairie city, proud of having just attained a population of 110,000 and a record of slaughtering 6,000 hogs in one day, had spared nothing to help stage a monster show. A looming wooden hall named the Wigwam had been built especially for the meeting and decorated by the city's Republican ladies with winding festoons, streamers, flowers and busts of heroes of all ages. The bare, ugly clapboard fronts of the main streets were aflame with bunting, and the city fathers assembled at the depots with brass bands and fireworks to welcome the state delegations that pulled in on as many as one hundred special trains a day, each with its crowds of hangers-on.

Some delegations, to add to the noise, brought along their own bands. Thurlow Weed's New York team arrived complete with a Seward cheering section that filled thirteen cars, captained by a prize fighter named Tom Hyer. Over a thousand saloons stood open to refresh the President makers. No one seemed to mind the stench of the nearby slaughterhouses, or the piles of garbage dumped into side streets, or the millions of rats that scurried under the city's wood-plank pavements. The actual delegates, who numbered less than five hundred, were submerged in a visiting swarm that may have numbered 40,000. Professional gamblers, pickpockets and prostitutes arrived in force to swell the city's own contingent, and Chicago's red-light district became so overcrowded that the mayor, at the height of the proceedings, felt it necessary to stage a police raid—in the course of which his men picked up a large number of delegates, including three gentlemen from Ohio, in one of the fancier establishments.

Weed, big, bland, hearty as ever, moved into Richmond House, where he began serving champagne and cigars to delegates from Maine to California while assuring them with blackslaps that Seward was sure to win. Across the way, the barrel-shaped, jovial bulk of Judge David Davis, Lincoln's manager, settled into Tremont House, from where he captained the thousands of downstate young bucks who had been herded into town to talk up "Old Abe" in the Wigwam galleries as well as in every saloon. At Tremont House, too, the wandering streams of politicos could encounter the aging, wizened, pint-sized Francis Preston Blair, Sr.—Republicanism's living link with Jacksonian Democracy—as he held forth in Edward Bates' headquarters. Beside him stood his son, Frank, Jr., tall, bronzed, athletic, with his twirling mustache, his keen eyes, his quick aggressive talk, and his phenomenal capacity for hard liquor. Other names, either already famous or soon to become so, moved up and down the milling corridors: here was the grandly bearded Gideon Welles, formerly a Democrat and now head of the Connecticut delegation, who was saying rebelliously that he would not go for Seward; Senator Hannibal Hamlin of Maine, a knotty, oaken man, holding his delegation tight in hand; Carl Schurz of Wisconsin, Germanic and intense, a Seward follower; the mild David Wilmot of Pennsylvania, still honored for the famous Proviso that for the first time had drawn up the lines of battle; and the fierce, unquenchable old abolitionist from Ohio, Joshua Giddings, who carried a price on his head in Virginia.

The great reporters and editors were all there: Bryant of the *Evening Post*, serious and subdued as always, busy exposing Weed's cash handouts and building up Lincoln; Raymond of the *Times*, cool, well dressed, deliberate, helping the Seward machine; the strutting, indestructible Colonel Webb of the *Courier and Enquirer*, also a Seward man; Murat Halstead of the Cincinnati *Commercial*, writing deft sketches of all the star performers; Medill of the Chicago *Tribune*, backing Lincoln against everybody; and Horace Greeley of New York—who was there not only as a correspondent, but also as a delegate and political mover on his own.

On the floor Greeley spoke not for New York—for Weed had refused to seat him among his stalwarts—but as a delegate from faraway Oregon, which had obligingly made a place for him. Three other Oregon delegates also let him share their room in crowded Tremont House, since he had come without bothering to make a hotel reservation. During the three noisy, jockeying days before the convention actually opened, he was to be seen in every hotel lobby and state headquarters, easily identifiable with his moon face, drooping specs, and loose-hanging, rumpled clothes, buttonholing delegations with amiable, short speeches. Thus, to a crowd from Kansas:

> I want to tell you boys . . . that you couldn't elect Seward if you could nominate him. You must remember as things stand today we are a sectional party. We have no strength outside the North; practically we must have the entire North with us if we hope to win. Now, there are states in the North that cannot be induced to support Seward, and without these states we cannot secure electoral votes enough to elect. So, to name Seward is to invite defeat. He cannot carry New Jersey, Pennsylvania, Indiana or Iowa, and I will bring you representative men from these states who will confirm what I say.

Then he moved on to the next group, grinning, exhorting, shaking hundreds of hands. He "looked like a well-to-do farmer fresh from his clover fields," one western delegate wrote of him, adding, "He seemed to find a place in our hearts at once." Strangers crowded in on him. Even Raymond's *Times* had to report that "Mr. Greeley has made a great sensation here." He was still on his rounds at midnight, and Murat Halstead, watching him make his progress through the packed lobby of Tremont House, had this to say:

The principal lions in this House are Horace Greeley and Francis Preston Blair, Sr. The way Greeley is stared at as he shuffles about, looking as innocent as ever, is itself a sight. Whenever he appears there is a crowd gaping at him, and if he stops to talk a minute with some one who wishes to consult him as an oracle, the crowd becomes dense as possible, and there is the most eager desire to hear the words of wisdom that are supposed to fall on such occasions.

Meanwhile, prevented by convention etiquette from being present at the show themselves, the rival contenders sat in their own home towns and nervously awaited what the next days might bring— Seward in Auburn, Bates on his estate outside St. Louis, Salmon P. Chase in Cincinnati, and Abraham Lincoln in his law office in Springfield. Three days of preconvention bidding had elapsed, tens or even hundreds of thousands of dollars had been spent, and many Chicago saloons had been drunk dry. The balloting could now begin.

7

Before Greeley went on the floor at Chicago, two things had happened elsewhere in America that bore on the Republicans' chances of success and on those of his own favorite, Bates. First, the Democrats had met in Baltimore and split wide open over their leading man, Stephen A. Douglas, just as Greeley had hoped and plotted all along that they should. While Douglas was nominated by their northern and moderate wing, the slaveholders' faction had bolted to run a man of their own, Breckinridge. Thereby the chances of a Republican victory were enormously increased. But at the same time there had been division on the other side, too, when irreconcilable old-line Whigs and Know-Nothings had placed *their* own man in the running, refusing to fall in line behind the Republicans. Whatever else this might lead to, it meant first of all that "old fogy" Edward Bates' chances at Chicago were now diminished.

In sum, then, 1860 now looked like a Republican victory year, but not like the year for Bates. Still, there was the block of pledged Bates votes on the convention floor. There were not many of them—only 48 in fact, out of a total delegates' roll call of 466—but they were a valuable trading counter. Everything depended, then, on holding them together. Thrown into the game at the proper moment, they might serve to carry a good man in, or at all events to keep the wrong man out.

The name of Seward—the wrong man, Greeley kept insisting—dominated the convention, and Weed claimed that he would poll nearly two hundred votes at the outset. The "stop Seward" forces, each with its own little nucleus of home-state votes for a favorite son, seemed hopelessly divided. Some were there obviously with the intention only of letting themselves be bought at a price. The well-drilled fifty-six men from Pennsylvania, for instance, were not seriously out to make their own chieftain, the slippery Simon Cameron, the party's nominee. Ohio and Indiana might fall into the market too. But Weed, who openly boasted that he was being subsidized by big eastern business interests, had the money, and Seward had the name.

On the day before the balloting began, Greeley had been called in to sit on the convention's platform committee. The drafting session took eight hours. Greeley worked "long and earnestly," he afterward said, to exclude from the document any planks "needlessly offensive or irritating" to the South. The party program, as presented to the Wigwam, simply denied the right of Congress or of territorial legislatures to legalize slavery in the territories, and spoke of their duty to prohibit it "whenever such legislation is necessary." Beyond this, the platform threw its net wide by promising tariff protection to northeastern industry and a homestead law plus a Pacific railroad to westerners. The Wigwam listened to the draft and quickly approved it.

Then Greeley went on his rounds again to see how the forces were shaping up for tomorrow. Among the anti-Seward leaders he found nothing but gloom. Weed was staging an exuberant pre-victory champagne banquet at Richmond House and sending well-lubricated brass bands bearing Seward banners to serenade other state delegations. Most of the seaboard states were already lined up behind Seward; so was Michigan. The big Pennsylvania crew, strutting about in the distinctive white hats which Boss Cameron had provided them, were dickering with Weed. Greeley canvassed the Ohio delegation and found them divided and irresolute. Indiana might switch either to Lincoln or Bates, but this was not enough. The Seward bandwagon rolled through the night. Greeley came back to Tremont House, discouraged. In an abysm of despair he hurried to the press desk and filed this message to his paper:

> My conclusion from all that I can gather tonight is that opposition to Governor Seward cannot concentrate on any candidate and that he will be nominated.

Then he climbed upstairs to the room of his lawyer friend, David Dudley Field, one of the few anti-Seward men present from New York. He threw himself down on a couch. "All is lost," he burst out; "we are beaten."

Field rallied him. "No," he shot back, "all is not lost. Let us up and go to work." It was midnight, and Greeley was exhausted. He managed to pull himself together, and they went downstairs to start out again on a final try. Just before they reached the lobby, the gargantuan bulk of Judge David Davis, Lincoln's man, was seen descending. He had been having a most important meeting in another room. His guests were the leaders of Simon Cameron's high-priced Pennsylvania crew. In the lobby, Medill of the Chicago *Tribune* buttonholed Davis to ask him what the result had been.

"Damned if we haven't got them," said Davis jovially.

"How did you get them?"

"By paying their price."

The price to be paid for getting Cameron's pivotal delegation to switch to Lincoln on the second ballot next day was that Cameron, in spite of his personal ill repute, was to be guaranteed a Cabinet post if Lincoln won. These terms, for the moment, were secret. But the rumor of the deal was enough to send Greeley and Field out into the night with the hope that there might be a chance now to stop Seward after all. Bates was definitely out. But Lincoln might conceivably be the man. Greeley, Field, and the elder Blair exhorted the Missouri men who were here for Bates to stick together until the moment of a planned switch. In the early morning hours Greeley went to work on the delegation from his native Vermont. Maine, where Greeley's private emissary, the *Tribune* correspondent James S. Pike, had been busy, had already moved over. New Hampshire showed signs of being ready to break for Lincoln on the second ballot—if the Seward men, in the meantime, did not stampede the convention.

Next morning, in the Wigwam, the contenders were placed in nomination. Seward's name was greeted by a great, organized cheer led by Tom Hyer and his big-voiced visitors from New York. Then came Lincoln's, and it was the signal for a roar so tumultuous that it astounded and virtually deafened the hall. This was Judge Davis in action: he had packed the galleries with leather-lunged Illinois hog callers. After the echoes died down, the first tally was taken. Seward was far out front, as expected, with 173½ votes; but Lincoln had amassed 102. Bates trailed with his 48.

Excitement rose in anticipation of the next round. Greeley bustled about the hall, rumpled, glistening, and exhorting the Bates men to stand together once more—except for a dozen who were to switch in a group to Lincoln. The Seward people were still confident, believing that no concerted force could mass against them. But tumult spread in the Wigwam when the second tally showed that Lincoln had climbed suddenly to 181 votes, with Pennsylvania, Indiana, New Hampshire and Vermont coming over to him. This placed him neck and neck with Seward, who had won 184½. Weed, sitting in a lobby, lost his composure. Now, suddenly, he needed the help of the Bates block if the tide toward Lincoln was to be stemmed. He needed Horace Greeley. Hurriedly he proposed a deal. But it was too late. The third ballot came. The well-marshaled Bates men went over in a body to Lincoln. Old Abe was nominated.

Amid the western yell that now shook the rafters, Greeley was observed sitting in his chair in the Oregon section wearing a beatific smile of victory. Delegates streamed past him up and down the hall, shouting and chanting out of sheer release from tension. Then crowds of them gathered around him too and cheered him. Not all understood just how the thing had happened, but a sense had spread across the floor that the odd-looking, cherubic editor had been instrumental in achieving it. More and more sweating men crowded in on him, pumping his hand and shouting through the din, as if he alone—without money or a machine to back him—were the hero of the hour. "Greeley has slaughtered Seward, but has saved the Republican party," exclaimed the chairman of the Indiana delegation. George William Curtis of *Harper's Weekly* wired home that Greeley's triumph was such as to make his *Tribune* "the great organ and censor" of the Republican party. Alvan Bovay, the pioneer Republican who had been Greeley's friend since antirent days, wrote him jubilantly that "It seems to be the style just now to discuss the sayings and doings of Horace Greeley . . . If it was through your efforts that William H. Seward was defeated, so much more glory and honor to you. It saved the Republican party and the country . . ." James Parton, Greeley's biographer of five years before, told him, "I believe that you are the most popular man in the northern states."

Some men, though, would never forgive him. There was Thurlow Weed, the vanquished boss, who was seen openly weeping in the Wigwam lobby when the final returns came through. There was William H. Seward back in Auburn, who had set up a saluting gun on his lawn to boom forth victory the moment the news was flashed to him, and who now had to order it hurriedly hauled away. There were pro-Seward politicians like Andrew ("Bray") Dickinson, who cornered Greeley before a crowd in Tremont House after it was all over and accused him of having betrayed his old New York friends. ("I never saw a man get such an awful dressing," said an eyewitness; "Greeley couldn't get a word in edgewise.") "The white-livered old cuss," another Sewardite called Greeley in a letter home; "to his venom the result was attributable."

In private Greeley enjoyed watching the confusion of his enemies. "Do you see how the heathen rage?" he wrote James S. Pike, who had worked hard with him. But in public he tried not to crow. He insisted that his role at Chicago was being exaggerated, and he added archly that it was through no fault of his own that the favorite Seward had gone down to defeat.

This was too much for Henry Raymond, Greeley's successor at the side of Seward, who now sat down to go to work on the rival editor with all the verbal resources at his command. Raymond had always excelled at sardonic, spiked attacks, and this, when it appeared in his paper next morning, was his best:

. . . With the generosity which belongs to his nature, and which a feeling not unlike remorse may have stimulated into unwonted activity, [Greeley] awards to others the credit which belongs transcendently to himself. The main work of the Chicago convention was the defeat of Governor Seward . . . and in that endeavor Mr. Greeley labored harder, and did tenfold more, than the whole family of Blairs, together with all the gubernatorial candidates, to whom he modestly hands over the honors . . .

Mr. Greeley had special qualifications, as well as a special love, for this task, to which none of the others could lay any claim. For twenty years he had been sustaining the political principles and vindicating the political conduct of Mr. Seward through the columns of the most influential political newspaper in the country. . . . His voice was potential precisely where Governor Seward was strongest —because it was supposed to be that of a friend, strong in his personal attachment and devotion. . . .

While it was known to some . . . that nearly six years ago— in November, 1854—he had privately, but distinctly, repudiated all further political friendship for and alliance with Governor Seward . . . no use was made of this knowledge in quarters where it would have disarmed the deadly effect of his pretended friendship for the man upon whom he was thus deliberately wreaking the long hoarded revenge of a disappointed office-seeker . . .

Being thus stimulated by a hatred he had secretly cherished for years, protected by the forbearance of those whom he assailed and strong in the confidence of those upon whom he sought to operate, it is not strange that Mr. Greeley's efforts should have been crowned with success . . .

We cheerfully tender for Mr. Greeley's use this record of his deserts, when he may claim at the hands of his new associates that payment for lack of which he has deserted and betrayed his old ones.

But Greeley had his answer ready. He did not roar back in print. He simply demanded—now that the subject of the dissolution of his partnership with Seward had been raised—that Seward release to the press the actual letter Greeley had written him on that occasion back in 1854. Under pressure, Seward complied. The six-year-old letter had listed all the injuries—real or fancied—done by the Albany chieftains to their junior *Tribune* partner, and had flatly declared that Greeley would work for them no more. Now the whole northern press carried the text, thereby parading Greeley rather than Seward as the party who had been aggrieved. Greeley felt wholly vindicated when showers of approving mail piled in on the *Tribune* office. "If ever in my life I discharged a public duty in utter disregard of personal considerations," he summed up, "I did so at Chicago."

XII. WARHAWK

1

"I cannot come to you, for Sunday is one of my great working days," Greeley wrote in August, 1860, to his close friend Bayard Taylor, who had asked him out to the country. "Dana goes away on Saturday and I write a good share of the paper for Monday. (Don't you remark that it is particularly spirited on that day?)" And he added, "There is no rest for me till after the Presidential Election. I must write and speak incessantly, tho' so weary that I can hardly stand. I spoke last night in Norwich, Conn., and must speak tonight in Haverstraw. Love to all."

He felt he had never worked so hard for a candidate or a cause as he was now doing for Lincoln. Sometimes he was on the platform twice a day before local labor unions, Wide-Awake clubs, outlying lyceum audiences, and groups of campaign workers. With his sister Esther's husband, John F. Cleveland of the *Tribune*, he put together a lengthy campaign manual packed with speeches, historical background and statistics, and this "textbook," as he called it, ran through nine printings. He had the *Tribune* shop issue basic Republican addresses and arguments in pamphlet form and distribute them across the country. At the same time he was running a newspaper, too. Its circulation soared during the campaign; it was by far the most influential Republican organ in the country. Most newspapers, to be sure, were showing election-year increases: Bennett's *Herald* was now selling more than 70,000 on weekdays and 80,000 on Sundays, while the New York *Sun* was up to 60,000 daily, the *Times* to 35,000, and Bryant's *Evening Post* to 20,000. Bennett was in fact running somewhat ahead of the daily *Tribune* in New York; but no rival could begin to approach the *Tribune's* weekly edition, which together with its semiweekly and Pacific Coast editions now swelled Greeley's total press run to fully 300,000.

And since the great bulk of his weekly copies went out to small-town and rural subscribers who generally passed their "*Try-bunes*" from hand to hand, Greeley was probably reaching at this time a total readership of over one million.

In his paper and on his platforms Greeley was now saying that Lincoln represented precisely what the country needed. Bryant, who had been saying it all along, looked down on Greeley as a latecomer, which bothered him not at all. He spoke of Lincoln as an authentic, earthy voice of the people and as the carrier of the popular, constitutional tradition of Henry Clay and Andrew Jackson. (Andrew Jackson had now been dead long enough to be taken safely into the Republican camp.) He claimed for Lincoln all the spaciousness of the West, the area of America's greatest hope, whose illimitable future itself promised death to the antique way of slavery.

Rising optimism and enthusiasm fired him all that summer, even amid the sharpening tensions across the land. He was certain that the sundered Democrats would be turned out of office. He sensed—or thought he sensed—an undercurrent of refusal among small folk in the South to go along with the extremist leaders who were talking secession from the Union in case Lincoln won. He himself had marshaled and published a great array of economic arguments to prove that secession would be suicidal for the South. He believed them. He thought he was making great numbers of southerners believe them too. He wrote of free land, of the great, waiting West, of the fair distribution of the nation's soil and natural riches. He himself had written into his party's platform a plank that promised a Homestead Act after Republican victory, and he felt sure of the resolving power of this appeal. Millions would stream to new homes. Industry would spread: protected in the North, factories would strike root also in the South. The outlived days of slave imperialism were nearing their inevitable end. The moral and material energies of the whole nation would pull together; and so, as he wrote in the *Tribune* in July, "The signs of the times indicate that the Republican President will be inaugurated, as it were, by universal consent, amid an era of good feeling."

2

It would be so because good sense and good morals would prevail. The slaveholding oligarchy, said Greeley, was in the toils both of bad morals and bad sense. He had pointed out, using economic logic, why it was absurd for a clique of cotton barons to think of cutting themselves adrift from the Union when their overworked, one-crop region could not possibly stay on its feet alone. The South, he had shown, actually stood in far greater need of the varied, industrial North than the North did of the South. Wouldn't the men of the South understand that?

Suppose, though, they didn't. Suppose that in the back of their minds ran another chain of logic—twisted, to be sure, but still identifiable as thought. They might be saying to themselves, when looking at their present condition, Look, our particular system has now become so highly developed, with all its capital committed into slaves, cotton land, and next year's crop, that it must have the full backing and underwriting of the government if everything we live by is not to come down crashing. This was, after all, only the southern equivalent of the argument which northern capitalists were making too, namely that our system of commercial undertaking has now grown to the point where it must absolutely dictate the program of government if its investment and its future growth are to be protected. Unquestionably, there was a certain rough logic on both sides. Yet there was only one government. Both sides could not control it at once. What did one do then?

Lincoln was elected. South Carolina's leaders at once made ready to pull their state out of the Union. Greeley scoffed at the spreading secession movement, saying that it lacked popular roots and that the "overawed, gagged, paralyzed majority" of southerners would refuse to follow a rabid minority on a desperate gasconade. This sounded reassuring, and he still believed it. He had to believe it; it was an article of faith. Progress, brotherhood and freedom had to win out over rank retrogression; good morals would surely overcome the bad. But then again—suppose they didn't?

Fight? Greeley abhorred the thought. Submit to the slaveholders' terms? He could not countenance that, either. Here was the dilemma that seized upon a man who was simultaneously an antislavery crusader and a pacifist. There must be no further compromises, deals, concessions, he said, for the slaveholders' object was always the same—to make the entire West their province. Yet neither, in this day and age, should an enlightened people resort to bloodshed to decide their differences. What was the answer? Better a Union **without** the South, Greeley thought, than a Union submissive to slaveholders. "Disunion, should it befall, may be a calamity," he wrote; "but complicity in slavery extension is guilt, which the Republicans must in no case incur." No yielding, then, but also no coercion. If the mass of southerners really wanted to quit the Union —something he still did not for a moment believe—it seemed to him that they had a right to do so. He opposed, he said, the idea of "a Union held together by bayonets." On the contrary: "We hold, with Jefferson, to the inalienable right of communities to alter or abolish forms of government that have become oppressive or injurious; and if the cotton states shall decide that they can do better out of the Union than in it, we insist on letting them go in peace."

He set forth his idea to President-elect Lincoln in a letter in December, 1860:

1. I do not believe that a State can secede at pleasure from the Union, any more than a stave may secede from a cask of which it is a component part.
2. I do believe that a people—a political community large and strong enough to maintain a National existence—have a right to form and modify their institutions in accordance with their own convictions of justice and policy. Hence if seven or eight contiguous States (not one small one) were to come to Washington saying, "We are tired of the Union—let us out!"—I should say, "There's the door—go! . . ."
3. If the seceding State or States go to fighting and defying the laws—the Union being yet undissolved, save by their own say-so—I guess they will have to be made to behave themselves. . . .

What he meant by this was that while he thought secession theoretically a right, it was one which could be exercised only in orderly fashion by the vote of the people of a large section after due, open discussion. But this, he said, was not happening in the South. Instead of giving time for public debate on the momentous step, virulent slaveowners' cabals were meeting in southern capitals, terrorizing their opponents and trying to "carry things by a sudden rush." Their very haste, he thought, revealed their fear of giving the latent Unionist sentiment of the southern common people a chance to come to the surface. The important thing now, he argued, was to encourage that Unionist sentiment. A show of arms would not do it; threats of force would simply give the southern ringleaders the opportunity they were looking for—an excuse to shoot. But a policy of steady calm and forbearance, granting to the cotton states collectively their right to secede but insisting upon patience, deliberation, and orderly process, might yet hold the South in line.

So Horace Greeley thought. He put his whole *Tribune* opinion-making machine to work behind his argument. The South by now had placed itself into a virtual state of siege, sealing itself off from outside influences by seizing northern mails and newspapers, denying free movement to travelers from the North, and threatening dissidents with lynch law. Greeley took this as another indication of the fear and insecurity of southern fire-eaters, and he proceeded to exploit it. He sent one of his most trusted reporters, Albert D. Richardson, into the South in disguise to report on the wide Unionist sentiment there which the leaders were trying to suppress. He managed to procure dozens of smuggled dispatches from southern capitals, all proving the same point. Southerners—or alleged Southerners—sent him letters from the outlying countryside, attesting their loyalty and personal hatred of slavery. (A few of these letters bore earmarks of having been composed in the *Tribune* office or in the countryside of Chappaqua. Here, said Greeley, are the facts of what is going on under the surface below the Mason and Dixon's line. Here, he went on, turning to the South itself, is the truth which your own ruling oligarchs want to hide. The mass of your slaveless, small southerners feel little in common with the slavocrats; but they feel much in common with the Union. Therefore—beware of rashness!

It was a skillfully conducted propaganda operation. There were only two flaws in it. The first was that Greeley, in spite of his wide travels, had never himself visited the South, and thus did not know how little his hopes corresponded to its realities. The second flaw was that his *Tribune*, with which he hoped to influence southern sentiment, was now being virtually boycotted there. Southern people did not want to be seen reading the organ of that "crafty old incendiary," as a Mobile paper called him.

3

His argument had already been undermined when South Carolina voted formally to quit the Union. Now Alabama, Florida and Mississippi, sparked by the Charleston convention, were about to follow. In county after county of the cotton states, militia companies were drilling and mounting the blue cockade of secession. Southern Unionist sentiment—which had in fact become visible, but only in isolated areas—was now being engulfed by the general tide.

Greeley, watching the dispatches with growing dismay, made the *Tribune* ready for another great turnabout. So a fanatical clique in Charleston was going to disrupt the entire Union. It simply could not be permitted, he now decided. A new argument occurred to him. The South Carolinians, in voting themselves out of the Union, were threatening to make off with national property inside their borders; they were threatening to seize Fort Sumter—a stronghold which belonged to the people of the entire United States. There was only one word for such a seizure, and that was treason. And to this there was only one answer: "Stand firm!" cried the *Tribune*. The Federal Government and the loyal states must arm at once "to protect the country from civil war." Force must be met with force. The nation's ranking pacifist editor dropped his outstretched hand and came forth sounding a drum roll: "Though we acknowledge prayer to be indispensable to the saving of individuals and nations, we nevertheless consider powder a good thing."

Not really. Greeley, in his alarm, was subject to spells of fright. He was in just such a state when he wrote Herndon in Springfield, on the eve of the new year, "I think it today an even chance that Lincoln will *not* be inaugurated at Washington on the 4th of March." As late as February, 1861, he was still saying intermittently that he thought secession was valid—in theory. "Whenever it shall be clear that the great body of the southern people have become conclusively alienated from the Union, and are anxious to escape from it," he said in his paper, "we will do our best to put forward their views." But the joker in this remark was the words "great body of the southern people"—the mass which he insisted had not yet spoken. And he now added another joker: the rest of the American people must speak out too before any such southern decision could be accepted, and must approve it in special convention. Obviously, the non–southern majority would not dream of approving it. Here was a new twist to the argument. No matter how it twisted the *Tribune* readers who tried to follow it, it seemed to satisfy Greeley's conscience and steady his nerve. For what he was really saying was that while secession was all right in theory, it would never do in practice. Then what was the present condition of the seceding states? It was simply one of "armed rebellion." Greeley swallowed hard and beat the drum again.

Many of his readers, by this time, had been left completely confused. There were letters attacking his "vagaries" and "gyrations."

But his audience, too, was gyrating—as was the entire North. Men who called for forceful action one day fell back into rank confusion the next, and on the third listened to politicians calling nervously for last-minute appeasement of the South. Appeasement was at least something that Greeley had ruled out for himself. In this he was strikingly different from William H. Seward, long the stern prophet of "irrepressible conflict," who had suddenly made a switch-over of his own in the opposite direction, and who now was to be found agreeing to the idea of surrender. Seward's partner, Weed, had suggested in his Albany paper that in the interest of peace, the Republican party go back on its campaign pledges against slavery extension and permit the South to carry slavery right across the trans-Mississippi West; and although Seward said that he was not to be held responsible for this proposal, he had at least encouraged it. "What I do, Weed approves," he was heard saying some time later; "what he says, I endorse. We are one."

President-elect Lincoln, watching and waiting in Illinois, was wholly against any such repudiation of his principles. But the pressure on him grew. Raymond, although calling his *Times* a Lincoln paper, came out for appeasement. New York merchants and bankers, so eager until yesterday to curb the South, now thought hard of the $150,000,000 or so they had advanced to southerners in long-term and crop loans—a sum they might never get back if the South deserted and then was faced with war. Senator Crittenden of Kentucky put up a proposal resembling Weed's in the Senate, and won wide attention for it in the North. Only the fewest wanted to fight. Greeley, once the pacifier, now sounded dangerously militant. James Gordon Bennett, taking the leadership of New York defeatist sentiment, came up with one of his most cynical proposals. The best solution of the crisis, suggested his *Herald*, might be for the North and the South to separate but thereupon to enter a close alliance for mutual commercial and empire-building benefits. Under this plan, Bennett said, the South would be encouraged to go ahead and take over Mexico, while the North would compensate itself by seizing Canada.

Such schemes aroused the *Tribune's* righteous horror and contempt. It kept hammering on one theme: no compromise, now or ever, on the central issue of slavery extension. In this, whatever his other excursions, Greeley remained firm and consistent. He wished he were as sure of Lincoln's consistency. There were too many rumors about the devious spoilsmen and fast operators moving in on the President-elect at Springfield. Lincoln was weak, Greeley kept thinking; he needed strong, dedicated spirits around him to energize him. He thought he had better go out to Springfield himself.

4

Sometime in midwinter every year, Greeley felt he had to go West on a lecture tour. This time, in January, 1861, he chose Illinois. He held forth in half a dozen towns on one of his standard subjects —"Self-made Men." Then, with an air of casualness, he shaped a course for Springfield. He arrived there on a blustery, snow-flecked day, and the President-elect came walking downtown to call on him at his hotel. They were alone together for several hours—Greeley apparently doing most of the talking. For this was the time when Lincoln was saying very little—so little, in fact, that many easterners who had already been inclined to look on him as an unlettered rustic wondered whether he had anything to say for himself at all. In his long, point-by-point policy letter to the President-elect a month earlier, Greeley had set down this final, commanding paragraph:

6. I fear nothing, care for nothing but another disgraceful backdown of the free states. That is the only real danger. Let the Union slide—it may be reconstructed; let Presidents be assassinated—we can elect more; let the Republicans be defeated and crushed—we shall rise again; but another nasty compromise . . . will so thoroughly disgrace and humiliate us that we can never again raise our heads.

This was what he wanted to talk to Lincoln about: to stiffen him against any last-minute deal with southern slaveholders such as might be pressed upon him by men like Weed, Seward, and the slippery Simon Cameron—all of whom had gathered close about the new chieftain. The fact that they had done so was in itself profoundly disheartening to Greeley. He looked on himself as a practical politician; but these men were entirely too practical for him.

Weed had stalked away from the Chicago convention with a look of dark embitterment, and the *Tribune* had concluded that the dethroned New York boss was through. But within a few weeks Weed had come back smiling, accepting an invitation to meet with

Lincoln and Judge Davis in Illinois, after which the indispensable Judge Davis had journeyed East for a return meeting with Weed. Greeley had watched all this with growing uneasiness, and before long his suspicions were confirmed. For at some point an agreement was reached assuring to Weed and his friends an inside place in the new administration in return for their full support in the campaign.

This meant that Seward, whom Greeley had tried so hard to eliminate, would be influential after all. For a while Greeley had tried to tell himself that it couldn't be so. Seward's term as senator was running out. Raymond had written a midsummer *Times* interview in which Seward, sulking on his Auburn lawn, had said he would not accept a Cabinet post under Lincoln. After the election, Greeley had still kept up his belief that Seward would be left out: "Between us," he wrote the editor Beman Brockway, "Seward will not be invited to take a place in Mr. Lincoln's cabinet, whatever else may betide. He will probably be offered a first-class Mission; but even that is not certain if he insists on being elected to the Senate. However, I only guess this; about the cabinet, I *know*."

But he did not know. A few weeks after he had written this, Lincoln was not only offering Seward a place in his Cabinet, but the top post in it—the Secretaryship of State. Back in the days of the Chicago convention the *Tribune* had congratulated itself on helping to block Seward "in the interest of purity and integrity of administration." Now the discredited New York machine was back with all its power. "Seward is a poor worthless devil," Greeley grimly wrote Colfax, "but Old Abe seems to have a weakness for such."

Lincoln also seemed to have a weakness for Simon Cameron; or rather, Boss Weed and Judge Davis between them would not let Lincoln forget that he owed the Pennsylvania chieftain a debt for having switched at the right moment at Chicago. Everyone who knew politics knew Cameron's reputation. The Philadelphia economist, Henry C. Carey, an old *Tribune* contributor, plainly warned Lincoln that "there exists throughout the state an almost universal belief that [Cameron's] fortune has been acquired by means that are forbidden to the man of honor . . . Most of all well-disposed fellow citizens look upon him as the very incarnation of corruption." Even so, Cameron would have to get a job. The only question was, which one? Here Weed had shown his colors by backing his Pennsylvania friend for the post of Secretary of the Treasury—a job in which, whether he properly watched over the Treasury or not, Cameron would at least take good care of his New York financial friends.

It was a picture calculated to arouse Greeley and make him doubt Lincoln even more than before. While the editor grumbled, Weed had been out spending two December days at Lincoln's Springfield homestead, sparring and spinning yarns over the breakfast sausages and hot cakes. (It is not recorded that Greeley ever shared a meal with Lincoln.) Other Lincoln men who did not want to see Lincoln become Weed's man were grumbling too. Republicanism had come into being partly as a movement to break away from the traffickers in vested privilege; yet here the same traffickers were on hand again, threatening to take over Republicanism. Men as different as William Cullen Bryant, the sage and serious Jacksonian of the *Evening Post*, and Charles A. Dana, the rising Republican stalwart on the *Tribune*, came together to press upon Lincoln the need of offsetting the power of the eastern party bosses and corruptionists. They proposed that he take into his Cabinet three men of unimpeachable character—Salmon P. Chase, Gideon Welles, and Judge Montgomery Blair, all of whom had been Democrats, yet all of whom had become vigorous free-soilers. Welles and Blair, moreover, like Bryant, were old-time Jacksonians. Now Horace Greeley could not get along with Bryant, and in the old days he had bitterly fought the Jacksonians; yet here was Greeley out in a Springfield hotel room with Lincoln, ardently promoting these same men for the new Cabinet. He badgered, he lectured; but he went away without knowing what results he had achieved—if any.

There was simply no point in telling Lincoln that he ought to keep clear of the Weed-Seward crowd. For Lincoln was constantly and acutely aware that he was a minority President—the winner only because of the number of entries in the field—and therefore in need of appeasing powerful rivals far more than of rewarding old friends. He would listen to all sides, Greeley's included, and try to do the best he could for everyone who had a claim. But he would not throw himself into the arms of any one side, for fear of losing the support of the other. And he certainly was not going to throw himself into Horace Greeley's arms.

For, in spite of wide areas of agreement, the two men at the moment differed sharply on two points. The first and major one concerned the American Union. Greeley had been able to say to Lincoln, "Let the Union slide—it may be reconstructed." This Lincoln could never for one moment consider. How he himself felt about the Union he was soon to reveal when he declared on his way to Washington:

I have often inquired of myself what great principle or idea it was that kept this Confederacy so long together. It was not the mere matter of separation of the colonies from the motherland, but that sentiment in the Declaration of Independence which gave liberty not alone to the people of this country, but hope to all the world, for all future time. It was that which gave promise that in due time the weights would be lifted from the shoulders of all men, and that all should have an equal chance.

The other immediate point on which they differed concerned Horace Greeley himself and his political ambitions. A seat in the Senate was to become vacant the moment that William H. Seward was elevated to the Cabinet. Thurlow Weed had his plans as to who should succeed to it. But Greeley also had a plan of his own, and this he communicated to Lincoln. He asked, in short, that the President-elect back him against the Weed-Seward machine in New York. Visions of a final personal triumph over his enemies rose in Greeley's mind. Lincoln listened. Privately, he did not think it a very good idea.

5

Hadn't Greeley learned by now how little fitted he was for holding public office? The answer was, Not at all. Nothing could be done to exorcise his passion for it. He had confessed his resurgent hopes to Beman Brockway right after the election victory: "As to myself, I *would* like to go to the Senate, and *would not* like to go into the Cabinet." (Not that anyone had remotely suggested to him that he might be picked for the Cabinet; but he said that he did not like its "official routine, with great, dull dinners" anyway.) The week following—having enlisted the help of Brockway, who was now editing the upstate Watertown *Reformer* and hurling shots at Weed— Greeley wrote again to say, "I thank you for what you have done in my behalf, but I do not know that I can encourage you to do more. I am very weary, overwhelmed with daily cares, cleared out in money by the expenses of the canvass, and every way under the weather. I am sure I can do nothing to make myself U. S. Senator, and I am not even sure that I would try very hard if sure of success." And next day, having let this tacit appeal for more aid sink into his friend: "I am very patient . . . I have only made up my mind to two things: first that I shall ask nothing of nobody. Second, that the Scripture rule, 'Ask and ye shall receive' will apply to this case, at least negatively."

Greeley did ask, though, and to his delight got encouragement from many New York State Republicans who shared his suspicion and resentment of Boss Weed. Greeley's own three-months' maladroitness in Congress twelve years ago had been all but forgotten. His successful maneuver against Weed and Seward at Chicago had won him national political renown. True, he had been accused of betraying his old allies and of being nothing but a paltry office-seeker himself; but he had managed to turn these attacks back against their makers by showing up Weed's bossism for what it had come to mean in terms of corruption, and to many New York citizens he now seemed the logical man to carry the fight against the Albany machine to its finish.

While Greeley was out West, talking about "Self-made Men" and badgering Lincoln, Dana was busily scurrying up to Albany for him and trying to round up votes in the state legislature to nominate and then elect him to the Senate. Anti-Weed chieftains like David Dudley Field helped along. Even Bryant, over at the *Post*, gave his blessing. Dana and his friends spread stories in the lobbies to the effect that Lincoln was for Greeley's candidacy. This enraged Thurlow Weed, who was at that moment busy lining up legislators behind his own choice for the post, the eminent but rather colorless lawyer, William M. Evarts. He protested at once to Lincoln's political fixer, Judge Davis, "This is a canard of the grossest sort." Davis answered, "The possibility of Greeley's election surprises me . . ." Seward, too, was wrought up, hearing that "Evarts is in danger, and that I ought to interpose for him directly, and secure Mr. Lincoln's interference." On whose side did Lincoln stand, anyway? A formal statement from Springfield was asked for. This was what Weed received, in the first week of February:

DEAR SIR: I have both your letter to myself and that to Judge Davis, in relation to a certain gentleman in your state claiming to dispense patronage in my name, and also to be authorized to use my name to advance the chances of Mr. Greeley for an election to the United States Senate.

It is very strange that such things should be said by anyone. The gentleman you mention did speak to me of Mr. Greeley in connection with the senatorial election, and I replied in terms of kindness toward Mr. Greeley, which I really feel, but always with an expressed protest that my name must not be used in the senatorial election in favor of anyone. Any other representation of me is a misrepresentation.

As to the matter of dispensing patronage, it perhaps will surprise you to learn that I have information that you claim to have my authority to arrange that matter in New York. I do not believe you have so claimed; but still so some men say. On that subject you know all I have said to you is "justice for all," and I have said nothing more particular to anyone. I say this to reassure you that I have not changed my position.

In the hope, however, that you will not use my name in the matter, I am,

Yours truly,
A. LINCOLN

Weed took note: Lincoln was not going to do his bidding, after all. Yet neither was Lincoln beholden to Greeley. Meanwhile the Republican caucus in the Albany legislature was meeting to choose between Greeley and William M. Evarts for the nomination. Weed, usually so amiable and serene as he moved through the lobbies with his stately gait and whitening hair, was worried this time. On the first ballots, Greeley was showing extraordinary strength. The boss retired to the Governor's room and bit his cigar. Fearing that Evarts might not pull through, Weed had given his blessing to a third entry in the race—the former antirenter, Judge Ira Harris—whom he kept in the background for possible emergency use. On the seventh caucus ballot, Greeley began pulling well ahead of Evarts, with the insignificant Harris trailing. Another ballot like this and Greeley might win against the whole machine. Hurriedly Weed issued his orders: all Evarts men were at once to switch their votes to Harris. It worked: Harris won the nomination and thereby the Senate seat. The victory "paid the first installment on a large debt to Mr. Greeley," crowed Weed. But he knew how near he had come to defeat.

6

Greeley, for his part, was not to forget how near he himself had come to a personal triumph. Nor was he to forgive Lincoln for having withheld the support that might have enabled him to overthrow the Albany machine. He met Lincoln again in the middle of that month, climbing aboard the President-elect's special train with his red-and-blue blanket roll in hand as it moved eastward in slow stages along Lake Erie to the inauguration. The Union was fast falling apart; Buchanan's flaccid administration had virtually collapsed; there was open talk that Lincoln would be assassinated before he ever reached the capital. Yet on the rear platform of the train, Greeley saw the President-elect wisecracking with crowds at whistle stops and making easy-going speeches that dismissed the nation's crisis as something "altogether artificial." To a man of Greeley's high-pitched intensity, such casualness in the face of national peril was horrendous. It seemed to confirm his earlier fears that Lincoln was irresolute and not to be relied on. He talked with Lincoln for twenty minutes amid the retinue of politicos. Then he left the train at Erie.

He saw Lincoln again making his progress through New York City and driving in his open carriage through a curious, silent sea of faces to a series of receptions by the city's elders. Then Greeley went on to Washington to see what impact the new Chief Executive would make there. The whole town was speculating on the names Lincoln might announce for his Cabinet. Greeley was apprehensive: "Seward surrounds him perpetually, and will lead him on to ruin," he told Brockway four days before the inauguration; "Seward will have the control of the Cabinet . . . I think we have fought through the nomination of Chase for the Treasury, but I am not sure . . . We are making a last despairing effort to put in Montgomery Blair, so as to have three—Blair, Chase and Welles, with Bates as the pivot or arbiter . . . Old Abe is honest as the sun, and means to be true and faithful; but he is in the web of very cunning spiders and cannot break out if he would." And he added this: "*Mrs.* Abe is a Kentuckian and enjoys flattery—I mean, deference . . ."

March fourth broke bright but blustery, and at noon the Presidential procession, surrounded by cavalry that beat up swirling dust clouds, started up Pennsylvania Avenue between somber crowds and silent houses. Infantrymen lined the rooftops to guard against possible trouble. Sharpshooters were perched high up in pairs among the columns of the unfinished Capitol, eyeing the crowd below as it waited to hear Lincoln speak. Among the frock-coated dignitaries who sat on the high, undraped platform was Horace Greeley, aware that a whole company of soldiers was crouching in the space beneath it. When Lincoln shuffled to his feet, manuscript in hand, Greeley saw Senator Stephen A. Douglas, in the front row, reach forward obligingly to hold his old rival's stovepipe hat while he spoke. He heard the March gusts carrying Lincoln's resonant tenor words: "We are not enemies, but friends . . . Though passion may have strained, it must not break our bonds of affection." He saw the aged Chief Justice Taney—a shriveled relic of Jacksonian days—move forward to administer the oath.

Next day Lincoln announced his Cabinet, and Greeley could breathe with relief: Chase, Welles, and Montgomery Blair all were safely in it. So his own work, and that of the other anti-Weed and anti-Seward leaders, had not been without avail. The New York *Tribune* warmed to the new President. His inaugural speech, it thought, would have "a happy effect on the country," revealing as it did both Lincoln's friendly sentiment toward the South and "the firmness with which he avows his determination to obey the simple letter of his duty." Furthermore, the trio of "no-compromise" men in his Cabinet would resist any attempt by Secretary of State Seward to make him weaken. Federal laws were to be upheld and Federal property secured, wherever it was. "NO COMPROMISE!" the *Tribune* rang out every morning, in a standing banner line at its masthead; "NO CONCESSIONS TO TRAITORS!—*The Constitution As It Is.*"

But within a few weeks the *Tribune's* enthusiasm for the new President paled. He had declared that "the Union is unbroken" and had promised to defend Federal property; yet in fact the Union was now broken, Federal forts were being seized, and at any moment strategic Fort Sumter might go. Why the inaction and delay? In mid-March, calling at the White House, Greeley said he saw the President "listening to the endless whine of office-seekers, and doling out village post offices . . . just as though we were sailing before bland breezes on a smiling summer sea." "Mr. President!" he blurted; "do you know that you will have to fight for the place in which you sit?"

No more temporizing with southern traitors, roared the *Tribune*. The only way to outface them was by assuming a posture that was "proud and manly." The honor of the nation demanded that Fort Sumter, isolated in Charleston Harbor, be kept out of rebel hands. Why this unconscionable delay in reinforcing it? "Let this intolerable suspense and uncertainty cease!" the *Tribune* trumpeted on 3 April. "The Country, with scarcely a show of dissent, cries out —If we are to fight, so be it."

Yet there was dissent, and it centered in the President's Cabinet itself—just as Greeley had feared it might. The trouble stemmed from his ambitious ex-partner, William H. Seward. It was not enough for Seward to be Secretary of State. Looking upon himself as by far the ablest and most distinguished man in the Administration—next to whom Lincoln was a well-meaning ignoramus who had somehow done him out of the Presidency—Seward wanted also to be Prime Minister and run the government on his own. Lincoln, in his incompetence, could hear of his decisions after he had made them. Seward almost got away with this—for a week or two. Flagrantly ignoring Lincoln's pledge to protect Fort Sumter, he assured a Confederate emissary on his own hook that his government, in order to preserve peace, was ready to surrender the Fort.

Greeley did not hear of this particular maneuver. Neither did Lincoln, until after Seward's sovereign word had been handed to the Confederacy. But the *Tribune* did get wind of a Cabinet meeting in late March at which Seward led a majority in opposition to the idea of relieving Fort Sumter by a naval expedition. The only men who had stood up for action that day were Salmon P. Chase of the Treasury and Postmaster General Blair—the two whom Greeley had been most anxious to boost into the Cabinet. Lincoln accepted their minority view, and the expedition was ordered South to Sumter. Thereby Seward's dream of accomplishing some new grand compromise after the style of Henry Clay was frustrated. But Seward did make one more attempt at it —even though again he seriously compromised his government in so doing. Taking advantage of Lincoln in a moment of preoccupation, he managed to get off a message to the departing naval force that detached its strongest ship for other duty, thereby leaving the expedition so weak that it might not fulfill its mission.

Greeley's suspicions were fully aroused. Yet he turned his guns on the President no less than on Seward. On 9 April, when there was still no news of the Sumter expedition, he let go. A government that submitted to any further southern insults, said the *Tribune*, "confesses itself a humbug and a bastard." On the same day he scribbled to Brockway, "Who shall deliver us from the body of this Old Abe? I don't feel like going through another four years of such government." Letters came in denouncing his warlike stand. Yet young Theodore Tilton, a former *Tribune* man who was now editing Henry Ward Beecher's religious weekly, the *Independent*, cheered him by calling upon him to "keep writing and pushing. . . . Go straight ahead—don't stop in these critical times. . . . If there were any other man whose words would be of equal weight with yours on the present condition of public affairs, I would ask him to write—but where is he?"

Four days later came the news that Confederate batteries had fired on Fort Sumter, beaten off its relief expedition, and forced the garrison to strike the United States flag. Lincoln had moved slowly—far too slowly, thought the *Tribune*—but at least, under pressure, he had moved. "Democrat as well as Republican, Conservative and Radical, instinctively feel that the guns fired at Sumter were aimed at the heart of the American Republic," Greeley's paper proclaimed; "it is hard to lose Sumter; it is a consolation to know that in losing it we have gained a united people . . . For Sumter is temporarily lost, but the country is saved. Long live the Republic!"

Greeley's old rival, Bennett of the *Herald*, had gone on arguing into mid-April, "A civil war . . . what for? To 'show that we have a Government? . . .' A war will only widen the breach, and enlarge and consolidate this southern Confederacy." This was the vein in which Greeley himself had once talked—months ago. The new Greeley was speaking another language. And while the *Herald*, after Sumter, grudgingly shook out a fresh set of sails and came about on a new prowar tack, the *Tribune* was steering far out ahead. There must be more action, more troops, more gunboats, younger generals, more determination, it signaled, if the rebellion was to be put down before it could gather momentum. Washington's strategy must be quick, dramatic, and had best follow this program:

First, the military occupation of Maryland, so far as prudence renders it necessary.

Secondly, an advance upon Richmond, and the armed holding of that city.

Thirdly, the military occupation of Norfolk, Charleston, Savannah, Mobile and New Orleans.

Fourthly, the proclamation of martial law in all the rebellious States.

Fifthly, the offering of large rewards for the arrest of Jefferson Davis and his chief conspirators.

Sixthly, their trial and execution under martial law, that being the only way that justice can reach them.

No delay, thundered the *Tribune*; the rebels should be "crushed out in blood and fire if necessary." Lincoln's first call for 75,000 volunteers was good, but not good enough; we needed more cavalry, more artillery. If we moved fast and decisively enough, "Jeff. Davis & Co. will be swinging from the battlements at Washington at least by the Fourth of July." But any sign of dawdling or indecision would protract the war—dangerously. Lincoln, said Greeley, was still slow, still surrounded by men of dubious purposes. "Instead of energy, vigor, promptness, daring, decision," he wrote later, "we had in our counsels weakness, irresolution, hesitation, delay." Moreover, he said, "I apprehend that Mr. Lincoln was very nearly the last man in the country, whether North or South, to relinquish his rooted convictions that the growing chasm might be closed and the union fully restored without the shedding of blood." No quarter, called the *Tribune*, in the face of disloyalty in Maryland: "Let troops be poured down upon Baltimore, and if need be, raze it to the ground." The sturdy civilian soldiers of the North should descend at once upon the arrogant "rebellious minority" and clean out their "foul nests." And then, when no descent materialized throughout the month of June, the *Tribune* pinned to its masthead this standing head:

THE NATION'S WAR-CRY

Forward to Richmond! Forward to Richmond!
The Rebel Congress must not be allowed to
meet there on the 20th of July!

**BY THAT DATE THE
PLACE MUST BE HELD BY THE NATIONAL ARMY!**

XIII. ERRANT KNIGHT

1

"Imagine Greeley booted & spurred with Epaulets on his Shoulders and with a whetted blade in his hands," a New York politician named James Nye snorted to his friend Seward early that year; "shade of a [Winfield] Scott defend us: The idea of Greeley turning warrior, is too ridiculous to be thought of."

The idea was sometimes disturbing to Greeley himself. The *Tribune*, once a pacifist organ, was now trying to tell the generals how to run a war. *"Forward to Richmond,"* Greeley exhorted the laggards, although he himself had a horror of bloodshed. Let the test of battle come quickly, then—and be over. He worried at the thought of a lengthy campaign. "I *do* want to see this war through," he underlined to Colfax in June, and then added nervously, "If the Seceshs [sic] are not whipped this winter, the Union is gone." In public he tried to conceal such trepidations. He had been accused of softness; now he must be hard. But sometimes this outward hardness carried its own suggestion of underlying stress. "Whoever asserts that the *Tribune* does not earnestly desire an early conclusion . . . of this war, defies the confutation of the most notorious facts," his editorial page sputtered one day; "whoever insinuates it aggravates cowardice by falsehood."

Perhaps, he had hoped, if the Union moved quickly enough, there would not have to be an actual drawn battle after all. The rank and file of the gathering Confederate armies might break and run. "The Confederate armies are cowed, if not disorganized," the *Tribune* assured the North in mid-June, when nothing more than skirmishing had happened; "they dare not step on the soil of the loyal states . . . They dare not meet the Unionists in fair and open battle." Why should the slaveless small farmers who were being enlisted on the southern side want to fight at all? "We do not believe," the paper said, "that the thousands forced into the rebel armies by conscription or terror of mob violence will choose to sacrifice their lives for a cause they abhor." This was published on 19 July, 1861. Two days later occurred the first battle of Bull Run.

Afterward, the question arose as to whether the *Tribune*'s "Forward to Richmond" slogan had helped bring on that battle. The banner had been flying at the paper's masthead from 26 June through 4 July—crucial days in the planning of Union strategy. Dana had been inveighing against the immobility of the Federal forces who were lingering along the Potomac "in idleness and dissipation" while the rebellious Virginia capital lay within reach. Greeley had gone a step further and placed the blame on their Regular Army commanders, many of whom, he charged, were of doubtful loyalty and did not want to fight. He was by no means alone in charging this; there was dismay throughout the North at the fact that over a third of the Army's regular officers had gone over to the Confederacy, and many a Republican applauded when the *Tribune* exclaimed that "West Point has long been a nursery for breeding traitors at public expense." The *Tribune*'s war cry echoed all the North's rising impatience and channeled it into a demand for one impetuous action. The pressure told on Washington. Lincoln's war council was acutely aware of it when it met on 29 June to speed up operations and try to devise some move that would supply quick victory for the headlines. Further south, the Confederate General Beauregard was fully informed about this pressure too. So his young army massed directly athwart the main route from Washington to Richmond, with a flanking force under Joe Johnston up in the Shenandoah Valley—and there it waited.

Another man who was conscious of the pressure was the dour, jowled General Irvin McDowell of the Regular Army, who had been given command of the Federal troops pointed against the Virginia lowland. But he was also conscious of his own problems on the ground: his raw, civilian infantry regiments had not yet been pulled together; he had no working brigade formations; he had no cavalry; the one thing he did have in abundance was colonels—most of these, however, being simply elected amateurs with an utter ignorance of warfare and a swollen sense of their importance. Under the pressure, though, McDowell thought he had better try an advance. His chief, the aged General Scott—ponderous, gilt-encrusted, half-palsied, but still alert—advised him to hold back until he was in stronger shape to move. But military experts ranging from Horace Greeley and Charles A. Dana to half a dozen other editors and Abraham Lincoln himself were pressing upon the unhappy McDowell. So he marched—or rather, his half-organized men ambled—through the midsummer heat upon the bristling Confederate positions along Bull Run stream at Manassas.

In midmorning of the 21st the *Tribune*'s reporter on the spot, E. H. House, saw McDowell's men swarm out of the scrubby woodland on the Confederate left and briskly beat down Beauregard's flank regiments. By early afternoon it looked as if the next Federal assault would also carry the battered Confederate center. The reporters sent off glowing rush stories by rider to the telegraph office in the capital. McDowell, too, felt so sure that the rebels were already doomed that he dispatched a signal to Washington proclaiming victory. Early next morning, the *Tribune* was put to bed carrying this account:

A great battle was fought yesterday at Bull's Run. . . . The Rebels had every advantage—position, numbers, and perfect knowledge of the ground over which the Unionists advanced to engage them. Yet all did not avail against the enthusiasm and well-directed valor of the national forces. The Rebel Batteries were ultimately silenced, and their ranks forced back inch by inch, until they were driven from Bull's Run, leaving their dead on the field and the National troops undisputed victors. . . .

There was only one discordant sentence in that triumphal dispatch. "It is morally certain," it ran, "that the enemy have been reinforced by the arrival of Johnston's army from Winchester." A reader of the *Tribune*'s first edition might have paused over this, and wondered.

Johnston's force had indeed arrived, taking the attacking Federals in the rear, and this, in addition to a surprising defense put up by a man who was thenceforth to be known as "Stonewall" Jackson, had turned the battle at the crucial moment in late afternoon. At six P.M. Washington confidentially learned the worst: McDowell's entire army had collapsed in confusion and rout. By that time the correspondents who had filed exuberant stories a few hours earlier were themselves caught up in the dazed swarm that choked the roads of retreat. Their editors heard nothing more from them that night. It was left to a young reporter of the New York *Herald*, Henry Villard—the same young man who had rescued Horace Greeley from his plunging mule one day in Colorado—to disengage himself from the fleeing horde after midnight and ride posthaste to Washington to write the first account of what had actually happened. He put it on the wire the moment the telegraph office opened at seven o'clock. An hour later the *Herald* was on the streets with it, and Greeley, picking up his rival's extra, read the story of disaster.

He had been beaten on a sensational piece of news. Yet this was not the moment to worry about that. He was seized with horror at the news itself. He was implicated in all that had led to Bull Run; he knew that. He had hung all his self-confidence on the outcome. Now the torn regiments were streaming back to Washington, their dead and wounded abandoned in the Virginia scrub. An appalling thought swept over him: he himself was part guilty; there was blood on his hands.

His right-hand man, Dana, was rattled too. For the morning of the 23rd he wrote an editorial that cried out, "We have fought and been beaten. God forgive our rulers that this is so . . . The 'sacred soil' of Virginia is crimson and wet with the blood of thousands of Northern men, needlessly shed. . . . A decimated and indignant people will demand the immediate retirement of the present Cabinet . . ." This outburst only made the paper's position worse. The *Tribune*'s arch-enemies—Raymond of the *Times* and Bennett of the *Herald*—at once struck back. How dare the *Tribune* blame the Cabinet, they exclaimed, when the *Tribune* had only itself to blame? The crime of Bull Run was Greeley's own; he and his "ferocious Jacobins" had brought it on.

Shaken and feverish, Greeley sat down to try to write a reply. The press revulsion against him spread across the North. His newspaper was in danger. He remembered that it was Dana, acting in his absence, who had posted the fatal "Forward to Richmond" slogan at the masthead. Yet he himself had not objected when he saw it. Again, it was Dana who had written the ill-found editorial demanding the Cabinet's dismissal. Yet again, he had approved—or at any rate, he hadn't disapproved. He had built up in the *Tribune* a great instrument of leadership, only to let it flounder now before all the world. Torn between self-defense and self-abasement, he dashed off these distraught paragraphs for next day's paper:

> An individual's griefs or wrongs may be of little account to others; but when the gravest public interests are imperilled through personal attacks and the coarsest implications of base motives, the assailed, however humble, owes duties to others which can not be disregarded. . . .
>
> I am charged with what is called "opposing the administration . . ." and various paragraphs which have from time to time appeared in the *Tribune* are quoted to sustain this inculpation. The simple fact that not one of these paragraphs was either written or in any wise suggested or prompted by me suffices for that charge. . . . It is true that I hold and have urged that this war can not, must not, be a long one; that it must be prosecuted with the utmost energy, promptness and vigor, or it will prove a failure . . . But the watchword, "Forward to Richmond," is not mine . . . So with regard to the late article urging a change in the Cabinet. . . .
>
> I wish to be distinctly understood as not seeking to be relieved from any responsibility for urging the advance of the Union grand army into Virginia . . . I thought that that army, one hundred thousand strong, might have been in the rebel capital on or before the twentieth instant. . . . And now, if any one imagine that I, or any one connected with the *Tribune*, ever commanded or imagined such strategy as the launching of barely thirty thousand . . . against ninety thousand rebels enveloped in a labyrinth of strong entrenchments and unreconnoitered masked batteries, then demonstration would be lost on his closed ear. . . .
>
> If I am needed as a scapegoat for all the military blunders of the last month, so be it. Individuals must die that the nation may live. If I can serve her best in that capacity, I do not shrink from the ordeal.
>
> Henceforth I bar all criticism in these columns on army movements. . . . Henceforth it shall be the *Tribune*'s sole vocation to rouse and animate the American people for the terrible ordeal which has befallen them. . . .
>
> The journal which is made the conduit of the most violent of these personal assaults on me attributes the course of the *Tribune* to resentment "against those who have ever committed the inexpiable offense of thwarting Mr. Greeley's raging and unsatiated thirst of office."
>
> I think this justifies me in saying that there is no office in the gift of the government or of the people which I either hope, wish or expect ever to hold . . .
>
> Now let the wolves howl on. . . .

Yet not even this public act of expiation could right Greeley's tumultuous emotions. Two sides of his being were clearly at war—the man who wanted to help lead a righteous cause, and the man who was fearful of its cost. The cause of the warring North was strong and moral; he was sure of that. But he had believed all his life long that moral causes inevitably prevailed. This one, so soon, had ignominiously failed. Was there something wrong, then, with its morals? Could it ever conquer? And, in the background, wasn't there always the dread thought that more slaughter might simply lead to a worse wrong?

He tossed about and wrung his brain. Every pent-up conflict of his years now lashed back at him. Each day told him that evil forces were gathering to destroy him and his *Tribune*; some that he saw were real, some were imagined. He grew feverish; he took to his bed; extraordinary, unbalanced letters began coming from him; and on 29 July, eight days after the battle, he was near delirium when he scrawled to the President this outcry:

DEAR SIR: This is my seventh sleepless night—yours, too, doubtless—yet I think I shall not die, because I have no right to die. I must struggle to live, however bitterly. But to business. You are now considered a great man, and I am a hopelessly broken one. . . . Can the rebels be beaten after all that has occurred, and in view of the actual state of feeling caused by our late awful disaster? If they can—and it is your business to ascertain and decide—write me that such is your judgment, so that I may know and do my duty. And if they can not be beaten—if our recent disaster is fatal—do not fear to sacrifice yourself to your country. . . .

If the Union is irrevocably gone, an armistice for thirty, sixty, ninety, one hundred and twenty days—better still for a year—ought at once to be proposed with a view to a peaceful adjustment. . . .

This letter is written in the strictest confidence, and is for your eye alone. But you are at liberty to say to members of your Cabinet that you know I will second any movement you may see fit to make. But do nothing timidly or by halves. Send me word what to do. I will live till I can hear it, at all events. If it is best for the country and for mankind that we make peace with the rebels at once, and on their own terms, do not shrink even from that. . . . Do the thing that is the highest right, and tell me how I am to second you.

Yours, in the depth of bitterness,
HORACE GREELEY

Later Greeley said that at the time when he wrote this, he was "all but insane." His doctor diagnosed his case as brain fever and put him to bed in a darkened room in the Nineteenth Street house. For a week he tossed and tumbled, unable to sleep more than two or three hours a night. But by mid-August he was working again. He cast aside all pleas that he go away for a while and rest: "I must stay about the *Tribune* now or let everything go to destruction." His flow of letters resumed, still high-strung, yet now rational again. "I have scarcely slept since Bull's Run," he wrote Brockway. ". . . But as to the *Tribune*: All it said about the way things were managed in regard to the War, Traitors, etc., was the naked truth—yet the *Tribune* should not have said it— certainly not in the *tone* it too often held. . . . Through the faults of several, mainly mine, the *Tribune as a power* is broken down; but I trust its usefulness is not all gone yet. If God decides that I shall live, I hope to make it still a minister of good . . ."

He pulled himself together and cast aside his fears. In the excitement of his returning strength he went to the opposite extreme and described himself as the North's most determined champion. "I guess there is nobody really in earnest in opposing the Jeff Davis rebellion but the *Tribune*," he told Sam Wilkeson, his new Washington correspondent; "and the Confederate States of America, backed by the Northern Democracy and the Catholic priesthood, make a pretty strong antagonist for one newspaper." He still saw himself as standing alone in a world of foes. Yet he felt that he was mending. Very few people knew the extent of his recent disorder. There was only one person who knew that in the course of it he had actually proposed surrendering the whole fighting cause of which he was popularly thought to be a leader. The man who knew was President Lincoln, who had himself opened the distraught message Greeley had sent him, read it, understood it for what it was, and tucked it away in a confidential corner of his desk. No one, Lincoln decided, should see it. Still, it was a valuable confession for him to have in hand—especially valuable because Greeley knew he had it.

2

In a sense Greeley never really mended. The schism in his mind never quite healed between what he had hoped for and what he saw the nation get. In periods when the war went well for the Union and seemed to promise an early decision, his hopes soared again and the *Tribune* became exuberant. But when long months brought only defeats and stalemate, he sank into doubt and depression and steered the *Tribune* in wavering, querulous courses. As a result he was widely looked upon, in his eminence at fifty, as erratic, unpredictable and irresponsible. His paper never fully won back the ground it had lost after the "Forward to Richmond" fiasco. Meanwhile across the way, at the corner of Broadway and Ann Street, the aging, crabbed James Gordon Bennett, at sixty-six, was making extraordinary headway with his *Herald*—even though a New York mob, enraged on the day after Fort Sumter by his proslavery stand, had threatened his *Herald* building and demanded that he run up the United States flag.

To Bennett, quickly hoisting the appropriate colors, the war became a colossal news story, and he covered it with his full genius for capturing each human detail. For Greeley it remained a moral struggle in whose toils he was deeply involved, and his attention kept shifting from its outward news content to the state of his own mind and conscience—a condition which changed so much as to keep him pretty busy reporting on that. Not that he let the paper neglect its news-gathering functions. He built up an expanded wartime Washington news staff around the deft and sometimes devious Sam Wilkeson. He assigned George W. Smalley, the toughest reporter on the paper, to the Army of the Potomac. He sent the daring, self-reliant Albert Richardson, who had supplied him with undercover news from the South, out West to organize a news service in the border areas and then assigned him to cover General Grant's first Mississippi campaign. He took Henry Villard away from Bennett's *Herald*, equipped him with three assistants, a servant, and full field equipment, and sent him out to report General Burnside's move on Fredericksburg. Yet he was always hard pressed to keep up with Bennett, who cast causes to the wind while concentrating on news beats, exclusives, and such audience-building devices as publishing his own stop-press casualty lists in advance of the War Department's—all this at a cost that ran upward of half a million dollars before the war was over. Bennett simply depicted, illustrated, and—when the mood was on him—sneered and savagely exposed. The *Tribune*, meanwhile, argued, scrupled, enthused, deplored, described with moral comment, and then also exposed. The *Tribune*'s formula, amid the daily stress and drawn-out weariness of wartime, was the more demanding, and at times the less rewarding. Bennett drew ahead in daily circulation.

Greeley could not help being upset about the role of Charles A. Dana, to whom he felt he had delegated too much power at the office. "No one man can manage a newspaper for another in such a crisis as this," he told Wilkeson; "and I am peculiarly unfortunate in this respect." The mischief was his own doing: he had spent too much time away talking, lecturing, and playing the practical politician. (Later a subsequent *Tribune* managing editor, John Russell Young, was to spot his chief's problem clearly when he remarked, "Mr. Greeley would be the greatest journalist in America if he did not aim to be one of the leading politicians in America.") And Greeley's worries about Dana's editorial power at the shop were increased by the knowledge of his growing financial power there, too. For the managing editor had now become one of the *Tribune*'s major stockholders. In fact, in the process of amiably parceling out shares to his employes, Greeley had let his own interest in the firm decline to the point where he now held only fifteen shares, while Dana held twenty. Samuel Sinclair, the new publisher, who had bought up Tom McElrath's holdings, was concerned about Dana's inordinate influence, too. He knew what was in Greeley's mind. Accordingly he rounded up several other stockholders in a move to force Dana out.

Greeley recognized in his strong-willed, imaginative managing editor the best newspaperman the *Tribune* had produced. Yet they had drawn temperamentally far apart: while Greeley still remained the surging enthusiast for a score of causes, Dana with the coming of middle years and prosperity had turned away from his early insurgency and toward solidity, conformity, and comfort. The blow fell, and Dana was out on the street. Yet he did not stay there long. The War Department called him in, and within a few months he was made Assistant Secretary of War.

3

So Lincoln had taken Greeley's discarded subordinate into his family. Greeley saw in the appointment an administration gesture directed against himself. It added to the strain that had been growing over the months between himself and the White House. Dana, for his part, circulated in Washington his own version of the *Tribune* break. "Mr. Greeley never gave a reason for dismissing me," he said, "nor did I ever ask for one. I know, though, that the real explanation was that while he was for peace I was for war, and that as long as I stayed on the *Tribune* there was a spirit there which was not his spirit."

Dana's story was frankly malicious. The true difference between Greeley and Dana had been not over peace vs. war, but over the kind of war that was to be fought. Greeley, recovering from his midsummer lapse, had found fresh hope in the way the Union armies were being reorganized and trained for a fresh assault. But he had also been asking himself the question, Victory—what for? What must we do now, while the iron is hot, to turn this sacrifice to some social good?

Restore the Union; that's enough for now! argued all the followers of Lincoln's moderation. One issue at a time! On the other hand the radical abolitionists were busy with their cry, Free the slaves! No union with slavery!—and they were pointing with revulsion to the fact that Union commanders in the field had orders to respect slaveowners' property even to the extent of restoring fugitive Negroes to their masters. Greeley had never before sided with this extreme group. Yet now, amid the drifting doubts of the war's first months, he felt the need of anchoring himself to some one moral certainty. In mid-June, 1861, his *Tribune* had still been able to say, "We have insisted that the War should not be perverted from its one avowed, legitimate, essential purpose [i.e., suppression of the rebellion] into a crusade against Slavery. If it should be, the zeal of many would be cooled, while thousands who are today for the Union would be driven over to the side of its adversaries." But by mid-autumn this argument was no longer good enough for Greeley. If the war was to be sustained by a winning moral purpose, he now felt, it must in fact become a crusade. That is, even while struggling toward its first objective—Union—it must proclaim the second: Emancipation.

The *Tribune* enthused when Greeley's old friend John C. Frémont, acting on his own responsibility as Union commanding general in divided Missouri, ordered the confiscation of the slaves of all who had taken up arms against the Union there. It was dismayed when Lincoln thereupon annulled the order. (So, among other antislave men, was Lincoln's long-time law partner, Herndon, himself: "Does the war go on to suit you?" he exclaimed; "It does not suit me. Frémont's proclamation was right. Lincoln's modification of it was wrong.") Greeley cheered, again, when Secretary of War Cameron—for whom he otherwise had no use—in midautumn authorized the use of fugitive slaves by Union commanders in the field. He began agitating for a general appeal to slaves to come over and join the Northern side against their masters. But then Lincoln toned down Cameron's program, too, and once again the *Tribune* grumbled. And in December, when Lincoln assured Congress in his first annual message, "I have been anxious and careful that the inevitable conflict . . . shall not degenerate into a violent and remorseless revolutionary struggle," Greeley felt sure that all his suspicions were right: the President had fallen into the hands of operators who did not wish to fight slavery at all.

He himself, six months before, had used precisely the same arguments that Lincoln was now using for going slow on drastic antislavery measures. But now he feared that the war was going slow on everything. Greeley, too, in times past had called for a strategy of moderation in order to hold the wavering tier of border states in line—which was precisely the thing Lincoln was doing now. But Greeley was through with that strategy; he felt it had given more than it got. His own patience had worn out; he feared that temporizing might be the worst breeder of disaffection; now there was no time to lose. Nothing about the President so amazed and estranged him as Lincoln's willingness to wait, to postpone decisions, to hold burning issues in abeyance, and to appear philosophical when matters went wrong. Why, Greeley remarked years later, speaking of the first battle of Bull Run, "the wanton rout of that black day cost the President but one night's sleep"—as if a stronger President would have tossed on his bed for weeks on end, like Greeley.

Lincoln was being all too philosophical, though, many people began to think, toward his new military favorite, the bumptious but still immobile General George B. McClellan, now commanding the fast-swelling Army of the Potomac. "Little Mac's" succession to the deposed McDowell's command had been greeted with enthusiasm, even on the part of the New York *Tribune*. But as autumn wore on and the highly praised drill master went on promising great battles without delivering any, the *Tribune* and a great part of the public began asking questions. What was wrong with the man whom Greeley had first acclaimed as "young Napoleon?" Didn't he want to fight? No, the radicals answered, he didn't; he was a conservative, a Democrat, a professional soldier who deplored all antislavery agitation—in other words, another West Pointer who couldn't be relied on. And in fact, while McClellan went on training and talking and keeping his big divisions safely in camp, a small Union detachment had been smashed and humiliated by Confederate riflemen at nearby Ball's Bluff. When was this sort of thing going to end? Greeley burst out again, at the sight of wasted blood. Did the generals and the politicians in Washington have any will at all to act?

"For half a year we have had one continued succession of disasters—all owing to the supineness and stupidity of the people at Washington," he exclaimed in October to James R. Gilmore, who called at his office one day while he was writing an editorial. The pen dropped and the high voice ran on: "Six months! And we worse off than when we began! Why, six weeks of such a man as Jackson would have stamped the whole thing out, and now it must go on till both sections are ruined, and all because we have no sense or energy in the Government. It pains, it grieves me to think of it; for I feel in a measure responsible for it. For you know it is said that but for my action in the Convention, Lincoln would not have been nominated. It was a mistake—the biggest mistake in my life."

Gilmore, who shared Greeley's antislavery views—but not his current opinion of Lincoln—had an idea. As a successful New York cotton broker before the war, he had traveled up and down the South and there had conceived a first-hand hatred of the whole slave system. Meanwhile, as a promoter with a writing flair, he had dabbled in backing magazines, and now he wanted to launch a propaganda monthly that would expose southern conditions and state the theme—as he put it to Greeley—that "The Union can't be saved without destroying slavery." Greeley was at once interested—especially since Gilmore wanted him to write for it. The promoter went on to say that the magazine also had the backing of one of Lincoln's closest advisers, the former senator, lobbyist and Kansas territorial governor, Robert J. Walker. Walker, an ex-Buchanan man who had turned into an ardent Unionist, stood so high in the President's estimation that Lincoln—so Gilmore said—"will naturally seek his advice on all important subjects that may, from time to time, come up." Then Gilmore clinched his point: "Lincoln will be forced to be open with him, and thus I shall know all the inner workings of the administration."

Greeley eyed him shrewdly. "For Walker will tell you all such things?"

"Of course. He has Mr. Lincoln's permission to do so."

The upshot was that Greeley agreed to write for the new *Continental Monthly* at twenty-five dollars an article. In exchange he blandly suggested that Walker and Gilmore pass on to him, for the *Tribune*, some of the inside information they were about to get.

This little play was duly communicated to Lincoln. He saw its possibilities right away. Here was a chance, by promising the *Tribune* a few tips from time to time, to recapture the editor for the administration and—as Walker put it—to "keep him from going off on tangents." If Gilmore's account is trustworthy, a meeting between Lincoln, Walker and himself thereupon occurred at which the President wholeheartedly fell in with the idea. Sitting down at once, he drafted a letter—nominally addressed to Walker but actually intended for Greeley's eyes—in which he proposed a most unusual arrangement. He promised to reveal fully to Walker "the policy of the Government—its present views and future intentions when formed—giving you permission to communicate them to Gilmore for Greeley." The source of these communications, of course, must be kept hidden, and Greeley was not to let any of his subordinates in on the secret. "[Greeley] will be, in effect, my mouthpiece, but I must not be known to be the speaker."

Then, having offered a giant favor, Lincoln gilded it with flattery. "I need not tell you," he went on in his letter to Walker, "that I have the highest confidence in Mr. Greeley. He is a great power. Having him firmly behind me will be as helpful to me as an army of 100,000 men." It was not difficult to see what effect that sentence would have on the man at the *Tribune*. "That he has ever kicked the traces has been owing to his not being fully informed. . . . If he ever objects to my policy, I shall be glad to have him state to me his views frankly and fully. I shall adopt his if I can. If I cannot, I will at least tell him why. He and I should stand together, and let no minor differences come between us, for we both seek one end, which is the saving of our country." And then —as if he had not poured on enough already—Lincoln added this closing touch: "Now, Governor, this is a longer letter than I have written in a month—longer than I would have written for any other man than Horace Greeley."

Gilmore, the intermediary, promptly brought this letter to New York to show to the man for whose eyes it had been designed. He observed Greeley's first reactions. The editor lit up, he reported, and beamed with a "simple joyousness." Greeley read it over again, thought awhile, and then exclaimed of Lincoln, "He is a wonderful man—wonderful. I never can harbor a thought against him, except when I keep away from him. You must let me keep this letter . . . I want it just to look at when I am downhearted."

4

That was in December, 1861. Now, for a while, the *Tribune* steered a course closer to the administration. Actually, there is no record that Lincoln passed on to Greeley any information of real value. Greeley in fact later complained that the President had welshed on the agreement and sent him nothing worth while at all. It was the letter itself that achieved Lincoln's immediate effect. But at the same time it also had the effect of making Greeley believe that his own ideas would be listened to receptively at the White House. So, while suspending outright criticism, he kept up his pressure for what he desired most—speed in operations and early steps toward Negro Emancipation. Privately he was still suspicious and subject to impatient outbreaks: "If the rebels are not whipped by June, they never will be," he told Colfax. But in public he remained calm. Lincoln and Walker thought they had won their game with the *Tribune*.

Greeley did go on attacking the overblown McClellan; he could not resist that. But he cast his argument for emancipation in shrewd terms that were calculated to persuade rather than antagonize the President. He knew that the administration was daily growing more fearful that Britain and France might recognize the Confederacy as a belligerent nation separated from the United States—a move that would have the severest moral and material repercussions in the North. He also knew—as did the administration—that the mass of people in those countries detested the slavery system. But if they were to discourage their governments from aiding the Confederacy, they must first be convinced that the North was in fact fighting a war against slavery and for human freedom. For this reason, then, if for no other, the administration must act forcefully and dramatically against slavery wherever its forces met it.

Numerous abolitionists had been making this point. Greeley threw the power of the *Tribune* behind it and developed it. The nation and the administration heard him. His correspondents abroad dwelt on the increasing danger of European intervention calculated to help the South. He picked up and spread curious rumors—such as the story passed on to him by the formidable antislavery lady novelist, Lydia Maria Child, to the effect that Mason and Slidell, the Confederate agents who had been seized on their way to England, were carrying secret instructions with them to hold out southern abolition of slavery to Britain and France as an inducement to an alliance. Here was a good propaganda point to make: If we wouldn't emancipate the slaves ourselves, Europe would do it for us! ("The question is, which party shall emancipate first," Lydia Child had remarked; "really, this is the Lord's doing . . . That two selfish parties should be forced by events into competition for doing what neither wanted to do! It is wonderful! Be of good cheer. God reigns!")

All this was grist for Greeley. He kept up the pressure. Sam Wilkeson buttonholed Washington lawmakers in his name. Then, in March, 1862, Lincoln stirred and proposed to Congress a scheme of partial, "compensated" emancipation. This was simply a program of buying out all slaveholders in those border slave states that had not left the Union. It was a small beginning, but the *Tribune* publicly thanked God that America had "so wise a ruler."

As it turned out, it was not much of a beginning: under counter-pressure from those same border states, the idea was shelved. The *Tribune* grew impatient again. Once more Greeley felt he had been right when he said, Stop coddling the border states; you'll get nowhere with it. Equivocal slaveholding Kentucky aroused him. "The cause of the Union will be stronger if Kentucky should secede with the rest than it is now," he is said to have told Lincoln one day in the White House. "Oh, I can't think that," was Lincoln's reply.

He laid on more pressure. At the end of March he received a peculiarly hesitant letter from Lincoln, arguing that compensated emancipation should be urged "*persuasively*, and not *menacingly* upon the South.*" He was "a little uneasy," Lincoln went on, "about the abolishment of slavery in the District [of Columbia], not but that I would be glad to see it abolished, but as to the time and manner of doing it. If some one or more of the border-states would move first, I should greatly prefer it . . ." And, significantly, the President added, "I do not talk to members of Congress on the subject—except when they ask me."

From Greeley's point of view, this was nothing but a confession of indecision and weakness. (Now both men had confessed to one another—a unique performance between two leaders who still would not admit that they might hold any worries in common.) The *Tribune* grew less friendly. At the same time General McClellan, well mounted and with fully a hundred thousand highly trained, eager troops in hand, had finally worked up enough self-confidence to launch his long-awaited grand advance upon Richmond. "I shall be in Richmond in ten days," he had boasted outside his tent flaps. That was back in mid-February. Yet in May he was still working his way cautiously along the Yorktown peninsula against smaller Confederate numbers. Then he settled down to drawn-out siege operations. "McClellan is a dear luxury," Salmon P. Chase told Greeley, in whom the Secretary of the Treasury was finding a kindred spirit; "fifty days—fifty miles—fifty millions of dollars—easy arithmetic but not satisfactory. If one could have some faith in his competency in battle . . . it would be a comfort."

The end of June saw the slaughter of the Seven Days' Battles before Richmond, without bringing the "young Napoleon" any nearer to his goal. As a result his whole grand assault was called off, and the commander removed. So the *Tribune* had been right all along about McClellan, Greeley could say, as the bloodied Army of the Potomac drew off northward. And if he had been right about those "military aristocrats" who lacked stomach for the cause, then wasn't he also in the right on the other immediate issue—emancipation? After McClellan's failure, Northern morale tumbled; a panic wave seized Wall Street; the President called for 300,000 fresh volunteers; and in the excitement Congress passed a law confiscating such slaves of rebel masters as came into Federal hands, and permitting their use in the Army. This looked like a big step forward; but Greeley thought he had evidence that the President and most of his commanders shrank from applying it—which, indeed, they did. He waited a few more weeks, and still the administration faltered. Then he decided to go ahead on his own and deal a propaganda stroke that would force the issue.

What he did not know was that Lincoln at the very same time

had decided on a bold public stroke too, and in the same direction. The two men's minds, outwardly in opposition, had a way of moving amazingly in concert. It was true that Lincoln had been worried by the new confiscation act and its provision for arming the Negroes. Yet on 22 July he had gone before his Cabinet with an even more revolutionary measure in hand. It was the draft of a proclamation written to declare that as of next New Year's Day, all slaves in rebel territory would be free. Seward was apprehensive and had counseled delay, arguing that such a document, if issued amid the present wave of defeats, might sound like the last gasp of northern desperation. His call for postponement had prevailed; but the great paper now lay ready in Lincoln's desk, approved in principle and awaiting only a battlefield victory to bring it out into the world.

Of this Greeley heard only that Seward once again had blocked an attempt by Lincoln to move in the way the *Tribune* wanted him to. He learned this through Sam Wilkeson's grapevine, and at once concluded that Lincoln's move had been blocked entirely. He knew Seward well—too well. He did not know Lincoln quite so well. Meanwhile the private information channel set up to carry messages from Lincoln to Walker to Gilmore to Greeley failed to function on this, its vital occasion. The champing editor thought that Lincoln quite definitely was not going to emancipate the slaves. Very well: all the more reason for staging a showdown now.

To Charles Sumner, the leader of the Senate "Radicals," Greeley wrote on 7 August, "Do you remember that old theological book containing this: 'Chapter One—Hell; Chapter Two—Hell Continued.' Well, that gives a hint of the way Old Abe *ought to be* talked to in this crisis of the Nation's destiny." That was the way he now resolved to talk. Gilmore, calling at the *Tribune* office, heard as much. Then Gilmore went to the White House to report.

"I infer from the recent tone of the *Tribune* that you are not always able to keep Brother Greeley in the traces," said Lincoln.

No, Gilmore admitted, he wasn't. But he said that Greeley's new managing editor, Sidney H. Gay, with whom he had been dealing, had at least "softened Mr. Greeley's wrath on several occasions."

"What is he so wrathy about?" asked the President—according to Gilmore's account.

"The slow progress of the war—what he regards as the useless destruction of life and property, and especially your neglect to make a direct attack upon slavery," said Gilmore. "On this last point I am told by Mr. Gay that he is now meditating an appeal to the country, which will force you to take a decided position."

"Why does he not come here and have a talk with me?" asked the President.

Gilmore answered that Greeley refused to come and had said that he didn't want to have Abraham Lincoln presuming to act as advisory editor of the New York *Tribune*. Would it be all right for Gilmore himself to run up to New York and tell Greeley about the forthcoming Emancipation Proclamation, in order to head off a *Tribune* storm?

At first the President was reluctant. He said he feared Greeley's "passion for news." He may also have feared that Greeley, if told the full story of this all-important document, might blackmail the White House into issuing it at once. Yet finally he agreed to let Gilmore go.

Gilmore started at once for New York. When he arrived next morning he picked up a copy of the day's *Tribune*. There he found splashed across its editorial page, under the startling heading, "The Prayer of Twenty Millions," a lengthy open letter addressed by Horace Greeley to President Lincoln, and beginning:

DEAR SIR: I do not intrude to tell you—for you must already know—that a great proportion of those who triumphed in your election, and of all who desire an unqualified suppression of the rebellion now desolating our country, are sorely disappointed and deeply pained by the policy you seem to be pursuing with regard to the slaves of rebels. I write only to set succinctly and unmistakably before you what we require, what we think we have a right to expect, and of what we complain. . . .

5

Now there was no way of keeping the two wills from clashing before the public ear. What Greeley was saying to Lincoln, in the name of his "Twenty Millions" (a number many times the actual size of his *Tribune* audience) was that he, as President, had been "strangely and disastrously remiss" in carrying out the terms of the recent Confiscation Act. He charged Lincoln with letting himself be "unduly influenced" by "certain fossil politicians hailing from the Border Slave States" who wanted him to forget that "Slavery is everywhere the inciting cause and sustaining base of treason."

He declared that a Union "so wantonly, wickedly assailed by rebellion as ours has been . . . cannot afford to temporize with traitors, nor with semi-traitors." He went on to say that "all attempts to put down the rebellion and at the same time uphold its inciting cause are preposterous and futile"; and he closed with a ringing demand that the President set aside all his qualms about the Confiscation Act and enforce it to the letter, giving immediate freedom as well as military employment to all rebels' slaves coming within the Union power.

The challenge was sweeping, imperious and direct. All the Union as well as the press of western Europe heard it. Lincoln read it and pondered. He had in his hands the one answer which would certainly trump it—his Emancipation Proclamation, lying secreted in his desk. But he was not to be pressured into issuing this paper simply on demand of the New York *Tribune*. He resolved, instead, on an answer that would try to defend his existing position and avoid any definite commitment. He knew he was grappling with a master propagandist, but even so, the more he thought about it the more he welcomed the chance of this confrontation. He wrote out a draft reply and read it aloud to some callers to gauge its effect. He waited two days. Then he released this letter to the press:

> Executive Mansion,
> Washington, August 22, 1862

HON. HORACE GREELEY:

DEAR SIR—I have just read yours of the 19th instant, addressed to myself through the New York *Tribune*.

If there be in it any statements or assumptions of fact which I may know to be erroneous, I do not now and here controvert them.

If there be in it any inferences which I may believe to be falsely drawn, I do not now and here argue against them.

If there be perceptible in it an impatient and dictatorial tone, I waive it in deference to an old friend whose heart I have always supposed to be right.

As to the policy I "seem to be pursuing," as you say, I have not meant to leave any one in doubt. I would save the Union. I would save it in the shortest way under the Constitution.

The sooner the national authority can be restored the nearer the Union will be—the Union as it was.

If there be those who would not save the Union unless they could at the same time save slavery, I do not agree with them.

If there be those who would not save the Union unless they could at the same time destroy slavery, I do not agree with them.

My paramount object is to save the Union, and not either to save or destroy slavery.

If I could save the Union without freeing any slaves, I would do it—if I could save it by freeing all the slaves, I would do it—and if I could do it by freeing some and leaving others alone, I would also do that.

What I do about slavery and the colored race, I do because I believe it helps to save this Union, and what I forbear, I forbear because I do not believe it would help to save the Union.

I shall do less whenever I shall believe what I am doing hurts the cause, and I shall do more whenever I believe doing more will help the cause.

I shall try to correct errors when shown to be errors, and I shall adopt new views so fast as they shall appear to be true views.

I have here stated my purpose according to my views of official duty, and I intend no modification of my oft-expressed personal wish that all men everywhere could be free. Yours,

A. LINCOLN

This letter, so shrewdly conceived and masterfully executed, did not actually answer Greeley's specific appeal. It simply outflanked his with a far warmer, subtler counterappeal of its own. Greeley knew at once that he had been outmaneuvered and outdone. Lincoln, he told Gilmore, had "added insult to injury by answering my 'Prayer of Twenty Millions,' which asked only for the honest enforcement of an existing law, as if it had been a demand for the abolition of slavery; thus adroitly using me to feel the public pulse, and making me appear as an officious meddler in affairs that properly belong to the government. No, I can't trust your 'honest Old Abe.' He is too smart for me."

Yet the game between them was not all one-sided. Greeley, too, had scored heavily on the mind of Abraham Lincoln, as well as on that of at least a weighty proportion of his "twenty millions." For the moment it might do for Lincoln to tell them that "if I could save the Union without freeing any slave, I would do it"; but this argument was wearing thin. Lincoln himself had already reached the moment—as he himself put it—"when I felt that slavery must die that the nation might live." Greeley had helped push him toward that still-unannounced decision. Now, with his ever-present threat of continuing the public pressure begun by his "Prayer," Greeley was pushing Lincoln toward converting that decision into action. Was the President of the United States to go on writing defensive letters to the press to cover up his postponement? There was only one way to silence Greeley and the radicals. That was by doing quickly what he had already decided he had better do.

First there must be a victory in the field, though, as Seward had insisted. Instead, late August brought a smashing defeat—and again at fatal Bull Run. Ragged but jubilant, Robert E. Lee's victorious Confederates now came streaming northward past Washington to try to cut the North in two. No, this was distinctly not the moment for an Emancipation Proclamation. What happened instead was that, other generals having failed, the cautious McClellan was called back to command. "Well, here we are besieged again in Washington," wrote Salmon P. Chase to Greeley, in one of those letters in which the ambitious Secretary tried to keep Greeley at odds with the President; "McClellan commands the army which defends the Capital against the powerful host of rebels who have invaded Maryland. I say powerful host. Perhaps the language is too strong. I do not believe that the number which has actually crossed into Maryland exceeds 75,000. . . . We outnumber them decidedly on the rolls. But we have too many stragglers, too careless officers, too little discipline, too little scope for *honorable* ambition to rise . . ."

Nevertheless, Little Mac, in mid-September, managed to pull his army's sprawling divisions together enough to stage a head-on collision with Lee on the narrow ground where Antietam Creek ran into the upper Potomac. The *Tribune* man, George W. Smalley, saw it all, while Matthew Brady took the world's first photographs of men in battle. When Hooker's and Mansfield's corps stormed the Confederate woods and Sumner's carried Bloody Lane, Smalley raced off the smoking field to ride the darkening road to Washington, flash the victory news to Lincoln personally, and then write a first-hand *Tribune* story that beat the entire nation's press. Lincoln, Greeley, and the whole North cheered. McClellan sluggishly failed to follow up his corps commanders' triumph and pin Lee down—but no matter. The occasion would do. The Emancipation Proclamation hurriedly came out of the President's drawer. On the 22nd the press had it. "It is the beginning of the end of the rebellion," Greeley's *Tribune* sang out as it splashed the news; "it is the beginning of the new life of the nation. . . . GOD BLESS ABRAHAM LINCOLN!"

6

Little Mac—who had lacked the energy to drive Lee back to where he came from—looked up angrily when he read the proclamation which the blood shed by his soldiers at Antietam had bought. "It is now a war for abolition," he grumbled. He wanted no part of that. Again he was removed—this time for good. "It's a stride!" Wendell Phillips enthused of Lincoln's state paper. James Gordon Bennett, on the other hand, flew into a rage. It signified an abject surrender to the "radicals," said his *Herald*; Greeley was a "seditionist," a "disunionist," a "political cheat" and a "hypocrite," while Lincoln was simply "an imbecile joker." Raymond, over at the *Times*, was of divided mind. The Emancipation Proclamation, he said coolly, reflected political necessities. Bryant at the *Evening Post* stood up to cheer those necessities. Greeley for his part sat back amiably and reflected on his part in bringing those necessities about. Good will for Lincoln now exuded from him. "Since the President has shown a disposition to go straight ahead so fast and so far as circumstances will warrant," he wrote Colfax in Washington, "I want to do all I can to strengthen him with the country." This was to be the *Tribune*'s official message to the White House. "I am willing to go slowly," Greeley added to Colfax for Lincoln, "provided I am sure of going at all."

All would be well, then—provided that Horace Greeley remained filled with moral certitude. For the moment he beamed. He predicted that the President's new emancipation policy would in itself assure an early triumph over the South. Moral force was the invincible weapon, after all; he repeated the principle on which he had always insisted.

The November Congressional elections that year did not seem to bear him out, for they showed an alarming swing in the North away from the administration and toward the equivocal Democrats. No matter. The *Tribune* took a deep breath and denied that this meant anything. If the elections had any significance at all, Greeley stoutly declared, they showed simply that the mass of patriotic young Republican voters had gone off to war and thereby lost their chance to vote, leaving the shirking Democrats behind to capture the polls.

Put this way, the story sounded passable. But Greeley's confidence died again in wintertime, when once more the road to Richmond blocked the Union's hoarded hopes. This time the blunderer was General Burnside, whose clumsy frontal assault came to nothing at Fredericksburg. Henry Villard was there for the *Tribune*. Ironically enough, he turned the news of this fresh disaster into another triumphant *Tribune* news beat. Breaking out of the press camp on which the beaten Burnside had imposed strict silence, Villard had rushed his story by boat and horseback to Washington and then on to New York by messenger, evading the telegraph censors at the capital. After filing his copy he had hurried over to the White House, still begrimed, to blurt the truth. "I hope it is not as bad as all that," Lincoln had remarked to him, since he had not yet heard the details from his generals. But it was as bad as that. In fact, it was worse.

The *Tribune* muttered against this latest ranking military incompetent who wore sideburns. Then, amid January floods, storms, and ice floes in the Rappahannock, Burnside ordered yet another frontal assault. Again the Federals were to charge across the river into the waiting Confederate rifle pits beyond. This was too much for the shaken Army of the Potomac, many of whose regiments now threatened mutiny. It was too much for Burnside's hardiest corps commander, "Fighting Joe" Hooker, who appealed to Lincoln to prevent another crazy massacre. It was definitely too much for Horace Greeley, who had heard from Villard the full story of what the Potomac generals had done to their army, and who now lost hope of victory. He took to thinking of an armistice, as he had done after the first Bull Run. Only this time he did his thinking in public.

Managing editor Sidney Gay could do nothing to stop Greeley from saying openly in the *Tribune* on 22 January, 1863:

> If three months more of earnest fighting shall not serve to make a serious impression on the rebels; if the end of that term shall find us no further advanced than its beginning; if some malignant Fate has decreed that the blood and treasure of the Nation shall ever be squandered in fruitless efforts,—let us bow to our destiny, and make the best attainable peace.

The whole North heard this. What was worse was that the South heard it too, and drew its own conclusions. If the Union's leading editor spoke in this way, it was surely a confession that the morale of the North was crumbling and that the government at Washington was near the end of its rope. Southern leaders swallowed their long-standing hatred of Greeley and now passed his editorial around as a tonic to raise flagging Confederate spirits. Richmond, Montgomery and New Orleans papers copied it. The mischief was done. Then Greeley went on in his gloom and did more.

Ten days before he wrote his defeatist editorial, he had received a four-page communication marked "Private" from one of Washington's most suspected residents—the handsome, shifty Clement L. Vallandigham of Illinois, recently retired from Congress for his pro-slavery opinions. This man, a minister's son who had inherited the language of non-resistance and studded it with grandiose apologetics in Latin and Greek, had set himself up as the North's "apostle of peace" and declared himself ready for martyrdom. But at the same time, amid all his Christian professions, he had proclaimed his preference for the slave system and entered into dealings with Confederate agents, going so far as to mobilize all northern defeatists he could find to agitate for a settlement on Southern terms.

Vallandigham, unstable and conspiratorial, thought he might find in Greeley a kindred spirit. "Evidently you and I have mistaken each other for some time past," he wrote him. "You thought me a secessionist, one willing to yield up the Union and aid the South in leaving it. I knew myself to be one of the truest of Union men; but one believing in a mode of saving the Union not very popular till of late—by peace and compromise. On the other hand, I have thought you a disunionist for years—and one especially who had rather break up the Union than have it 'endure part slave and part free.' You are no doubt satisfied now that Slavery cannot be abolished by fighting—or Proclamations." If only Greeley would take the next step of agreeing that the whole agitation to abolish slavery should be called off, "we shall not differ greatly at last." He played on Greeley's horror at the cost of battle: "If the war keeps on, the end will be slavery everywhere. . . . Worse will follow, too—universal revolution in the free states; and the men who are now in power, or have aided them through the press or otherwise, will perish." The price of reunion, then, was simply "slavery on the old basis." "Is it not worth the price?" he asked. He called upon Greeley to join him in a covert campaign for mediation: "*You* can do much. . . . Do nothing against peace in the *Tribune*; but do what you desire to do for it, *first outside*." And in a postscript he added confidentially, "I could talk much more fully."

Greeley had despised the slippery figure of Clement Vallandigham. Yet now he entered into communication with him. He evidently thought that the ranking Copperhead of the Midwest might serve him as a carrier of an armistice offer to the South. Vallandigham, for his part, clearly looked upon Greeley as an amiable innocent who might be wrapped in his coils. Just what they said to one another is unknown. But the results became evident enough to compromise Greeley before the nation.

Shortly after receiving Vallandigham's first message, the editor of the New York *Tribune* proceeded to Washington to meet privately with a foreign emissary—the representative of Emperor Napoleon III, Henri Mercier. Napoleon was at this moment working up a scheme to "mediate" the American civil conflict—not for humanitarian reasons, to be sure, but simply in order to divide the United States permanently in two and thereby advance his own colonial ambitions in neighboring Mexico. The State Department had learned this on 15 January, and was on its guard. Greeley appears to have been informed, too; but at all events, his own guard was down. Ever since Margaret Fuller had written for the *Tribune* her first-hand account of the Little Napoleon's siege of republican Rome, Greeley's paper had been a noisy foe of the Emperor's unconscionable foreign adventures. It had denounced his current efforts to take advantage of American wartime distraction at home and build himself a puppet empire in the morass of Mexico. It was thoroughly aware of the monarch's leaning toward the Confederacy and his desire to win it as a benevolent partner. Yet the *Tribune* took this moment to hint that foreign mediation might be the only way to end the war, in case the Union could not win an early victory in the field. This was precisely what the devious Bonaparte and his minister wanted to hear.

One night, on an Albany-bound boat, Greeley ran into Henry Raymond, who was traveling upriver to see Weed. The two editors who had called each other so many names leaned at the rail for a talk. According to Raymond's account of it, Greeley opened up frankly and unburdened himself. He said it was time that either

France or Switzerland or a concert of European powers intervene and mediate, and added that he was out to persuade Washington to accept the idea. "You'll see," he declared; "I'll drive Lincoln to it."

He went to Washington to have a confidential talk with Mercier. He appears to have assured Napoleon's minister that there was a growing sentiment throughout the North that would welcome mediation. Mercier's instructions, meanwhile, had been to promote just such sentiment as this. It was important for Napoleon's purposes that the initial move for mediation appear to come from Washington rather than from Paris. Through popular pressure the administration was to be inveigled into appointing peace commissioners ready to treat with the South—at which point the Emperor would gracefully offer his help and move in.

Secretary of State Seward, his wits sharpened by two years of dealing with foreign, pro-southern interventionists, understood the French game and would have none of it. When Napoleon's proposal was formally presented at the State Department, he brusquely tossed it aside. Then Mercier told the Secretary that Horace Greeley, the nation's leading Republican editor, had himself privately suggested mediation—which caused Seward to explode. Furthermore, Seward learned that Greeley had set forth his ideas in a letter to Mercier which the French diplomat in turn had read to his Russian colleague in Washington, Stoeckel, and that when Mercier "came to the concluding paragraph, which was a protest that [Greeley] could not favor any mediation which should hazard the Union, he said, 'That's all bosh, of course.'"

So, at least, Seward told his friend Raymond of the *Times*. Greeley was manifestly getting out of hand. Here he was setting himself up as a special, private emissary of the American people, and thereby embarrassing if not actually undermining his government. Seward uttered dark threats. There was the sixty-year-old Logan Act, he said, which prohibited American citizens from dealing with foreign governments in any manner such as this. Greeley had laid himself open to prosecution under it.

The government did not take action against him, but word of his strange actions spread fast. In Washington the fiery, swashbuckling Polish republican exile, Count Adam Gurowski, who had attached himself to Lincoln as a sort of household oddity, went around snarling that Greeley was "an ass, a traitor and a coward." (There had been other tensions between Gurowski and Greeley, too;

Greeley had fired the Count from the *Tribune*, where he had been employed as a European political specialist, and Gurowski had never gotten around to repaying a loan of $300 which the editor had advanced him.) What hurt Greeley more was the flood of letters from readers and friends that now streamed into the *Tribune* office, voicing amazement and dismay at his performance. "I was pained to see even the admission in the *Tribune* that such a thing [i.e., a peace of appeasement] could be possible, and I will not for a moment believe it," wrote one correspondent. Another, James W. White of New York, addressing the editor as "My dear Friend," inveighed against his "suicidal course on the subject of the war. I had a letter this morning from Washington from a friend who states that every Representative in both houses is denouncing you and declaring that you shall be held to a reckoning with the People yet for striking hands with Vallandigham and the rest of that crowd in their effort to break up the country." White hoped it was only a "momentary aberration" from which his friend would soon recover.

Greeley did recover—to a degree. The early months of 1863 brought no further military disasters. By April he was feeling restored enough to reassure his private listener Margaret Allen that the war would end this year—"and I think before the 4th of July. I may be too sanguine in this, but I am determined to see the end of it before the Copperheads can get into power and make a new compromise that will bind us all to the bootstool of slavery evermore." The first hints of spring came. He warmed when the revived Army of the Potomac, sporting still another commander, marched off for still another strike at Richmond. Two weeks of suspense followed. Then the massive host led by Joe Hooker collided with Lee and Stonewall Jackson at Chancellorsville. "My God! it is horrible—horrible!" Greeley cried out, ashen and shaking, as he read the bulletins of this latest disaster; "To think of it—130,000 magnificent soldiers cut to pieces by less than 60,000 half-starved raggamuffins!"

Greeley searched his soul. Back in January he had written, "It is almost impossible to make a good War or a bad Peace." Yet he wanted a good peace, although he hated a bad war, by which he meant a bloody one. Here was the moral dilemma, and he saw no way out of it. Charles Sumner of Massachusetts, the most learned and remorseless foe of slavery in the entire Senate, was caught up in it too; hadn't Sumner himself said years ago that "There is no war which is honorable, no peace which is dishonorable"? In action, this was not true; a peacemaking Vallandigham did lead to dishonor; yet how and for how long was one to drown one's scruples?

Other leaders were more fortunate: they never felt any. There was the towering, relentless Thaddeus Stevens, stalking through the Capitol corridors as a mighty hater of the slave system and as a successful Pennsylvania ironmonger besides. Next to him came Senator Ben Wade of Ohio, a rough, barrel-chested crusader for emancipation as well as for Midwest commercial interests, who beat his gavel and shouted down all waverers as the Senate's chief inquisitor on the conduct of the war. In their train followed the hearty, hard-drinking Senator Zach Chandler, Detroit's drygoods king and political boss, who also clamored for the extremest measures—and for the spoils that were to follow. All were firm, all were vengeful, and all were also hard-shelled, practical operators. They were ranking Republicans and Radicals—the latter word in the meantime having been capitalized or set inside quotation marks. They meant business.

Now came the start of July of the year 1863. Lee's conquering army was streaming up through Maryland and into Pennsylvania to deal the deciding stroke. "I hope Meade will fight no decisive battle till he gets everything in hand," Greeley darkly wrote Colfax; "I tremble lest Bull Run strategy should result in another Bull Run defeat. If so—where are we?" Two days later Sam Wilkeson, standing on the field of Gettysburg at the side of the terrible-tempered Meade after the collapse of Pickett's final Confederate charge, heard a Union band break out with "Hail to the Chief" and turned to the commander: "Ah, General Meade, you're in very great danger of becoming President of the United States."

The *Tribune* cheered. Now there must be no more idle peace talk, Greeley admonished his readers—and himself—after Gettysburg. For now the chances were that the rebellion would be quickly "stamped out."

7

Another bloody clash at once followed, though, and it took place in the streets of the City of New York. Greeley was caught in the midst of it. It was a battle different from anything that had happened so far: the attackers were ordinary city slum dwellers who had been enraged by the new draft law, whose provisions callously favored the rich by offering them exemption if they would simply pay substitutes to serve in their stead. Many of the new rebels were Irish-American laborers who hated and feared the competing Negro—especially since employers had brought gangs of freed slaves into New York to serve as strikebreakers. Some of their leaders were Tammany Democrats anxious to do everything possible to undermine the Republicans' war effort. Well supplied with frenzied racial slogans and drink, the mob struck at everything that seemed to embody the Republican order. It went out especially after Horace Greeley—the "niggers' friend."

Drawing of draft names by lottery had begun on 11 July at the Enrollment Office on Third Avenue and 46th Street. Sullen crowds massed around the building all day. Next morning and afternoon there were secret meetings and speeches throughout the city's slum districts. Then, when the Enrollment Office opened again on Monday morning, a mob of thousands stormed it, wrecking the lottery machine and driving off police details and a guard of invalided soldiers. A second draft office downtown was fired by crowds armed with guns, clubs and paving stones. In the afternoon more men poured forth from factory shifts and shipyards and took to looting stores, raiding saloons, and burning warehouses, crying "No Draft!"—"Kill the niggers"—and bearing such placards as "The poor man's blood for the rich man's money." One gang went off to wreck the Fifth Avenue home of the city's Republican mayor. Policemen and soldiers were clubbed to death; dozens of Negroes were seized and strung up to trees and lampposts, one of them being left to roast slowly over a fire set in Clarkson Street. A rifle factory on Second Avenue was raided. The growing mobs, setting fresh fires as they went, drove the police off the streets.

At this point Horace Greeley's friend and biographer, James Parton, heard gangs on 14th Street taking up the cry, "To the *Tribune* office! We'll hang old Greeley to a sour apple tree!" He hurried downtown to try to beat the crowd to the building on Printing House Square. But other rioters had already gathered there, across the way from City Hall. Sidney Gay, the *Tribune*'s managing editor, heard them yelling "Down with the *Tribune*! Down with the old white coat that thinks a nigger as good as an Irishman!" He hurried into the building to warn Greeley and tell him that the place should be armed. "This is not a riot, but a revolution," he burst out.

"It looks like it," Greeley said, dropping work to look out over the seething mass in the square. "It is just what I expected, and I have no doubt they will hang me; but I want no arms brought into the building."

Gay tried to persuade his chief to slip out of the building by the back door and leave town as fast as he could. James Gilmore—Greeley's and Lincoln's recent intermediary—was on hand to join in the argument. The gentle Charles Congdon, Greeley's favorite editorial writer, prodded him. Finally Greeley said he would go out—for dinner. "If I can't eat my dinner when I'm hungry, my life isn't worth anything to me," he barked. He clapped on his hat, took Theodore Tilton of the *Independent*, who had been calling on him, by the arm, and stepped out into seething Printing House Square. The editors watched him stalk through the crowd arm in arm with Tilton, hat pushed back on head, specs hanging on his nose, and his face wearing its expression of unshakable benignity. No one in the mob touched him. He steered Tilton into Windust's Restaurant nearby.

Stones flew and smashed the *Tribune* windows. At dusk the mob charged, battered in the doors, and smashed up the building's ground floor. But before they had a chance to wreck the presses or get at the editorial rooms upstairs, a countercharge by massed policemen coming up Nassau Street threw the rioters out. That night Gilmore, the ever-ready fixer, busied himself persuading Army Headquarters on Governor's Island to rush a consignment of old muskets to the *Tribune* building the first thing in the morning. Then he managed to wheedle a howitzer and some bombs out of the commandant of the Brooklyn Navy Yard. So when Greeley arrived next noon from his Nineteenth Street house through the barricaded, smoke-filled streets, he found to his amazement that the upstairs editorial office overlooking the square had been turned into an arsenal.

He exploded at once at the sight of the arms. "Take 'em away! Take 'em away! I don't want to kill anybody, and besides they're a damned sight more likely to go off and kill us!" But in the meantime a fresh crowd was yelling and threatening outside. Reporters slipped in with stories that pitched battles were going on uptown between mobs and army contingents. Once again Greeley braved the turmoil in the square to stride over to City Hall to hear an address to the crowds by Governor Horatio Seymour of New York—a Democrat—who expressed sympathy with them. Again Greeley got back safely. But he said he could not go on working with all those arms about. So he moved out into the city room and amid the nervous reporters scratched away at his daily editorial. The men took heart at his presence in their midst. Toward evening he started to leave the beleaguered building again, apparently intending to take a horsecar uptown. Finally Gay and Gilmore hustled him into a private carriage.

By the morning of the third day, the city's dead numbered perhaps four hundred. The vanguard of thirteen regiments hurriedly ordered east from the battlefields of Gettysburg were arriving at the depots. The pall of smoke hanging over burned-out buildings began to lift. Troops with field artillery marched up the avenues to pick up the corpses swelling in July heat. The *Tribune* published extras. Then, when order was restored, Greeley took the train to Chappaqua for a Saturday's rest. There he found that his wife, alone on the farm with Ida and little Gabrielle, had been threatened too. Drunken rioters from nearby Sing Sing on the river had started moving on to the farm, only to find its gates closed and to hear that a train of gunpowder had been laid across their path. A Quaker neighbor of the Greeleys, Edward Quinby, is said to have told the rioters, "Heed my warning, my brethren. Horace Greeley is a peace man, but Mary Greeley will fight to the last." The men dispersed, while Mary—alone, unstable, and ignorant of what was happening in the city—sat firmly and grimly behind her shuttered windows.

On Sunday, as always, Greeley returned to town to work. The city was pulling itself together. From his Unitarian pulpit the Reverend Octavius B. Frothingham, a friend of Greeley's since old transcendentalist and Brook Farm days, was saying:

> The one man who, before and above all others, was a mark for the rage of the populace . . . the one man who was hunted for his blood as by wolves . . . was a man who had been the steadfast friend of these very people who hungered for his blood; their most constant, uncompromising, and public friend; thinking for them, speaking for them, writing for them; pleading their cause through the press, in the legislature, from the platform; excusing their mistakes and follies, asserting and reasserting their substantial worth and honesty and rectitude, advocating their claims as working people, vindicating their rights as men. . . . I need not speak his name—you know whom I mean, Horace Greeley.

XIV. PEACEMAKER

1

After Gettysburg and Grant's victory at Vicksburg came the great Union stand at Chickamauga and finally a shining triumph at Chattanooga. By now the *Tribune* had fallen back joyfully into line. It called upon all good men to "trust our Government; it is doing its very best." Lincoln was appreciative: "I do not suppose I have any right to complain," he remarked one day to a *Tribune* reporter; "Uncle Horace agrees with me pretty often after all; I reckon he is with us at least four days out of seven."

Still, there were the other three days of the week. On these Greeley stayed off on his own, and his trips took him far afield. He went out roving for new political game—specifically for a new candidate with whom the party might replace Lincoln when he came up for renomination in 1864. Greeley was looking both for a stronger President and a more pliant one—stronger in the sense that he would resist any compromise in the conduct of the war, and more pliant in the sense that he would follow whatever advice was given him by Horace Greeley. The trouble with Lincoln, said Greeley, was that he seemed not to understand that the cause of the rebellion was the concentration of southern power in the hands of a landed few, and that these vast slave baronies must be broken up. Here was Lincoln talking about returning all real property to any Confederate who simply swore an oath of loyalty—which would mean allowing the old order to reestablish itself after the blood bath. What was the excuse for fighting the war, asked Greeley, if not thoroughgoing social reform? Lincoln might be trying to do his best, but he was "not one of those rare great men who mould their age." "Has Mr. Lincoln proved so transcendently able a President," the *Tribune* asked, "that all consideration of his merits, abilities and services of others should be postponed or forborne in favor of his reelection? ... We answer ... in the negative. Heartily agreeing that Mr. Lincoln has done well, we do not regard it as at all demonstrated that Governor Chase, General Frémont, General Butler or General Grant cannot do *as* well."

Any one of these men—even the raucous, uncouth Ben Butler—would make a more suitable President in 1864 than Lincoln, thought Greeley. Yet these were not his very first choices. In 1863 he had become absorbed with the idea of promoting for the highest office Major General William S. Rosecrans, a western campaign veteran who just then enjoyed repute as one of the few senior Union commanders who had not blundered conspicuously in the field, and who, besides, had an imposing look on horseback. But Rosecrans' looks were more imposing than his performance, and when he finally did blunder at Chickamauga, leaving the subordinate George H. Thomas to save the day, the *Tribune* quickly helped drop Rosecrans out of sight.

Unlikely as his first choice had been, Greeley had not been alone in suggesting it. Hardheaded politicians of the stripe of Charles Sumner and Ben Wade had joined him in the thought, remembering the success of Seward and Weed in another day in making themselves the bosses of General Zachary Taylor. Now the militants began casting about for another savior. The domed, ministerial countenance of Secretary Salmon P. Chase gazed at them hopefully. Deeply religious and intensely evangelical, the Secretary of the Treasury hated slavery and looked down on all who compromised with it. From his earnest height he also looked down on Lincoln. Like Seward, his Cabinet colleague, he still felt humiliated that a man of Old Abe's humble caliber should have done him out of the 1860 nomination. But unlike the jovial Secretary of State, Chase was pontifical and could not unbend; or rather, when he did bend down, his high collar creaked and he seemed to fawn. This endeared him to ambitious men anxious to manage him, but not to the general public.

Chase had been bowing steeply to Greeley for a year or more, hoping that the editor would help him into Lincoln's chair. In 1862 he had unctuously thanked Greeley for his "generous and disinterested support"—something he appreciated all the more, he said, because of Greeley's "earlier unfavorable judgments, which ... perhaps had more justice in them than I was willing to admit." But he also made obeisance before the brilliant young Philadelphia banker, Jay Cooke, who had special intentions of his own. Cooke, acting as a chief promoter and salesman of government war bonds, had sold so many that Secretary Chase had made him the Treasury's chief fiscal agent and let him in on advance top-level information—an arrangement that soon proved of great practical benefit to the firm of Jay Cooke & Co. Grateful for this, and for the government commissions he was collecting at the rate of $3,000,000 a year, Cooke had volunteered to do whatever he could to advance his patron's fortunes. He threw his nationwide network of bond salesmen into action as advance agents for a Chase presidential boom. Next he advanced Chase some money. The righteous Secretary of the Treasury, when you looked closely, was apparently not so strict after all.

Of Chase's private dealings with Cooke, Greeley appears not to have known. In the winter of 1863-64, the *Tribune* started to campaign for Chase for President. Again, Greeley was not alone. Powerful insurgents like Sumner, Thaddeus Stevens and Wade were also taking up the idea. Lincoln's closest political friends—above all the Blair brothers, Montgomery (the Postmaster General) and Frank, Jr. (now a congressman and brigadier general)—became disturbed. They went to work trying to rebuild fences between the White House and the *Tribune* building. "Montgomery Blair has been friendly and wonderfully deferential to me of late," Greeley told Colfax; "always comes to the *Tribune* office as he passes through our city. . . . Frank called twice . . . I don't think he was ever in the office before." But Greeley was not to be bought off. At a public meeting in December he stood up to acclaim Chase as "the largest brain and the steadiest arm" in the service of the Union. According to John Hay, Lincoln was "greatly amused" when he read this. Actually he was not amused at all.

Among those who now joined the effort to find a replacement for Lincoln were such ranking voices of conscience as Wendell Phillips and William Cullen Bryant. But the difficulty of these ardent spirits was that they could not fully agree on a man. When they came down to it, they could not even communicate with one another. Phillips, although he looked on the *Tribune's* editor as a colossal mischief-maker, could at least bring himself to speak to Greeley. But Bryant could not. At a reformers' Sunday breakfast party given by John Gray early in 1864 at which Greeley and Bryant were both present, along with Phillips and E. L. Godkin, the host turned to Bryant to ask, "Don't you know Mr. Greeley?" "No, I don't," answered Bryant in a stage whisper; "he's a blackguard—a blackguard."

Chase, these assorted men thought, looked good—although not too good. Unctuously the Secretary of the Treasury asked the *Tribune's* editor for advice: "The simple fact that I am named in connection with the next choice of President brings upon me the most unscrupulous attacks of the Postmaster General and his brother," he complained. The Blair brothers' hatchet-work could not really hurt him, he said, but it might "impair my usefulness"; and, "except for usefulness, I do not want the Presidency." What, then, should he do? Withdraw from the race? Or give up the pretense of being a loyal member of Lincoln's administration and strike out on his own? "Give me your counsel." Greeley paused before answering; but the Republican voters of Chase's home state of Ohio did not. They took a quick vote and decided that Chase did not look as good to them as Lincoln, at all events. That collapsed the Chase boom overnight.

Once more the militants cast about. The somewhat tarnished Pathfinder of 1856, John C. Frémont, now put his case forward, aided by his enterprising wife Jessie. Frémont, like so many adventurers, was now a major general, although he had not won a battle. Instead, he had created havoc as chief of the Department of the West by issuing orders that violated Lincoln's policies; but it was just these orders, breathing an uncompromising spirit against slaveowners, that had made him again a favorite of the militants. True, there were some stories about Frémont's private financial dealings that Greeley did not like, and there was a story about his relations with a servant girl in California which made Bryant bridle. But no matter; the Pathfinder might serve. Greeley and Bryant, although still not on speaking terms, propagandized for him. Wendell Phillips helped in New England. The sudden campaign gathered force so quickly among the restless that Greeley was amazed to find that four hundred assorted reformers, including the billowing Elizabeth Cady Stanton, were on their way to stage a rump political convention of their own, at which they went recklessly ahead and nominated Frémont as their own candidate for President.

President Lincoln had not gone far enough ahead in his war policies: that was what the Fremonters were trying to tell America.

But on the other hand there were many Republicans who thought he had gone too far. These men, also bemused by soldiery, were suddenly seized with the idea of running General Grant. On still another side stood the northern Democrats, dominated by all the "Peace Democrats" or "Copperheads" who wanted to call off the war at once, and who were being marshaled by the scaly figure of Vallandigham. That seemed to leave, for the moment, very few men who actually wanted Lincoln. The Republican party might break up, with several tickets in the field. Greeley became worried: "We must save the government from the Copperheads if possible; for I see no difference between their triumph and that of the outright rebels." He began to regret the whole Frémont affair. Boss Thurlow Weed, cool and collected while he profited from war contracts, had regretted it all along. He had resented Lincoln's failure to throw him more political patronage, but he swallowed this and decided that Old Abe should be the man for 1864 after all. The practical politicians around Weed took up the word. They moved in on the Republican national convention in Baltimore and helped bring about a quick renomination.

Yet even then, in the early summer of 1864, Lincoln's chances looked poor. The Union cause had reached its lowest ebb: wartime paper "greenbacks" had fallen in value to forty cents on the gold dollar. General Grant, leading the Army of the Potomac for still another strike at Richmond, had lost nearly 70,000 men in barely six weeks, only to find himself stopped in front of Lee's trenches at Petersburg. Greeley was not the only one to recoil from such bloodletting. "My God! my God! I cannot bear it!" cried Lincoln himself, when he learned of the slaughter in the Wilderness.

2

Heat and apprehension settled upon New York with the coming of July. The *Herald*'s rush casualty lists ran to two, sometimes three columns. Lincoln was about to call for another half-million volunteers. Furthermore, the administration had split wide apart over Lincoln's veto of the Wade-Davis Bill—a measure pushed through by the Radical bloc to deprive the President of any say in the handling of the South after its defeat. To many people it looked as if it might not be the South at all that would be the defeated side. Greeley tried hard to keep his own depression out of his editorials. But the tension grew on him. He tried to find refuge in a deluge of work on other subjects. He was already writing a weekly article on the side for Beecher and Tilton's *Independent*; now he took to lecturing again, talking about those old stand-bys, Temperance and Self-made Men, and one Sunday he delivered a guest sermon in Dr. Chapin's church. He locked himself for whole afternoons in an uptown office he had taken in Bible House, across the way from A. T. Stewart's department store on Fourth Avenue, where *Tribune* callers could not reach him. There he threw himself into still another project—the writing of a high-speed, two-volume journalistic history of the slavery crisis and the war. ("The materials are very imperfect," he told the widow of his old friend, Obediah Bowe, "and the generals on both sides lie fearfully.")

Then, on the hot morning of 6 July, a letter reached him that sent him spinning. It came from William C. Jewett, a shadowy figure from Colorado who had set himself up as another go-between trying to promote peace overtures on both sides. Greeley had corresponded with him before, offering to help get negotiations started. Now Jewett came back with startling news. Writing from Niagara Falls, he told Greeley in strict confidence that "two ambassadors of Davis & Co." had arrived just across the border in Canada "with full and complete powers for a peace," and that they wished to confer with him personally. They asked that Greeley either come to the Canadian border to meet them or else procure from Lincoln a safe conduct that would enable them to come and meet him. The whole matter, he went on, "can be consummated by me, you, them, and President Lincoln."

For Horace Greeley that morning, Jewett's message was irresistible. To be sure, it was strange that two Confederate "ambassadors" should come all that way to deal with him personally rather than with an accredited spokesman of the United States Government. But his suspicions were not aroused. He knew his fame and power as an editor; and it seemed conceivable that the "ambassadors," knowing this also, might look on him as an even more influential man than the Secretary of State. To outdo William H. Seward was always an exciting prospect for Greeley. Luckily, though, this time he did remember the Logan Act.

He rushed Jewett's message to Lincoln, covering it with a personal appeal of his own. He was in a state of high excitement when he wrote it, and began by reminding the President that "Our bleeding, bankrupt, almost dying country . . . longs for peace—

shudders at the prospect of fresh conscriptions, of further wholesale devastations, and of new rivers of human blood." Next he referred to a "widespread conviction" among citizens "that the government and its prominent supporters are not anxious for peace" —a sentiment which, he feared, might well lose Lincoln the coming election. It was not enough, he went on, for our side to desire peace; we must publicly demonstrate it, and avoid giving the impression of intransigence. "I entreat you . . . to submit overtures for pacification to the southern insurgents, which the impartial must pronounce frank and generous . . ."

Thus far it was Greeley, the hater of war, speaking. But then, even while writing his letter, his fears subsided and Greeley, the staunch antislavery man, took over. He was talking about overtures to the South, peace conditions, terms. He suggested a few—and made them firm. The first, obviously, must be that "The Union is restored and declared perpetual." The second, he thought, should state flatly that "Slavery is utterly and forever abolished" throughout the Union. Any other terms must depend on these. Nothing less would be "consistent with the national integrity and honor."

The letter, reaching Lincoln's desk, clearly revealed the stormy conflict in Greeley's mind—and Lincoln knew that it was a state by no means confined to Greeley. The editor had tried to clinch the two sides of his argument by saying that no matter how stiff Union terms were, peace talks should be begun anyway—if only to place upon the South the onus of rejecting them. Here was Greeley, the professional propagandist, speaking. Lincoln thought differently. He saw that any discussion of peace terms at all at this low stage of the war might simply seem to be an admission of northern weakness. He wished this mysterious business at Niagara had not come up. Besides, he doubted that these "ambassadors" were genuine. Yet he must not turn down Uncle Horace flatly, or there would be trouble with the *Tribune*. An inspiration struck him. If Greeley was so anxious for peace negotiations, why not just encourage him to go ahead and involve himself at Niagara Falls on his own? Then, if the intrigue collapsed and the public heard about it, Greeley would have no one to blame but himself. So Lincoln wrote back to Greeley, instructing him to go upstate to investigate in person. ("I just thought I would let him go up and crack that nut for himself," Lincoln later told Senator Harlan.)

Greeley, reading the reply, in his turn sensed a trap. "[Lincoln] thinks me a damned fool," he had told Gilmore some time before; "but I am never fooled twice by the same individual." "If you can find any person, anywhere," Lincoln was instructing him, "professing to have any proposition of Jefferson Davis in writing, for peace, embracing the restoration of the Union, and abandonment of slavery . . . say to him he may come to me with you. . . ." Back from Greeley to Lincoln went a note: "Whether there be persons at Niagara (or elsewhere) who are empowered to commit the rebels by negotiation, is a question; but if there be such, there is no question at all that they would decline to exhibit their credentials to me, much more to open their budget and give me their best terms. Green as I may be, I am not quite so verdant as to imagine anything of the sort . . ." He suggested that if there was to be any counterapproach, it be done not through him but by official Washington. Yet before he finished the letter, his desire to go ahead and act overtook him anyway. All right, he said, he would run up to Niagara—just to take a look.

Then he learned—reliably, he thought—that the Confederate agents across the border were actually empowered to treat for peace. He reported this to Lincoln. By telegraph, Lincoln urged him on: ". . . I was not expecting you to send me a letter but to bring me a man or men." Something in Lincoln's tone made Greeley suspicious. He feared he might be going off on a fool's errand, and that Bennett's *Herald* might be waiting for just such a story as this. On the other hand he could not turn down even the slimmest chance for bringing peace. He hoped Lincoln understood his sincerity and his desire to win at least some moral advantage for the North. Then John Hay, Lincoln's secretary, arrived in New York bearing a personal, confidential note for the editor. "I am disappointed," the President said in it, "that you have not already reached here with those commissioners. . . . I not only intend a sincere effort for peace, but I intend that you shall be a personal witness that it is made."

"This curt and peremptory missive"—so John Hay himself described it, recalling his own part in the play—"was delivered to Mr. Greeley early on the morning of the 16th [July]. Mr. Greeley was still somewhat reluctant to go; he thought someone not so well known would be far less embarrassed by public curiosity; but said finally that he would start at once if he could be given a safe conduct for four persons, to be named by him. Major Hay communicated this to the President, and received the required order in reply."

So Greeley hurried by train to Niagara Falls, and there sent a message to the supposed "commissioners" waiting on the Canadian side tendering them a Presidential safe-conduct to Washington. Their reply at once showed him that Jewett's messages had deceived him. They hedged; they said they were not empowered to treat at all; they proposed referring the whole matter back to their chiefs in Richmond—in such a way, no doubt, as to make it appear to the public that it was the Union, and not the Confederacy, that proposed stopping the war.

Greeley had neatly been caught between two fires. He stalked furiously back into his room near the sound of the falls, sent off a telegram to Lincoln asking for new instructions, and waited. Two days later, the youthful, ever-amiable John Hay arrived from the White House to look over the scene and handed Greeley this message which he was to transmit in person to the agents across the bridge:

> EXECUTIVE MANSION, WASHINGTON, July 18, 1864
> *To whom it may concern:* Any proposition which embraces the restoration of peace, the integrity of the whole Union, and the abandonment of slavery, and which comes by and with an authority that can control the armies now at war against the United States, will be received and considered by the executive government of the United States, and will be met by liberal terms on other substantial and collateral points, and the bearer or bearers thereof shall have safe conduct both ways.

If Greeley had been upset before, he was enraged when he read this text. Not that he objected to its overall peace conditions; they were, in fact, precisely the same as those which he himself had proposed to Washington. But he thought this was entirely the wrong way to go about presenting them. His own plan had been to bring the "commissioners" to Washington without mentioning terms at all to them, and to involve them deeply in negotiations before revealing any. He appears, moreover, to have suggested to them at the border that no terms had been fixed. He had tried to play his game shrewdly—too shrewdly, it now turned out. Lincoln had outplayed him. The President's barbed message would obviously have the effect of discouraging any talks at all—and it would leave Greeley standing, as a discredited intermediary, at the Falls.

Nevertheless, the message now had to be delivered. Greeley refused to do so unless Hay himself would accompany him across the international bridge as a witness. The angry editor and the young, bright-eyed assistant headed across the chasm. They handed Lincoln's note to one of the southern agents, James Holcombe of Mississippi. Then Greeley got on a train as quickly as he could and made away for New York.

The tenor of the Confederate agents' reply could have been foreseen. But Holcombe and his fellow agents were even more skillful than Greeley now feared they might be. Adroitly, they addressed themselves personally to him, rather than to Lincoln, in a letter which they gave to the press. They reminded him of the promising start of their negotiations and of the President's "rude withdrawal of a courteous overture for negotiation." They declared that the Lincoln message which had been brought to them across the Niagara bridge was of so insulting a nature as to make it impossible for them even to transmit it to Richmond "without . . . dishonoring ourselves and incurring the well-merited scorn of our countrymen." And in closing, amid regrets, they offered thanks to Horace Greeley for "the solicitude you have manifested to inaugurate a movement which contemplates results the most noble and humane . . ."

The last touch was deadly—especially when Bennett's *Herald* and Raymond's *Times* got hold of it. Both papers exploded into righteous wrath at Greeley's "cuddling with traitors," and together they led a chorus of northern jeers at his "meddling," his "bungling," and his supposed willingness to compromise the United States Government. Bennett's own war record, to be sure, was hardly that of a militant believer in the northern cause. Raymond's was stronger —and, besides, he had now been made chairman of the Republican National Committee. But even Raymond, at the very time when he was denouncing Greeley's peace moves, was busy preparing a peace proposal of his own for Lincoln's private eye. His own terms were far softer than Greeley's: he suggested that the southern states be allowed to perpetuate slavery if they would simply agree to come back into the Union. Yet the public did not know of these thoughts of Raymond's. It heard only the outward rage of every editor who hated Greeley. Bryant announced that the whole affair was "sickening." Charles A. Dana—ex-*Tribune*—chuckled at the outcry in his office of Assistant Secretary of War. Lincoln grinned too. "I sent Brother Greeley a commission," Dana heard him say; "I guess I am about even with him now."

3

Greeley went on muttering distractedly into late summer. Lincoln had invited him to come down to Washington to talk things over. Greeley answered that he saw no point in it so long as the President was surrounded by men like Seward. "I fear that my chance for usefulness has passed," he exclaimed; ". . . what, then, can I do in Washington? Your trusted advisers nearly all think I ought to go to Fort Lafayette for what I have done already. Seward wanted me sent there for my brief conference with M. Mercier. The cry has steadily been, No truce! No armistice! No negotiation! No mediation! Nothing but surrender at discretion! I never heard of such fatuity before. There is nothing like it in history. It *must* result in disaster . . ." In another letter to Lincoln he demanded, "Do not let this month pass without an earnest effort at peace." He thought that perhaps a one-year armistice between North and South might help.

He was obviously shaken again. Yet his senses, torn as they were, had not quite left him. Lost in the uproar over the Niagara affair was the fact that Greeley, in introducing it, had actually suggested peace terms of basic importance. They challenged the set ideas of northern militants and conservatives alike. He had set down as the prime requirement the total abolition of slavery—a point which the Republican Radical bloc looked on as a matter of course, and to which Lincoln had gradually become converted. Yet leaders on the conservative side, such as Thurlow Weed, Seward and Henry Raymond, were still willing to do without it, and they resented Greeley's efforts to keep the President committed to it. Then Greeley had gone on to propose as his next point that a general amnesty be extended to all who had joined the Confederacy, and that the rebellious states be readmitted at once to full political privileges. Here the alignment was the other way round: these principles were welcome to most moderate or conservatively inclined men, but they were bitterly opposed by the militants led by men like Sumner, Stevens and Ben Wade. Yet, again, they were principles to which Lincoln had already attached himself and was already trying to apply in southern sections that Union armies had overrun.

As a result one could not definitely classify Greeley as between "conservative" and "radical." Neither could one classify Lincoln. Some called Greeley a ruthless Jacobin, a destroyer of order, a fomenter of Negro revolution; others saw in him simply a quavering compromiser. Tossed about by all the swirling currents of northern feeling, he stood somewhere in midstream. There, too, stood Lincoln—although, to be sure, he stood on a more stable rock. Some ranking Republicans, like Thurlow Weed, were quite ready to forget about putting down slavery. Others, like Thaddeus Stevens, were insistent not only upon putting down slavery but on tearing apart the whole fabric of southern life along with it. Lincoln and Greeley were two of those who wanted to bear down hard on slaveholders but not on the South as a whole. Neither Lincoln nor Greeley, for all the passions the war had unloosed, could accept the notion that the rebellious states had lost their old rights of statehood and therefore should be treated henceforth as conquered provinces. Neither of them, for all their earlier calls to battle, could bear the thought of mass vengeance afterward. Lincoln, the President, and Greeley, the radical editor, were equally disturbed by the demands made for the whole South's ruthless subjection by northern men who had a commercial reason for doing so. They had not reckoned on the rising power of these men; Lincoln, in fact, had talked of restoring the Union "as it was." The eyes of the President and the editor remained fixed more on the morals of the situation than on its economics. In spirit, thereby, they drew together. It was their special dilemma, when they came to face each other, that they could not draw together in practice.

The fault, again, lay on both sides. That summer Greeley's *Tribune* had supported Lincoln in his veto of the Wade-Davis postwar reconstruction bill, much to the annoyance of the Radical camp. This had served as an indication to the President that while the *Tribune* had been one of the stiffest critics of his conduct of the war, it might well become one of the staunchest defenders of his plans for peace. Yet Lincoln had failed to act on that sign. He still could not forget Greeley's imperious airs and volatile ways. Privately he wrote off the editor as "an old shoe—good for nothing now, whatever he has been." And he went on with his game of tripping up Uncle Horace at Niagara. The game came off. But, in a way that Lincoln had not foreseen, its very success hit back. Greeley, grown surly, decided in the next month to heave a brickbat at the President. He communicated with Wade and Davis, the authors of the disputed bill which Lincoln had shelved. Not that he had swung around to full agreement with them; but still, chafing from his

Niagara wounds, he thought it well to lend them a ready hand against the White House. So they wrote and he published in the *Tribune* on 5 August this blasting manifesto:

.... The President, by preventing this bill from becoming a law, holds the electoral votes of the rebel states at the dictation of his personal ambition. . . . A more studied outrage on the legislative authority of the people has never been perpetrated . . . This rash and fatal act of the President is a blow at the friends of his administration, and at the rights of humanity and the principles of republican government. . . . But he must understand that our support is of a cause and not of a man; that the authority of Congress is paramount and must be respected; that the whole body of Union men of Congress will not submit to be impeached by him . . . and if he wishes our support, he must confine himself to his executive duties—to obey and execute, not to make the laws—to suppress by arms armed rebellion, and leave political reorganization to Congress.

4

The Peace Democrats met under Vallandigham's leadership to put up the deposed General McClellan for the Presidency on a platform that called the Union cause a "failure." Raymond told President Lincoln that "The tide is setting strongly against us." Greeley, still aroused at Lincoln's failure to deal with Confederate emissaries, if only to put them in the wrong, warned him that "Nine-tenths of the whole American people, North and South, are anxious for peace—peace on almost any terms." Many Republicans who had gone along with Lincoln's renomination began to think, now that a dismal fall was approaching, that maybe they should set aside their candidate and try someone else. The idea was unprecedented and it was audacious. Greeley fell in with it.

In mid-August an extraordinary, secret meeting was held in New York in the house of David Dudley Field, the influential lawyer who had worked with Greeley for Edward Bates at the party's Chicago convention of 1860. The purpose of the present evening was frankly to work up sentiment for scuttling candidate Lincoln and for calling a new, last-minute presidential convention. A unique mixture of dissident idealists, parliamentary Radicals, and assorted practical operators was on hand. Greeley spoke for the *Tribune*. Parke Godwin, Bryant's son-in-law, spoke for the old, Jacksonian *Evening Post*. Theodore Tilton, young, handsome, religious, intense, was there for the Protestant *Independent*. The Republican Mayor Opdyke of New York appeared. So did Henry Winter Davis, the vengeful coauthor of the postwar reconstruction bill Lincoln had vetoed. Francis Lieber, a leading liberal spokesman of German-Americans, was there. Salmon P. Chase and Thaddeus Stevens, although not present, had hinted their interest. Messages came in from the West. The rising star of the Cincinnati *Gazette*, Whitelaw Reid, for instance, was keen on the move.

The insiders agreed that a new national convention should be called for late September. "Mr. Lincoln is already beaten," Greeley told Mayor Opdyke; "he cannot be elected. We must have another ticket to save us from utter overthrow." He proposed Grant, William T. Sherman, or General Benjamin F. Butler for President, with Admiral Farragut—fresh from Mobile Bay—as running mate. Chase, Sumner, Wade and many others of the Radical bloc joined in the conversations. Even Thurlow Weed was heard to tell President Lincoln that his popular appeal had grown small.

Then General Sherman, one of the dissenters' favorite sons, spoiled their plans—by his triumph at Atlanta. General Phil Sheridan, the Union Army's new-found cavalry genius, was running the Confederates southward along the Shenandoah. The last rebel forts in Mobile Bay fell. The North, abject in August, cheered its leaders wildly in September. Maybe Lincoln would do after all. The convention to replace him was called off. Its leaders backtracked shamefacedly toward the White House. Greeley went with them. It had taken him a long time to learn that he belonged at Lincoln's side, but he knew it now.

According to one account, what actually made Greeley find this out was a practical inducement held out to him during that crucial fall by the anxious Lincoln. If the narrative of George G. Hoskins, an upstate New York politician who saw both men, is to be believed, the President set out to appease the editor in the one way that Greeley would surely find irresistible. Hoskins had been in to see Greeley and had found him generally out of sorts with Lincoln—so much so, in fact, that the editor had flatly declined a presidential invitation to come down to Washington for a talk. Then Hoskins went on to see Lincoln himself, hoping in some way to repair the breach. According to Hoskins' account, the President took him by surprise and "began at once to express his lifelong admiration of Mr. Greeley, asserting . . . that he regarded him as the ablest editor in the United States, if not in the world, and believed that he exerted more influence in the country than any other man, not excepting the President." Then Lincoln proceeded to call Greeley "the equal if not the superior of Benjamin Franklin"—a remark which led the President to say that he had long had in mind offering to Greeley the very post which Banjamin Franklin had first held, namely that of Postmaster General.

Hoskins, amazed by all this, asked the President whether he meant it seriously. Of course, said Lincoln; and he instructed Hoskins to go back and convey the Cabinet offer to Greeley in his name as a "solemn promise" to be fulfilled after his reelection.

Hoskins took the next train to New York and delivered the offer to Greeley that same night. "Do you believe that lie?" Greeley asked him in his queasy voice; "I don't."

"I will stake my life upon it," said Hoskins.

Greeley sat and thought awhile. He said nothing, but next morning the *Tribune* came out solidly for Lincoln for President.

So, at all events, runs Hoskins' story. No other certain evidence supports it. If Greeley was actually offered the Postmaster-Generalship—a post for which he had hankered ever since William Henry Harrison's victory in 1840—nothing was later done about it. Lincoln, to be sure, was holding out some very odd plums at the moment. He offered to James Gordon Bennett, who had called him "an imbecile joker," the post of United States Minister to France. This offer was instrumental in bringing Bennett's *Herald* around into the Lincoln camp just before election. But it was probably something else than a Cabinet offer that made the *Tribune* proclaim, on 6 September,

> Henceforth, we fly the banner of ABRAHAM LINCOLN for our next President. Let the country shake off its apathy; let it realize what is the price of defeat—a price neither we nor the world can afford; let it be understood how near we are to the end of the Rebellion, and that no choice is left us now but the instrument put into our hands, and with that we CAN and MUST finish it. . . .

5

The *Tribune* swung into action as in its old, hardest campaigning days. Slogans, cartoons, jingles, fat headlines, enlivened it. In November, Lincoln carried the day. The paper turned to thoughts of the possible peace ahead. Signs of Confederate disintegration were now multiplying; one last big push would surely bring Jefferson Davis' house down. Once more Greeley thought of accomplishing this through words and gestures that might prevent further bloodshed. He was certain now that if the southern people could be shown that the Union was offering them a peace settlement, they would quickly lay down their arms, no matter what their own leaders in Richmond said or did. He knew that Jefferson Davis was fast losing his hold (two out of every three Confederate soldiers were absent from the ranks, Davis had admitted—"most of them without leave") and that Lee's beleaguered army at Richmond was fast dwindling away. His mind turned inevitably to a new peacemaking gesture. This time he would not venture to undertake it himself. He cast about for some other eminent figure who might carry it through. In Washington, amid his books and his memories, sat the wizened, undersized father of the "Blair boys"—Francis Preston Blair the elder, now almost seventy-five, an adviser of Presidents since Andrew Jackson's day, and renowned in North and South alike. To him Greeley proposed the idea. Old Blair took it up at once. "The suggestions of your letter," he told Greeley, "tempt me to tender to the President a plan for this purpose to which my thoughts have been drawn for some time—a plan to deliver our country from the *cause of the war*—the *war itself*—and the *men and means* essential to carrying it on against us. You see, I am very *radical*; but if my scheme should ever be sufficiently developed to explain itself, it will be found to be extremely *benevolent* as well as radical."

What Blair proposed to Lincoln was that he be permitted to cross the picket lines before Richmond and try to reach some arrangement on broad Union terms with the Confederate leaders there. Lincoln, although skeptical, agreed to let the veteran go ahead on his own. So Blair set off on his laborious journey. "Our plot thickens," he told Greeley. The *Tribune* cheered him on his way and publicized his mission with all its stops out. But these organ tones, intended to be helpful, served to make so loud a noise as to frighten off Jefferson Davis and his men when they received Blair at their capital. The conversations led only to an odd, groping meeting at Hampton Roads between President Lincoln and his old friend and colleague in the House of Representatives, Vice-President Alexander Stephens of the Confederate States of America, which in turn led to nothing.

Once more, the *Tribune* had to subside. The sinister shape of Clement Vallandigham emerged from his retreat in Dayton, whispering into Greeley's ear: "*You* at least know that the South is able and determined, if driven to extremities, to carry on the war for an indefinite time herself." Again Vallandigham raised the bogy of European intervention on the side of his Southern friends, and as the outcome a triumphant, independent Confederacy holding "at least the lines of the Potomac, the Ohio and the Missouri, to be further followed . . . by the accession of the Northwestern States." On the other side Bennett and Raymond, neither of them always steadfast or warlike in their day, banded together to belabor their *Tribune* rival for his latest efforts to bring about peace. This time Greeley listened neither to the oily Vallandigham nor to the newfound bitter-enders. After many tortuous intellectual turnings and explosions, he had at last returned instinctively to the middle position of the people whom he had served and whom he had helped lead—a position compounded of moral earnestness, lingering scruple, and an impulse toward charity. A final battle needed to be fought, he said, but then the war must end—and, if possible, end generously. A few weeks dragged on. General Lee's thinning, threadbare army found it could no longer hold on at Richmond. Grant turned the screws of the Union vise. Finally Lee broke out, only to end at Appomattox.

Greeley put aside his old differences with Lincoln and went down to Washington to see the President amid his somber triumph. They talked. Just what they had to say to one another is not recorded. It was, apparently, at last a close and friendly meeting. This we know only because a sudden, surprising tenderness appeared in the description which Greeley wrote of the war President as he now saw him. He had met Lincoln often. Yet Lincoln's face now had nothing in it of "the sunny, gladsome countenance he first brought from Illinois." It was now a face "haggard with care and seamed with thought and trouble . . . tempest-tossed and weatherbeaten, as if he were some tough old mariner who had for years been beating up against the wind and tide, unable to make his port or find safe anchorage. . . . The sunset of life was plainly looking out of his kindly eyes."

On the morning after Lee's surrender, Greeley sat down in New York to write an editorial. He headed it "MAGNANIMITY IN TRIUMPH." This was to be his ruling idea in victory. It was Lincoln's, too, he knew. "We plead," he wrote, "against passions certain at this moment to be fierce and intolerant. . . . We plead for a restoration of the Union, against a policy which would afford a momentary gratification at the cost of years of perilous hate and bitterness. . . . We have done what we could—of course, not always wisely—to baffle, to circumscribe, and ultimately to overthrow the slave power. . . . At length . . . the end which we sincerely hoped but hardly expected to see, is plainly before us. . . . Let us take care that no vindictive impulse shall be suffered to imperil this glorious consummation . . ."

Hopes filled and stirred him when he spoke thus in public. Yet he could not escape certain private doubts and apprehensions amid the new day that he had helped bring about. In some degree, Lincoln perhaps shared them. They may have discussed them at the long-delayed, final talk which aroused so much of Greeley's emotion. Otherwise, there were few friends now in whom Greeley could confide. He looked away from New York and back to Vermont, to forgotten Westhaven, and he wrote his boyhood friend, Mrs. Whipple, who lived there:

I have not usually believed that we should win, because I could not believe that we *deserved* to win. We are a pro-Slavery people today. In the great city of Philadelphia, which gave Lincoln nearly 10,000 majority in '60 and again in '64, a black Union soldier is not allowed to ride the street-cars. I tried to pilot through a most respectable colored clergyman, but was obliged to give it up. By all ordinary rules, we ought to have been beaten in this fight and the more consistent and straight-forward worshippers of Satan triumph. Our great triumph is God's answer to the prayers of the Colored People; it is not *our* victory, and the result will show it . . .

I am becoming still more alienated from the religion which passes among us for Orthodox and Christian. Its teachers and leading professors are loudest in the cry for bloodshed and vengeance as against the beaten, prostrate Rebels. They want to erect the gallows all over the South and hang the baffled traitors whom we have not killed in battle. I am sure Jesus of Nazareth is not truly represented in this spirit.

As for me, I want as many Rebels as possible to live and see the South rejuvenated and transformed by the influence of Free Labor. . . . I see great trouble in the future growing out of our partial, tardy, enforced conversion to the Gospel of Equal rights. I fear more calamity is needed to convert us to the true faith that wrong done to the humblest, most despised, is an injury and peril to all.

If you are not with me, adieu.

He sent the letter off on 13 April. Next evening, at about eleven, Tom Rooker's pressmen were locking up the *Tribune*'s main news page when an A.P. bulletin from Washington electrified the city room. Orders went downstairs to hold the edition. In the capital, Sam Wilkeson got on the wire to ask that the story be stopped until he confirmed it. Soon he did. More bulletins poured in. Rooker's men got ready to run heavy black borders down the front page. President Lincoln, shot in Ford's Theatre, was sinking.

XV. THE OLD WHITE HAT

1

While Richmond lay half in ruins, New York City boomed. The *Tribune,* when war news came to an end and slavery was gone, tried to take stock of the vast changes that had come over the city during the years of crisis. New streets, new mansions, new fortunes, were to be seen on every hand. Up until the eve of the war, most of the avenues north of Forty-Second Street had still been roads running raggedly off between knots of houses into open country, and horsecars had served them only at hourly intervals. But by 1866, brownstone fronts were pushing on to Fifty-Seventh Street and beyond, and the *Tribune* was hailing the new proposal of building an elevated railway line to carry fast traffic above the crowded streets. Within a decade New York had added to its number more people than had made up its whole population back in the year when Horace Greeley had first set foot in it. Within only three years, money transactions through the New York Clearing House had doubled. Financing railroads was the downtown fever of the hour—heightened when insiders bought them up and consolidated them. When Greeley took the New York & Harlem train to Chappaqua, he was now riding Cornelius Vanderbilt's road. When he took the Broadway horsecar down to the *Tribune* office or Bible House, he was also paying his fare to Vanderbilt.

The old Commodore, so long the raw, piratical ruler of New York Harbor, still lived in his miserly, run-down house on Washington Place, although his fortune was estimated at over $20,000,000. William B. Astor, who had run up lines of tenements on hundreds of acres of city land bought with his father's fur-trading earnings, still functioned in an old-fashioned cubbyhole office in Prince Street, where he took in annual profits exceeding $1,000,000. But the magnificent A. T. Stewart, whose department-store business had netted him $5,000,000 in the war year 1864, was moving to a white marble palace he had built for himself on Fifth Avenue. The Fifth Avenue Hotel on Madison Square—called "Eno's Folly" when it was put up in 1859, because men thought it had been placed too far uptown ever to succeed—had become the glittering, gaslit center of social and political dining out. Carriages stood until late at night in front of the Union League Club nearby, the headquarters of young Republicans. There the members spoke with awe of the newest celebrities who had arisen in New York's midst—Pierpont Morgan, not yet thirty, who had made a wartime fortune in gold speculation and munitions sales; Jay Gould, small, foxlike and furtive, already feared as one of the most ruthless of market operators; and Jim Fisk, the fat, flamboyant ex-peddler from Vermont, who had made killings out of war contracts and cotton deals across the lines.

On any bright Sunday such new faces—the dour Morgan, the diamond-studded Jim Fisk, and their friends and retainers—could be seen taking the air up Fifth Avenue, riding past the new mansions into the freshly landscaped Central Park at the margin of the city. There, on occasion, Horace Greeley of the New York *Tribune* could also be seen bouncing unsteadily down the bridle path— sometimes with his new friend and protégé, Whitelaw Reid, beside him. In such new surroundings, among the gleaming carriages and finery, the ramshackle editor looked oddly out of place. It was as if everything in town had changed but he himself. He still wore the rustic and rundown clothes that looked as if he had put them on in the dark. If the years had altered his round face at all, they had merely made it rosier, and not all the strains and angers he had been through had disturbed its quaint air of simple gentleness. It was a "hopelessly peaceable face," thought the editor E. L. Godkin, wondering how a man with such a look could ever have aroused so much storm and stress. "To see him walking up Broadway," Godkin added, "you would take him for a small farmer of the Quaker persuasion, who had lost all the neatness of the sect, but had appropriated in his disposition a double portion of its meekness."

He was a fixture about town by now—a veteran of so many years of editing that there were many middle-aged people in New York who had read Horace Greeley regularly ever since they had been in their teens. Some called him crude, obstreperous, irresponsible, and grown seedy with the years. But others had warmed to him just because of his infectious enthusiasms, his rousing angers, his turnings, his twistings, his pointing a moral finger, his returning good humor, his air of hope, his wide-eyed wonder, his touches of comedy, and his intermittent despair. These people by now had taken him to their hearts. For good or ill, he was their Uncle Horace. They deplored much of his political infighting. But they seemed to find a needed voice in his broad, unquenchable humanity. He lectured them, he belabored them with his personal warfare against drink, tobacco, free trade, dancing, Democrats, and divorce, and still they read him. They laughed at him as well as with him—sometimes doing both at once. And they told endless stories about him.

He still lacked the bearing of a gentleman. Well-educated, well-spoken men like Bryant, John Bigelow and Godkin looked down on him because of this. The story went around that one day a wealthy, pompous visitor had called at the *Tribune* office, demanding to see Greeley in order to remonstrate against something he had published. The office boy told the visitor to go right on in, but he insisted on first presenting his visiting card. When shown in to the editor's cubicle, he opened up with a vigorous "Good morning" and then launched into his speech. Greeley, at his desk, meanwhile kept right on writing. Getting no response, the visitor spoke his piece again, only to find the editor still scratching away. He tried once more. Finally he burst out, "Mr. Greeley, I have sent my card to you, like a gentleman. I have spoken to you three times, like a gentleman. Now, if you continue to pay no attention to me, I shall be obliged to conclude that you are no gentleman."

Greeley looked up at last from his writing and beamed, "Well, who in hell ever said I was?"

One could never tell what might happen when one went to try to get something out of Greeley. One day a fashionable lady arrived to ask him for a contribution to her favorite charity. Greeley was known all over town as an easy giver. But this lady had evidently bothered him before. He went on writing while she told her story. Finally, without answering, he grabbed the speaking tube that connected him with the downstairs office of Samuel Sinclair, the publisher, and shouted into it, "Sam, Sam, for God's sake send me up five dollars and let me get rid of this pesky woman!"

But on the other hand, one winter night two poorly dressed women came in to try to get a moment with him at a time when he was busy, with callers waiting. Seeing them in the outer office, Greeley at once stopped work and asked, "Ladies, what can I do for you?"

They turned out to be workers in a hoop-skirt factory who had just gone out on strike for higher wages, and wanted to tell him their story.

"What pay do you get?" asked Greeley.

"Three and a half dollars per week."

"And how much of that goes for your board?"

"Three dollars."

"Do you mean to say that you have only fifty cents a week for your clothes and other necessaries?"

"That's all," answered one of the women. From her look and gesture Greeley understood at once what she had been forced to do in order to make ends meet. "It's a shame—a burning shame!" he exploded. "You want me to expose these men, and I'll do it. They shall have a column in tomorrow's *Tribune*." And they got it. But before the women left the office Greeley had slipped them each twenty dollars.

The staff, too, had extraordinary run-ins with their unpredictable editor, and these became the basis of further yarns. On one occasion —as Joseph Bucklin Bishop, a *Tribune* reporter, recalled it— Greeley had written an editorial advocating the running of an early morning milk train from Westchester County to New York City. But the compositor especially trained to decipher Greeley's "worm-fence" handwriting was away, and his substitute read for Greeley's word "milk," the word "swill." After the editorial was published, an angry delegation of Westchester farmers descended on Greeley. Greeley, in turn, in high rage scrawled a note to the composing-room foreman ordering that the incompetent who had misread his copy be fired. Of this message nothing was legible to the average reader save the signature. The dismissed compositor got permission to take it away with him as a keepsake. When he went across the street to the *Times* to apply for a new job, he answered inquiries as to previous employment by showing the note, and the mere name of Greeley on it—all else being illegible—was accepted as a good enough recommendation in itself. He used that same note many times over, so the story ran, and always got the job.

On another occasion Greeley found what looked like a flagrant typographical error in a piece on the New York Board of Trade, and called in foreman Tom Rooker to give him a dressing down. Rooker objected that the compositor had correctly followed copy. "Then the man who wrote the copy should be kicked!" Greeley sputtered. Rooker got the copy and showed him that he himself had written it. Greeley apologized and said, "Tom Rooker, come here and kick me quick."

And then there was the evening when William Winter, the paper's drama critic, had given a pair of theatre tickets to a young *Tribune* reporter who wanted to take his girl to a show. At the last minute the reporter was ordered to cover a lecture by Horace Greeley that same night out in Harlem. "What is Uncle Horace going to lecture about?" Winter asked the unhappy reporter. When told the subject, he reassured the young man, "That's easy. I've heard him talk on that subject many times, and know just what he'll say. Take your girl to dinner and the theatre, as you have planned. Then meet me at Browne's restaurant and I will dictate a report of his lecture to you." This was done, and next morning the *Tribune* set forth in half a column what Greeley had said to his Harlem audience. Later that day Greeley appeared at the city editor's desk and squeaked, "What infernal fool wrote that?" The reporter arrived, and Greeley began to dress him down. The city editor interrupted: "But you know, Mr. Greeley, you are a difficult man to report." "Report!" snorted Greeley; "I didn't lecture!"

2

The yarns about Greeley grew and became legends. He was supposed to be so absent-minded, for instance, that he detailed an office boy to keep him informed as to whether he had had anything to eat that day or not. A *Tribune* man, Junius Henry Browne, picked up a sheaf of such stories in a popular compendium he published of New York life in 1869, and in which he devoted a whole chapter to Greeley. Later, a group of *Tribune* pressroom veterans printed another selection of their own in a pamphlet they called *Fun From Under the Old White Hat*. The word "old" had inevitably settled on him, even though at the time the war ended he was not yet fifty-five. The aging that men saw in him lay less in his appearance than in his mannerisms, his crotchets, and his old-fashioned way of running a newspaper.

The aging could be seen, too, in his newspaper itself. The *Tribune* and its staff showed distinct signs of weariness. Ten years of concentrating on fighting the slavery issue had left its chief men exhausted and its whole organization run down. Uncle Horace had let many sides of management slip; he no longer governed as closely as did Bennett and Bryant down the street—and Bennett and Bryant were both more than fifteen years older than he. The *Tribune*'s whole physical plant looked worn-out. Looking over the musty, creaking shop, Greeley recalled a word he had used long ago to describe a home of his, and called it the "old rookery."

Even before the war, the aspiring New York *Times* had moved from its first location to a newer, bigger building on Printing House Square. But the *Tribune* stayed on in the cramped, old quarters which the antidraft mobs had come near wrecking in sixty-three. According to one reporter, Joseph Bucklin Bishop, they were "the most ill-furnished and ill-kempt suite of rooms imaginable. There was scarcely a desk in any one of them that had not been for many years in a state of hopeless decrepitude, and scarcely a chair with a full complement of its original legs. . . . There were only about half enough chairs and desks to go round. Reporters and even editors were obliged to take turns in writing their copy, and each man secured a share of a desk only after a considerable period of service. One of my earliest recollections is hearing Isaac H. Bromley say to Clarence Cook, who was the most merciless of art critics, 'Cook, are you through with that desk? If you are, scrape off the blood and feathers and let me come.'"

With its disorder, its inefficiency, its open doors and its low, dirty partitions, the *Tribune* office struck Bishop as "a thoroughly democratic place." He loved it for all its old-time confusion. Although Greeley during the war had moved his office away from the fourth-floor city room and the nightly reporters' noise to a little cubicle tucked away on the second floor, the significance of this retirement escaped a young man like Bishop. The editor's old spell enveloped him: "Ill-furnished and ill-kept as the *Tribune* office was in those days," Bishop recalled many years later, "it harbored a moral and intellectual spirit that I met nowhere else during my thirty-five years of journalistic experience. Every member of the force, from reporter to editor, regarded it as a great privilege to be on the *Tribune* and to write for its columns, and there could be no higher ambition than to write for the same page as that for which Horace Greeley wrote."

Famous *Tribune* writers, contributors and friends passed into the inner office before Bishop's eager eye: besides familiar faces like George Ripley and Bayard Taylor he watched new names such as Whitelaw Reid, E. C. Stedman, Charles Dudley Warner, Mark Twain, John Hay, Bret Harte, William Winter, Joaquin Miller. Yet Bishop's very listing showed the thinning out of Greeley's old associates and the arrival of a new generation straining to supersede him. Ripley, the veteran of Brook Farm, had grown garrulous and diffuse as he carried on the functions of the *Tribune*'s literary critic toward the age of seventy. Bayard Taylor, middle-aged and prosperous as America's favorite travel lecturer, wrote for the paper only occasionally. Greeley's brilliant city editor of the 1850's, F. J. Otterson, was now a burned-out man who puttered about the office at odd jobs. Sidney Gay, Dana's successor as managing editor, had broken down too under wartime overstrain. Henry Villard, the paper's crack war correspondent, had drifted off into businesses of his own: he would be heard from next as a railroad promoter and land agent for the great Jay Cooke. Sam Wilkeson, too—the bustling Washington bureau chief whose office opposite Willard's Hotel had become a center of politicians' and Army officers' gossip—had gone off to work as a publicity man for Cooke. That left only a few veterans on hand to shoulder the weight—above all George Smalley, whose famous news beat at Antietam had won him promotion to an editorial desk, and the brusque, forceful Albert Richardson, now back on assignment as a roving reporter after having been captured by the Confederates and held for a year as a dangerous man.

Clearly, the paper needed rejuvenation. Carl Schurz helped out for awhile as Washington correspondent. But above all, a new managing editor was needed—another Dana. Greeley shopped around for one, anxious to unload his daily responsibilities, and turned up John Russell Young, a brash, aggressive Irishman, aged twenty-six—who got the job. The new man, overwhelmed by the importance of his post, at once bore down hard. At the daily one o'clock editorial conferences which he held he rapped out assignments, ordered the older men about, and laid down the line, while Greeley stayed apart in his cubicle. Then Young flooded the office with new hands who were special friends of his and posted on the *Tribune*'s bulletin board daily numbered ukases such as these:

Order No. 56.—There is too much profanity in this office.

Order No. 57.—Hereafter the political editor must have his copy in at 10:30 p.m.

Greeley had never minded profanity. He was probably the profanest man in the shop himself. As for the "political editor" whom Young was ordering to get on his toes, he was Amos J. Cummings —another Irishman. Cummings had climbed up in the business from the job of an apprentice printer, and he was not easily cowed. In response to Young's Orders Nos. 56 and 57, he posted on the bulletin board his own "Order 1234567," reading:

Everybody knows _____ well that I get most of the political news out of the Albany *Journal* and everybody knows _____ _____ well that the *Journal* doesn't get here until eleven o'clock at night, and anybody who knows anything knows _____ _____ well that asking me to get my stuff up at half past ten is like asking a man to sit on a window-sill and dance on the roof at the same time.

                    Cummings

Cummings' comeback lost him his job. But it also helped to show that Young was not the right man for his own. Greeley began looking about again. In the meantime, sobering up, Young did accomplish some historic beats during the three years he was managing editor. In the summer of 1866 the first cable was laid under the Atlantic, and at once the *Tribune* decided to beat Bennett to the use of it—no matter what the cost. Heretofore American papers had relied entirely for European news on dispatches sent to them by ship by foreign space writers and occasional roving correspondents of their own, together with items lifted from two-week-old overseas newspapers. Now the *Tribune* rushed its crack George Smalley to London to open its own European news bureau—the first to be set up by an American paper. The summertime Austro-Prussian War was about to end, and on 1 August the *Tribune* received this laconic message from its man in London—the first cable dispatch to reach an American news desk:

Peace was certain at Berlin on Saturday. Bismarck and the King return this week.

Prussia carries all her points. The Liberals support Bismarck's foreign policy.

Austria's naval victory is much overrated.

The Hyde Park riots and the movement to form exclusive Reform League meetings have perilled the Derby government.

But this cable innovation, while giving the *Tribune* two weeks' news start over its slower competitors, turned out to be extremely costly. Its first fifty-word dispatch alone cost $200 to transmit. At the end of the year Samuel Sinclair, down in the business office, was shocked to find that the paper's wire tolls for 1866 had soared to almost $60,000—a rise of nearly $40,000 over the year before.

This was not the only trouble. In one year the *Tribune*'s paper bill had jumped by $100,000: newsprint that had cost ten cents a pound before the war was now bringing almost twice that price. Editorial expenses, too, were $30,000 higher in 1866 than the year before, as salaries, "stringer" fees and Associated Press charges followed the general inflation. Local reporters who had made fifteen or twenty dollars a week before the war were now getting thirty or more; and the *Tribune* had over thirty of them in its city room. Tom Rooker's fifty-odd compositors downstairs were also drawing better pay: at lineage rates the most skilled could now take home five or six dollars a day—which was the most journeyman Greeley, three decades ago, had been able to earn in a week. In order to meet the general rises the *Tribune* had jumped its price twice— first to three cents during the war, and then to four; but the boost in income was not keeping pace with the climbing outlays. Last year, over-all expenses had run to $646,000. This year they were almost $250,000 higher. Last year the stockholders had pocketed a comfortable $170,000 profit. But this year, *Tribune* earnings had dropped to $24,000. In 1867, at this rate, the company would go deeply into the red.

For this, Samuel Sinclair in his ground-floor office directly blamed Greeley. A sharp, flinty man, Sinclair had risen from a clerk's desk to replace the easygoing Tom McElrath both as publisher and chief *Tribune* stockholder. But he had never won McElrath's place in Greeley's affections, and between the two men ran a current of daily hostility. Greeley had early learned from his experience with Dana the hazards of letting such large blocks of stock fall into the hands of others. In Sinclair he saw a financial power who could at any time outvote and unseat him. Sinclair, for his part, appears to have seen in Greeley a famous name who was past his prime, and whose tradition of personal journalism conducted from under his hat was out of date in an era of big enterprise. Greeley was notoriously improvident—both as to his own and his newspaper's resources. He had never let the thought of loss of *Tribune* profit interfere with his taking an unpopular stand. But now, Sinclair warned him, there were outside stockholders to be considered—men like J. C. Ayer, the Massachusetts patent-medicine man, to whom Dana had sold his block on quitting the paper. These men were arguing that the *Tribune* property had outgrown the editor who had founded it. They were not to be deprived of their annual return from it. The paper must be modernized, made smoothly efficient, and protected as a safe investment. In short, it was time for a new management to take over.

Greeley sensed the danger, and tried to forestall it. Again the problem: he needed a crack managing editor who would carry on for him. In late 1867 he thought he had found his man. He was the slim, soft-spoken Whitelaw Reid, already an established correspondent and newspaper investor at thirty.

Reid, reared in an Ohio family of means, was a college graduate, and Greeley had always said he had no use for men of the educated class in the rough-and-tumble of journalism. With his chiseled head, his well-turned, dark mustache, his groomed clothing, and his general air of polish and reserve, the young Cincinnati newspaperman looked as if he had little in common with turbulent Greeley. Yet Reid could dig for news, move fast, stay on top of a story: that had become evident in his brilliant firsthand reports from the battlefield of Shiloh and then in his work as Washington writer for a string of Ohio papers. In Washington he had been shrewd enough, too, to get himself the part-time job of librarian of the House of Representatives, which let him in on inside floor news and gossip. He had made friends with Greeley during the Chase presidential boom which they had both promoted in sixty-four. Since the war Reid had casually dropped in on Greeley now and then. Not that he needed a job: he was prospering as the co-owner of the Cincinnati *Gazette* and as an investor in southern cotton lands.

The young man had grace, presence, and every indication of supple will. His charm captured Greeley. Letters began flowing from the elder editor to the younger. Thus in January, 1866: "Friend Reid: Supposing you should have a good chance to come to this city on the *Tribune*, would you do so? And how much would you think a fair compensation? . . . I write this apropos to nothing in particular, but with a view to possibilities. You will answer as tardily and cloudily as you please—or even not at all." Reid showed interest, but cautiously did not bite. Then Greeley raised the inducement. He wrote that before long he intended to retire as active editor of the *Tribune*—a clear hint to an ambitious young man to come in now and make good. In late 1867 he was even holding out stock participation: "I hope you will authorize me to buy one or two *Tribune* shares for you. I believe it will pay, even in 1868 and thereafter. And I believe you are mistaken as to my withdrawing from the active direction of the *Tribune* in 1869. I guess I shall be able to do it. At all events, I hope to try." Now Reid had two pretty definite commitments in hand. Still he waited. Then another letter: "I will be in Cincinnati during the winter. Will you try to be there when I am? If the mountain will not come to Mahomet, etc. . . ."

Next spring Reid finally agreed and came in as "first writing editor"—which meant chief editorial writer. But it was obvious to the staff that he was being held in reserve for a higher job. Soon, in 1869, the moment came. Managing Editor Young was discovered using his position to slip Associated Press copy from the *Tribune* to a Philadelphia paper in which he had an interest, but which was not a member of the Association. The ax fell. Up on the bulletin board went a famous announcement:

> The office of Managing Editor is abolished, and Mr. Whitelaw Reid will see that Mr. Greeley's orders are obeyed, and give instructions at any time in his absence to subordinates.

3

Uncle Horace took time off from his first love, newspapering. Up at Bible House on Fourth Avenue he had been finishing the second volume of his *American Conflict*. Then he wrote his *Recollections of a Busy Life* as a serial for Robert Bonner's popular New York *Ledger*. Next, letting his mind drift back to life in Chappaqua, he undertook a tract called *What I Know About Farming*, in which he tried to capture in print all the pleasure and fulfillment which had been denied him on his own land at home. When he traveled upriver one day to Highland Falls to visit Bryant's urbane and elegant partner on the *Evening Post*, John Bigelow, he disconcerted his host by talking all through dinner about practical agriculture while he wolfed his food.

For long periods now he lived apart from his family in the Nineteenth Street house. Late in 1865 Mary Greeley had gone to Cuba for the winter, suffering from "throat and consumption," and taking seventeen-year-old Ida with her. Little Gabrielle, aged nine, was left in a convent at Manhattanville. ("These are all that remain to us of our seven children," Greeley bitterly remarked to Mrs. Bowe.) Next summer, showing no recovery, Mary was back at the farm. "There remains my very sick, sad wife—fighting death," Greeley told Margaret Allen; "she grows visibly weaker, thinner, sadder . . . but, in the average, she fights dauntlessly. Still, she fades, and any week may be her last." "I expect soon to go up [to Chappaqua] oftener than weekly," he added. But he didn't. He even spent the Fourth of July in town, working on a book.

Mary lived through the summer, went South again, and survived the next summer. That year she talked of taking Ida to Europe in the fall. Life with her on the farm had become increasingly difficult: now she refused to let any tree around the house be cut or trimmed to admit sunlight, and she ordered that no cow on the place that had given milk to her children ever be destroyed, no matter how old and sickly it had become. The aged cattle "fell down sometimes and wanted to die," Margaret Allen remarked after a visit, "but Mother would not let them and kept a man to lift them up and care for them."

Next year Greeley was reporting to another of his steady correspondents, Mrs. Whipple, that Mary "seldom leaves her room, but she is up and at work some hours of almost every day. Up at the farm, she rarely came down to her meals but took them in her sick chamber." Several months later he found her "weaker," but added that "she says she is good to live till cold weather returns, anyhow." Then he put in a surprising touch: Mary was, he told Mrs. Whipple, "as vigorous and clear in mind as ever." She had in fact improved in mental state in this year of her decline. Greeley, looking for signs of hope, was inclined to exaggerate the betterment. Words of affection for Mary began to appear again in his letters concerning her. But then Mary, feeling stronger, took Ida off for another long stay in Europe, leaving the farm deserted and the house on Nineteenth Street uncared for. "I will try to see you on Sunday as usual," he wrote Margaret Allen, months after they had left.

Without a home to hold him, he continued on his restless travels and faraway lectures. Without children around him, he became a sort of mentor at large to the younger generation, handing out moral precepts in articles and letters. "I *try* to commend to the rising generation Industry, Temperance, Diligence and true Republican simplicity," he wrote a Brooklyn correspondent who had come to him for advice. "These are not in accordance with the spirit of the times, yet I trust some hear and heed me." A young woman in Kennett Square, Pennsylvania, laid her personal problems before him, and he answered: "You ask me if it would be right for one to borrow money in order to establish in trade. I answer that I consider it highly unadvisable . . . I cannot realize that it is your duty to support your parents and educate your sister. . . . I conclude that you ought not to run into debt." Bonner's *Ledger* asked him to write a series of hortatory essays for young men at $500 an installment. "Believe firmly in God," he told them. "Take care of your health. . . . Be a good citizen. . . . Never be ashamed of frugality. . . . Owe no man anything but good will. . . ." He needed Bonner's money, especially since he had lent or given away so much of his own. The improvident Cornelius Vanderbilt, Jr., still in disgrace with the Commodore, had touched him for another $2,000, pleading "that you not now desert me; on no account give any information to Father or family in relation to the past or present." And that other prodigal, Jonas Winchester—now the quack proprietor of "Winchester's Hypophosphites and Specific Remedies" —had gotten him to sink still more money in another of his mining schemes, blandly remarking that "I fancy you are $10,000 out of pocket on my account—perhaps much more." So Greeley sat down and wrote for Wood's *Household Magazine* an article on the virtues of thrift.

He seemed content to play the part of an elderly oracle, amiable and benign, and to have done with the political ambitions that had so long troubled him. He avowed this one day in 1868, when he turned up at a banquet in Montreal to remark,

Daniel Webster was not only a gentleman, but he had the elements of moral greatness; and he had faults as well. He failed only in one respect, and in this respect I differ from him—he wanted to be President, and I don't. . . . [Cheers and laughter.] We have seen our greatest man, Mr. Chase, making the same blunder. I have seen men who had the disease early, and died of it at a very old age. [Laughter.] General Lewis Cass died at about eighty-two, and up to the day of his death he wanted to be President. No one ever escapes who once catches the disease; and he lives and dies in the delusion. Being a reader and an observer at an early age, I saw how it poisoned and paralyzed the very best of our public men, and I have carefully avoided it.

That same year New York's leading editors and writers banded together to give a public banquet to honor Charles Dickens, who had just arrived in triumph as the English-speaking world's most renowned author. In casting about for the man who could most appropriately preside over the festivity at Delmonico's, they turned first to William Cullen Bryant, whose four decades on the *Evening Post* made him the city's senior editor, and who, besides, had served as host to Dickens on a visit twenty-six years before. But Bryant, in a huff, refused to serve—reportedly because Dickens had failed to pay him a call. The editors debated a second choice. Greeley? There were objections: rival editors feared that Greeley might insult them from the chair, or that he might abuse any Democrats at the dinner. Moreover, he might object to the serving of wine. Still, Greeley's name was approved and on the appointed evening the aging Dickens entered the banquet hall amid applause and cheers, leaning on the arm of the editor of the *Tribune*.

Far from being in a combative mood when he arose to speak, Greeley launched into mellow reminiscence. Going back to *New Yorker* days thirty years ago, he recalled:

In looking about for matter to fill my literary department I ran against some sketches from a cheap English periodical which I at once transferred to my paper. Those sketches were by a then unknown author who wrote under the name of Boz. So I think I can claim to be the first who introduced Mr. Dickens to this country.

Raymond, Dana, and the other editors present breathed easier. Greeley did manage to startle a few of them, though. In order to forestall the wine waiter, Greeley had placed into his claret glass a deep red rose, "whose perfume he would now and then inhale," John Russell Young recalled, "to the scandal of many nearsighted guests who saw with their own eyes that he was sipping wine."

4

Next spring, just when he had made Whitelaw Reid his second-in-command, Greeley received a startling piece of news. Henry Raymond, his first assistant in pioneer *Tribune* days, had died suddenly at the age of fifty. The circumstances were peculiar: two friends with whom Raymond had been out drinking had brought the editor home and deposited him at his front door on Ninth Street in what they took to be a state of drunken stupor. Early next morning he was found there, dying of apoplexy. Greeley forgot his dislike of the "little viper" who had become his ablest rival and had the *Tribune* eulogize him by saying, "We doubt whether this country has ever known a journalist superior to Henry J. Raymond . . . Genial, unassuming, and thoroughly informed by study, observation and travel, Mr. Raymond was a delightful companion . . ." Standing beside two other enemies—Thurlow Weed and James Watson Webb—Greeley served as pallbearer at Raymond's funeral. The splendid Henry Ward Beecher rose before them to deliver one of his rolling orations:

. . . . This great thundering city is like the ocean, and as when one falls overboard and gives one outcry, and the flying water is disturbed, but the huge waves pass over, the wrinkles are smoothed out, and the sea is no fuller than before, so the great multitude forget him and pass on. You who are so important today may be insignificant tomorrow.

Raymond's death had one immediate result: it brought Charles A. Dana, Greeley's other early lieutenant, into his kingdom. Five years of government service had left Dana itching to get back into his profession. He had just raised the money to buy Moses Beach's declining New York *Sun*. As a newsman trained in Greeley's school he was Raymond's equal, and now he had his chance.

Greeley, watching the *Sun* take on radiance under Dana, was left to muse over his own long history and the fates of the men whom he had started. He was gratified to hear that at least Dana had hung his picture on the *Sun's* editorial wall. He thought back to their old socialist days together. Dana had long since laughed off their past utopian ventures. Greeley, for his part, was never to be convinced that the ideas behind them were so laughable. Fifteen years of absorption in the slavery conflict had turned his mind into other channels, that was all. Now, after victory, he began to toy again with projects for a better life—some of them fanciful, others faraway. "One of these days, if I live," he had written Margaret Allen's daughters in Detroit in 1866, "I am going out as a missionary to call for the planting of Vineyards, Fruit Gardens, etc., in order to give pleasant and paying employment to our poor young girls around the villages and cities; and I want to point to some ladies competent and willing to give instruction in the practical art." And in 1869 he was deep in plans for setting up a new model colony—this time far out in Colorado. Once again, at fifty-eight, he dreamed of a utopia.

His partner in his newest scheme was the *Tribune's* agricultural editor, Nathan C. Meeker, a gray-haired, benevolent westerner who had been swept up in the Fourierist enthusiasm twenty-five years before and had carried something of it around with him ever since. Meeker sounded like an old-time survival as he preached to the *Tribune*'s war-hardened, expansive farm audience of the late sixties the dangers of unbridled individualism and the virtues of a communal society. Yet he was also a practical farmer and a traveler of the Great Plains areas which were now being opened fast to settlement. He applied his communal argument to what he saw on the semiarid land and advised settlers going out there to think in terms of working together on large-scale irrigation and scientific agriculture. He took as his text the flowering Mormon oasis at Salt Lake. Greeley cheered him on: here was the refrain "Go West" again, with all his own cooperative overtones. Then Meeker, stagecoaching over the high, empty country along the eastern barrier of the Rockies between Laramie and Boulder, Colorado, found a stretch that made him dream of founding his own equivalent of Salt Lake. He hurried home and began drawing up plans. "Go ahead," said Greeley, "and I will back you in the *Tribune*." He added some advice: "Have no rum and no fences in your colony."

So Meeker published in the *Tribune* a call to high-minded "temperance men ambitious to establish a good society" to subscribe to a common colonizing fund and receive acreage allotments in return, together with the benefits of a church, school, library and town hall to be built with joint proceeds. "A location which I have seen is well watered with streams and springs," he announced; "there are beautiful pine groves, the soil is rich, the climate is healthful . . . Mineral springs are near . . . Deer, antelope, wild turkeys, prairie chickens and speckled trout abound . . ."

Within a few weeks, a flood of subscriptions totaling almost $100,000 swamped the *Tribune* office. A young office boy named Daniel Frohman was kept busy opening as many as a hundred letters a day. An organizing meeting for the proposed Colorado colony was held at Cooper Union, with Horace Greeley in the chair. "This is a meeting of persons who propose emigrating in a colony to the West," the chairman began. ". . . There are many men working for wages who ought to emigrate. . . . New York is filled with people, yet there are thousands who do not want to come hither, never thinking that the cost of living eats up the greater part of their earnings. . . ."

It was like the old days twenty and more years ago. "The greatest enthusiasm prevailed," the *Tribune* reported, "and all agreed that they had never attended a more harmonious meeting." Meeker outlined his project in detail, Greeley remarking that "Mr. Meeker does not wish to give the locality of the place where it is proposed to establish the colony, for speculators will flock in and buy up all of the desirable land." The "Union Colony" was established, with Meeker as president and Greeley as treasurer. Then Meeker went out again and in its name bought up some 12,000 acres of railway land along the Cache la Poudre River. He gave his planned townsite a name: it was to be called Greeley, Colorado.

Next year, in 1870, Greeley went out to see Greeley, Colorado, for himself. It was not as Meeker had described it; what Greeley found there was simply a "bare, bleak prairie." The first band of communal settlers had been bitterly disappointed, too; "there were no buildings," he wrote Margaret Allen, "and nothing whereof to erect them, and the soil could not be cultivated to any purpose without irrigation." But Greeley was not easily to be disheartened when it came to the West. He knew its overstatements and was inclined to chuckle at them. He knew for instance that Sam Wilkeson, functioning as the chief publicity agent of Jay Cooke's railroad through the mountainous Northwest, was lying outrageously when he told immigrants of the region's orange groves and balmy climate —"a cross between Paris and Venice." Yet no matter. Even amid frauds and failures, the West would prove itself. Pushing through the dismal mud of Greeley, he grew cheerful: "Here we have already some seven hundred families, three hundred houses built or nearly finished in the village, one hundred or more scattered on the prairie around, and probably two thousand persons in all, with more daily arriving. We have an irrigating canal which takes water from the Cache . . . and distributes it over one thousand acres, as it will do over several thousands more . . . We are soon to have a newspaper (we already have a bank) and we calculate that our colony will give at least five hundred majority for a Republican President in 1872 . . ."

5

Down at the "old rookery," meanwhile, young Reid ran the daily show. His manner was gracious, but his hand was firm. He knew how undisciplined the stable of strong-willed *Tribune* writers had often been under his predecessors, and he had heard many a story of how Greeley had let them have their heads. Albert Richardson, for instance, in early 1865 had gone to the length of writing President Lincoln a letter of protest against his own chief's "Magnanimity in Triumph" editorial—and hadn't been fired for it. Sam Wilkeson, always deep in his own intrigues while serving as the *Tribune's* Washington man, had met with Radical Republican leaders right after Lincoln's death and had promised them that he would "put Greeley on the war path" against any conciliation of the beaten South. Greeley had let Wilkeson stay and talk. And in 1868, John Russell Young had taken advantage of Greeley's absence on a lecture tour in Minnesota to reverse the paper's stand on the proposed impeachment of Lincoln's successor, Andrew Johnson. Greeley had been against impeachment; Young came out for it; when Greeley returned from the Northwest woods he protested, "Why hang a man who is bent on hanging himself?"—but he stuck by Young's turnabout, knowing that the damage had now been done.

This was far from Whitelaw Reid's idea of how to run a newspaper. The brilliant, persuasive new managing editor at once showed that he was intent on leading a tightly knit, well-ordered team. He pulled the floundering Washington bureau together. He gave Smalley in Europe new, skilled assistants. One of these, Joseph Hance, became the first man to telegraph to America a battle dispatch from the Franco-Prussian War, while another scored a sensational news beat with an exclusive story of the capture of Emperor Napoleon. The funny young author of western comic sketches, Mark Twain, sometimes contributed. So did another highly original Californian, Henry George. Articles on women's fashions and cooking brightened the paper.

Greeley himself, closeted in his second-floor cubicle or in his uptown diggings, contented himself with writing editorials and sending Reid short scribbled chits about their daily business. He would call for statistics on rainfall or crop yields for some piece he was drafting. He would warn Reid against some boring caller: "This fellow is the biggest humbug and nuisance in or out of Bohemia. Beware of him." Sometimes, after scanning the morning's *Tribune*, he would deliver an old-time blast:

I want to ascertain what reporter of a late Democratic Union Convention talked of that Convention going through the "farce" of making up a ticket. Whoever doesn't know what is a reporter's business, and that it is not that of editing the paper—ought to find some other place.

Yet gradually, week by week, Greeley let the controls slip out of his hand. He lost a good friend at the end of 1869 when the eruptive Albert Richardson, to whom he had once offered the managing editorship, was shot down in the office by a jealous rival named McFarland, with whose divorced wife Richardson was said to be living. The *Tribune*'s moral readers were scandalized by the affair; but this was nothing compared to their horror when Henry Ward Beecher, grasping for the limelight, dramatically married the dying Richardson to Mrs. McFarland. And to make matters even worse, Beecher thereupon defended his action by saying that Horace Greeley had put him up to it—which brought on one of the editor's most profane public rages. More and more new faces at the *Tribune* took the place of the old. And the man whom Reid now brought in as his own especial confidant and friend was one calculated to rub Greeley at his most sensitive spot. He was John Hay, the late President's secretary, and his presence on the *Tribune* reminded Greeley of the worst fiasco of his career—the affair at Niagara Falls.

A legend had it that the debonair Hay, a skilled diplomat and aspiring belles-lettrist, came to the paper at Greeley's own behest. It was said that Hay dined one night with his friend Reid at the Union League Club and then came along to the *Tribune* office to watch the managing editor run over the evening news copy, in the course of which Reid tossed him a European dispatch and asked what he thought should be said about it. Hay, drawing on his recent experiences in legations abroad, sat down, unlimbered his pen, and in a twinkling turned out an editorial of which Greeley remarked when he saw it next day, "I have read a million editorials, and this is the best of them all."

Such was the legend. Actually it appears that Reid hired Hay as an editorial writer without Greeley's knowledge, and that Greeley, on returning from another of his perennial tours, was upset to find this first-hand witness of Niagara on the payroll. Yet Hay, turning out engaging literary and political copy, made an immediate hit with the readers, and within a few weeks Reid had jumped his pay from $50 to $65 a week—a high figure at that time for a new man. The serious Reid and the high-spirited Hay began that close

comradeship-in-arms which was to advance them both through
decades to come. Next spring Hay turned in to Reid a new poetic
effort of his own entitled "Jim Bludso," and soon thousands of
Tribune readers were repeating the first of his *Pike County Ballads*:

> Whar have you been for the last three year
>   That you haven't heard folks tell
> How Jimmy Bludso passed in his checks
>   The night of the Prairie Belle? . . .

Reporters recited it in the bars down on Frankfort Street. Horace
Greeley read it to visitors at Chappaqua. Another bright star had
risen on what the staff now called the "G.M.O."—Greeley's "Great
Moral Organ."

The *Tribune* climbed again. Greeley himself seemed to be
declining. He approached his sixtieth year. One reporter remarked
to John Bigelow that "Horace is constantly . . . letting things be
done in the paper which he says he does not approve of." He let
them slide. Reid would solve routine chores for him. And Reid
continued to address him with what seemed filial devotion. "I am
always sorry when you leave [town]," he wrote Greeley in 1871,
"and delighted when you get within consulting distance. I am
willing to do any amount of work and would gladly relieve you
of four-fifths of that which harasses you when here, but I feel
more comfortable when once in twenty-four or forty-eight hours I
can go to you for advice and counsel." There was only one problem
immediately ahead. The staff had now been brought firmly into line.
But what about the editor himself? What if Greeley suddenly
struck off on some new political tangent of his own? How much
longer would the stockholders and the younger leaders on the staff
go on looking at the *Tribune* as Uncle Horace's personal organ to
be carried around with him wherever he went?

XVI. THE PARTIES' CHOICE

1

The fact was that Greeley, in spite of his outward air of benignity, was growing restive again. He had helped found the Republican party. He had helped shape the central issues of the Civil War. Yet the more he now witnessed the practical results of either, the more he decided that he did not like what he saw.

Some old crusaders had said all along that matters could not possibly turn out as Greeley had fondly hoped. Just before the war, in 1860, he had been assailed by one of his old confederates of early land-reform and antirent days, the redheaded, flaming Tom Devyr, who had denounced the whole Republican party as a fraud and Greeley's part in it as dishonest. The new party, Devyr had exclaimed in an abusive pamphlet, was simply a thinly disguised businessman's machine designed to replace southern agricultural slavery by an equally harsh industrial slavery in the North. Its adoption of the land-reformers' homestead idea was nothing more than an attempt to seduce the working classes while actually throwing open the whole West to reckless exploitation. As for a civil war over slavery, Devyr had added months later, he would have none of it; the moral professions of northern businessmen were not to be believed, and the whole crusade was merely a device to throw the American people into the hands of industrial monopolists and stockjobbers.

At the time, Greeley had enjoyed answering Devyr's insults with a letter calculated to crush him:

Mr. T. A. Devyr:

The only favor I shall ever ask of you—and I never asked one before—is, that you procure and read Benedict Arnold's letter to his betrayed countrymen after he escaped from West Point to the British camp, and then take a steady look at your own face in the mirror. I loathe you too much for your treason to the rights of man, to speak of you: but for what you have said or may say about me I care nothing.

I remain, glad that you have ceased personally to infest me,

Horace Greeley

Years later, Greeley still had no use for Tom Devyr. But there were times when he wondered whether everything the angry Irishman had said was wholly wrong, after all. The Republican party and its cause had triumphed; all should be well. Yet just before Lincoln's death Greeley had written Rebekah Whipple a confession of his own forebodings, and the years that followed had deepened them. Some men could be philosophical amid the disappointments of victory. Yet Greeley felt himself profoundly involved as one progenitor of that victory; all his strength and all his hopes had been committed there; and besides, he was an activist rather than a philosopher. That is, he talked in terms of moral actions rather than of moral reflections, and he had assumed all along that a good action would bring an early, good result. Now the results were there. But the haunting question was— were they good?

For many years—for decades now—he had preached business expansion, westward movement, "internal improvements," and a self-sufficient, industrialized America. All these things were now being rushed to their fulfillment. Yet he had hoped to see them all invested with a high, ethical purpose. Business progress, he had been sure, would lead to moral betterment. Black slavery, an obsolete vestige of the past, would disappear. Enlightened employers, safeguarded in a fast-spreading home market, would find it to their advantage to raise wages and secure to the worker a fair share of their increment. The ideal of cooperation and brotherhood between classes, so long set forth in the name of reform, would take hold at last. Unions and cooperatives, working with rather than against "good" employers, would set standards of workmanship, wages and prices that would shame and discredit the cutthroats and laggards. And as a final guarantee against human exploitation, free homesteads in the great West would provide a safety valve for escape from the overcrowded immigrant labor markets of the eastern seaboard.

Such was the dream. Great physical strides since 1860 seemed to point toward its realization. The *Tribune* reported with enthusiasm that during just three war years, 180 new factories had been opened in Philadelphia alone. Two transcontinental railroad lines to the Pacific were building, and more were being surveyed. Inside of three years of Drake's oil-drilling discovery in Pennsylvania, eleven hundred oil companies had been formed, with a capitalization of more than half a billion dollars. Wealth at the rate of $100,000,000 a year was coming out of Nevada's silver mines. And the $2,700,000,000 worth of securities which the government had issued to finance the war had created a great new capital fund with which industry could expand—a fund doubly valuable to its holders since it now looked as if the government would pay off on the notes in hard gold dollars, although many investors had bought them with cheap, inflated wartime paper money.

Amid such a war-born bonanza, it was upsetting for Greeley to find that in New York, unskilled male laborers were still earning only three to five dollars a week—and this at a time when their living costs had doubled since 1860. Women workers could not be sure even of that much: in 1864 it was found that the average pay of women employed by Army clothing contractors was just $1.54—per week. The *Tribune*, that same year, had sent a reporter around to look into the conditions prevailing in the blocks of city tenements which William B. Astor had thrown up to house the hordes arriving annually from Europe. He described whole families crowded in windowless rooms in fetid cellars without toilets or running water—and this at a time when Astor was earning $1,000,000 a year from his holdings. Something appeared to be going wrong with the dream.

Labor unions, undermined by falling real wages and mass immigration, had fallen apart during the war—almost as they had back in the 1837 depression. Scores of employers had imported gangs of freed Negroes from the South to depress wages further and break strikes—hardly a sign of emerging brotherhood. On the other hand the promised Homestead Bill had been passed, but it was not advancing the worker either in the way Greeley had hoped it would. The further West had indeed been thrown open—too wide open,

Greeley now thought, as he looked with dismay on the huge acreage grabs and land-office swindles that were being reported from Kansas all the way to the Coast. How had it happened, for instance, that one man had won title to 40,000 acres of Nebraska public land, when the law was supposed to divide up that land among small, bona fide homesteaders? What were Thaddeus Stevens and Ben Wade doing lobbying a bill through Congress that would hand over to a Montana iron-mining company in which they were interested a domain of 13,000 acres at the homesteaders' nominal price of $1.25 an acre? "Go West!" Greeley had cried. But look at the people who were getting in there first!

Ever since Henry Clay's day, Greeley had preached that the Federal Government should provide aid to the most productive and useful forces of society; but the ruling Republicans, in following this advice, were now growing generous to a fault. Timber, cattle and mining interests were all winning huge handouts; soaring tariffs assured great profits to favored textile and manufacturing groups; veterans were getting their cut in the form of record pensions, and farmers theirs in land; but the biggest plums by far were going to the transcontinental railroad companies and their rings of promoters—some 20,000,000 free public acres to the Union Pacific group, and another 47,000,000 to the Northern Pacific. "Congress has been voting away the richest lands of the earth," Greeley's *Tribune* exclaimed, "and the wise and necessary prize of a railroad to the Pacific has been made to cover the most shameless legislation that ever disgraced Congress."

All this went under the heading of progress, but the price seemed very high. The worst of it was that not many people now seemed to care how progress was achieved, so long as it paid a dividend. Some of the elder Radical Republicans, for all their desire to see their northern business friends triumph, had at least been moved by a moral idea. Their leader, Thaddeus Stevens ("a *leetle* too savage a politician," Greeley had remarked of him as early as 1840), had fought like a raging Jacobin for Negro equality and the Negro's right to share in the ownership of southern land. But there was nothing Jacobinical about the tough-fisted "Black Jack" Logan, boss of the veterans' lobby; or about Senator Boutwell of Massachusetts, who denounced southern "aristocrats" but ran errands for northern ones; or about Oliver Morton, the lantern-jawed, flag-waving, one-man ruler of Indiana, who made a political living out of calling Democrats "murderers" and "traitors" and helping loyal profiteers; or about the golden-haired, gorgeous Senator Roscoe Conkling, the rising new boss of New York, whose flamboyant clothes, windy speeches, general air of a sporting spoilsman, all told of his readiness to deliver what his friends wanted. These were the men who were now taking over control of the Republican party. Apparently nothing could be done to stop them. Even Simon Cameron, whom Lincoln had put out of his Cabinet and whom Greeley had publicly attacked for his war-contract frauds, was back in power, running Pennsylvania in the name of his own coal and railroad interests. Schuyler Colfax, Greeley's confidant of so many years, had fallen in with the gang too: He had now become "Smiler" Colfax, the unctuous and complaisant Speaker of the House, in which capacity he coolly accepted a block of stock from the Union Pacific Railroad while it was busy defrauding the government.

2

The conscience of America was tired; perhaps that was it. Now that the war was over, many leaders who had spent their best years fighting the stirring battles that led up to it wore a look resembling that of the *Tribune* building: they were run down and worn out. William Lloyd Garrison—once a "universal reformer"—thought that with Negro emancipation his work was done, and that he could now quit the scene and rest. Others looked away deliberately from the aftermath; some held their noses. Young Henry Adams was to remark cynically that "President Grant's administration was the dividing line between what we hoped for and what we got." Herman Melville cut himself off from a world in which his dark prophecy of evil seemed to have been fulfilled, and poured out his scorn in stories which no one read. Even Walt Whitman dropped his buoyant façade to voice his sadness at the "measureless viciousness" of the times. The reforming impulse, insofar as it survived at all, seemed now to have resolved itself into a genteel concern with such matters as the condition of almshouses and the morals of delinquent girls. Twenty years before, the intellectual heirs of Puritanism had asked themselves in strenuous sermons and debates why there should have to be alms and poverty at all when there could be enough to go around for everybody, and just how young factory girls were to escape delinquency so long as their wages averaged two dollars a week. But these were embarrassing questions which few ventured to ask today. Minds that had once tested their mettle on the challenges of socialism or the heady school of Emerson now were found sitting back comfortably between the aspidistras in their parlors, writing out checks from time to time for the advancement of foreign missions and the prevention of cruelty to animals.

These minds had grown old. But that still left one asking, Where were the young minds that might have been expected to pick up the earlier enthusiasms and carry them on? It was this that exercised Greeley; not the aging of his friends. He lectured and stumped the country, looking for a fresh response. He saw a busy generation—not too busy to stop for a moment and listen to him, to be sure, but otherwise entirely absorbed in its own pursuit of money. The young generation was in business. There was no harm in that: Greeley had expansively applauded businessmen and wanted to see them prosper. Business, in turn, was in politics. There was no harm in that either: Greeley had always been realist enough to see that the motive power behind politics was economic self-interest, and he had argued before the war that northern commerce and "free labor" were underrepresented as against the southern planter oligarchy. But business and its particular interests now seemed to be dictating the entire politics of Republicanism. That was something else again. Greeley had not counted on that. He had dreamed of balance, not monopoly. Today, however, business had not only grown big, but it had outgrown the Republican party in ultimate power. So the roles were now reversed. Business did not depend on Republicanism for its advancement. Republicanism depended on business. The politicians who had talked so well now stood hat in hand before the owners' counter, awaiting their share of the reward.

Years before, Greeley had attacked Thurlow Weed in print for involving himself in the crooked deals of Peter B. Sweeny's New York street-railway ring and then for profiting as an insider from war-contract swindles. But the aging Weed's involvements were small compared to those of his successor, Roscoe Conkling, one of whose masters was Jay Gould. Gould, Cooke, Vanderbilt and William B. Astor were all eminent businessmen, and they now paid the Republican party's chief campaign bills, but they did not thereby produce an eminent politician. Instead, they produced General Grant—a bemused pensioner who gave them all they wanted.

3

President Andrew Johnson, the man who had succeeded to Lincoln's chair while Grant was still resting after Appomattox, had foreseen the new issue that was now arising. In 1866 he had bluntly declared to Congress, "We now find that an aristocracy of the South, based on $3,000,000,000 in Negroes, has disappeared and their place in political control of the country is assumed by an aristocracy based on nearly $3,000,000,000 of national debt . . . The war of finance is the next war we have to fight." These were words which the apprehensive Greeley could understand. Yet it was very difficult for him to understand Andrew Johnson. The *Tribune* could sympathize with Johnson's inherited, Jeffersonian feeling for the class of small farmers from which the new President had sprung, and for Johnson's native desire to follow Lincoln's humane precepts and avoid bitter reprisals against the South. But it was apparent to Greeley, too, that Johnson's tenderness toward the region arose in part from his being a border southerner himself, and that his leaning toward the South's white farmers reflected his inborn dislike of the Negro in their midst. It was hard, Greeley found, to side with the dour, ill-favored, often mulish Johnson against the powerful, vengeful Radicals. He could not help calling Johnson at one point an "illiterate." Besides, the man drank too much. Greeley could love a farmer, but not a crusty, southern one like this. (Johnson, for his part, could not bear Greeley; he called him "all heart and no head . . . a sublime old child.")

Nevertheless, Greeley tried for a while to get along with the new President, reasoning that he was trying in his way to carry out Lincoln's program of pacification. He did not like Johnson's first show of reluctance to admit Negro freedmen to the ballot. Yet he called upon Speaker Colfax to "take care that we do nothing calculated to drive the President into the arms of our adversaries. Let us respect his convictions and thus impel him to respect ours." But when Johnson went on refusing to yield on the matter of Negro suffrage, Greeley took to warning in his paper that "It looks as though the President has made up his mind to go whole hog with those who predicted that 'the blacks cannot live among us except as slaves,' and are striving to make good their prophecy." Unreconstructed southerners were moving into Johnson's camp along with such equivocal figures as Raymond of the *Times*. This was no place for Greeley, so for a while he switched over and found refuge among Thaddeus Stevens' Radicals. But when he saw their spoilsmen, their carpetbaggers, and their other vengeful rowdies at work, he knew he did not belong there either. Neither he nor his readers were sure just where he did belong. His political morale reached low ebb. He drifted doubtfully along with the Radicals' attacks on Johnson. But then, suddenly reviving, he stood against the current. He chose the worst possible moment to do it; but this could not be helped. A challenge had been thrown down, and he, for one, felt that he could not escape it. He picked up the gauntlet, leaving his readers thunderstruck.

In the spring of 1865, at the height of the North's fury at the assassination of Abraham Lincoln, a posse of Federal cavalry had pursued the escaping President of the defeated Confederacy, Jefferson Davis, and seized him in Georgia. Manacled as if he were a fugitive criminal, Davis had been thrown into Fortress Monroe, charged with treason and complicity in murder. Legally, though, the charge had left a good deal to be desired. There was not the slightest evidence of any involvement of Davis in the attack on Lincoln. And the more Federal prosecutors thought about the matter, the less basis they could find for singling out Davis as a traitor, when a whole section of the nation had rebelled. They wished that the Union's overzealous cavalry had never captured him and thereby embarrassed their courts. But they knew that to release him would be embarrassing, too. So, month after month, they had let him rot in jail without a trial.

This, thought Greeley, just would not do. By the spring of 1867, Davis had been living behind bars for two full years. The question of his right to trial did not disturb the northern majority; they were content to have him stay just where he was. Greeley, for his part, could look back to a time in 1861 when he himself had called in the *Tribune* for the court-martialing and hanging of men like Davis. But that had been 1861. Now two years had passed since the war's end. The main thing now was to heal its wounds. They could never be healed, though, so long as Jefferson Davis sat as a Federal prisoner. His release, if it could be arranged—since no one had the slightest intention of trying him—would be a token of reunion and goodwill.

The opportunity arose when the United States Circuit Court in Richmond, Virginia, finally agreed to let Jefferson Davis out on bail if a group of reliable citizens in various parts of the nation would go bail for him. Greeley jumped at the chance. His Republican friends warned him against it, and told him that he would be mad to fly in the face of ruling opinion. There was a scene at the office. "I know about all the things that may happen to me," Greeley barked, "but what I am to do is right and I'll do it."

When the names on the $100,000 Jefferson Davis bail bond were published, Greeley's stood out above all the rest. The reaction in the North was immediate and staggering. Greeley had been attacked for his and Dana's "Forward to Richmond"; he had been reviled for "cuddling with traitors" at Niagara; but he had never been submerged under an outcry such at this. Abusive letters swamped the paper; old friends cut him; thousands of subscribers to the new volume of his *American Conflict* canceled their orders; and many more thousands canceled their *Tribune* subscriptions —which in turn caused a storm in his business office and among the *Tribune*'s stockholders. Greeley was called upon to recant, to clear himself from complicity with the man who was the very "fountainhead of treason," and to raise the Union flag he had insulted. He refused. Thirty-six stalwart Republican members of the Union League Club of New York, to which he belonged, drew up a formal demand that he appear before the full membership and face charges of disloyalty. He declined to do that, too. But in refusing, he wrote the thirty-six men a letter which he thought might be worth publishing:

GENTLEMEN: I was favored, on the 16th inst., by an official note from our ever-courteous President, John Jay, notifying me that a requisition had been presented to him for "a special meeting of the club, at an early day, for the purpose of taking into consideration the conduct of Horace Greeley. . . ."

Mr. Jay continues: ". . . I beg, therefore, to ask on what evening it will be convenient for you that I call the meeting . . ."

Gentlemen, I shall not attend your meeting. . . . I do not recognize you as capable of judging, or even fully apprehending me. You evidently regard me as a weak sentimentalist, misled by a maudlin philosophy. I arraign you as narrowminded blockheads, who would like to be useful to a great and good cause, but don't know how. Your attempt to base a great, enduring party on the hate and wrath necessarily engendered by a bloody civil war, is as though you should attempt to plant a colony on an iceberg which had somehow drifted into a tropical ocean. I tell you here, out of a life earnestly devoted to the good of human kind, your children will select my going to Richmond and signing that bail-bond as the wisest act, and will feel that it did more for freedom and humanity than all of you were competent to do, though you had lived to the age of Methuselah.

I ask nothing of you, then, but that you proceed to your end by a direct, frank, manly way. Don't sidle off into a mild resolution of censure, but move the expulsion which you purposed, and which I deserve if I deserve any reproach whatever. All I care for is, that you make this a square, stand-up fight, and record your judgment by yeas and nays. I care not how few vote with me, nor how many vote against me; for I know that the latter will repent it in dust and ashes before three years have passed.

Understand, once for all, that I dare you and defy you, and that I propose to fight it out on the line that I have held from the day of Lee's surrender. So long as any man was seeking to overthrow our Government, he was my enemy; from the hour in which he laid down his arms, he was my formerly erring countryman. So long as any is at heart opposed to the national unity, the Federal authority, or to that assertion of the equal rights of all men which has become practically identified with loyalty and nationality, I shall do my best to deprive him of power; but whenever he ceases to be thus, I demand his restoration to all the privileges of American citizenship.

I give you fair notice that I shall urge the re-enfranchisement of those now proscribed for rebellion so soon as I shall feel confident that this course is consistent with the freedom of the blacks and the unity of the Republic, and that I shall demand a recall of all now in exile only for participating in the rebellion, whenever the country shall have been so thoroughly pacified that its safety will not thereby be endangered. And so, gentlemen, hoping that you will henceforth comprehend me somewhat better than you have done, I remain

Yours,
HORACE GREELEY

The thirty-six Union League clubmen, having read this communication, decided not to go ahead with their punitive meeting. Millions of other Americans read the letter too. Even editors who had been laying into Greeley could not resist picking it up

—simply as a letter. Some people with good memories agreed that it was the kind of thing Abraham Lincoln himself might have written. In fact, when you read it over, some of the very phrases sounded remarkably like Lincoln's. Hadn't Lincoln written a famous public letter that breathed the very same spirit—and even the very same cadences—to Greeley himself, back in 1863, when the editor of the *Tribune* had belabored him with his impetuous "Prayer of Twenty Millions?"

4

The letter to the thirty-six, however, did not take Greeley back into the camp of Andrew Johnson. It left him dangling midway in political empty space. He felt only repulsions, and could find no point of new attraction. When the Radical rulers of Congress in early 1868 voted to impeach the President, Greeley was away lecturing in his old refuge, the West. He had even let himself drop off telegraphic contact with his office. In Greeley's absence his managing editor, Young, threw the paper's support on the side of impeachment. All that Greeley did on his return was to mutter some regrets over this at the office and to say that he did not like to see the Radicals resorting to "reprehensible French methods." But he drifted along with Young. He even let Young print a snarling editorial impugning the motives of the seven senators on the Republican side who voted to acquit the unhappy Johnson:

> All we know is that money was used to secure the acquittal of the President. . . . The verdict is tainted, and the men who made it must remove the taint in their own way and time.

This was a very low point indeed for the *Tribune* and Horace Greeley.

He floundered in indecision for another year and a half. Then it was Johnson's successor, President Grant, who made up his mind for him. Remembering the other generals he had seen in the White House, Greeley had not expected much of this new soldier and had given him only reluctant support. But the spectacle of the hero of Vicksburg and Richmond being dazzled by the splendor of Jim Fisk and sitting slothfully by while his administration sank into seas of corruption soon repelled the *Tribune*. It attacked him first for letting many of his officials connive in

Fisk and Gould's "Black Friday" raid on the New York Stock Exchange. It attacked him again for the misrule of his carpetbag regimes in the conquered South. It called for an end to Radical Reconstruction which failed to reconstruct, and demanded that disfranchised Southern whites get back their voting rights. By 1870 Greeley was saying privately that Grant was "impossible." Early next year another scandal broke when a group of shady promoters and adventurers inveigled Grant into supporting their plan of buying up the Republic of Santo Domingo. The incorruptible Charles Sumner, Chairman of the Senate Foreign Relations Committee, savagely denounced Grant for this, as a result of which he was purged from his committee post. "Grant is done for and the Republican Party probably ditto," Greeley went around remarking. Then, in April, the *Tribune* broke publicly with the President, declaring that it was opposed to his reelection.

Greeley's enemies spread the story that the break had really been caused simply by the editor's old weakness—personal ambition for office. It was true that Greeley, who could never cease regarding himself as a practical politician of the first water, had gone fishing again—first for a senatorial nomination in 1866, and then once again for the New York governorship early in 1870, in both cases without success. Being denied these awards, he had insisted at least that as a reigning New York Republican he be consulted on the distribution of ripe local political plums to others —above all, the Collectorship of the Port of New York, a post that carried with it great powers of patronage and, if the wrong man got it, phenomenal chances for graft. Grant, however, was not in the least inclined to listen to Greeley. He appointed to the Collectorship one of "Sandy" Conkling's most crooked henchmen, Thomas Murphy, who at once lived up to expectations and organized a private ring to loot the Port. This provided Greeley with some of his most sensational exposure stories—and also with another reason to bolt the rule of Grant.

With an effort at cunning, the President had tried to appease Greeley cheaply by holding out to him the Ministership to the Court of St. James's—a post that would also get the troublesome editor out of the way. But Greeley notified Schuyler Colfax— Vice-President Colfax, now—that he would have none of it. "All we want is to be let alone," said Whitelaw Reid, speaking for his *Tribune* chief. Nevertheless, Grant tried again to bring Greeley back into line by cajolery, even as Lincoln had. He, too, used an intermediary. To John Russell Young, who had remained Greeley's friend even after being ousted from the *Tribune,* Grant addressed a letter intended for the editor's eyes. "Mr. Greeley is an honest, firm, untiring supporter of the Republican Party," he wrote expansively. "He means its welfare at all times. But he is a free thinker; jumps at conclusions; does not get the views of others who are just as sincere as himself . . . I have long desired a free, full talk with Mr. Greeley, because I have confidence in his intentions. I have thought at times of inviting him to Washington for that purpose; but I have been afraid that the object might be misinterpreted." Greeley made no answer. To a political friend, L. U. Reavis, who had also been invited to go see Grant, he wrote, "I advise you to let him severely alone . . . At all events, I shall."

But if you broke with Grantism, where else were you to go? Victorious Republicanism, like other revolutions before it, had devoured its young. The Chandlers, the Mortons and the Conklings, sitting on the lid of Grant's regime, were preventing a new leadership from springing up from below. Disaffected men like Carl Schurz, Charles Sumner and Lyman Trumbull stood no chance against the machine. A few had already drifted over to the Democratic party, in spite of the fact that to millions of Republicans it was still "the party of treason." The younger Frank Blair had even gone so far as to run as the Democrats' choice for Vice-President in 1868. To Greeley, such a desertion was inconceivable; for the Democratic party was also the party of free trade, Tammany and liquor interests—the last being an especially high offense, as he saw it. ("I never said all Democrats were saloon-keepers," he once declared; "I only said that all saloon-keepers are Democrats.")

And if the Republican party had its corrupt Camerons, Conklings and Tom Murphys, the Democratic party in New York now had its Boss Tweed and Oakey Hall. Which side was the more dishonest? It was hard even for the *Tribune* to tell. The Democratic state leader, the eminently respectable Samuel J. Tilden, struck Greeley as being simply a false front for the thefts and vote frauds of Tweed's municipal gang. In 1869, he had written Tilden one of his most commanding open letters:

> You hold a most responsible and influential position in the councils of a great party. You could make that party content itself

with the polling of legal votes if you only would. . . . Mr. Tilden, you cannot escape responsibility by saying, with the guilty Macbeth,

> "Thou canst not say I did it;
> Never shake those gory locks at me."

for you were at least a passive accomplice in the giant frauds of last November. . . . On the principle that "the receiver is as bad as the thief," you are as deeply implicated in them today as though your name were Tweed . . . or Oakey Hall. . . . Now, Mr. Tilden, I call on you to put a stop to this business. You have but to walk into the Sheriff's, the Mayor's, and the Supervisor's offices in the City Hall Park, and say that there must be no more of it. . . . Will you do it? If we Republicans are swindled again as we were swindled last fall, you and such as you will be responsible to God and man for the outrage.

Tilden had made no reply to this letter. The *Tribune* took to attacking the leadership of both parties. Whitelaw Reid thought it would be best at this point for the *Tribune* to "hold itself above party" entirely.

But that had never been Greeley's way, and it was not to be now. He had to mix in with the struggle on the ground. He had been watching a Republican revolt making up in the Middle West, where disgusted liberals like Carl Schurz were calling for independent political action by people of their own kind. Something might well come of this in the election year 1872. It might be the only way out of the morass. One could not tell yet where the new movement was heading. But it might possibly—just possibly —lead in the direction of Horace Greeley.

5

He had to act, move, agitate, and try once more to command. He could not sit back in Chappaqua. The place was deserted now; Mary Greeley, throughout 1871, was still abroad with Ida. "I have hardly known what home meant for years," Greeley wrote Margaret Allen, "and am too busy to enjoy anything." He had few friends, he told her; of those he did have, "most are women, and these I am proud of." Some of them, though, like his sister Esther, had "gone over to the Catholics," and now he felt lonelier than ever; only with Margaret herself was he still "in full religious sympathy." His life had been "too hurried," he confessed. In another letter he summed up, "My life is all a fevered march."

There was one brief interlude in Arcadia, though, before he drove into the gathering political storm. The date was late April, 1871. Greeley had just passed his sixtieth birthday. Forerunners of spring had come early to the Westchester farm that year. He made up a party to go out and spend the day there, taking along Margaret Allen and his favorite younger couple, Theodore and Elizabeth Tilton. Theodore, handsome, romantic and intense, had climbed from his days as a *Tribune* fledging and as Henry Ward Beecher's protégé on the *Independent* to become one of the nation's top crusading editors, campaigning for Negro rights, woman suffrage, and the overthrow of the Grant regime in the pages of both his *Independent* and his *Christian Union*. His wife, "Liz," small, dark-eyed, and submissive, seemed even more earnest and devotional than he. Tilton, like Greeley, liked to go off on long, strenuous lecture tours, leaving Liz and the children behind. Liz, a former Sunday-school teacher, worshiped ardently at Dr. Beecher's church, and during Theodore's long absences Beecher also ministered privately to her.

"Mrs. Tilton I fell in love with at first glance," Margaret Allen remembered of their springtime visit to Chappaqua; "she is a frail little creature ... and is just coming back to life after a long sickness. She looks up into your face with such loving, sincere, trustful eyes, that you feel like kissing her every time you meet her glance." Greeley led the party over his acres. "The day was one of the happiest I ever spent," said Margaret. "Dear old Horace's face fairly beamed with happiness. We rode all over 'Mother's land,' up hill and down ravines, and over to see his woodland where he spends every Saturday chopping. He and Tilton kept up a fire of jests ... There was lots of fun aboard.

"I'll never say again Mr. Greeley isn't queer," she rattled on. "He drove slow, of course, and such driving you never saw. His old horses knew him, no doubt, and they paid not the slightest attention to his chirps and gentle shakes of the lines. He held one line in each hand with elbows sticking out, and his hat on the back of his neck, while his horses went all ways but in the road, and sometimes took us over stumps, to the no small risk of an upset."

Then they visited the tumbling brook in Greeley's woods and drank from it. It was "the purest and sweetest water in the world," he said. They trooped back to the house over a field of which he said that it "used to be the wickedest frog pond you ever saw, all cabbage, and so springy you could not walk over it with safety." Margaret Allen found it to be "a beautiful field now, but the old man's face, beaming in pride of it, was much more attractive to me."

Back at the empty farmhouse, Greeley said he was sorry he could not offer them dinner there, and took them over to the inn near the Chappaqua station instead. Then they rode back to New York and to the Nineteenth Street house, where Greeley read poetry to them all evening, beginning with Whittier's "My Psalm" and then going on to John Hay's "Jim Bludso," recently published in the *Tribune*.

There was one thing about that day of seeming sunny calm before storm, though, that Margaret Allen did not know. It was that Theodore Tilton, several months before, had confronted his patron and idol, the Reverend Dr. Beecher, and accused him of adultery with his wife Liz. Liz had confessed to Tilton, and finally so had Beecher. While they tramped over Greeley's acres, bearing their secret, the Tiltons knew that at any moment it might break out before the public. Within only a few weeks, in fact, the first hints of it were to be published by Victoria Woodhull, the explosive feminist, birth-control reformer, spiritualist, business promoter and general busybody. The revelation that America's greatest preacher had transgressed with the wife of his best friend was to wreck Beecher, the Tiltons, and the faith of thousands who had hung on their lofty words.

That day in Chappaqua was one of Greeley's last happy ones. Old ties were breaking up; his world grew lonely. Mary had decided to spend another winter abroad on her never-ending search for health, taking the children from England to the south of France. Greeley said he was not sure just how the girls now looked. "In the spring, they will return," he hoped. "Ida and Gabrielle take turns in caring for their helpless, suffering mother, who is disabled by rheumatism from walking or even standing, though mind and voice are as strong as ever. I grieve for Ida's worn, anxious youth, which never can be regained."

Ida, reserved and distant from him, was content to be away tend-

ing her mother. Gabrielle, impetuous at fourteen and closer in spirit
to her father, wished she were home: "I *hate* it over here and I fully
appreciate America," she wrote him from Tours. Her mother and
elder sister took her in hand. "Mother wishes to express her mind
at some length regarding Gabrielle and her general behaviour," Ida
addressed her father coolly. "I told her it was quite useless to
say anything because you always think that Gabrielle behaves
beautifully except when she is with us and that it is because
we are so hard on her that she gives us trouble." Christmas
found them in Rome, with no thought of coming home. Ida wrote
her father that this was "the happiest Christmas I ever spent."

That spring, Greeley had been out lecturing as far west as
Texas. In the fall he had set out again for Iowa. He had complained of neuralgia and told Margaret Allen from on tour that
he would "almost enjoy this vagabond life" if it was not that "I
get so weary sometimes that I can hardly stand up." But in
December he was on the road once more:

. . . . That night I sat four hours in a depot [in Clyde, Wayne
County, New York] awaiting a belated train, and next day wended
to Perry, N. Y., where the mercury stood 26 below that morning.
The last nine miles were made by sleigh, and I was called at four
next morning, to make six miles more in an open cutter to meet
a train at six a.m. so as to reach my next appointment without
mistake. Then three hours more of waiting to catch a train that
would take me home . . .

He spent his sixtieth Christmas alone in the half-closed Nineteenth
Street house and went to church with Barnum. Then, in February,
1872, he was out traveling once more:

I rode all night from a lecture in Maine, arriving late on a
broken-down train in a blistering snowstorm. I worked all day,
and then stood up four hours shaking hands.

6

All this time, the thought of a bolt from the Republican fold had
been on his mind, tormenting him. He had been watching the
signs multiply of a liberals' revolt against Grant. He had heard his
own name mentioned as a possible presidential candidate on a third-
party, "Liberal Republican" ticket. He had been intrigued and
tempted by the notion—and had gone forth into the snows to cool

off. He had seen third-party revolts before—those of the Liberty men in 1844 and the free-soilers in 1848, in particular—and he had fought shy of them, believing that one must work inside the established parties rather than outside them. Yet, on the other hand, he had gone over to the pioneer Republicans—and what were they, at the start, but a third party? Mightn't there be a chance now, again, for a fresh coalition that would sweep the country up from its political dry rot —especially if a man like Horace Greeley headed it?

Not much of a chance: that was clear to him when he thought realistically. For the men who were gravitating toward each other in their rumblings against Grant were an odd assortment, conspicuous far more for their differences than for what they had in common. At one end of the group one could find a smattering of old-time insurgents of Jacksonian origin such as Bryant of the *Evening Post*, walking together with young western radicals like the homemade Minnesota utopian, Congressman Ignatius Donnelly. At the other one encountered high-minded eastern conservatives such as the thin-lipped Charles Francis Adams, Jr., and the superior E. L. Godkin of the *Nation*—men who looked down fastidiously on the vulgar excesses of Grantism and who thought that civil-service reform on a gentlemanly basis might solve everything. Somewhere in the middle wandered homeless veterans like Gideon Welles, late Secretary of the Navy, and the inescapable Salmon P. Chase, now Chief Justice, who so far had been in and out of no less than eight different political parties. Some of the reformers were high-tariff men, while others were low-tariff men; many, like Murat Halstead of the Cincinnati *Commercial* and Henry Watterson of the Louisville *Courier*, were rank political amateurs, while others, like the gamy Reuben Fenton of New York, were rank professionals. Some had been Democrats, others had denounced Democrats, and still others were rapidly on their way toward striking up bargains with Democrats—which meant that as reformers they would find themselves making deals with the unconscionable Democratic boss, Tweed.

Probably no political combination more unlikely than this had ever been attempted in America, and Greeley knew it. He himself was in disagreement with some of its members because he had never been a Jacksonian; with others, because he was neither well bred nor conservative; with still others, because he could not bring himself to believe in lowering the tariff; and with others, again, because he mistrusted all Democrats and had waged lifelong war upon them. Yet he had helped build other American combinations that had also looked diffuse and confused at the start. Here was another; and the thought of starting all over entranced him.

Clearly, even if it pulled itself together and triumphed over Grantism, it would be a reform movement for very limited aims. Its spokesmen had no intention of looking far under the skin of American society and of proposing drastic remedies; they were concerned simply with treating certain surface wounds. Wendell Phillips, a lonely, unwearying survivor of past crusades, might continue his searching criticism by analyzing the "incoming flood of the power of incorporated wealth" and warning America that great corporations, "unless some power more radical than that of politics is found, will rule [the nation] inevitably." But the reformers of 1872 were interested chiefly in getting Grant out and a better class of men in. "Man is more valuable than money," the unquenchable Phillips kept on pounding, arguing for a socialist solution, and in this Greeley at heart agreed with him; but such sweeping challenges had now become submerged in the measureless tide of self-aggrandisement, and Greeley reasoned that a little moral gain at this point was better than none at all. Perhaps, in fact, the new reform movement might be successful just because it was so very mild.

Even so, when it came to making his outright break with regular Republicanism, Greeley was hesitant. While other men like Carl Schurz, Lyman Trumbull, Sumner and the Adamses went boldly ahead, he asked himself what would happen to the *Tribune* if he jumped the traces. "If I owned it I would not mind," he wrote Brockway. At one time he had owned it—or half of it, which was enough—but now, as a minority holder whose only power lay in his editorial hand, he worried about his rights and duties to those who had a greater money stake in the paper than he. "You see that I am drifting into a fight with General Grant," he confided to Margaret Allen; "I hate it; I know how many friends I shall alienate by it, and how it will injure the *Tribune*, of which so little is my own property that I dread to wreck it." Yet, he went on, "I should despise myself if I pretended to acquiesce in his reelection." At times he wished he could escape his dilemma and retire both from politics and editing entirely: "Too much care is wearing me out," he told Nathan Meeker in Colorado. But at other times he was intrigued with the idea of promoting himself: "I want a candidate who can get on with less liquor [than Grant], if such can be had, to say nothing of tobacco," he whimsically told Rebekah Whipple, who no doubt knew by this time which particular teetotaler he had in mind. Meanwhile Thomas Nast, the sharp and popular cartoonist of *Harper's Weekly*, made it quite clear to the public what was on Greeley's mind. Greeley had just published his pamphlet, *What I Know About Farming*. Now Nast came back with a cartoon entitled *What I Know About Horace Greeley*, in which he drew a lumpy, loutish Uncle Horace gazing in jealously through the White House doorway at the solidly seated figure of President Grant.

7

A national nominating convention of the insurgents was called to meet in Cincinnati in May. "I feel like fighting," Greeley had told Brockway a month before; "I shall favor the Cincinnati convention, and am inclined to support its candidates unless this should require me to oppose protection to home industry. *That* I can't do, even tho it would make me President."

Very few of the assorted civil-service reformers, tariff reformers, practical politicians, and agitators for southern amnesty who made their way to Cincinnati had the slightest idea of making Horace Greeley President. The reformers, captained by the brisk, commanding, Germanic Carl Schurz (with young Joseph Pulitzer, then editor of Schurz' St. Louis *Westliche Post*, acting as his lieutenant), had their eye on the elder Charles Francis Adams, a man of faultless background, political distinction, and civic virtue. Adams, however, in order to show that he was not just another paltry office seeker, had just sailed away for Europe, and this show of disdain did not help the reformers. The practical politicians, for their part, were putting forth as their man the shrewd, Falstaffian hulk of David Davis, the politician-judge who had managed Lincoln's first campaign and in reward had been elevated to the Supreme Court. His backers did not pretend that the jovial judge could be presented at Cincinnati as an apostle of purity. But they had been negotiating with Democratic party leaders and had reason to think that they could present him as an affable, conciliatory character whom the Democrats would themselves endorse for President.

As for Horace Greeley, the chief organized sentiment in favor of him as a candidate came from Horace Greeley himself. He whispered, he hinted, he privately explained the shortcomings of both Adams and Davis, and then he went publicly through the telltale motions of disavowing any desire to run. The fastidious John Bigelow, watching all this, had advised his friend Whitelaw Reid to do all he could do to stop it. "Greeley is an interesting curiosity which everyone likes to see and to show and in whom we all feel a certain amount of pride, but I do not think anyone can seriously believe in his fitness for any administrative position whatever. If they do, they know as little of him as he knows of himself." Reid also had been apprehensive at first of any further excursions on Greeley's part. Yet Greeley's earthy enthusiasm for a fight and a campaign was working on him. He became intrigued by the idea of seeing Uncle Horace run. And he saw a remote possibility that Greeley might actually carry off the nomination at Cincinnati: the Adams backers and the Davis backers were obviously at loggerheads. It would take some very shrewd management, though, to put Greeley across. Rising to the opportunity, Reid volunteered to do that managing himself. He hurried out to Cincinnati to act as his *Tribune* chief's agent on the floor. One matter had already been agreed on between them. In the event of nomination, Greeley would retire entirely from the paper for the duration of the campaign, leaving Reid in full command. It went without saying that in case Greeley was elected President, Reid would continue in command.

Carl Schurz, looking like a German Ph.D., presided over the Liberal Republicans when they met in Cincinnati's Music Hall, and he opened the proceedings with the words, "This is moving day." It was not quite clear who was to do the moving, though, and what the new day was to be like. Henry Watterson, the Confederate ex-soldier and young editorial light who was heading the Louisville *Courier*, described the incongruous crowd:

> A livelier and more variegated omnium gatherum was never assembled . . . There were long-haired and spectacled doctrinaires from New England, spliced by stumpy and short-haired emissaries from New York—mostly friends of Horace Greeley, as it turned out. There were brisk Westerners from Chicago and St. Louis . . . There were a few rather overdressed persons from New Orleans brought up by Governor Warmouth, and a motley array of Southerners of

every sort, who were ready to clutch at any straw that promised relief to intolerable conditions. The full contingent of Washington correspondents was there, of course, with sharpened eyes and pens to make the most of what they had already begun to christen a conclave of cranks.

Not only were all the famous newspaper names there, but four of them—Samuel Bowles of the Springfield *Republican*, Murat Halstead of the Cincinnati *Commercial*, Horace White of the Chicago *Tribune*, and Carl Schurz of the German-language *Westliche Post* —had organized themselves into a pressure group for the purpose of shutting Judge Davis out and putting the absent Adams in. No one challenged their right to maneuver thus in the lobbies and on the floor, for almost all delegates were alike in that they represented only themselves. The four-man junta dined and drank together, pursuing their cause, until Whitelaw Reid appeared on the scene to ask suavely why it was that in a newspaper combine like this, the representative of the New York *Tribune* had not been included. The four men—all editors-in-chief—were inclined to look down on Reid as a mere subordinate. But the captivating Reid from the East persisted, and finally Henry Watterson, who had been sitting with them, remarked, "Now, gentlemen, in this movement we shall need the New York *Tribune*. If we admit Reid we clinch it. You will all agree that Greeley has no chance of a nomination, and so by taking him in we both eat our cake and have it." They agreed. Later they were to regret it.

The newspaper clique, riding high in the convention, now agreed to limit the field to Adams, Lyman Trumbull of Illinois, and —simply as a *pro forma* concession—Horace Greeley of New York. Between them, by the ready use of their newspapers as propaganda instruments, they managed to undermine and then collapse the Davis boom. But beyond that, they could not work in concert. One night the stately, handsome Alexander K. McClure, editor of the Philadelphia *Times* and chief of the Pennsylvania delegation, appeared in their midst to hear them out. They talked rapidly and at cross-purposes, and McClure shot holes into their arguments. Afterward Watterson asked him, "McClure, what in hell do you want anyhow?"

"What?" said McClure; "With those cranks? Nothing."

Charles Francis Adams, so right and so superior, lacked appeal on the floor. Once Judge Davis had been eliminated, the convention got out of hand. Young Reid, with Theodore Tilton and a group of New York professional politicos in his wake, moved quickly amid the delegations. He persuaded the journalistic four horsemen who thought they were running the convention to agree to omit any tariff-reform pledge from the party platform—thereby opening the way for the nomination of Greeley, an unalterable protectionist. Frank Blair, nominally a Democrat, arrived on the scene at the strategic moment to help throw toward Greeley the weight of Missouri, where the third-party movement was strongest. Stacks of the latest *"Try-bunes"* flooded the convention hall. Homely, patriarchal pictures of Uncle Horace went up. On the first ballot Adams led Greeley, but then for several they ran abreast. Finally, in confusion, the assorted Midwest followers of Adams, Schurz and free trade gave way. Within another hour Greeley received a one-word rush telegram in New York from his man on the floor: "Nominated. W.R."

Amos Cummings, the man who had lost his job at the *Tribune* after tangling with John Russell Young, was the first reporter to interview the nominee when the news was flashed. He came for Dana's *Sun*. The familiar Greeley sat before him, scratching away at an editorial amid the accumulated litter of his desk, with clippings and manuscripts falling out of its open drawers and the ancient shears swinging from their chain. But when he looked at the editor's clothes, Cummings saw a surprising change: today Greeley was decked out in a suit of neat black, with china studs glistening on his starched shirt front and his tie correctly in place. Cummings asked him whether he had expected the nomination. No, answered Greeley, he could not say that he had.

"Have you read the platform?" asked Cummings.

"I have read what has been telegraphed."

"Have they run a tariff plank into the platform?"

Greeley smiled shrewdly. "They have done just what I thought they should have done, and just what I advised—referred the whole tariff business to the people, to be settled in congressional districts."

"If the convention had adopted a free trade plank, would you have accepted the nomination?"

"I would not. I telegraphed that if the free-traders got control of the convention I would not accept. . . ."

"I see you were nominated on the sixth ballot, Mr. Greeley."

"Yes. I think it more creditable to be nominated on the sixth than on the first ballot. It is an evidence that our friends had bottom, and that their bottom didn't fall out."

At this point a sudden roar from outside shook the windows. The saluting cannon in City Hall Park were going off in Greeley's honor. Smoke drifted across the park. Crowds gathered before the *Tribune* building—the biggest assemblage on this side of the square since the days of the draft riots. They cheered: "Yee-ay, Horace! Go it, Uncle Horace!" The editor stood in his window, specs drooping, and waved.

8

In Cincinnati that night, several upset men sat down to dinner. Reid, all smiles, had insisted that the four horsemen join him at a victory banquet. "Frostier conviviality I have never sat down to," Henry Watterson recorded; "Horace White looked more than ever like an iceberg, Sam Bowles was diplomatic but ineffusive, Schurz was as a death's head at the board . . . We separated early and sadly, reformers hoist by their own petard."

Still dazed by what had happened, the "cranks" asked themselves what force had hit them. Skilled political management had intervened—cynical management, they told themselves—and, after watering down their program, it had stolen the prize for a man whom some regarded as America's master crank. Millions of plain readers might love old Horace for all his crotchets, his homeliness, and his daily parading of his changing conscience; but could anyone seriously believe that the amiable old editor was fit to be President or even to conduct a campaign? Godkin was astounded when he heard the news. "We suppose," he wrote in the *Nation*, "that a greater degree of incredulity and disappointment . . . has not been felt . . . since the news of the first battle of Bull Run." Bryant was equally overwhelmed on learning of his old rival's triumph: "I should at any time beforehand have said that the thing was utterly impossible—that it could not be done by men in their senses," he wrote; "but bodies of men as individuals sometimes lose their wits, and . . . the average reason of a large assembly is sometimes sheer insanity." Even Alexander McClure of Philadelphia, a warm admirer of Greeley, was upset and apprehensive: "I had known him for many years, and loved him as a brother. As his friend I sought to prevent his nomination at Cincinnati because I regarded it as simply crucifixion . . ."

Carl Schurz, muttering in Missouri, unloosed upon the candidate an eleven-page letter of abuse in which he threatened to bolt the ticket on the ground that "the first fruit of the great reform movement, so hopefully begun, was a successful piece of political huckstering, and that the whole movement had been captured by politicians of the old stamp." Meanwhile Thomas Nast at *Harper's Weekly*, already famous for his deadly caricatures of the bloated Boss Tweed, went to work with equal savagery on candidate Greeley, drawing him as an aged rural comic. Senator Roscoe Conkling sneered at Greeley as "grotesque and harmless." And James A. Garfield, another rising, regular Republican, threw up his hands: "Was ever the like known in the history of politics?"

The laughter and the caricatures were in the minds of the Democrats when they met in Baltimore in July for their own national convention. Yet there was not much they could do now. If their party was to stand any chance at all against Grant, it must avoid putting up a candidate of its own who would merely split the opposition vote. It must take Greeley—even though he had written to one of their men, "I am ferociously protectionist; I am not the man you need." So the party which Greeley had fought, for almost forty years, duly nominated him for President. Not only that, but it endorsed the entire Cincinnati platform, with its demands for equal Negro rights, for amnesty in the South, for civil-service reform, for "sound" currency, and for an end "to all further grants of lands to railroads or other corporations."

"The medicine was nauseous," Greeley wrote Margaret Allen of the Democrats' action, "but the patient was very sick." He grew "dizzy," he told her, at the thought of finding himself being endorsed by the party he had assaulted so long. And he was even more impressed by the Democrats' adoption of his entire platform. "Whatever the result of the contest," he ended, "the Liberal movement is a step in human progress. I do not believe it can ever be retraced."

XVII. THE SAGE OF CHAPPAQUA

1

"Our Presidential contest goes on well," Greeley wrote Margaret Allen as the summer began; "it looks as though we were bound to win." Alexander McClure called on him and found him brimming with happiness. Yet he was tired and complained of "something like brain fever," for which his doctor ordered him away for several days' rest. He retreated to Chappaqua, only to be pursued by reporters who disrupted his brief quiet there.

He had been advised to conduct his campaign in the usual front-porch manner of his predecessors, staying at home, showing himself to visitors, and making few speeches. It was still thought undignified for a presidential nominee to appear to exert himself too strenuously for the office; his friends and agents should do that work for him. The idea of a cross-country speaking tour was unheard of. It would also be far better for Greeley's health, his doctor said, if he followed the accepted practice. But there was one weakness in all this persuasion: weary or not, Greeley was never the man who could resist the idea of a grand tour. Besides, what he now learned of the growing forces arrayed against him made him decide that he had better go forth and fight—fight harder, in fact, than any presidential candidate before him had ever done.

In the meantime, after almost two years abroad, Mary Greeley came home to stand at his side. Going down the bay to meet her and Ida on the Lloyd steamer *Rhein* (Gabrielle had returned alone in advance of them), Greeley found his eyesight so poor that he could not recognize Ida on deck until long after she had spotted him. Mary was in her stateroom below, by now far gone in her invalidism. The band played Vienna waltzes as the ship came up the bay. "Mother is not so badly broken as I feared she would be," Greeley wrote Rebekah Whipple, "but has lost nearly all her teeth and looks very old and thin. She cannot walk, but we carry her in a chair, and her mind is as clear and strong as ever."

He took her to the St. Cloud Hotel on Broadway at 42nd Street, and then, when she was able to move further, to Chappaqua. There at the start of July, he felt encouraged. "She has had one or two severe attacks since, with difficulty of breathing," he told Margaret Allen, "but, tho she will never walk again, she seems as likely to live for years as at any time since 1865." Back at the old homestead, in spite of all its memories of past estrangement, her spirits rose. She found Horace cheerful and mellow amid bustle and excitement. Visitors overran the place; but, far from shunning them, she tried after her long isolation to share in Horace's present life with them. It cost her great physical effort; but she tried.

One day in mid-July, some three hundred of Horace's political friends and campaign workers—including Theodore Tilton and Cyrus McCormick—came up from New York to descend on the farm. It was a golden day for Greeley. He trooped down to the station to receive them. "The vigorous form of the philosopher himself [so one visitor described him] with his broad white hat slammed on the back of his caput, his head up and gold spectacles glittering in the sun, was discerned coming in his jerky trot down the hill." Then the trainload of guests walked with him up the wooded road, while a few dropped quietly off along the way at the inn for a quick drink, knowing that they would get nothing at Greeley's. They reached his hillside cottage, followed him in Indian file up a rocky glen to his highly prized spring, duly sampled the purling water, followed him down again over his reclaimed fields, admired his ditches, dikes and reservoirs, and then assembled under the trees around the house to consume lobster salad, potted pigeon, ice cream, fruits and lemonade.

Ida Greeley, pale, harassed and overworked, had supervised the arrangements, while her mother lay upstairs. But before the guests had finished picnicking, a carriage appeared from around the side of the house bearing Mary Greeley herself—"her clear complexion appearing almost transparent, and her large eyes dark as night," one visitor remarked. "She looked like a ghost, as she reclined in her carriage," Greeley himself said, "but talked as if young and hearty." She asked especially that any visitors from the South be introduced to her; her mind had been going back to her early schoolteaching days in North Carolina. Then Horace Greeley stood up, inevitably, to address the crowd. He talked of farming and ways of improving it—a subject especially interesting to Cyrus McCormick, who sat leaning against a tree. Other speeches followed. Finally the host drew out a huge gold watch—it was the one presented to him years ago by the New York Printers' Union—and told the guests that it was time for them to catch their train back to town.

2

At the start of August Greeley broke off playing the role of "the sage of Chappaqua" and hit the road. He carefully revised his outward appearance for the purpose of the tour, setting out in a black swallowtail coat and trousers with a black velveteen vest and a white muslin string necktie, and he took care to groom his whiskers. Joseph Bucklin Bishop of the *Tribune* watched this transformation at close hand and mistrusted it; its artificiality, he said, reflected that of the whole campaign. Bishop was upset to see windy reforming enthusiasts like Victoria Woodhull and her sister, Tennie Claflin, swarming around him hand in hand with tough, cigar-smoking professionals who looked on this as just another political operation. Greeley, for his part, was more concerned about those who failed to rally round. For not all the Liberal Republicans had accepted his candidacy; some, like Bryant and Godkin, would have none of him, and Carl Schurz was threatening to call a fresh convention and start all over. Nor had all the Democrats fallen into line; some southern irreconcilables who looked on him as a "nigger lover" talked wildly of staging a rump convention of their own. Charles Sumner was with him, but his old friend Beecher was against him, and the insurgent Wendell Phillips—of all people—had come out for Grant. Grant, thought Phillips in a moment of utter confusion, had at least been kind to Indians.

The campaign as a whole was more than confused; it was so entangled amid cross-purposes and inherited hates as to become weird. Greeley's managers thought that all would go well if the candidate would talk protectionism in the East, labor's rights in the big cities, civil-service reform to Liberal Republicans, and southern amnesty to Democrats below the Ohio. On the other hand, Greeley was under attack in the North as a conciliator of "rebels," and in the South as a past abolitionist and warmaker. While Carl Schurz looked on him as the mere instrument of machine politicians, Thomas Nast drew him brutally as the doddering companion of Boss Tweed. Others at the same time pilloried him as a radical eccentric who wanted to usher in a socialist revolution and free love. A whole anthology of past *Tribune* editorial statements—all of them assigned to Greeley, and many of them self-contradictory— was published under the title *What I Know About Politics*, the purpose being to show that he knew nothing. Dana's *Sun*, Manton Marble's *World*, and Bryant's *Evening Post* all turned their guns on him. "If anyone could send a great nation to the dogs, the man is Greeley," said the New York *Times*, which was now commanded by Greeley's boyhood friend from East Poultney, George Jones. The only voice missing in the New York newspaper line-up against him was James Gordon Bennett's. Bennet had died that June.

Nevertheless, Greeley was full of hope when he struck out for New England, sometimes speaking fifteen and twenty times a day to audiences along the circuit that he had covered so often since his first days as a temperance lecturer. In mid-August he thought New Hampshire safe, along with Connecticut and Rhode Island. He took time between speeches to climb Mount Kearsarge and write home about it. Then he swung westward, speaking at least twenty times in Pennsylvania. Thus, at Pittsburgh:

> They talk about Rebels and traitors. Fellow-citizens, are we never to be done with this? We demanded of our adversaries in the great civil war that they surrender their arms and go to their homes . . . Everything has been done that we asked; everything has been conceded; and still they tell us, "Why, we want them to repent." Have they not brought forth works meet for repentance? Theirs is a lost cause, but they are not a lost people . . . We want peace, not vengeance . . .

Then on to Cincinnati, where the fiercely mustached Henry Watterson met him and acted as his escort to Louisville and Indianapolis. "He was in a state of querulous excitement," Watterson recorded, but added that "before the vast and noisy audiences which he faced he stood apparently pleased and composed, delivering his words as he might have dictated them to a stenographer." At Covington, Kentucky, he spoke to a great assemblage of border southerners:

I believe that the day is at hand when we shall very generally realize that henceforth it becomes us to banish all bitterness and hatred, and forget our past conflicts and struggles against each other, and to remember only the blessed legacy of liberty and independence bequeathed to us by an illustrious ancestry. In behalf of these truths I have dared to alienate friends whom I loved, and who loved me . . . When I first, at the close of our great war, declared that our country must be rebuilt on the foundations of universal amnesty and impartial suffrage, I knew that platform was not acceptable at the North nor at the South. . . . Very well, said I, I can wait; and I have. . . .

At Dayton, Ohio, he addressed thousands of farmers who had come in to town in their buggies just after harvesttime:

We are one people, and shall evermore remain one people. Shall we be a harmonious people? Shall ours be a Union cemented only by bayonets, or shall it be a Union of hearts and hopes and hands?

At Jeffersonville, Indiana, to a small open-air audience, he talked familiarly about himself:

I was in the days of slavery an enemy of slavery, because I thought slavery inconsistent with the rights, dignity and highest well-being of free labor . . . I was anxious first of all for labor—that the laboring class should everywhere be free men. . . . My life has been an open book; all could read it.

Henry Watterson, who had been highly skeptical of Greeley as a candidate, watched these performances and found himself stirred by them. "They were marvels of impromptu oratory," he wrote, "mostly homely and touching appeals to the magnanimity of a people not ripe or ready for generous impressions; convincing in their simplicity and integrity; unanswerable from any standpoint of sagacious statesmanship or true patriotism if the North had been in any mood to listen and to reason." And Watterson was only one of many whom Greeley converted. The Democratic Senator Voorhees, until now another doubter, rose to exclaim that "for elevation of thought . . . broad philanthropy and general benevolence," Greeley's speeches had "no parallel in American history." Thousands who had been taught to believe that Greeley was simply a lovable old eccentric—or, if they followed Nast's cartoons, a floundering old buffoon —were startled and moved by the warmth and substance of his wayside talks. Even hostile papers like the New York *World* praised them. And in September Dana's *Sun* overcame its grudges to proclaim on its front page:

THE VOICE OF A STATESMAN

Magnificent Speeches of
Dr. Horace Greeley

Ohio and Kentucky Boiling
Over With Enthusiasm

His audiences swelled. He laid into the corruptions of Grantism; he spoke of man's right to fair government, of the need for equality between races and sections, and of labor's right to a full share of American reward. Sometimes he sounded as he had back in the eighteen-forties—forgetting, for the moment, that these were the eighteen-seventies.

3

But the reigning chieftains around Grant hit back ferociously, and money was on their side. Oliver Morton waved the "bloody shirt" against the South and all Democrats. Handsome "Sandy" Conkling called down curses upon the "traitors" who had bolted the party—a faction, he said, that included "every thief and cormorant and drone . . . every baffled mouser for place and plunder . . ." Zach Chandler, chief of the Congressional Campaign Committee, shook down railroad magnates and stock promoters for round after round of contributions, warning them that the radical Greeley would surely put an end to the Federal handouts which had netted them tens of millions. He might even investigate the circumstances under which so much national wealth had been handed out. "Who knows what Greeley might do?" Chandler rumbled alcoholically into apprehensive ears.

Jay Cooke, for one, had reason to be worried. He had floated the huge Northern Pacific Railroad stock syndicate, counting on continued Federal benevolence to cover its reckless watering and wastage of funds. Now, unless the government would go on backing him, he saw himself faced with bankruptcy. In showering gifts of stock upon America's prime movers and opinion makers, he had bestowed $20,000 worth upon Horace Greeley; how ungrateful for the editor now to turn against him and threaten to expose his hold upon the Treasury and the legislature! In order to stop Greeley, Jay Cooke came through to Chandler with cash contributions that probably exceeded $30,000 and may have reached $50,000.

This money went to work throughout the North and West to mobilize other men of property against the Greeley threat. In the South it paid carpetbag governments to hold their states safely in line for Grant. In early September, in the midst of his barnstorming, Greeley was still moderately hopeful: "The money and office-holding power arrayed against us are fearfully formidable; but we *ought* to win, so I guess we shall." Yet a week later, his doubts were growing: "The Grant folks are full of money and are using it with effect." He tried to cover up his fears of defeat with whimsical touches: "While there are doubts as to my fitness for President, nobody seems to deny that I would make a capital beaten candidate." Indiana elected a Democratic governor in October, but regular Republican money was winning in the South, where several state elections that preceded the national poll were duly bought for Grant. Greeley's managers tried to shrug off the setbacks. They hoped that more speeches, slogans, editorials and exposures would still manage to offset the money being poured into doubtful states by men like the promoters of the Crédit Mobilier and the Whiskey Ring. But the candidate himself was an old hand at feeling political pulses and forecasting elections. He did not let himself be deceived any longer.

At the start of October, already half-resigned, he had remarked to Margaret Allen, "As to the election, I am only anxious that my friends shall say after it is over, 'He did not throw his chance away by any blunder. He *ought* to have won.'" Nevertheless he went on speaking, writing, smiling, shaking hands, although his gestures grew more and more mechanical and he voiced his irritation at reporters and local politicos who boarded his train at all hours, leaving him no rest. He wrote to Margaret of his exhaustion. Then, while pushing on between towns, he received some ill news he had not expected. It came from Ida in Chappaqua. Her mother, she said, had suffered a relapse.

He had assumed that all was well at Chappaqua—or at any rate, as well as could be expected. He had last seen Mary revived in spirits when his long tour began, and for the first time in many years had felt her presence helping at his side. Yet in September, when speeches crowded him, he had failed to go back to the farm to see how Mary fared. He had been too busy pursuing his ambition and leading a cause whose hopelessness he now saw. Bitter remorse seized him. He canceled his final speaking engagements and hurried to her bedside. "I may soon have to shed some tears for my wife, who seems to be sinking at last," he wrote Margaret Allen, "but I shall not give one to any possible result of the political canvass." Four days later, when he wrote Rebekah Whipple, Mary's state had worsened: "My sky is darkened in many ways," he burst out, "but more especially in my home. My wife is going at last. . . . I am glad that the election will soon be over. My home trouble is enough to make me forget it."

He moved Mary into town in order to bring her nearer to good doctors, and stayed with her at the house of their friend Alvin S. Johnson, the publisher, on Fifty-Seventh Street. There he tried to write, to keep up his correspondence, to draft outlines of closing campaign talks; the election was now barely two weeks away. It was all no use; he was resigned. He saw failure approaching, hand in hand with death. He passed nights in sleeplessness and the final days in near-stupor. Suddenly he confessed to Margaret, "I wish [Mary] were to be laid in her grave next week and I to follow her the week after. But say nothing of this."

Reid, Tilton and the rest tried to rally him. But it was too late. On 30 October, Samuel Sinclair received this stark note at the office from Fifty-Seventh Street:

DEAR SINCLAIR:
Mrs. Greeley died at 4 this morning.
HORACE GREELEY

A second note to Sinclair that day, written in a shaky hand, ordered arrangements for Mary's funeral. Then there was silence from Fifty-Seventh Street. Outside, the professional orators rolled on, Thomas Nast drew a final withering cartoon, Jay Cooke wrote out a last-minute check, and the campaign reached its inevitable end. On 4 November, two days before the voting, Greeley mustered the strength to promise Sinclair that he would come downtown next day. "Though I am in agony there is work that must be attended to." But on the same day, in a disturbed hand, he wrote Margaret Allen:

I am not dead, but wish I were. My house is desolate, my future dark, my heart a stone. I cannot shed tears; they would bring me relief. Shed tears for me, but do not write again till a brighter day, which I fear will never come.

"Very private," he marked this letter, adding, "Show this note to no one and destroy it."

General Grant won the election, piling up almost 3,600,000 votes as against Greeley's 2,800,000. Conkling, Morton, Chandler and their allies crowed: the threat of Reform had been put down for many years to come. Greeley, that day, sat mourning in his friend's house.

4

"My life has been a fevered march." Now the truth of that sank in. The marching stopped suddenly; he felt as one cast upon the rocks. He had passionately loved the exercise of politics—only to find himself so savagely traduced that he said he hardly knew whether he had been "running for the Presidency or the penitentiary." And now he was destroyed politically. He had passionately loved his *Tribune*; but perhaps he had now led that to its destruction, too. Between these two loves he had virtually forgotten Mary and the fact that he had loved her as well, in spite of all their estrangement and the years apart; and now Mary was gone. He had never brought himself to love anyone else. At any rate, he had never admitted to himself that what he felt for any other woman was anything more than intellectual attraction. He and Mary had disappointed one another and had learned at times to resent and even hate one another; yet they had made seven children together, and at the end they had returned to one another, tentatively, uncertainly, yet with a quiet, autumnal glow of affection—and then it was too late.

Nothing was left to him now but the *Tribune*. Yet the *Tribune* was no longer really his. He became obsessed with the thought that men were conspiring to take it away from him, to throw him out and ruin him, or possibly to ruin him and it together. He detected scheming foes all about him. He felt he could trust no one—not even in his own office. "I am far beyond tears," he scrawled in anguish to Margaret Allen. "Nor do I care for defeat, however crushing. I dread only the malignity with which I am hounded, and the possibility that it may ruin the *Tribune*. My enemies mean to kill that; if they would only kill me instead, I would thank them lovingly."

Sleepless and tortured, he stalked down to the *Tribune* office to reassert himself in command. He wrote out a signed editorial leader announcing his return to "the editorship of the *Tribune*, which he relinquished on embarking on another line of business six months ago." Henceforth, he went on, his effort would be "to make this a thoroughly independent journal. . . . Since he will never again be a candidate for any office, and is not now in full accord with either of the great parties . . . he will be able and will endeavor to give wider and steadier regard to the progress of science, industry and the Useful Arts, than a partisan journal can do . . ."

It was apparent to Reid, to business manager Sinclair, and to the others who saw him at the office that the editor was a sick man. They had expected that before he attempted to resume his old job he would go away for a long rest. Sinclair, a calculating man with a promoter's mind and little respect left for Greeley, had laid his own plans for what he might do during that rest: he was thinking of a stockholders' coup that would unhorse the editor for good. So Greeley's feverish suspicions had substance, after all. Greeley turned to Reid, who had loyally supported him throughout the campaign. But at this moment, either through accident or extraordinary misjudgment, Reid let into the paper a piece that could be read as a patronizing insult to its founder and editor, and thereby turned Greeley's suspicious wrath against himself.

The piece—an editorial called "Crumbs of Comfort," by John R. G. Hassard of the *Tribune* staff—was probably meant to be innocuous. It did no more than voice whimsical satisfaction at the fact that the *Tribune*, now being finished with practical campaign politics, would no longer find itself pestered by endless office seekers, seeking support. But it contained passages like these:

> There has been no time until now, within the last twelve years, when the *Tribune* was not supposed to keep, for the benefit of the idle and incapable, a sort of Federal employment agency . . . Any man who ever voted the Republican ticket believed that it was the duty . . . of the editor of this paper to get him a place in the custom-house. Every red-nosed politician who had cheated at the caucus and bought at the polls, looked to the editor of the *Tribune* to secure his appointment as gauger, or as army chaplain, or as minister to France . . .

Greeley, already at the breaking point, exploded on reading this, staged a scene with Reid, and demanded a published retraction. He wrote out a statement so strong that Reid protested. According to John Bigelow, who got the story from Reid a few days later, "Greeley ... whined and cried and went on like a baby. He called himself over and over again 'a black fraud,' said he was ruined, the *Tribune* was ruined, begged the trustees to turn him out, turn Reid out, turn anyone out, to save the paper." Greeley rewrote his disavowal, toning it down somewhat, and handed to Reid for next morning's paper a statement beginning, "By some unaccountable fatality, an article entitled 'Crumbs of Comfort' crept into our last unseen by the editor, which does him the grossest injustice . . . The article is a monstrous fable based on some other experience than that of any editor of this paper . . ." This, too, Reid declined to publish. Greeley stormed out of the office. Then he took to writing furious letters to outsiders, declaring that Reid had betrayed him and was trying to seize control of the paper.

It was true that Reid regarded himself as the heir apparent to the chair of the *Tribune* and that besides, having faithfully followed Greeley through all his late "vagaries," he felt it was now time to put the paper firmly back on a solid Republican track. But it was not true that Reid was conspiring against his chief. The source of the true conspiracy was Sinclair, who was trying to unseat both Greeley and Reid and turn the paper over to a syndicate of new investors who would buy him out at a high price. He himself owned twenty of the *Tribune* Association's one hundred shares and these he had quietly arranged to sell to William Orton, president of the Western Union Telegraph Company, for $10,000 a share. In addition he was busy rounding up other stockholders—notably the Clark family, who owned twelve shares, and J. C. Ayer, the medicine man, who owned fifteen—and getting them to agree to sell out to Orton too. It was understood that once Orton was in control, the man who would be brought in as editor was none other than "Smiler" Colfax, the former Indiana editor who had risen high in Republican politics only to involve himself in the corruption of the Union Pacific Railroad ring and their Crédit Mobilier—a connection so flagrant that even Grant had decided to drop him as Vice-President. Behind Orton and Colfax, in turn, stood the predatory figure of Jay Gould, who was putting up some of the money and was anxious to get in on another good thing.

Of the details of this, Greeley knew little. But he knew that in any struggle for power with Sinclair, Reid and his friends in and about the *Tribune* could muster money too, while he himself, with only six of all his original shares now remaining in his hands, stood alone and near the bottom of the list. He saw the rival groups contending for high stakes, and felt the helplessness of his own condition. For a few days more he stumbled in and out of the *Tribune* office, confused and dazed. Then he could go on no longer. On 12 November, still sleepless and pursued by nightmares, he threw himself into bed at Alvin Johnson's and called for doctors. On the thirteenth he fell into spells of delirium.

All that day he wrote, spattering purple ink over sheet after sheet of *Tribune* notepaper. He started letters, wills, testaments, assignments of property, broke off, and began again. Scratching away in bed, on one sheet he agreed to sell to his host, Alvin Johnson, "in consideration of the sum of $30,000, which he agrees to pay to my daughter Ida, for her own and her sister's use and benefit, all the stock in the *Tribune* Association owned by me, being six shares therein . . ." Taking up another sheet, he proceeded to sell to Alvin Johnson for another $10,000 his various real-estate holdings:

1. Eighty acres of woodland in the townships of Mt. Pleasant and Newcastle near the east line thereof, bought by me of Robert S. Hart.

2. My farm in Buckingham Co., Va., near Gravelly Ford, consisting of 500 acres, more or less.

3. My lands in Greeley, Colo., consisting of one five-acre tract planted with forest trees and one wild tract of forty acres.

4. A mortgage on the farm of my nephew, Horace Greeley 2nd, in the township of Jackson, Ocean Co., N. Y.

5. My ten acres of land in the northeast of Madison, Conn.

He grasped another sheet. Now he made over to Alvin Johnson "all my right, title and interest in the following notes . . . now owned by me"—and then listed obligations by Edward Bayard in the amount of $5,000; George and Albert Brisbane, for $2,500 and interest; and four other acceptances endorsed and paid by himself to a total of $10,000. Next, he made over to the same Alvin Johnson "my right and title to an undivided interest in the Positive Motion

Power-Loom invented and patented by Thos. Norfolk, Salem, Mass." Then he wrote John R. Stuart of Tarrytown, N. Y., ordering him to "take possession of Mrs. Greeley's farm at Chappaqua" and sell all its stock, crops and movable property.

In increasing confusion, he started over once more, now obsessed with notions that he himself had defaulted and had disgraced his family: "I, Horace Greeley, finding myself bankrupt without hope, do hereby sell, assign and make over to Alvin S. Johnson in trust for my wife's estate to which I owe many thousands of dollars beyond the value of my property, this being the oldest and most sacred of all my debts, the following property . . ." He started a wild letter to Cornelius Vanderbilt, entreating his "mercy for my innocent children" and reminding him of the amounts his son Cornelius had once borrowed from Greeley: "I never had and never made any claim on you therefore. But, now that I have beggared and forever disgraced my innocent daughters, I beg you to take up these notes at their face value, giving the money to my children . . ." He broke off midway, reached for another *Tribune* letterhead, and scrawled on it, "*Out of the Depths*: Utterly ruined beyond hope, I desire, before the night closes its jaws on me forever, to say that, though my running for President has placed me where I am, it is not the cause of my ruin." Then he cast that sheet aside, too, and began afresh, splotching the paper with ink and tears:

I stand naked before my God the most utterly, hopelessly wretched and undone of all who ever lived. I have done more harm and wrong than any man who ever saw the light of day. And yet, I take God to witness that I have never intended to wrong or harm anyone . . .

My total vice has been a readiness to believe and trust every flattering, plausible villain. These have come to me in succession with their plausible stories and borrowed from me hundreds of thousands in all, which was often not mine to lend. . . . My ruin is beyond all example.

He exculpated his *Tribune* associates from "any knowledge of my wrongdoing." He apologized to the Liberal Republican leaders for having disgraced their cause: "My crimes will bring reproach on them which is utterly undeserved." He confessed that he "had been tempted by the glittering bait of the Presidency," when he should have put his own house in order. "And now," he hurried on, in ever bigger strokes of his shaken pen, "having done wrong to millions while intending only good to hundreds, I pray God that he may quickly take me from a world where all I have done seems to have turned to evil, and wherein each hour has long been and henceforth must be one of agony, remorse, and shame."

5

He was taken quickly to Dr. George S. Choate's private home for mental patients at Pleasantville, only three miles from Chappaqua. Famous brain specialists attended him there. The *Tribune* explained that he was suffering from "nervous prostration." John Bigelow was more brutal. "I think he has been crazy for years," he told his diary on 24 November; "Now . . . the fact cannot be disguised. I was told a week ago he was out of his head. Yesterday it was currently reported upon good authority, that application had been made for his confinement at Bloomingdale . . . I am the more disposed to credit it, as Reid and Hay both had quite prepared me for such a catastrophe."

He lingered on until the end of the month, sometimes lucid, often delirious. Ida, blanched, wan, prematurely aged after attending her mother through years of sickness, now nursed her father. Her younger sister Gabrielle, sturdier, round-faced, more stolid and more likable in Greeley's eyes, stood by. Old friends called— foreman Tom Rooker of the *Tribune* composing room, and Patrick O'Rourke of the pressroom, both of them hands who had been with Greeley for thirty years. Reid came in—the heir apparent. But there was no hope. Greeley sank into coma. What he murmured then became a source of legend—Greeley's last. A pious version had it that he muttered, "I know that my Redeemer liveth." Another had it that he swore unconscionably at those who he thought were trying to seize control of his paper. On the 28th of November he was sinking. Next day he died.

He had left instructions for a simple funeral and burial. As for a memorial, "Let it be a plain marble slab," he had written; "no Latin—no embellishments. State when nominated and when deceased. Get Gen. Cochrane to write epitaph—his style is so simple —Whitelaw will distribute locks of my hair—Be kind to Tilton—he is foolish, but young. Plant me in my favorite pumpkin arbor, with a gooseberry bush for a footstone."

Nevertheless, it was decided that the final honors to Horace Greeley must be fitting and grandiose. Three preachers officiated at the funeral services on Fifth Avenue. One of them was Dr. Chapin, Greeley's old Universalist pastor, who delivered a long, learned eulogy from the pulpit. But the star of the hour was the Reverend Henry Ward Beecher, who disdained Chapin's pulpit and advanced among the banks of flowers on the floor of the church to deliver another of his warm, tremulous orations. He spoke in "a musical, low-pitched, moving voice," Joseph Bucklin Bishop remembered, without recalling just what he said. Among the mourners sat Theodore Tilton, Greeley's favorite young friend and now Beecher's deadly enemy. Phineas T. Barnum was there. Old Tom Rooker's *Tribune* composing-room force filled up four pews. Whitelaw Reid and his lieutenant, John Hay, came in together—both young, lean, mustached, and dressed in proper black as they paired off against Sinclair and his candidate for the editorship, "Smiler" Colfax. Stockholders in their pews could weigh the rival factions. Jay Gould, in his uptown mansion, was weighing them too. Now he was toying with the Orton-Colfax crowd; but within a few weeks he was to shift his winning weight to the side of Reid.

Thurlow Weed was on hand as a pallbearer—white-haired, a little stooped, but still a tall and commanding presence. His partner of many years, William H. Seward, who had missed the Presidency too, was not there: after seven years of high service as Secretary of State, Seward had retired, had declared himself neutral in the last election, had gone home to rest in Auburn, and there, in October, had died. But Seward's old rival, Salmon P. Chase, now Chief Justice of the United States, was present, as were the governors of New York, New Jersey and Connecticut. Dana, Bryant, George Jones of the *Times*, Manton Marble of the *World*, and even George William Curtis of *Harper's Weekly*—whose cartoonist, Nast, had hounded Greeley throughout the late campaign—had all delivered themselves of the appropriate eulogies. The mayor of the City of New York was on hand. At noon the funeral procession formed and policemen lined the crowded streets. City churches rang their chimes and all business stopped as the cortege passed down Fifth Avenue, heading for Greenwood Cemetery in Brooklyn. On Madison Square the people of New York stood twenty deep to watch Horace Greeley go by. The New York Police Band played the Dead March from *Saul*. In the first carriage following the family mourners rode General Ulysses S. Grant, President of the United States.

BIBLIOGRAPHY

1. GENERAL SOURCES

Greeley was his own fullest biographer. With the run of his own editorial page for almost forty years, he spread over it day by day and week after week a public story of his personal opinions, encounters, discoveries and political adventures. Then, before shutting down for the night, he usually went to work laying bare his private story by hurrying off notes and letters packed with incident, argument, confession, and expostulation to a string of confidants. Greeley's published work in itself provides an ample basis for narrative. His private letters provide another, and there are over a thousand of them extant.

Almost his entire correspondence with his wife, written during their frequent, protracted absences from one another, has been destroyed or lost. But it is doubtful whether he ever opened his mind as fully in writing to Mary Greeley as he did to intimates such as Beman Brockway, Emma Whiting Newhall, Rebekah Whipple and Margaret Allen, all of whom devotionally preserved scores of letters which he wrote to them, while Greeley for his part also preserved the lengthy messages they sent him. His interchanges with Brockway, Mrs. Whipple and Mrs. Allen are now to be found in the Greeley manuscript collection in the Library of Congress, which also includes letters to and from a large assortment of occasional correspondents, as well as Greeley's office jottings and outbursts to Charles A. Dana, together with lecture notes, press clippings, and transcripts of his letters to Mrs. Newhall.

This collection is complemented by the Greeley Papers in the New York Public Library, a mass which consists of (1) the Greeley-Colfax correspondence, a file of the editor's frank exchanges with one of his closest political associates over a period of two decades, and (2) the Ford Collection of letters to and from Greeley, along with notes, miscellaneous manuscripts and pictures, many of them acquired from the

Greeley estate. Richer than the Library of Congress file, the Ford Collection ranges over both Greeley's personal and political correspondence, including exchanges with close friends like B. F. Ransom, Obediah Bowe, and Mrs. Newhall, as well as with William H. Seward, Edward Bates, Salmon P. Chase, William H. Herndon, the Blair family, Simon Cameron and many others. Correspondence on *Tribune* business with Thomas McElrath, Bayard Taylor, Samuel Sinclair, Samuel Wilkeson, Whitelaw Reid, and others rounds out this invaluable store.

A smaller collection in the New York Historical Society Library contains, among others, exchanges with Thurlow Weed. Greeley's letters to Margaret Fuller are preserved in the Harvard University Library. Other letters to Weed as well as to William H. Seward are in the Rush Rhees Library, Rochester, New York. Some of Greeley's letters to Lincoln are among the Lincoln Papers in the Library of Congress, and others in the Lincoln Collection of the University of Chicago Library. Letters to Theodore Parker are in the Massachusetts Historical Society Library, Boston, and miscellaneous other letters repose in the collections of the Boston Public Library, the New York State Library in Albany, and the Yale University Library. Still others, now undiscoverable in the original, are available only in the form of printed texts published during or after his lifetime.

Greeley wrote his own story in the form of a series of newspaper articles thrown together hurriedly in the 1860's and published in book form as *Recollections of a Busy Life* (New York, 1868). The work is a prime source for the history of his early years and family background, but in approaching the chronicle of his maturity Greeley became either so distracted or inhibited that there his narrative loses all but incidental value. For the real story of what Greeley thought and did publicly, the biographer turns inevitably to the files of his own regular publications—the weekly *New Yorker* (22 March, 1834–20 November, 1841), the weekly *Jeffersonian* (3 March, 1838–9 February, 1839), his weekly *Log Cabin* (1 May, 1840–20 November, 1841) and the daily and weekly New York *Tribune* (beginning 10 April, 1841).

But these files by no means exhaust Greeley's published utterances. The complete file of his writings, large and small, includes a sixteen-page campaign pamphlet, *Protection and Free Trade: the Question Stated and Considered* (New York, 1844, published by Greeley & McElrath); campaign songs and doggerel in *Whig Songs for 1844* (also published in that year by Greeley & McElrath); a pamphlet reprint of his debate on Fourierism with Henry J. Raymond, *Association*

Discussed: or, the Socialism of the Tribune Examined (New York, 1847); a "Sons of Temperance" tract entitled *Alcoholic Liquors: their essential nature and necessary effects on the human constitution* (New York, 1849); a collection of his moral lectures, speeches and editorials, *Hints toward Reforms* (New York, 1850); a reprint collection of his European correspondence to the *Tribune* entitled *Glances at Europe* (New York, 1851); an edited version of Epes Sargent's *Life and Public Services of Henry Clay*, with seven chapters added by Greeley (Auburn, N.Y., 1852); his summary *History of the Struggle for Slavery Extension or Restriction in the United States, from the Declaration of Independence to the Present Day* (New York, 1856); a reprint of articles written on his western tour, *An Overland Journey from New York to San Francisco in the Summer of 1859* (New York, 1860); his two-volume, journalistic *The American Conflict: a History of the Great Rebellion in the United States of America, 1860-64* (Hartford, Conn., 1864-66); a pamphlet entitled *An Address on Success in Business* (New York, 1867); another tract on protectionism, *Essays designed to elucidate the Science of Political Economy* ("while serving to explain and defend the policy of protection to home industry, as a system of national cooperation for the elevation of labor"—Boston, 1870); still another travel-article reprint, *Mr. Greeley's Letters from Texas and the Lower Mississippi* (New York, 1871); and a final, lengthy exercise, *What I Know About Farming* ("A series of brief and homely expositions of practical agriculture as an art based upon science"—New York, 1871.)

As a celebrity in his early forties, Greeley received his first book-length biographical attention in James Parton's *The Life of Horace Greeley* (New York, 1855, and revised in subsequent editions). Privately Greeley said of this book that "some of it is untrue, much of it is ridiculous; it is full of idle gossip which Parton picked up by inquiring at all the places where I had lived." Yet it is just this first-hand roving inquiry by the energetic Parton, at a time when Greeley's first employers and the elder neighbors who knew his family history were still living, that gives Parton's book unique value as a source. The subsequent biographies by Francis N. Zabriskie (1890) and William A. Linn (1903) were hardly comparable in originality and insight. Whitelaw Reid's brief memoir, *Horace Greeley* (New York, 1879), brought forth much authentic *Tribune* detail. Charles Sotheran's *Horace Greeley and Other Pioneers of American Socialism* (New York, 1892) is full of interesting tractarian matter on Greeley's Fourierist and land-reform associations. A report published under the auspices of the New York State Historian under the title *Proceedings at the Unveiling of a Memorial to Horace Greeley at Chappaqua, N.Y.* (Albany, 1915) is a storehouse of first-hand recollections, transcripts, photographs, and other Greeley memorabilia. Both of Greeley's more recent biographers, Don C. Seitz (1926) and Henry Luther Stoddard (1946) offer much new material obtained from manuscripts, letters and people who knew Greeley, but Stoddard is often highly inaccurate in his transcription of sources. Ralph R. Fahrney's monograph, *Horace Greeley and the Tribune in the Civil War* (Cedar Rapids, Iowa, 1936), fills in many gaps left by earlier studies, and Jeter Allen Isely's *Horace Greeley and the Republican Party, 1853-1861* (Princeton, 1947) is an outstanding work of scholarship.

Contemporary glimpses of Greeley the newspaperman, and of the journalistic world in which he moved, appear first of all in memoirs written by other newspapermen—many of them *Tribune* veterans, and others outside friends or rivals. Especially illuminating among these are John Bigelow, *Retrospections of an Active Life*, 5 vols. (New York, 1909-13); Joseph Bucklin Bishop, *Notes and Anecdotes of Many Years* (New York, 1925); Beman Brockway, *Fifty Years in Journalism* (Watertown, N.Y., 1891); Charles T. Congdon, *Reminiscences of a Journalist* (Boston, 1880); James R. Gilmore, *Personal Recollections of Abraham Lincoln and the Civil War* (Boston, 1898); Edwin L. Godkin, *Life and Letters*, ed. by Rollo Ogden, 2 vols. (New York, 1907); James S. Pike, *First Blows of the Civil War* (New York, 1879); Bayard Taylor, *Life and Letters*, ed. by Marie Hansen-Taylor and Horace Scudder, 2 vols. (Cambridge, 1884); Henry Watterson, *"Marse Henry,"* 2 vols. (New York, 1919); Henry Villard, *Memoirs*, 2 vols. (Boston, 1904); and John Russell Young, *Men and Memories*, 2 vols. (New York, 1901). The "Extracts from the Journal of Henry J. Raymond" published in *Scribners Monthly Magazine* for November, 1879, and January and March, 1880, touch briefly but importantly on Greeley. Other books by *Tribune* hands in Greeley's day that help round out the picture are Junius Henry Browne's *The Great Metropolis* (New York, 1869); Congdon's *Tribune Essays, 1857-1863* (New York, 1869); Solon Robinson's *Facts for Farmers* (New York, 1864); Albert D. Richardson's *The Field, the Dungeon and the Escape* (Hartford, 1869); Bayard Taylor's *At Home and Abroad* (New York, 1860); and George W. Smalley's *Anglo-American Memories*, 2 vols. (London, 1911-12).

Other memoirs, written by preachers, lady poets, men of fashion, and politicians, also touch colorfully on Greeley and his friends and rivals. Of these one can best single out Mary C. Ames, *A Memorial of Alice and Phoebe Cary* (New York, 1874); Theodore L. Cuyler, *Recollections of a Long Life* (New York, 1902); John W. Forney, *Anecdotes of Public Men*, 2 vols. (New York, 1873-81); Octavius B. Frothingham, *Recollections and Impressions, 1822-1890* (New York, 1891); Philip Hone's *Diary*, ed. by Allan Nevins, 2 vols. (New York, 1927); George W. Julian, *Political Recollections, 1840-1872* (Chicago, 1884); and the *Diary* of Gideon Welles, 3 vols. (New York, 1911). On the subject of Greeley's complex and troubled relationships with the political firm of Weed & Seward, valuable information from the partners' side is preserved in Thurlow Weed, *Life of . . . including his Autobiography and a Memoir*, ed. by Harriet A. Weed, 2 vols. (Boston, 1884), and William H. Seward, *Autobiography, from 1801 to 1834, with a Memoir of his Life . . . to 1846*, ed. by Frederick W. Seward (New York, 1877), followed by William H. Seward, *Seward at Washington, 1846-1861*, ed. by Frederick W. Seward (New York, 1891).

No adequate biography has yet been published of Greeley's first protégé and subsequent rival, Henry J. Raymond of the New York *Times*; but Augustus J. Maverick's *Henry J. Raymond and the New York Press for Thirty Years* (Hartford, 1870), written by a man who worked for both editors, is full of interesting if haphazard information about them. Greeley's second brilliant protégé, Charles A. Dana, has fared better in Candace Stone's *Dana and the Sun* (New York, 1938). An incisive picture of Greeley's bitterest enemy is given in Oliver Carlson's *The Man Who Made News: James Gordon Bennett* (New York, 1942). Royal Cortissoz's *Life of Whitelaw Reid*, 2 vols. (New York, 1921) suffers the handicaps of an "authorized" biography. Among studies of other men close to Greeley, Glyndon G. van Deusen's *Thurlow Weed: Wizard of the Lobby* (Boston, 1947) is invaluable for its study of the "triumvirate." Greeley's dealings over the years with Lincoln are documented at length in J. G. Nicolay and John Hay, *Abraham Lincoln, A History*, 10 vols. (New York, 1890), and interpreted with much engaging matter in Carl Sandburg, *Abraham Lincoln*, 6 vols. (New York, 1929-39).

Political and other studies that bear on particular phases of Greeley's career are cited under chapter headings below. Studies of journalism that cast light on his role and environment throughout are Frederic Hudson, *Journalism in the United States* (New York, 1873); Alfred McC. Lee, *The Daily Newspaper in America* (New York, 1937) and Frank Luther Mott, *American Journalism* (New York, 1941), along with Elmer Davis, *History of the New York Times* (New York, 1921); Allan Nevins, *The*

Evening Post: A Century of Journalism (New York, 1922); and, particularly, Harry W. Baehr, *The New York Tribune Since the Civil War* (New York, 1936).

2. PARTICULAR SOURCES

(LC=Library of Congress; NYPL=New York Public Library; NYHS= New York Historical Society Library. HG=Horace Greeley.)

CHAPTER I: *Journeyman*

For Greeley genealogy and origins: HG, *Recollections*; autobiographical letter to Moses A. Cortland, April, 1845, in NYPL; Parton, *Life*. Genealogical and local detail in Joseph Merrill, *History of Amesbury, including the first Seventeen Years of Salisbury* (Haverhill, Mass., 1880); Edward L. Parker, *The History of Londonderry, New Hampshire* (Concord, N. H., 1883); John Farmer, *Historical Sketch of Amherst in the County of Hillsborough, N. H.* (Concord, 1837); Joseph Joslin and others, *A History of the Town of Poultney* (Poultney, Vt., 1840). Timothy Dwight quoted on Westhaven, from Dwight, *Travels in New England and New York* (New Haven, 1821-22). HG articles of apprenticeship, from original in LC. Col. W. L. Stone quoted on Syracuse, from Stone, "Journal of a Tour from New York to Niagara in the Year 1829," *Buffalo Historical Society Publications*. Vol. XIV; see also Moses C. Cleveland, "Journal of a Tour from Riverhead, L. I., to the Falls of the Niagara in June, 1831," *New York History*, Vol. XXVII.

CHAPTER II: *New Yorker*

For contemporary background and description of New York City, especially Hone, *Diary*; John Disturnell, *Guide to the City of New York* (New York, 1833); Tyrone Power, *Impressions of America* (Philadelphia, 1836). For detail on economic changes, Robert G. Albion, *The Rise of New York Port* (New York, 1939). James Parton letter to HG on Poultney, MS. in NYPL. Figures on technological revolution in printing, from A. M. Lee, *op. cit*. James Gordon Bennett background, based chiefly on Carlson, *op. cit*. Thurlow Weed's exchange with Croswell, from van Deusen, *Weed*. Weed on his method of running the *Evening Journal*, from Weed, *Autobiography*. For contemporary newspaper background and atmosphere, also Rufus W. Griswold, *Passages from the*

Correspondence and other Papers of . . . (Cambridge, 1898), and Merle M. Hoover, *Park Benjamin: Poet and Editor* (New York, 1948). Henry J. Raymond quoted on HG, from Maverick, *op. cit.*

CHAPTER III: Whig

For HG's relations with Mary Greeley, especially HG letters to B. F. Ransom, Obediah Bowe, and Emma Whiting Newhall in NYPL. Esther Greeley quoted on Mary, from Seitz, *op. cit.* For Workingman's and Locofoco movements, Seth Luther, *Address to the Working-Men of New England* (Boston, 1832); Frances Wright, *What Is the Matter?* (New York, 1838); Arthur M. Schlesinger, Jr., *The Age of Jackson* (Boston, 1945); Richard Hofstadter, "William Leggett, Spokesman of Jacksonian Democracy," *Political Science Quarterly*, Vol. LVIII; William Trimble, "The Social Philosophy of the Loco-Foco Democracy," *American Journal of Sociology*, Vol. XXVI. Figures on Rhode Island factory conditions, from Norman Ware, *The Industrial Worker, 1840-1860* (New York, 1924). For formation of Whig party in New York, Dixon Ryan Fox, *The Decline of Aristocracy in the Politics of New York* (New York, 1918).

CHAPTER IV: Campaigner

For HG's Albany role, HG *Recollections*; Weed, *op. cit.*; Seward, *Life and Letters* and MS. papers; van Deusen, *op. cit.*, together with files of *Jeffersonian* and *Log Cabin* and letters to Bowe. HG letter to Seward, text in *Recollections*.

CHAPTER V: Tribune

For New York press war on Bennett, Hone, *Diary*; Merle Hoover, *Park Benjamin*; Carlson, *op. cit.* HG's instructions to a country editor, from A. M. Lee, *op. cit.* HG's letters to Rufus Griswold, in LC; to Bayard Taylor, in NYPL. McElrath on the early *Tribune*, in letter to the *Tribune*, 1887. For Greeley's working methods, office, appearance, and personal habits, especially memoirs of Bishop, Brockway, Godkin, Taylor and Young cited above; other descriptive matter in Parton and Stoddard, *op. cit.*, and in George W. Bungay, *Crayon Sketches and Off-hand Takings* (Boston, 1852) and Thomas L. Nichols, *Forty Years of American Life* (London, 1864). New York *Herald* reporter's description of HG as lecturer, from Carlson, *op. cit.* HG's temperance lecture notes, from HG Memorial *Proceedings*. Concluding HG letter in chapter, to Schuyler Colfax, March, 1850.

CHAPTER VI: *Utopian*

Ralph Waldo Emerson cited on reform convention, from Emerson's *Works*, Centenary ed., Vol. X. For the Fourierist movement in America: Albert Brisbane, *The Social Destiny of Man* (Philadelphia, 1840) and *ibid.*, *Association; or, A Concise Exposition of the Practical Part of Fourier's Social Science* (New York, 1843); Parke Godwin, *Democracy, Pacific and Constructive* (New York, 1844); HG and Henry J. Raymond, *Association Discussed*; and miscellaneous matter in Sotheran, *op. cit.* Further, on Brisbane: Redelia Brisbane, *Albert Brisbane, A Mental Biography* (Boston, 1893); Charles A. Madison, "Albert Brisbane: Social Dreamer," *American Scholar*, Vol. XII; Arthur Eugene Bestor, Jr., "Albert Brisbane—Propagandist for Socialism in the 1840s," *New York History*, Vol. XXVIII. For Brook Farm, Lindsay Swift, *Brook Farm* (New York, 1900). George Ripley cited on resigning his pulpit, from Octavius B. Frothingham, *George Ripley* (Boston, 1883). Charles A. Dana cited on the same, from J. H. Wilson, *Life of Charles A. Dana* (New York, 1907). For general background of intellectual reform movements, William Henry Channing, *Life of William Ellery Channing* (Boston, 1880); Henry Steele Commager, *Theodore Parker: Yankee Crusader* (Boston, 1936); Odell Shepard, *Pedlar's Progress: The Life of Bronson Alcott* (Boston, 1937).

CHAPTER VII: *Lover*

For HG home life and relations with Margaret Fuller: *Recollections*, Parton, *Life*, HG letters to Emma Whiting Newhall, and Mason Wade, *Margaret Fuller: Whetstone of Genius* (New York, 1940). Margaret Fuller cited on Emerson, from Wade. Description of Anne Lynch's soirees, from *Memoirs of Anne Charlotte Lynch Botta*, ed. by Vincenzo Botta (New York, 1894). HG cited on divorce, from pamphlet *Love, Marriage and Divorce, and the Sovereignty of the Individual* ("A discussion between Henry James, Horace Greeley and Stephen P. Andrews, including the final replies of Mr. Andrews, rejected by the *Tribune*," ed. by S. P. Andrews, New York, 1853). HG letters to Margaret Fuller, in Harvard University Library. HG descriptions of "spirit-rapping" seance and "spirit" conversation with Pickie, MSS. in NYPL.

CHAPTER VIII: *Triumvir*

Weed to Seward on HG ("I can never comprehend him"), letter cited in Isely, *op. cit.* HG letters to Weed, in NYHS. For land-reform and "antirent" agitations, Thomas A. Devyr, *The Odd Book of the Nineteenth Century* (Greenpoint, N. Y., 1882); D. R. Fox, *op. cit.*; Henry Christman, *Tin Horns and Calico* (New York, 1945). Further material on Alvan E. Bovay, from MS. study of Bovay by Henry Christman. HG's beliefs as a land-reformer, from chapters "The Emancipation of Labor" and "The Organization of Labor" in HG, *Hints toward Reforms*. For HG's relation to land-reform movement, R. M. Robbins, "Horace Greeley: Land Reform and Unemployment, 1837-1862," *Agricultural History*, Vol. VII; John R. Commons, "Horace Greeley and the Working Class Origins of the Republican Party," *Political Science Quarterly*, Vol. XXIV; Earle D. Ross, "Horace Greeley and the West," *Mississippi Valley Historical Review*, Vol. XX. Alexander McClure cited on HG at 1848 convention, from McClure, *Our Presidents and How We Make Them* (Philadelphia, 1901). For Whig nativism, Ray A. Billington, *The Protestant Crusade, 1800-1860* (New York, 1938).

CHAPTER IX: *Mover*

HG to Seward concerning New York *Times*, letter in LC; Seward to HG, letters in NYPL. For Karl Marx and Dana, with comment by Engels, Franz Mehring, *Karl Marx* (New York, 1935). Beecher sermon cited, from Paxton Hibben, *Henry Ward Beecher: An American Portrait* (New York, 1927). Description of P. T. Barnum, from M. R. Werner, *Barnum* (New York, 1923). Walt Whitman cited ("I hail with joy"), from Whitman, *Democratic Vistas*. HG to Seward on Weed ("I have tried to talk to Weed"), letter in Seward Papers, Auburn, N. Y.; HG to Seward on dissolution of partnership, letter printed in *Recollections*; HG to Seward ("My political life is ended"), letter in LC. For HG's political evolution and formation of the Republican party, John R. Commons, *op. cit.*, and George W. Julian, "The First Republican National Convention," *American Historical Review*, Vol. IV. For general political development, Allan Nevins, *Ordeal of the Union*, 2 vols. (New York, 1947).

CHAPTER X: *Shaker*

William Allen Butler cited, from R. R. Wilson and O. E. Wilson, *New York in Literature* (Elmira, N. Y., 1947). Greeley on Ida ("She is reserved"), in letter to Emma Whiting Newhall. Figures on *Tribune* profits and stock participation of HG and others, from records in possession of the New York *Herald Tribune*. HG letter on Poe autograph, as printed in *Tribune* staff pamphlet *Fun From Under the Old White*

Hat ("written by old-time editors and reporters of the *Tribune*," New York, 1872). Whitelaw Reid's comments on HG, from Reid memoir, *Horace Greeley*. Letters from Jonas Winchester and Cornelius Vanderbilt, Jr., to HG, in NYPL; figures on other loans by HG, from canceled checks, statements and acknowledgments in NYPL collection. E. C. Stedman on his meeting HG, and text of poem submitted, from Laura Stedman and George M. Gould, *Life and Letters of Edmund Clarence Stedman*, 2 vols. (New York, 1910). Dialogue between Mary Greeley and caller, from Brockway, *op. cit.* Theodore Parker to W. H. Herndon on HG, cited in Isely, *op. cit.* HG proposing Republican "harmony" strategy in 1856 ("This country ought to be . . ."), letter to W. M. Chace and others, NYPL. Detail on HG's role during the Kansas crisis, from Isely, *op. cit.*, and William H. Isely, "The Sharps Rifle Episode in Kansas History," *American Historical Review*, Vol. XII. HG on his western tour, letters to the *Tribune* as reprinted in *An Overland Journey*, and other observations in *Recollections*. Henry Villard quoted, from Villard, *Memoirs*.

CHAPTER XI: *President Maker*

HG on Douglas ("a low and dangerous demagogue"), letter to F. Newhall, transcript in LC. For Herndon-Greeley interview in 1858, William H. Herndon and Jesse W. Weik, *Herndon's Lincoln*, (Springfield, Ill., 1921); HG on same, letter to Colfax, NYPL. Herndon letters to HG, in NYPL; Lincoln on HG ("I have believed"), letter to Charles L. Wilson; Herndon on HG ("Horace is with us"), letter to Lyman Trumbull, in Trumbull Papers, LC. HG to Joseph Medill, letter copied in Lincoln's hand and printed in D. C. Mearns, ed., *The Lincoln Papers*, 2 vols. (New York, 1948). Herndon to Theodore Parker on HG, letter in Massachusetts Historical Society; Seward in 1858 on HG ("I know how hard it is"), letter to R. M. Blatchford, NYPL. Murat Halstead's description of Seward and Chase, cited in William Baringer, *Lincoln's Rise to Power* (Boston, 1937). James Fell remarks to Lincoln, from Sandburg, *Lincoln: The Prairie Years*. For Republican personalities and strategy before and during the 1860 convention, especially Baringer, *op. cit.*; Murat Halstead, *Caucuses of 1860* (Columbus, 1860); Henry M. Field, *The Life of Dudley Field* (New York, 1898); Addison G. Proctor, *Lincoln and the Convention of 1860* (Chicago Historical Society pamphlet, Chicago, 1918); Reinhard H. Luthin, *The First Lincoln Campaign* (Cambridge, 1944); Burton J. Hendrick, *Lincoln's War Cabinet* (Boston, 1946). HG speech to Kansas delegation, from Proctor. HG talk with

Dudley Field, from Field, *op. cit.*; Medill-Davis interview, from Sandburg, *op. cit.* Letters from Bovay and Parton to HG, in NYPL. Sewardite outburst against HG ("The white-livered old cuss"), in Washbourne MSS., LC. HG letter to Pike, in Pike, *First Blows.*

CHAPTER XII: *Warhawk*

HG to Bayard Taylor, letter in NYHS; HG letter to Lincoln, December, 1860, text in Nicolay and Hay, *Lincoln,* Vol. III. For HG's shifting policies toward the South, almost daily editorials in the *Tribune* from early December, 1860, through March, 1861; studies and interpretations of the same in Isely, *op. cit.*; Fahrney, *op. cit.*; and David M. Potter, "Horace Greeley and Peaceable Secession," *Journal of Southern History,* Vol. VII. Seward comment on himself and Weed, from Welles, *Diary.* Henry C. Carey, reporting on Simon Cameron, cited in Harry J. Carman and Reinhard H. Luthin, *Lincoln and the Patronage* (New York, 1943). HG meeting with Lincoln in Springfield, from Herndon, *op. cit.*, and Henry Villard, *Lincoln on the Eve of '61,* ed. by Harold G. and Oswald Garrison Villard (New York, 1941). Letters of Judge Davis, Seward and Lincoln on HG's senatorial hopes, from Weed, *Memoir.* Weed on his victory over HG, letter in Weed Papers, cited by van Deusen, *op. cit.* Tilton to HG, letter in NYPL.

CHAPTER XIII: *Errant Knight*

Nye to Seward, letter in Seward Papers, cited in Isely, *op. cit.* HG letter to Lincoln after Bull Run, text in Nicolay and Hay, *op. cit.*, Vol. IV. HG outburst after Bull Run ("I must stay"), in letter to Samuel Wilkeson, in NYPL; other letters to same, also in NYPL. Dana on his leaving the *Tribune,* from Dana, *Recollections of the Civil War* (New York, 1899). Herndon, cited as criticizing Lincoln, from Sandburg, *Lincoln: the War Years,* Vol. I. HG conversations with Gilmore, and Lincoln meetings with Gilmore and Walker, from Gilmore, *Personal Recollections.* Lincoln letter to Walker, also in Gilmore, *op. cit.*, and N. W. Stephenson, ed., *An Autobiography of Abraham Lincoln* (Indianapolis, 1926). Lydia Maria Child to HG, letter in NYPL. HG exchange with Lincoln on Kentucky, from Sandburg, *op. cit.*, Vol. III. Letters from Salmon P. Chase to HG, in NYPL. Lincoln letter replying to HG's "Prayer of Twenty Millions," text from Henry Steele Commager, ed., *Documents of American History* (New York, 1934). For HG's 1863 peace moves, letter from Clement L. Vallandigham in NYPL; Nicolay and Hay, *op cit.*,

Vol. VI; Raymond, "Journal"; James L. Vallandigham, *A Life of Clement L. Vallandigham* (Baltimore, 1872); Elbert J. Benton, *The Movement for Peace Without a Victory During the Civil War* (Western Historical Society Publications, No. 99). For HG and New York draft riots, Gilmore, *op. cit.*; Parton, *op. cit.*; Congdon, *Reminiscences*; J. B. Bishop, *Notes and Anecdotes*; and O. B. Frothingham, *Recollections*.

CHAPTER XIV: *Peacemaker*

Lincoln on "Uncle Horace," from Sandburg, *op. cit.*, Vol. I. Bryant comment on HG at breakfast, from Godkin, *op. cit.* For HG and Niagara episode, texts of Lincoln's instructions and HG's replies in Nicolay and Hay, *op. cit.*, Vol. IX. Also Frank H. Severance, *Peace Episodes on the Niagara* (Buffalo Historical Society Publications, Vol. XVIII); HG, *The American Conflict*; Seitz, *op. cit.*; William Roscoe Thayer, *The Life and Letters of John Hay*, 2 vols. (Boston, 1915). Lincoln to Senator Harlan, remark cited in Ida M. Tarbell, *The Life of Abraham Lincoln* (New York, 1900), Vol. III. Lincoln comment on HG ("an old shoe"), from Welles, *op. cit.* HG letter to Lincoln ("Nine-tenths of the whole American people"), from Nicolay and Hay, *op. cit.* For details of HG's activities to replace Lincoln by another candidate, *The Secret Movement to Supersede Abraham Lincoln in 1864* (letters in the New York *Sun*, 30 June, 1889). Francis Preston Blair, Sr., messages to HG, in NYPL.

CHAPTER XV: *The Old White Hat*

For descriptions of the postwar *Tribune* and the later HG: in addition to newspaper sources cited above (especially Bigelow, Bishop, Godkin, and Young) Stedman, *op. cit.*; Charles A. Page, *Letters of a War Correspondent* (Boston, 1899); William Winter, *Old Friends* (New York, 1909); Julius Chambers, *News Hunting on Three Continents* (New York, 1921); Parton, *Life* (revised ed., 1872). Some HG stories and legends from *Fun From Under the Old White Hat*; details on the changing *Tribune* from Baehr, *The Tribune Since the Civil War*; figures on *Tribune* costs and profits, from Hudson, *Journalism*. HG 1866 letter to Reid, in NYPL; 1867 message to Reid and announcement of his promotion, in Cortissoz, *Life of Reid*. HG letters to correspondents seeking advice, in NYPL. HG letter to Margaret Allen's daughters, in LC. For account of Nathan C. Meeker's plan and settlement of Greeley, Colorado, recollections by Ralph Meeker in HG Memorial *Proceedings*. Story of Hay's coming to the *Tribune*, from W. R. Thayer, *op. cit.*

Bibliography

CHAPTER XVI: *The Parties' Choice*

HG letter to Devyr, text in Christman, *op. cit.* For postwar economic and social change, Gustavus Myers, *History of the Great American Fortunes*, 3 vols. (Chicago, 1907-1909); B. H. Hibbard, *A History of the Public Land Policies* (New York, 1924); Louis M. Hacker, *The Triumph of American Capitalism* (New York, 1940). For Reconstruction politics and politicians, especially Claude G. Bowers, *The Tragic Era* (Boston, 1929). HG on Grant ("Grant is done for"), from George W. Julian MS. Diary, cited by Bowers. Grant letter to Young, from Young, *op. cit.* HG letter to Reavis, in NYPL; HG letter to Tilden, text in Denis T. Lynch, *"Boss" Tweed* (New York, 1927). HG describing his lecture trips, in letters to Margaret Allen in LC. Wendell Phillips quoted, from Vernon Louis Parrington, *Main Currents in American Thought*, Vol. III (New York, 1930). For Liberal Republican movement in 1872, Carl Schurz, *Reminiscences*, 3 vols. (New York, 1908); Henry Watterson, *op. cit.*; Alexander McClure, *Recollections of Half a Century* (Salem, Mass., 1902). Bigelow on HG to Reid, from Bigelow, *Retrospections*, Vol. V. Bryant on HG's nomination, letter cited in Parke Godwin, *Life of Bryant* (New York, 1880).

CHAPTER XVII: *The Sage of Chappaqua*

HG complaining of "brain fever," in letter to Samuel Sinclair, NYPL. Description of HG's Chappaqua party, from Charleston, S. C., *Daily News*. For 1872 presidential campaign, Schurz, *op. cit.*; Watterson, *op. cit.*; *Harper's Weekly*; HG speeches as reported in the *Tribune* and reprinted in part in pamphlet form in *The True Issues of the Presidential Campaign: Speeches of Horace Greeley* . . . (New York, 1872). Also anti-Greeley campaign literature, especially *The Greeley Record: Showing the Opinions and Sentiments of Horace Greeley on Office Seeking—the Presidency—the Democratic Party* . . . (pamphlet, published by the Union Republican Congressional Executive Committee) and *Horace Greeley, "The Chappaqua Sage": What He Knows About Partisan Politics—Glances at His Political Record* (folder, no source given). On Greeley's side, especially Amos J. Cummings, ed., *Greeley Campaign Songster* (New York, 1872). HG letters during campaign ("The money and office-holding power," *et seq.*), to Margaret Allen, in LC and Joel Benton, ed., *Greeley on Lincoln, With Mr. Greeley's Letters to . . . A Lady Friend* (New York, 1893); HG letters to Sinclair, in NYPL. For Sinclair-Orton-Colfax maneuvers to gain control of the *Tribune*, Baehr, *op. cit.* Notes, unaddressed memoranda and instructions written during HG's final illness, MSS. in NYPL.

INDEX

Adams, Charles Francis, Jr., 331-336
Adams, Henry, 318
Adams, John Quincy, 10
Advertising in *Tribune*, 71-72
Agrarianism, 37, 138
Albany *Argus*, 21
Albany *Evening Journal*, 17, 21, 22, 44-45, 47, 53, 54
Alcott, Bronson, 93, 97
Allen, Margaret, 183, 215, 270, 305, 310, 327-330, 332, 338-340, 345-347
American Conflict, 304, 322
American Laborer, 87
American Monthly, 20, 49
American progress, 213-214
(*See also* Greeley, Horace, on American progress)
American Quarterly Review, 36
Amherst township, N. H., 3
Antietam, 264, 265
Appomattox, 291
Associated Press, 76
Association, Fourierist, 103-104
Astor, John Jacob, 106
Astor, William B., 294, 316, 319
Ayer, J. C., 303, 349

Banks, Nathaniel P., Jr., 171, 173
Barnum, Phineas T., 94, 123, 156-158, 175, 182, 330, 353
Bates, Edward, 215-218, 220-223, 239, 287
Bayard, Dr. Edward, 187, 350
Beach, Moses Y., 106, 308
Beauregard, Gen. Pierre Toutant de, 245

Beecher, Henry Ward, 88, 115, 156-158, 242, 280, 308, 312, 328, 329, 341, 353
Benjamin, Judah P., 143
Benjamin, Park, 20, 29, 49, 64, 91
Bennett, James Gordon, 21, 63, 73, 251
  death of, 342
  defeatism of, in war, 232, 242, 247, 265, 284
  description of, 23-25
  and Greeley, 23-25, 45, 251, 291
  Herald founded by, 25
    (*See also Herald*)
  and Lincoln, 289
  on slavery, 170
Benton, Thomas Hart, 163
Bigelow, John, 296, 313, 334, 349, 352
Birney, James, 133
Bishop, Joseph Bucklin, 84, 297, 299, 341, 353
Blackwell, Lucy Stone (*see* Stone, Lucy)
Blair, Francis Preston, Sr., 23, 73, 163, 170, 216, 218, 220, 222, 224, 290
Blair, Francis Preston, Jr., 164, 170, 216, 218, 224, 277, 278, 326, 336
Blair, Montgomery, 164, 170, 216, 224, 235, 239-241, 277, 278
Blanket sheets, 22
Bliss, Amos, 8-11, 18
Bonner, Robert, 304, 306
Bossange, Hector, 176
Boston *Atlas*, 54
Boston *Journal*, 198
Boutwell, Sen. George S., 317
Bovay, Alvan E., 136, 139, 165, 223

Bowe, Obediah, 12, 34, 41, 45, 53, 54, 62, 76, 81, 85, 90, 119, 179, 186, 280
Bowles, Samuel, 335, 337
Brady, Matthew, 264
Breckinridge, John Cabell, 220
Brisbane, Albert, 91, 92, 97-100, 102-103, 105, 187, 350
Brisbane, George, 350
Brisbane, Redelia, 91
Brockway, Beman, 4, 13, 82, 154, 180, 236, 239, 241, 250, 332, 333
Bromley, Isaac H., 299
Brook Farm, 84, 100-103, 109
Browne, Junius Henry, 298
Bryant, William Cullen, 20, 21, 38, 39, 101, 115, 170, 214, 219, 227, 235, 237, 265, 277, 278, 284, 296, 307, 331, 341, 342, 353
(*See also Evening Post*)
Buchanan, James, 194, 195, 239
Bull Run, battle of, 245-247, 254, 264
Burnside, Gen. Ambrose E., 251, 266
Burr, Aaron, 16
Bush, Margaret, 187
Business, big, age of, 213
  in politics, 319
Butler, Benjamin F., 276, 288
Butler, William Allen, 177

Calhoun, John C., 132, 143
Cameron, Simon, 221, 222, 233, 254, 318, 326
Carey, Henry C., 234
Carlson, Oliver, 76
Cary, Alice and Phoebe, 87, 182
Chandler, Zach, 271, 344, 345, 347
Channing, William Ellery, 93
Channing, William H., 105
Chapin, Dr., 353
Chappaqua (*see* Greeley, Horace, at Chappaqua)
Chase, Salmon P., 143, 164, 209, 210, 220, 235, 239-241, 259, 264, 276, 278, 288
  Chief Justice, 331, 353
  presidential boom for, 277-278
Cheney, Mary (*see* Greeley, Mary Cheney)
Chicago *Tribune*, 219, 335
Child, Lydia Maria, 258
Choate, Dr. George S., 352
Christian Union, 328

Cincinnati *Commercial*, 198, 209, 219, 331, 335
Cincinnati convention, 1872, 335-339
Cincinnati *Gazette*, 288, 303
Claflin, Tennessee, 341
Clark family, 349
Clay, Cassius M., 134
Clay, Henry, 35, 54-55, 74, 76, 86, 87, 100, 107, 127-128, 132, 140, 142, 143, 159
Cleveland, John F., 118, 226
Coggeshall, James, 65
Colfax, Schuyler, confidant of Greeley, 77, 78, 84, 104, 125, 129, 132, 135, 140, 141, 144, 153-156, 166, 169, 178, 180, 184, 185, 188-190, 193, 195, 203, 204, 208, 244, 257, 265, 271, 277
  as Congressman, 81, 174, 211
  editor of *St. Joseph Valley Register*, 74
  as Speaker of the House, 318, 320
  Vice-President, 325, 349
Commercial Advertiser, New York, 13, 20-21
Confiscation Act, 261, 262
Congdon, Charles T., 84, 186, 189, 273
Congressional Campaign Committee, 344
Conkling, Sen. Roscoe, 318, 319, 325, 326, 338, 344, 347
Continental Monthly, 256
Cook, Clarence, 299
Cooke, Jay, 277, 300, 310, 319, 344-346
Cooper, James Fenimore, 16, 37, 72
Cortland, Moses, 31
Courier and Enquirer, 21-23, 43, 63, 66, 100, 103, 127, 219
Crash of 1837, 40-41
Croswell, editor of *Argus*, 21
"Crumbs of Comfort," 348, 349
Cummings, Amos J., 84, 215, 301, 336
Curtis, George William, 84, 223, 353

Dana, Charles A., as Assistant Secretary of War, 252, 284
  at Brook Farm, 32, 97, 100, 103, 105
  and Greeley, 171-174, 237, 246, 252-253, 353
  Republican views of, 235

Index

Dana, Charles A.—*Continued*
  Sun bought by, 308
  (*See also Sun*)
  on *Tribune*, 80, 108, 143, 145
  as managing editor, 80, 83, 84, 153-155, 171-174, 185, 235, 247
Davis, David, 218, 222, 223, 234, 237, 334, 335
Davis, Henry Winter, 288
Davis, Jefferson, 143, 243, 250, 282, 290
  in prison, 321-322
Day, Benjamin, 25
Democracy in America, 36
Democratic party, 163, 326, 338
Devyr, Thomas A., 136, 139, 193, 314, 315
Dial, The, 109
Dickens, Charles, 27, 307
Dickinson, Andrew, 224
Donnelly, Ignatius, 331
Douglas, Stephen A., 159-162, 164, 194, 195, 202-206, 220, 239
Draft-law riots in New York, 271-274
Drake, Edwin, 213
Dred Scott decision, 194
Duff, Mrs., 19
Dwight, Rev. Timothy, 7

East Poultney, Vermont, 8, 9, 147, 342
Emancipation Proclamation, 261, 262, 264, 265
Emerson, Ralph Waldo, 93, 95, 97, 98, 109, 113, 115, 174
Engels, Friedrich, 155
Erie *Gazette*, 12, 13
Evans, George Henry, 136-137, 139, 164
Evarts, William M., 237, 238
Evening Journal, Albany (*see* Albany *Evening Journal*)
Evening Post, New York, 20-22, 38, 39, 101, 219, 287, 304, 307, 331, 342
Evening Signal, New York, 54, 64
Evening Star, New York, 63-64
Everett, Edward, 88
Express, New York, 63
Eytinge, Rose, 184

Factory system, 37
Farming, What I Know About, 178, 304, 333
Farragut, Adm. David G., 288

Fawkes steam plow, 213
Fell, James, 210
Fenton, Reuben, 331
Field, David Dudley, 222, 237, 287
Fillmore, Millard, 141, 144
Fisher, Burke, 40
Fisk, Jim, 295, 324, 325
Fort Sumter, firing on, 242
"Forward to Richmond" slogan, 244-248, 251, 322
Fourier, Charles, 91, 92, 97-98, 104
Fourierist association, 103-104
Fox sisters, 94, 123
Franklin, Benjamin, 16
Fredonia *Censor*, 51, 54
Free Soil party, 141-142
Free-soilers, 169-170, 331
Frémont, Jessie, 278
Frémont, John C., 193, 253, 276, 278, 279
Friends of Universal Reform, 93
Frohman, Daniel, 309
Frothingham, Rev. Octavius B., 274
Fuller, Margaret, 32, 84, 108-123, 130, 145, 268
  on *Tribune*, 113-115
  as Rome correspondent, 121-122
Future, The, 91

Garfield, James A., 338
Garrison, William Lloyd, 93, 105, 133, 162, 171, 193, 318
Gay, Sidney H., 260, 261, 266, 272-274, 300
George, Henry, 311
Gettysburg, Battle of, 271
Giddings, Joshua, 130, 131, 219
Gilmore, James R., 255-257, 260, 261, 263, 273, 274, 282
Godkin, E. L., 84, 85, 128, 189, 278, 295, 296, 331, 337, 341
Godwin, Parke, 88, 101, 104, 287
Goethe, 97, 115
Gould, Jay, 295, 319, 325, 349, 353
Graham, Dr. Sylvester, 25
Grant, Ulysses S., General, 251, 276
  at Richmond, 291
  Greeley defeated by, 347
  liberals' revolt against, 330-332, 338
  nomination of, 279, 288, 320
  President, 324-326, 341, 344, 345, 353

Index

Gray, John, 277
Greeley, Colorado, 310
Greeley, Arminda, 12
Greeley, Arthur ("Pickie"), 112, 116-124
Greeley, Barnes, 12, 187
Greeley, Esther, 6, 12, 25, 32, 34, 116, 118, 226, 327
Greeley, Ezekiel, 2
Greeley, Gabrielle, 180, 274, 305, 329, 330, 352
Greeley, Horace, What I Know About, 333
Greeley, Horace, as adolescent political orator, 10
  on American progress, 36, 315-316
  apprenticeship of, with *Northern Spectator,* 8-11
  arrival of, in New York, 15-16
  and Beecher and Barnum, 156-158
  belief of, in "spiritual manifiestations," 123-124
  and Bennett (*see* Bennett, James Gordon, and Greeley)
  birth of, in Amherst township, N. H., 3
  and Bryant, comparison of, 38
  as campaign editor, 44-45
  as campaigner, 46-62
  campaigning of, for Lincoln, 226-228
  at Chappaqua, 125, 177-182, 328-329, 339-341, 345
  and Clay, 127-128
  and Colfax (*see* Colfax, Schuyler, confidant of Greeley)
  as Congressman, 130-132
  and Dana (*see* Dana, Charles A., and Greeley)
  and Davis, 322
  death of, 352-353
  defeat of, by Grant in presidential election, 347
  and Devyr, 315
  and Douglas, 202-206
  early youth of, 4-5
  in East Poultney, Vermont, 8
  editorials of (*see New Yorker; Tribune*)
  for emancipation, 253-259
  in Erie County, Pa., 12
  financial troubles of, 184-188, 350-351

Greeley, Horace—*Continued*
  handouts, 186-187
    (*See also Tribune,* control of)
  first job of, 8-9
  in New York, 17
  as foreign correspondent, 144-146
  and formation of Republican party (*see* Republican party, formation of)
  "Forward to Richmond" slogan, 244-248, 251, 322
  and Fuller, 113-123
  "go West," 195-196, 309, 310
  at Graham House, 25, 30
  Jeffersonian founded by (*see Jeffersonian*)
  on labor, 105-107
  on land reform, 119, 134-139, 141
  lecture tours of, 88-90, 184, 280, 330, 342-343
  and Lincoln (*see* Lincoln, Abraham, and Greeley)
  Log Cabin founded by (*see Log Cabin*)
  at McGoldrick's shelter, 15
  marriage of, 32-34
    (*See also* Greeley, Mary Cheney)
  for mediation, 266-270
  method of, as editor, 83-84
  New Yorker founded by (*see New Yorker*)
  and Niagara Falls affair, 280-285, 322
  nomination of, for President, at Cincinnati convention, 335-339
  in Paris, 175-177
  for peace negotiations, 280-285
  personality of, 38, 295-296
  physical appearance of, 1-2, 4-5, 77-78, 295, 340
  political ambitions of, 127-132, 166-167, 236-238, 325, 333-334
  political apprenticeship of, 47-49
    (*See also* Weed, Thurlow, and Greeley)
  political strategy of, 202-206, 216
  in politics, 170
  "Prayer of Twenty Millions," 261-264, 324
  as president maker, 202-225
  presidential campaign tours of, 341-346
  protectionist views of, 336, 338

Greeley, Horace—*Continued*
  Raymond vs. (*see* Raymond, Henry J., vs. Greeley)
  real-estate holdings of, 350-351
  and reformist schemes (*see* Reformist schemes)
  and Reid (*see* Reid, Whitelaw, and Greeley)
  as Republican manager, 171-173, 314
  on role of editor, 64-66
  schooling of, 4-6
  and Seward (*see* Seward, William H., and Greeley)
  on slavery (*see* Slavery issue)
  and socialism, 42, 92, 100-102
  style of, 85-86
  and tariff issue, 133-134
  on temperance, 10, 89
  tour of West, 196-201
  Tribune founded by (*see Tribune*)
  at Turtle Bay farm, 111-112
  varied activities of, 175
  in war years, 244-293
  and Weed (*see* Weed, Thurlow, and Greeley)
  in Westhaven, Vermont, 7
  and Whigs, 38, 42, 127-147
Greeley, Horace, 2nd, 187
Greeley, Ida, 125, 168, 177, 180, 184, 274, 305, 327, 329, 339, 340, 345, 352
Greeley, Mary Cheney, 30-34, 62, 90, 109-126, 168, 176, 177, 179, 183, 274, 304-305, 327, 329, 339, 340, 346, 347
  personality of, 180-182
Greeley, Mary Woodburn, 3-5
Greeley, Raffael, 125, 168, 177, 180
Greeley, Zaccheus, 2-5
Greeley & McElrath, 107, 112, 133
Greeley & Story, 24
Greeley & Winchester, 26
Green, Duff, 21
Griswold, Rufus W., 68
Gurowski, Adam, 187, 269, 270

Hale, David, 18, 22, 23, 40, 63, 66
  (*See also Journal of Commerce*)
Hall, Oakey, 326, 327
Hall, Willis, 67
Halstead, Murat, 208, 219, 220, 331, 335

Hamlin, Hannibal, 219
Hance, Joseph, 311
Harlan, Sen. James, 280
Harper's Weekly, 223, 333, 338, 353
Harris, Ira, 238
Harrisburg *Chronicle*, 54
Harrison, William Henry, 55-61, 67
Harte, Bret, 300
Hassard, John R. G., 348
Hawthorne, Nathaniel, 20, 97, 100, 113, 115
Hay, John, 84, 277, 282, 283, 300, 312, 313, 329, 353
Hegel, Friedrich, 97
Heine, Heinrich, 97
Helper, Hinton R., 191
Herald, New York, 25, 63, 64, 66, 153, 242, 247, 251
Herkimer *Journal*, 53
Herndon, William H., 191, 204-206, 215, 231, 253
Hildreth, Richard, 84
Hoffman, Charles Fenno, 20
Holcombe, James, 284
Homestead Bill, 131, 316
Hone, Philip, 17, 20, 21, 23, 53, 57, 63, 139
Hooker, Gen. Joseph, 264, 266, 270
Hosford, Harlow, 11
Hoskins, George G., 288, 289
House, E. H., 246
Household Magazine, Wood's, 306
Hyer, Tom, 218, 223

Illinois Republicans, 204-207
Independent, 242, 273, 280, 288, 328
Industrial Congress, 139
Irish News, New York, 187
Irving, Washington, 20
Isely, Jeter A., 156

Jackson, Andrew, 10, 35, 227
Jackson, Stonewall, 246, 270
James, Henry, 119, 189
Jefferson and Jackson, 47
Jeffersonian, 46-54
  attack of, on Jacksonians, 48
  political sermons in, 49
  and Seward campaign, 50-54
Jewett, William C., 280, 283
"Jim Bludso," 313, 329
Johnson, Alvin, 346, 350, 351
Johnson, Andrew, 130, 311, 320, 321, 324

Johnston, Albert Sidney, 200
Johnston, Gen. Joseph, 245, 246
Jones, George, 11, 147-149, 342, 353
Journal of Commerce, New York, 18, 22, 40, 63, 66

Kemble, Fanny, 17, 19
Kirby, Georgiana, 125
Knickerbocker Magazine, 20
Know-Nothings, 152, 169-171, 192, 194, 220

Labor movement, 95-96
Labor unions, 316
Land reform, 119, 134-139, 141
Lechesne, 175
Ledger, Philadelphia, 304, 306
Lee, Gen. Robert E., 264, 265, 270, 271, 279, 291
Leggett, William, 21, 22, 39
Liberal Republican Party, 333-334, 338, 341, 351
Lieber, Francis, 288
Lincoln, Abraham, 1-2, 130, 170, 191, 195, 202, 204-207, 209, 220, 222, 223, 232, 246, 279
  assassination of, 293, 321
  Cooper Union speech, 214
  Emancipation Proclamation (*see* Emancipation Proclamation)
  and Greeley, 210-212, 229, 233-235, 237-239, 243, 249-250, 256-265, 280-283, 285, 286, 288-289, 291, 324
  nomination of, 223
  presidential campaign of, 226-228
  on the Union, 235-236, 240
  and Weed and Seward, 235
Lind, Jenny, 123
Locofocos, 37, 43, 53, 57, 86, 96, 101
Log Cabin, 56-62, 64, 65, 69, 162
  circulation of, 59, 61
  and Harrison campaign, 57-62
Logan, John, 317
Logan Act, 269, 280
Longfellow, Henry Wadsworth, 114-115
Louisville *Courier*, 331, 334
Lowell, James Russell, 93, 115
Luther, Seth, 37
Lynch, Anne, 115

McClellan, Gen. George B., 254, 255, 257, 259, 264, 265, 287

McClure, Alexander K., 141, 335, 337, 339
McCormick, Cyrus, 146, 213, 340, 341
McDowell, Gen. Irvin, 245, 246
McElrath, Thomas, 70, 71, 77, 87, 100, 156, 174, 252, 302
Mann, Horace, 130
Mansfield, Gen., 264
Marble, Manton, 342, 353
Martineau, Harriet, 17, 101
Marx, Karl, 154-155
Mason, John Y., 258
Masquerier, Lewis, 136, 139
Maverick, Augustus, 75, 76, 149
Meade, Gen. George G., 271
Meagher, T. F., 187
Medill, Joseph, 204-206, 216, 219, 222
Meeker, Nathan C., 309, 310, 332
Mehring, Franz, 155
Melville, Herman, 318
Mercantile gazette, 22
Mercier, Henri, 268-269, 285
Miller, Joaquin, 300
Minot, Christopher, 7
Missouri Compromise of 1820, 159
Morgan, Pierpont, 295
Morning Post, 24
Morton, Oliver, 317, 344, 347
Murphy, Thomas, 325, 326

Napoleon III, 122, 268, 269
Nast, Thomas, 333, 338, 342, 346, 353
Nathan, James, 118
Nation, 84, 85, 331, 337
National Intelligencer, 74
National Reform Association, 139
Nevins & Company, 40
New England Magazine, 20, 49
New England Workingmen's Association, 105
New York *American*, 21
New York City, 15-16, 19-20, 156, 294
  draft-law riots in, 271-274
New York *Commercial Advertiser*, 13, 20-21
New York *Evening Signal*, 54, 64
New York *Herald* (*see Herald*)
New York *Irish News*, 187
New York *Journal of Commerce* (*see Journal of Commerce*)

374 Index

New York *Sun* (*see Sun*)
New York *Times* (*see Times*)
New York *Tribune* (*see Tribune*)
New York *World*, 343, 353
New Yorker, 25-30, 45, 53, 62, 64, 65, 69
  on capital and labor, 36
  condition of, in crash of 1836, 40-41
  debts of, 54
  editorials in, 28-29
  financial opinions in, 39
  poetry in, 26-27
  political ideas in, 28
  public events in, 28
  on state of nation, 35
Newhall, Emma Whiting (*see* Whiting, Emma)
News, New York, 63
News beats, 73-77, 266
Newspapers in 1830, 21
Niagara Falls affair, 280-285, 322
Noah, Mordecai, 64, 72
North American Phalanx, 99, 100, 103, 104
Northern Spectator, Greeley's apprenticeship with, 8-10
Nye, James, 244

Opdyke, Mayor of N. Y., 288
O'Rourke, Patrick, 352
Orton, William, 349, 353
Ossoli, Giovanni Angelo, 110, 122
Otterson, F. J., 153, 217, 300
Owen, Robert, 104, 105

Panic of 1819, 6
Parker, Theodore, 93, 96, 98, 162, 168, 170, 171, 191, 193, 206
Parton, James, 4, 8, 9, 18, 224, 272
Phalansteries, 99
Philadelphia *Times*, 335
Phillips, Wendell, 105, 169, 171, 265, 277, 278, 332, 341
Pickett, George E., 271
Pigeon expresses, 76
Pike, James S., 84, 154, 222, 224
Pike County Ballads, 313
Poe, Edgar Allan, 115, 186-187
Politics, What I Know About, 342
Polk, James K., 107
Power, Tyrone, 17
Powers, Hiram, 145
"Prayer of Twenty Millions, The," 261-264, 324

Prohibitionists, 152
Pulitzer, Joseph, 333

Quinby, Edward, 274
Quincy, Josiah, 93

Ransom, B. F., 11, 27, 34, 40
Raymond, Henry J., 183-184
  for appeasement, 232
  chairman of Republican National Committee, 284
  conservatism of, during war, 284, 285
  on *Courier and Enquirer*, 103, 127
  death of, 307-308
  on Emancipation Proclamation, 265
  vs. Greeley, 103-105, 115, 148-150, 153-155, 160, 183, 224-225, 268-269, 284, 285, 291
  for Johnson, 321
  lieutenant governor, 153
  Times founded by (*see Times*)
  on *Tribune*, 29-30, 68, 69, 91
  as managing editor, 80, 83, 84, 100
  news beat of, 74-75
  Whig views of, 138
Reavis, L. U., 326
Recollections of a Busy Life, 5, 108, 124, 177, 304
Redfield, J. S., 18
Reformist schemes, 92-100, 308, 309, 318, 347
  (*See also* Brook Farm; Land reform)
Reforms, Hints toward, 138
Reid, Whitelaw, at Cincinnati convention, 334-337
  on Cincinnati *Gazette*, 288
  and Greeley, 185, 295, 303-304, 346, 348-350
  heir to *Tribune*, 84, 185, 352, 353
  on *Tribune*, 300, 310
  as managing editor, 307, 310-313, 325, 327
Republican convention, Chicago (1860), 217-225, 287
Republican party, 192-195, 314, 315, 318, 330
  and Democratic party, 326, 331
  formation of, 164-165, 168-171, 173, 190
Republicans, Illinois, 204-207
  Liberal (*see* Liberal Republicans)

Richardson, Albert D., 84, 198, 199, 230, 251, 300, 311, 312
Ripley, George, 84, 93, 96, 102, 105, 108, 109, 153, 300
Ripley, Sophia, 100
Robinson, Solon, 84, 154
Rockefeller, John D., age of, 213
Rooker, Thomas, 67, 78, 81, 185, 293, 298, 302, 352, 353
Rosecrans, Gen. William S., 276
Russell, Amelia, 102
Rust, A. J., 172

St. John, D. B., 151, 152
St. Joseph Valley Register, South Bend, 74
St. Louis *Westliche Post*, 333, 335
Sargent, Epes, 87, 127
Schurz, Carl, 84, 155, 219, 300, 326, 327, 332-338, 341, 342
Scott, Gen. Winfield, 55, 128, 144, 159 246
Seances, 123-124
Secession, 228-231
Seitz, Don C., 183
Seward, Frederick, 52
Seward, William H., 50-54, 56, 57, 75, 91, 132, 140, 143, 147, 165, 193, 207, 220-225, 353
  description of, 208-209
  and Greeley, 51-52, 144, 151, 166-167, 208
  as Secretary of State, 234, 239-241, 260, 269, 280, 285
  for compromise, 241
  and Weed (*see* Weed, Thurlow, and Seward)
Seymour, Gov. Horatio, 273
Shepard, H. D., 24
Sheridan, Gen. Philip H., 288
Sherman, Gen. William T., 288
Sinclair, Samuel, 185, 252, 296, 302, 346, 348-350, 353
Slavery issue, 133, 142, 144, 157, 160-163, 168, 191, 192, 232, 253-254
Slidell, John, 258
Smalley, George W., 84, 251, 264, 300, 301, 311
Snow, George, 68, 185
Social Destiny of Man, The, 91
Socialism, 42, 92, 98, 100-102
Spirit of the Times, 18, 19, 24
Springfield *Republican*, 335

Stanton, Elizabeth Cady, 183, 278
Stedman, E. C., 84, 188, 300
Stephens, Alexander, 130, 290
Stevens, Thaddeus, 57, 271, 277, 285, 286, 288, 317, 321
Stewart, A. T., 106, 295
Stoeckel, 269
Stone, Col. W. L., 13, 20
Stone, Lucy, 179, 183
Story, Francis V., 24, 26
Stowe, Harriet Beecher, 157
Sumner, Charles, 143, 164, 170, 260, 264, 270, 271, 276, 277, 285, 288, 325, 326, 332, 341
Sun, New York, 21, 25, 63, 64, 66, 308, 342, 344
Sweeny, Peter B., 319

"Table rappings," 123-124
Taney, Roger B., 240
Tappan, Arthur, 40
Taylor, Bayard, 77, 82-84, 115, 145, 153, 182, 185, 187, 188, 226, 300
Taylor, Zachary, 128, 132, 140, 141, 144, 276
Thomas, George H., 276
Thoreau, Henry D., 88, 93
Tilden, Samuel J., 88, 326, 327
Tilton, Elizabeth, 328, 329
Tilton, Theodore, 84, 242, 273, 280, 287, 328, 329, 336, 340, 346, 353
Times, New York, 11, 219, 220, 247, 342, 353
  founding of, 30, 69, 147-149
  and *Tribune*, founding of, contrast in, 148-149, 153
Tocqueville, Alexis de, 36
Toombs, Robert, 130
Transcendentalists, 97
Tribune, New York, 65-90, 100, 125, 153-156, 160, 161, 251, 348
  advertising in, 71-72
  circulation of, 144, 174
  control of, 332, 347-350, 353
  crusading of, 158
  Dana on (*see* Dana, Charles A., on *Tribune*)
  editorials in, 87, 158, 188-189
  expenses of, 302
  European news bureau, 301
  founding of, 66
  vs. *Herald*, 153-155

Index

Tribune—Continued
  Marx on, 154-155
  prowar, 242-243, 244
  Raymond on (see Raymond, Henry J., on Tribune)
  Reid on (see Reid, Whitelaw, on Tribune)
  on secession, 230
  signs of weariness on, 298-299
  staff of, 84, 300
    (See also particular staff member)
  vs. Times (see Raymond, Henry J., vs. Greeley)
  weekly, 70, 162, 226
Tribune Association, 185, 349, 350
Trumbull, Lyman, 326, 332, 335
Turtle Bay farm, 111-112
Twain, Mark, 201, 300, 311
Tweed, Boss, 326, 327, 331, 338, 342
Tyler, John, 61, 68

Union, 72
Union Colony, 310
Utopias (see Reformist schemes)

Vallandigham, Clement L., 267-268, 270, 271, 279, 287, 291
Van Buren, Martin, 47, 57, 59, 141
Vanderbilt, Cornelius, 16, 80, 106, 294, 319, 351
Vanderbilt, Cornelius, Jr., 187, 306
Verity, William H., 196
Villard, Henry, 84, 198, 199, 247, 251, 266
Voorhees, Senator, 343

Wade, Ben, 271, 276, 277, 285, 288, 317
Wade, Mason, 118
Wade-Davis Bill, 279, 286-287
Walker, Robert J., 255-257, 260
Ward, Enoch, 75
Warner, Charles Dudley, 300
Washington Globe, 23, 73, 74
Washington Telegraph, 21
Watertown Reformer, 236
Watterson, Henry, 331, 334, 335, 337, 342, 343
Webb, James Watson, 21-23, 43, 63, 66, 73, 100, 103, 138, 219, 308
  (See also Courier and Enquirer)
Webster, Daniel, 44, 48, 57, 75, 88, 142

Weed, Thurlow, and Clay, 55
  editor of Albany Evening Journal, 17, 21, 22
  and Greeley, 44-47, 52, 65, 91, 100, 151-152, 169, 170, 319, 353
  and Lincoln, 234-237, 279, 288
  in Republican party, 234-237, 285, 286
  and Raymond, 308
  and Seward, 50-52, 128, 129, 147, 165-166, 217-218, 221, 224, 232, 233
  in Whig party, 128-135, 139, 140, 191
Welles, Gideon, 218, 235, 239, 240, 331
West, John T., 17
Westhaven, Vermont, 7, 292
Westliche Post, St. Louis, 333, 335
Whig, The, 54
Whig party, 163, 171
  failure of, 191-192
Whig Songs for 1844, 107
Whiggism, 42-44, 47, 127-147
Whipple, Mrs. Rebekah, 183, 215, 292, 305, 314, 333, 340, 346
White, Horace, 335, 337
White, James W., 270
Whiting, Emma, 33, 34, 120, 124, 126, 178, 179, 182, 183
Whitman, Walt, 77, 105, 157, 318
Wilkeson, Sam, 250-252, 258, 260, 271, 293, 300, 310, 311
Wilmot, David, 140, 219
Winchester, Jonas, 26, 29, 185-186, 306
Windt, John, 95, 136
Winter, William, 84, 298, 300
Woman in the Nineteenth Century, 112
Wood's Household Magazine, 306
Woodburn, John, 3
Woodburn, Mary (see Greeley, Mary Woodburn)
Woodhull, Victoria, 329, 341
"Workies," 36, 37, 43, 51
Working Man's Advocate, 136
World, New York, 343, 353
Wright, Frances, 36, 94, 101, 104, 108, 136

Young, John Russell, 66, 84, 252, 300, 301, 304, 307, 311, 324, 326, 336

E 415.9 .G8 H17 1950

Hale, William Harlan, 1910-1974.
Horace Greeley